CATHOLICS WRITING THE NATION IN EARLY MODERN BRITAIN AND IRELAND

Catholics Writing the Nation in Early Modern Britain and Ireland

CHRISTOPHER HIGHLEY

OXFORD

UNIVERSITY PRESS

OXFORD
UNIVERSITY PRESS

Great Clarendon Street, Oxford OX2 6DP

Oxford University Press is a department of the University of Oxford.
It furthers the University's objective of excellence in research, scholarship,
and education by publishing worldwide in

Oxford New York

Auckland Cape Town Dar es Salaam Hong Kong Karachi
Kuala Lumpur Madrid Melbourne Mexico City Nairobi
New Delhi Shanghai Taipei Toronto

With offices in

Argentina Austria Brazil Chile Czech Republic France Greece
Guatemala Hungary Italy Japan Poland Portugal Singapore
South Korea Switzerland Thailand Turkey Ukraine Vietnam

Oxford is a registered trade mark of Oxford University Press
in the UK and in certain other countries

Published in the United States
by Oxford University Press Inc., New York

British Library Cataloguing in Publication Data

Data available

Library of Congress Cataloging in Publication Data
Highley, Christopher.
Catholics writing the nation in early modern Britain and Ireland / Christopher Highley.
p. cm.
Includes bibliographical references and index.
ISBN 978–0–19–953340–4 (alk. paper)
1. Catholic literature.   2. Nationalism–Religious aspects–Catholic Church.
3. Great Britain–Church history–16th century.   4. Great Britain–Church
history–17th century.   5. Ireland–Church history–16th century.
6. Ireland–Church history–17th century.   I. Title.
BX880.H54   2008
320.540941088′28209031–dc22
2008008626

Typeset by SPI Publisher Services, Pondicherry, India
Printed in Great Britain
on acid-free paper by
Biddles Ltd., King's Lynn, Norfolk

ISBN 978–0–19–953340–4

1 3 5 7 9 10 8 6 4 2

For Susie, Alex, and Greg

Acknowledgments

This book has benefited greatly from the generosity of friends and colleagues who have read drafts of various chapters, answered questions, and offered suggestions. I wish to thank, in addition to Oxford's two anonymous readers, Christopher Brown, David Cressy (and members of his Early Modern Seminar in the Department of History at The Ohio State University), Frances E. Dolan, Richard Dutton, Denise Fett, Steve Galbraith, Donna Hamilton, the late Nick Howe, John N. King, James Lenaghan, Colm Lennon, Arthur Marotti, Geoffrey Parker, Phoebe Spinrad, and Arthur Williamson. I am also grateful for support from The Ohio State University College of Humanities. Two people deserve special recognition: Mark Rankin for his unusually generous comments, and, above all, Susie Kneedler for her scrupulous attention to the manuscript and her unwavering support at every stage of the project. This book is immeasurably better for her help.

C.H.

The Ohio State University
January 2008

Contents

List of Illustrations

List of Abbreviations

AR A. F. Allison and D. M. Rogers ed. *The Contemporary Printed Literature of the English Counter-Reformation between 1558 and 1640*, vol. 1: *Works in languages other than English*; vol. 2: *Works in English* (Aldershot: Scolar Press, 1989–94).

CSP *Calendar of State Papers*

ERL *English Recusant Literature, 1558–1640*, ed. D. M. Rogers (Menston, York: Scolar Press, 1971–9).

ODNB *Oxford Dictionary of National Biography* (online edition, 2007).

All primary works are published in London unless otherwise noted. I have silently amended "u" to "v" and "i" to "j" when quoting early modern texts.

Here lies Robert Peckham, Englishman and Catholic, who, after England's break with the Church, left England because he could not live in his country without the Faith, and, having come to Rome, died there because he could not live apart from his country.

(English draft of Latin inscription in S. Gregorio, Rome: *The Other Face: Catholic Life under Elizabeth I*, ed. Philip Caraman (London: Longmans, 1960), 141)

1

Introduction: English Catholics and Discourses of the Nation

This book examines early modern Catholic imaginings of the nation, a perspective neglected by previous accounts of the period. I concentrate on the writings of English Catholics from around 1554 to 1625, glancing occasionally at texts by Welsh, Scottish, and Irish Romanists when they help to illuminate the contours of Catholic Englishness or Britishness. Since Catholic texts were often written to provoke Protestants or in response to Protestant provocations, my approach foregrounds the confessional dialogues or conversations in which Catholic texts are situated. My primary sources are an eclectic mixture of under-studied works, including historical and ecclesiastical narratives, polemical and controversial tracts, theological treatises, martyrologies, correspondence, and government propaganda. While this is not a book about the Catholic literary tradition in the mould of Alison Shell's *Catholicism, Controversy, and the English Literary Imagination, 1558–1660*, I try where appropriate to gesture to nominally canonical works of literature. One of the main purposes of this study, though, is to alert readers to the neglected corpus of non-canonical Catholic material in print and manuscript that has fallen outside the scope of "literary" investigations.[1]

Until recently, scholars of early modern England have assumed that the imagining of the nation was an exclusively Protestant endeavor. We are told that once the reformed faith gained official sanction under Elizabeth, and as a religiously conservative, confused, or apathetic population was gradually "Protestantized," so Catholicism became irrevocably associated in the cultural imagination with the non-English.[2] Catholicism comes to seem antithetical to the very idea of English nationhood. This is the narrative that underpins even the best of recent literary-historical work like Richard Helgerson's *Forms of Nationhood*. Because

---

[1] Alison Shell, *Catholicism, Controversy, and the English Literary Imagination, 1558–1660* (Cambridge: Cambridge University Press, 1999).

[2] Jeremy Gregory, "The Making of a Protestant Nation: 'Success' and 'Failure' in England's Long Reformation," in Nicholas Tyacke (ed.) *England's Long Reformation 1500–1800* (London: University College London, 1998), 307–34; Tony Claydon and Ian McBride, "The Trials of a Chosen People: Recent Interpretations of Protestantism and National Identity in Britain and Ireland," in Tony Claydon and Ian McBride (eds.), *Protestantism and National Identity: Britain and Ireland, c.1650–c.1850* (Cambridge: Cambridge University Press, 1998), 11.

Helgerson accepts *a priori* the notion that the English nation is a Protestant construct, there is no room for Catholic voices in his analysis of the cultural practices and literary genres that help to define and interrogate an emerging sense of English identity.[3] At the same time, the latest historical studies of the period, while alerting us to the complex range of identities, agendas, and meanings encompassed by the ideologically amorphous entity we call "Catholicism," tend not to look at the ways Catholics imagined themselves within larger national communities by actively shaping the discourses of Englishness. This is the gap in the current scholarship that my book aims to fill.[4]

My discussion of competing Catholic and Protestant visions of national identity presupposes, of course, that the concept of a national identity is a meaningful one in the context of early modern England. Questions of when and how an English nation, national consciousness, or a sense of national identity took shape have been lively topics of debate among sociologists and historians of the nation in recent decades. Leah Greenfeld's influential view that the English invented the concepts of the nation and nationalism in the mid-sixteenth century has been attacked by critics who wish either to postpone these developments until later centuries or to push them back to even earlier ones.[5]

Krishan Kumar and other "modernists," cannot imagine real nations and nationalist movements existing before the nineteenth century.[6] Borrowing Benedict Anderson's formulation, Kumar argues that genuine nationalism required the English people to see "themselves as an 'imagined community,' as a horizontally integrated group of like-minded individuals occupying the same cultural and political space." For Kumar, nationalism in this sense can be said to exist only once the majority of a population in a delimited territorial unit displays primary loyalty to the nation rather than to competing sources of allegiance like class, region, religion, state, or sovereign. According to these criteria, nationalism does not exist in Elizabethan England, which Kumar defines as a "patrimonial" state—one in which allegiance is given to the monarch, the embodiment of the state. Only can a secularizing, democratic, and industrialized society with well developed forms of mass communication inspire true nationalism.

---

[3] Richard Helgerson, *Forms of Nationhood: The Elizabethan Writing of England* (Chicago: University of Chicago Press, 1992). Also see Claire McEachern, *The Poetics of English Nationhood, 1590–1612* (Cambridge: Cambridge University Press, 1996).

[4] Anne Dillon, *The Construction of Martyrdom in the English Catholic Community, 1535–1603* (Aldershot: Ashgate, 2002); Michael C. Questier, *Catholicism and Community in Early Modern England: Politics, Aristocratic Patronage and Religion, c.1550–1640* (Cambridge: Cambridge University Press, 2006). For an overview of recent developments in Catholic historiography, see Ethan H. Shagan (ed.), *Catholics and the "Protestant Nation": Religious Politics and Identity in Early Modern England* (Manchester: Manchester University Press, 2005), 1–21.

[5] Liah Greenfeld, *Nationalism: Five Roads to Modernity* (Cambridge: Harvard University Press, 1992). On medieval discourses of the nation, see Kathy Lavezzo (ed.), *Imagining a Medieval English Nation* (Minneapolis : University of Minnesota Press, 2004).

[6] Krishan Kumar, *The Making of English National Identity* (Cambridge: Cambridge University Press, 2003), 101–3.

If, however, we think in looser terms than English "nationalism" conceived as an "ideology and movement," but instead about a sense of national identity, of national consciousness, and national sentiment, then the picture looks quite different. As Adrian Hastings and Anthony D. Smith argue, a sense of national identity can predate nationalism by centuries.[7] In the case of England, Medieval and Anglo-Saxon scholars have identified the emergence of a national consciousness at various moments before the Reformation. Several commentators have held up Bede's *Ecclesiastical History* as the earliest representation of England as a unified nation, despite the fact that politically and territorially "England" was still divided into several kingdoms, each with its own ruler. Bede imagines an overarching national community that transcends local administrative divisions, based in the shared ethnos of a single people, a "gens Anglorum," blending together Saxons, Angles, and Jutes.[8] For Bede, the essential unity of the English people derived not just from their common Germanic roots but also from the language they shared. Reinforcing these unifying ethnic and linguistic elements was a single ecclesiastical structure centered on Canterbury and organized upon a diocesian system.

As the foregoing suggests, the language of national identity in the medieval and early modern world overlapped in complicated ways with concepts of race or ethnic identity. The word "race" itself appears to have entered the English language only in the early sixteenth century, for the *OED* cites a passage from John Foxe's *Actes and Monuments* as the earliest recorded usage: "Thus was the outward race and stock of Abraham after flesh refused."[9] The concept of race, however, existed well before the sixteenth century: it was one of the implied meanings of the medieval Latin word "gens"—a term, like "natio," of considerable semantic flexibility that could also connote a people, nation, or tribe.[10] Robert Bartlett argues that it makes sense to talk about medieval (and I would add early modern) ideas of "race" if we keep in mind that before the late eighteenth century race was not understood as a genetic or biological category whose principal marker was skin pigment or physiognomy. While races in the medieval and early modern world may have been associated primarily with particular bloodlines, they were also seen as mutable constructs shaped by external factors like geography and

---

[7] Anthony D. Smith, "'Set in the Silver Sea': English National Identity and European Integration," *Nations and Nationalism* 12 (3) 2006, 441–2.

[8] Adrian Hastings, *The Construction of Nationhood: Ethnicity, Religion, and Nationalism* (Cambridge: Cambridge University Press, 1997), 35–9.

[9] See Margo Hendricks, "Race: A Renaissance Category?," in Michael Hattaway (ed.), *A Companion to English Renaissance Literature and Culture* (Oxford: Blackwell, 2000), 690–8.

[10] Robert Bartlett, "Medieval and Modern Concepts of Race and Ethnicity," *Journal of Medieval and Early Modern Studies* 31 (2001), 39–56. The medieval idea of the "natio" could mean various things in various contexts, but it suggested above all not the political structure organizing a people in a delimited territory, but the people itself, its "language, laws, habits, modes of judgement and customs" (Hastings, *Construction of Nationhood*, 17, quoting a 12th-century Norman bishop using the term "natio" to describe the Welsh).

identified in terms of language, culture, and political affiliations.[11] Thus when I talk about the English, Welsh, Irish, Scottish, and Spanish "races," in this study, I am thinking about them principally as self-imagined descent groups whose genealogical histories may be either separate from or interwoven with the ancestries of other groups. The persistence of a genealogical habit of mind in the early modern period shows itself in the myths of origin that people continued to tell themselves about their race's or nation's founding figures like Brut, Hercules, or Gathelus and Scota.[12]

Ultimately, questions of whether late sixteenth-century England constituted a nation according to demonstrable criteria, interest me less than the "sentient history" of how England's Catholic subjects imagined the territory, history, culture, and people of a place they called variously England or Britain. I focus on the Catholic preoccupation with "national self-imagining."[13] In recovering the "national self-imagining" of English Catholics, I rely mostly on the texts they produced "beyond the seas" while living in exile. My study thus fills a gap in recent scholarship on early modern Catholics that has overlooked the exiles in favor of other groupings within the Catholic community like martyrs or Church Papists.[14] I place the exiles at the center of this book about religion and national identity because like other groups of people forcibly displaced from their homelands, the exiles were urgently confronted by questions of national belonging.[15] The exiles' need to think though what it meant to be English and Catholic was driven not just by the fact that they were in unfamiliar surroundings but by an awareness that they shared those surroundings with exiled neighbors from other parts of the British Isles and Ireland.

The space of exile, then, often represented a multicultural contact zone in which English émigrés might feel their own sense of national distinctiveness under threat from both the host culture as well as exile populations from Wales, Scotland, and Ireland. English exiles were perhaps most conscious of living among other peoples and cultures when in Rome, "alwaies the citie of refuge and

---

[11] Robert Bartlett, "Medieval and Modern Concepts of Race and Ethnicity," *Journal of Medieval and Early Modern Studies* 31 (2001), 39–56.

[12] Roger A. Mason, "Scotching the Brut: Politics, History, and National Myth in Sixteenth-Century Britain," in Roger A. Mason (ed.), *Scotland and England 1286–1815* (Edinburgh: John Donald, 1987), 60–84.

[13] Smith " 'Set in the Silver Sea'," 438; Hastings, *Construction of Nationhood*, 18.

[14] Peter Guilday's ground-breaking study, *The English Catholic Refugees on the Continent, 1558–1795* (London, 1914), is subtitled Volume 1, "The English Colleges and Convents in the Catholic Low Countries, 1558–1795." Guilday never published further volumes. For studies of martyrs and church papists, see Dillon, *The Construction of Martyrdom* and Alexandra Walsham, *Church Papists: Catholicism, Conformity, and Confessional Polemic in Early Modern England* (Woodbridge: Boydell, 1993).

[15] Alexandra Walsham, *Charitable Hatred: Tolerance and Intolerance in England, 1500–1700* (Manchester: Manchester University Press, 2006), 186.

recourse of al Christians out of al Nations."[16] Here English exiles found colleges, hospitals, and churches specifically reserved for the use of pilgrims from different countries and cultures, including French, Portugese, Germans, Flemings, Polonians, Slavonians, Indians, Armenians, Greeks, and Hebrews. The Spanish were the largest of all the stranger nations in Rome with their own hospital and several churches devoted to their national saints.[17] Rome, as the universal city, was in theory a place where people could sublimate their national and cultural differences into a common overarching identity. But the close neighborhood of such a variety of peoples undoubtedly stimulated heightened national self-consciousness.

The category of "Catholic," as my references to exiles, martyrs, and Church Papists suggests, is a broad one, covering an array of heterogeneous identities, subgroups, and factions. The main split within the stay-at-home lay Catholic community was between the conformists (Nicodemites) or Church Papists who attended Church of England services, and the recusants who refused to attend. Within these broad categories there were different degrees and kinds of conformity, compromise, and resistance, as well as the possibility of movement among positions. Conformists, for example, might attend the official church occasionally, refuse to communicate when present, and perform acts of proscribed Catholic piety during sermons. The problem with trying to identify different groups within the Catholic community in England is that labels like "church papist," as Peter Lake argues, are early modern polemical constructs rather than "precise analytical categor[ies]." As such they are likely to tell us more about the prejudices of the contemporary user than about the purported identity of the observed.[18]

Questions of terminology prove most problematic when trying to describe the precise religious positions of stay-at-home lay Catholics. The problems are perhaps less evident when dealing with the exiles, who because they either chose or were forced to leave England, rather than conform to the Protestant status quo and live under heresy, were by definition recusants. This is not to say, however, that the diverse collection of men and women, aristocrats and commoners, religious and lay, seculars and regulars, who constituted the exile community were in any way ideologically unified. Like their Catholic counterparts in England,

---

[16] William Allen, *An apologie and true declaration of the institution and endeuours of the two English colleges, the one in Rome, the other now resident in Rhemes* (Rheims, 1581. *ERL* 67), 17[r].

[17] Gregory Martin, *Roma Sancta (1581)*, ed. George Bruner Parks (Rome: Edizioni di Storia e Letteratura, 1969), 194–5.

[18] "Religious Identities in Shakespeare's England," in David Scott Kastan (ed.), *A Companion to Shakespeare* (Oxford: Blackwell, 1999), 72. For a longer perspective on how the term "Catholic" was appropriated by both supporters and opponents of the schism from Rome, see Peter Marshall, "Is the Pope Catholic? Henry VIII and the Semantics of Schism," in Shagan (ed.), *Catholics and the "Protestant Nation"*, 22–48.

the exiles adopted a spectrum of political positions from groveling loyalty to the Elizabethan regime at one extreme, to advocating violent opposition to that regime at the other. Individual exiles might also change their political ideology as circumstances changed. William Allen, for example, for many years urged Catholics to obey Elizabeth in secular affairs, only to reverse this stance at the time of the Armada by urging them to overthrow her.[19]

The Catholic exiles scattered across early modern Europe constituted a diaspora—a term originally applied in the Old Testament to the Jews after their expulsion from Israel and their forced resettlement in alien societies. The term diaspora usually describes displaced minority populations (whether the Old Testament Jews or Cubans in modern America) that have a common ethnicity, language, and cultural identity, and that are significantly larger in numerical terms than the few hundred Catholic exiles living abroad at any given moment during the later sixteenth and early seventeenth centuries. But as William Safran argues, diasporas are defined less by their size than by the shared characteristics of their members: "they, or their ancestors, have been dispersed from a specific original 'center' to two or more 'peripheral,' or, foreign regions; . . . they retain a collective memory, vision, or myth about their original homeland—its physical location, history, and achievements; . . . they believe that they are not—and perhaps cannot be—fully accepted by their host society and therefore feel partly alienated and insulated from it; . . . they regard their ancestral homeland as their true, ideal home and as the place to which they or their descendents would (or should) eventually return—when conditions are appropriate; . . . they believe that they should, collectively, be committed to the maintenance or restoration of their original homeland and to its safety and prosperity; . . . and they continue to relate, personally or vicariously, to that homeland in one way or another, and their ethnocommunal consciousness and solidarity are importantly defined by the existence of such a relationship."[20] In every respect, the Catholic exiles of early modern England fit these criteria of the classic diaspora.

Even as I focus on the Catholic diaspora, I do not want to make too absolute a distinction between its members and their stay-at-home co-religionists because of the deep interdependence of the two communities. People, books, devotional objects, information, and money passed constantly back and forth between Catholic groups at home and overseas. For the most part, the exiles organized their lives in order to serve the perceived needs of the faithful back home, whether this meant praying for the reconversion of England, educating English Catholic youth in Continental establishments, or seeking military intervention from foreign rulers to overthrow heresy in England.

[19] Peter Holmes, *Resistance and Compromise: The Political Thought of the Elizabethan Catholics* (Cambridge: Cambridge University Press, 1982).

[20] "Diasporas in Modern Societies: Myths of Homeland and Return," *Diaspora* 1.1 (1991), 83–4.

STAY-AT-HOME CATHOLICS AND NATIONAL IDENTITY

Whereas the physical separation of exiled Catholics from England spontaneously fostered thoughts of home and a preoccupation with what it meant to be English and Catholic, stay-at-home Catholics were not immune from the same vexing questions of national belonging. They too needed to reconcile their Catholic faith and their Englishness under a Protestant regime that tried to prise these concepts apart. In a way the stay-at-home Catholics were exiles in their own right, albeit internal or "intellectual exiles," whose experience of estrangement from their ancestral home was different only in degree from that of their counterparts overseas.[21]

Stay-at-home Catholics, forced from the public arenas of parish and church into the private and secretive world of the household and other "unofficial" spaces, needed to preserve the "myths, memories, symbols and values" that defined their sense of themselves as Catholic Englishmen and women.[22] As Elizabeth's reign progressed and the possibility that the country would return to the "old religion" receded, Catholics feared that without regular access to priests, sacraments, and proper instruction, future generations of co-religionists would forget or misremember their religious heritage.[23]

One anonymous Catholic author, afraid that his fellow believers were in danger of lapsing into a collective religious amnesia, jogged their memory by publishing his "notes . . . concerning the observation of certaine Holy-daies and Fasting-daies and other Feasts in England." *A treatise with a kalendar* (1608. *ERL* 109) was the product of over forty years work spent assembling information about "the auncient customes of our Country."[24] The author, assisted by "an auncient and learned Priest" ordained under Queen Mary, aimed to reverse the "decay of devotion, both in the common people and others" that had resulted from "neglect" of the country's traditional holidays. The author claimed that he had already issued a table of holy and fasting days around the year 1576; his decision to now produce a more authoritative text with additional proofs was the result of the appearance of "certain English Kalendars and Rules" containing "many thinges very prejudicial to our Provincials." These anonymous printed calendars were allegedly causing uncertainty among English Catholics about which of the "laudable customes of our Country" were still permitted and which had been proscribed. As a result of this confusion about feasts and fasts, the

---

[21] Nancy Bradley Warren, "Dissolution, Diaspora, and Defining Englishness: Syon in Exile and Elizabethan Politics," in *Women of God and Arms: Female Spirituality and Political Conflict 1380–1600* (Philadelphia: University of Pennsylvania Press, 2005), 139.

[22] Smith, " 'Set in the Silver Sea'," 438.

[23] See Lisa McClain, *Lest we be Damned: Practical Innovation and Lived Experience among Catholics in Protestant England* (New York: Routledge, 2004).

[24] *A treatise with a kalendar*, (1608) (*ERL* 109), 3. See J. T. Rhodes, "English Books of Martyrs and Saints of the Late Sixteenth and Early Seventeenth Centuries," *Recusant History* 22 (1994), 7–25.

author complained, some Catholics now "neglect[ed] all."[25] The *kalendar's* desire to clarify the "laudable customes of our Country" was part of an ongoing debate within the Elizabethan Catholic community about the proper identity of their faith. Given the heterogeneity of belief and practice in an underground Catholic community that lacked any ecclesiastical hierarchy or structures of authority, who was to say what constituted English Catholicism?

One of the major faultlines within the stay-at-home Catholic community divided adherents of a home-grown English Catholicism based on "deep-rooted custom" from followers of a newer Counter-Reformation brand of the faith inspired by the rulings of the Council of Trent.[26] Defenders of a native English Catholicism exhibited what John Bossy calls "ecclesiastical patriotism": a "loyalty to the national church as a historic institution...[and] the instinct to defend [it]...against threats from all comers, including those, perhaps especially those, from Rome."[27] "Ecclesiastical patriotism" appeared early in Elizabeth's reign when clerical disputes broke out between non-conforming priests ordained under Mary and a younger generation of Continentally trained seminary priests. The Marian priests embodied a conservative Anglo-Catholicism, whereas the seminarians adhered to the reforming doctrines of Trent and a fierce loyalty to the papacy.[28] Many of the Marian priests were suspicious of what they considered the "new-fangled" doctrine imported into England by the missionaries back from Europe, including their intolerant attitude to lay Catholics who attended "heretical" services.[29] While the seminary priests wanted the laity to embrace full recusancy by abandoning all contact with the Church of England, the older Marian clergy had a more relaxed attitude to acts of occasional conformity that allowed timid or pragmatic Catholics to avoid fines and other penalties.

These disagreements over the identity of "English" Catholicism among native and foreign trained priests affected all areas of religious life, especially the nature of the calendar and the observation of feast and fast days.[30] The seminary priests, citing Tridentine reforms, wanted English Catholics to follow the universal Roman rite governing calendrical observances rather than the old Sarum

---

[25] *A treatise with a kalendar*, 7.

[26] Francis Edwards, SJ, ed. and trans., *The Elizabethan Jesuits: Historia Missionis Anglicanae Societatis Jesu (1660) of Henry More* (London: Phillimore, 1981), 66–7. For overviews of the Council of Trent, see Michael A. Mullett, *The Catholic Reformation* (London: Routledge, 1999), 29–68; and Robert Bireley *The Refashioning of Catholicism, 1450–1700: A Reassessment of the Counter Reformation* (Washington, DC: Catholic University of America, 1999), 45–69.

[27] John Bossy, "Catholicity and Nationality in the Northern Counter-Reformation," in Stuart Mews (ed.), *Religion and National Identity* (Oxford: Blackwell, 1982), 288.

[28] My comments are indebted to Bossy's work on the "Separation of Meats and Days: Fast and Feast," in his *The English Catholic Community, 1570–1850* (Oxford: Oxford University Press, 1975). Also see Patrick McGrath and Joy Rowe, "The Marian Priests Under Elizabeth I," *Recusant History* 12 (1984), 103–20.

[29] Christopher Haigh, "The Continuity of Catholicism in the English Reformation," *Past and Present* 93 (1981), 63.

[30] Rhodes, "English Books of Martyrs and Saints," 10.

rite of the Medieval English church.[31] Defenders of England's ancient religious traditions, on the contrary, claimed that the decrees of the Council of Trent had never been officially introduced into England and, until they were, Catholics could freely observe local customs.[32] The controversy was eventually taken up by a secret Catholic synod in 1580 involving secular clergy, prominent laymen, and the newly arrived Jesuit missionaries. The synod ruled that the old English fasting customs should be upheld. The Jesuit Robert Persons justifies this decision by referring to England's "converter St Augustine," who had upheld local religious traditions wherever he went: "when [Augustine] was in Milan," explains Persons, "he followed the particular use of that Church for divers particular fasts, and when he was in Rome and Africa he saith that he followed the use of those Churches where he was, and so we see that at this day in Europe many vigils and feasts are observed in Spain that are not in Italy, and in France and Germany that are not in Spain."[33] This national variation in religious customs was especially marked in England because, as Persons comments, St Augustine "did bring in and plant in England the flower of all works of piety that he had noted to be observed in any other nation by which he had passed."[34] Persons imagines the faith that Augustine had brought to Britain to be a cosmopolitan patchwork of different customs garnered from various stops on his European wanderings. Although in this account, English Catholic practice had a pan-European rather than an indigenous etiology, Persons recommended allowing Catholic clergy and laity a relative autonomy in their religious observances, rather than imposing a uniformity from outside that could only cause local resentment. By allowing flexibility at the local level, the Roman Church hoped to retain the loyalty of even its most distant communicants.

Catholics who remained in England constructed their national–religious identities (or had them constructed by others) out of a rich tapestry of often competing traditions, doctrines, and imperatives. A vivid instance of this process is provided by the *Vita* of one extraordinary Catholic woman, Lady Magdalen Browne (1538–1608), written by her priest Richard Smith. Smith—a Continentally trained secular priest who was as intolerant of the Jesuits as he was disenchanted with the surviving Marian clergy—depicts Magdalen as constantly torn between

[31] Henry Foley, *Records of the English Province of the Society of Jesus* (7 vols. in 8, London, 1877–83), 1: 393–6; Dennis Flynn, "The English Mission of Jasper Heywood, S.J.," *Archivum Historicum Societatis Jesu* 54 (1985), 45–76. See esp. 55–9 and 67–76. "Until the imposition of the *Book of Common Prayer*, the Sarum use was employed throughout most of the kingdom. It differed from the more common Roman rite in the breviary, in other parts of the liturgy, and in the severity of its fasts and abstinences" (Thomas M. McCoog, SJ, *The Society of Jesus in Ireland, Scotland, and England, 1541–88: "Our Way of Proceeding?"* (Leiden, 1996), 144).

[32] Alexandra Walsham, "Translating Trent: English Catholicism and the Counter Reformation," *Historical Research* 78.201 (2005), 288–310; the author of *A treatise with a kalendar* states that England unlike "Spaine and al other Provinces" had not yet "received the Councel of Trent" (73–4).

[33] Robert Persons, "Of the Life and Martyrdom of Father Edmund Campion," *Letters and Notices* 12 (1878), 37.

[34] Ibid.

her devotion to native Catholic traditions and to the newly-minted Tridentine doctrines associated with the Continental Counter-Reformation and a passionate loyalty to Rome. Smith explains that early in Elizabeth's reign, Magdalen received permission to attend heretical services from the old Marian priest, Alban Langdale (confessor to her husband, Anthony Browne, first Viscount Montague). Smith excuses Magdalen's conformity by imputing it "to the defect of instruction than want of zeal" on Magdalen's part.[35] Under Smith's superior guidance, Magdalen reforms: she gives up the scandalous habit of church attendance, surrounds herself with sound advisers, and builds in her home a private chapel complete with an elevated railed altar, a choir, and "a pulpit for the priests." These acts of Catholic piety prompt Magdelan's Protestant neighbors to dub her house "Little Rome."[36] Ironically, the idea of a "Little Rome" in the Sussex countryside reflects Magdalen's own ideal of bringing Rome home to England, grafting a Continental strand of Catholicism on to a native English one.

If Smith succeeded in persuading Magdalen to follow the dictates of Rome by abandoning heretical English services, he was less successful in weaning her from the traditional English fasting regime that Langdale and other Marian priests had promoted. "Although she was by privilege of her age exempted from fasting, yet did she piously observe all the fasts of the Lent, the Ember days, and whatsoever other, either commanded by the Church or introduced by the pious custom of the Country, as are the fasts of Fridays and some others, to all which of her own devotion she added some Wednesdays."[37] In "her last infirmity," Magdalen heeds the "counsel of her physician and . . . admonition of her confessor" to eat flesh on Ash-Wednesday, "which she never did in her life before, and did piously abhor it." In struggling to choose between priestly advice on the one hand and "her own will and her most ancient and religious custom" on the other, Magdalen reluctantly submits to her ghostly father but only with the utmost "caution and fear of scandal."[38]

Smith's hagiographical treatment of Magdalen depicts her as harmoniously embodying the potentially conflicting impulses represented by a traditional English Catholicism with its stress on outward observances and the Counter-Reformation emphasis on a more intense spiritual life. Thus, even as she observes "the pious custom of the Country" in terms of fasting, she displays in public "her

---

[35] *An Elizabethan Recusant House, Comprising the Life of the Lady Magdalen, Viscountess Montague (1538–1608). Translated into English from the Original Latin by Cuthbert Fursdon, in the Year 1627*, ed. A. C. Southern (London: Sands, 1954), 21, 41.

[36] *An Elizabethan Recusant House*, 43. On Smith's conflict with the Jesuits, see Questier, *Catholicism and Community in Early Modern England*, 207–32, 264.

[37] *An Elizabethan Recusant House*, 48. Alexandra Walsham explains how "the secular priest Richard Smith sought to divert the penitential zeal of Viscountess Montague away from practices like excessive fasting which smacked of superstition and empty externalism" ("Translating Trent," 297).

[38] *An Elizabethan Recusant House*, 37–8.

beads or cross which she used to wear about her neck," practices extensive "private devotions" with a zeal that astonishes even her priest, and exhibits an affective piety exemplified by the "abundance of tears" she sheds when contemplating her sins, and the "external reverence and humiliation of body" she shows during Mass.[39]

Magdalen's investment in traditional English Catholic customs is reflected not only in her devotion to fasting. When "humbly on her knees morning and evening" she asks the benediction of her priests, she is reviving, Smith tells us, an "honour exhibited to our priests from the beginning of the English Church (as testifyeth holy Bede in the third book of his history and twenty-sixth chapter), but long time intermitted."[40] Magdalen's respect for this ancient English custom points to her larger, divinely appointed, role of resuscitating discarded elements of English Catholic culture. This role is revealed allegorically in the narrative when the "body of a religious man" is found under the floor of the family chapel. The discovery of the priest represents a miraculous sign to the household since his body, "lapped in linen and bound hard with cords," remains "sound, flexible, and of so lively a colour, as it seemed alive." Magdalen herself reaches into the corpse's mouth and "did a little pull out his tongue, which was fleshly red and dry; and another [person] with a knife cut a flash in the flesh, which within seemed very sound and fatty, no sign appearing either of balm or any other thing that could conserve the body from corruption."[41] While Smith does not speculate on the meaning of the incident, allowing readers to draw their own conclusions, committed Catholics could have had little hesitation in construing the strange discovery as an allegory of their persecuted church in England and of Magdalen's own role in protecting the Catholic community in her household in "Little Rome." The priest's body, mysteriously "bound hard with cords," suggests the severe restrictions under which England's Catholics labor during this time of heresy. The body of Catholic believers, like the individual priest's body, exists in a liminal state between life and death, neither fully vital nor totally extinct. Magdalen's act of opening the priest's mouth and grasping his tongue, suggests her own special responsibility for making the True Faith speak again by bringing the Catholic past into the Protestant present.[42]

The discovery of the dead priest, "there buried many years before," the incarnation of the oppressed Church, connects Magdalen and her household to an immemorial religious past, one perhaps as ancient as the beginnings of the Roman faith in England that had been described by Bede. Even as Smith places Magdalen within the arc of sacred time, he also inserts her in the context of recent dynastic and religious history. Magdalen, Smith observes, is a living reminder of a brief happy interlude during the "turbulent" reigns of Henry VIII,

---

[39] Ibid. 44, 47, 49, 51.   [40] Ibid. 49.   [41] Ibid. 42.

[42] Other miracles and wonders associated with Magdalen and the Battle community appear at ibid. 52–7 and 60–1. By associating Magdalen with the miraculous, Smith could be laying the ground for her later canonization.

Edward, and Elizabeth when Mary Tudor "expell[ed] perfidious heresy, [and] re-established the ancient and true religion."[43] Magdalen's service as a Lady of Honour at Mary's court makes her into a sort of sacred relic, the embodiment of a longed-for past that besieged Catholics can now revere.

Smith also reminds readers of England's glorious Catholic past and of its fragmentary survival into the present in the figure of one of Magdalen's household priests, "M. Thomas More, great grandchild and direct heir of that famous Sir Thomas More, sometime Lord Chancellor of England and a most worthy martyr."[44] On every side, Smith surrounds Magdalen with signs of England's Catholic heritage and the promise that one day this "crooked and perverse nation," this "land of Hus, where is the hour and power of darkness, where piety is sharply impugned, and freedom given to vice," will return to the faith of its forefathers. Like St Paula (to whom Smith relates Magdalen typologically), the Viscountess lives "without reprehension" "as a light in the world."[45] Outside of "little Rome," England has abandoned its heritage and become a place of strange religious practices, a Protestant German state—'the land of Hus'—unnaturally transplanted to native English soil.

MARY AND PHILIP

Smith's allusion to Mary Tudor's queenship as the time when "the ancient and true religion" last flourished in England is worth pausing over because the reign of Elizabeth's half-sister is consistently discussed in modern historiography as a pivotal moment in cementing the alliance between Protestantism and English national identity. David Loades argues in "The Origins of English Protestant Nationalism" that Mary's Protestant opponents successfully created the perception that this daughter of a Spanish mother and wife of a Spanish king was working against the national interest, a betrayal of England fostered by her Roman Catholic faith.[46] Protestants thus fused their much-trumpeted devotion to England with their still unpopular religious ideas, even though, ironically, these ideas themselves were largely derived from reformist sources outside England.

Protestants were arguably more successful in establishing a received connection between their religion and loyalty to England, given how ideas of England as essentially Protestant have dominated academic narratives of the nation as well as popular consciousness. But English Catholics worked no less strenuously to identify their religion with English patriotism. My project will delineate the many forms the imaginative struggles of English Catholics took to retain control of discourses of national and cultural identity. Mary's marriage to Philip and her subsequent reconciliation of England with Rome are the two acts that signaled

---

[43] Ibid. 41, 12.   [44] Ibid. 43.   [45] Ibid. 70.
[46] *Politics, Censorship, and the English Reformation* (London: Pinter, 1991), 39–48.

to Protestants Mary's betrayal of Englishness. But for Catholics these same acts were on the contrary seen as ways of strengthening the nation and revitalizing Englishness. I want to discuss the arguments developed by Mary's Catholic subjects around the marriage and reconciliation because, as the following chapters will show, later generations of English Catholics would return to these arguments in response to changing religio-political circumstances.

THE SPANISH MATCH

Most opponents of Mary's controversial marriage to Philip claimed to be motivated not by religious ideology but by a patriotic desire to ward off foreign interference in English affairs and the resulting contamination of what they imagined to be a pristine Englishness. Philip was suspected, not unreasonably, of seeking an alliance with the English as a way of consolidating Habsburg power against the perennial enemy of France. The marriage, its opponents charged, could only embroil England in Habsburg political and military machinations, dragging England into wars that were not in the nation's interest. Mary's Catholic apologists responded to these arguments by claiming that the opponents of the Spanish match were only using the idea of an endangered English purity as an ideological screen behind which to promote either their pro-French or their pro-Protestant agendas. The Marian apologist John Proctor offered a stark choice: either Mary could marry a benevolent Spaniard or England could fall prey to the wicked French:

we know most certenly that ther is ment no maner of evil to us by those strangers [the Spanish], but rather aide, profit & comfort against other strangers our auncient enemies [the French], with whom they [the rebels] as most arrant & degenerate traitors do in dede unkindly & unnaturally joine: we in her graces defense wil spende both life & what we have beside to the utter most peny against them.[47]

For Proctor, England's "auncient enemies," the French, were far worse than any Spaniards. Another Marian apologist, John Christopherson, accused Thomas Wyatt and the rebels who had tried to depose Mary, of using the proposed marriage to Philip as a "Spanishe cloke to cover their cursed devys" of re-establishing the "new religion."[48] Although Wyatt and his followers were in fact religious conservatives, the Marian regime sought an advantage by portraying them as adherents of the "new religion" and as thus constituting a far greater threat to English national integrity than a handful of high-ranking Spaniards.[49]

---

[47] *The historie of wyates rebellion* (1554), 22.

[48] *An exhortation to all menne to take hede and beware of rebellion* (1554), Nviii[r].

[49] Ibid. Qviii[v]. See also Loades, "The Enforcement of Reaction, 1553–8," in *Politics, Censorship*, 33; Loades, "The English Church during the Reign of Mary," in John Edwards and Ronald Truman

After all, from a Catholic perspective, the new religion was itself a foreign innovation. While Protestants charged that Catholicism was essentially a non-English religion because its figureheads like the pope, the Holy Roman Emperor, and the king of Spain were all foreigners, Catholics responded in kind that Protestantism was a foreign heresy. From the beginnings of the Reformation in Europe, the defenders of orthodoxy had invariably characterized heresy as something that originated beyond their own national borders. Luther's antagonists, for instance, accused him of polluting the German homeland with a foreign heresy identified with the enemy territory of Bohemia and its native son, "the arch-foreigner" Jan Huss. As David Bagchi explains: "the accusation of 'Bohemianism' ... triggered a series of associations and reverberations within the German national consciousness, of treachery as much as heresy, of social disorder and border clashes as much as schism. Above all, 'Bohemia' was the very quintessence of what was foreign to Germany."[50]

In English Catholic discourse, Bohemia and Germany were also seen as the wellsprings of the new religion polluting England. John Christopherson urged his readers to examine these countries if they wanted to see the social and economic chaos unleashed by Protestantism.[51] And in John Proctor's pro-Marian *The historie of wyates rebellion*, the suffering figure of Lady England invokes "my sister Boheme" as a salutary warning to Englishmen of "what I maye come to, and am like to be if you cease not this your willfull and desperat outrage."[52] The Marian apologist Miles Hogarde invokes Germany and Switzerland, rather than Bohemia, as the sources of England's heresies:

O develysh libertie, I wold to God Germany might have kepte the styll: so Englande had never bene troubled with the. I would to God thou haddest had all our Englyshe bier too drynke dronke with Hance and Jacob in Strasborowe, upon condicion London had never reteyned the. I would to God thou haddest remayned in Swicherlande a conquerour, so that thou haddest never had conquest in Englande. For sythe thy arrivall hether, many poore men by thy ungracious marchaundise are undoone. Many a good Englyshe man at the first glad to entertaygne the, for curtesie as a straunger, wold now be rydde of their gueste, but they cannot. But I truste shortly to see the bankeroute and glad to flye the realme.[53]

(eds.), *Reforming Catholicism in the England of Mary Tudor: The Achievement of Friar Bartolomé Carranza* (Aldershot: Ashgate, 2005); Loades, *The Reign of Mary Tudor: Politics, Government, and Religion in England, 1553–1558* (London: Benn, 1979), 224–51, 321–64.

   [50] David V. N. Bagchi, *Luther's Earliest Opponents: Catholic Controversialists, 1518–1525* (Minneapolis: Fortress Press, 1991), 105–6. Bohemia was actually surrounded by German territory: "It was no distant threat; rather it evoked that mixture of hatred, fear, and fascination reserved for the enemy within" (106).

   [51] *An exhortation to all menne*, Xviii[v]. The anarchy and rampant covetousness unleashed by heresy in the German states portended the decay of England's aristocracy, yeomanry, and commons (Aaii[v]).

   [52] *The historie of wyates rebellion*, n1[r].

   [53] *The displaying of the Protestantes* (1556), 116[r–v].

Hogarde's conceit follows contemporary characterizations by associating heresy with self-indulgence and disorder. As a hard-drinking companion, heresy might be at home among the stereotypically bibulous Germans and Swiss, but he is an incongruous figure in polite English society. Only when heresy undoes itself will England be free again.

Catholic rhetoric about the infiltration of heresy into England from overseas was already circulating before Mary's reign. As Diarmaid MacCulloch notes, during Edward VI's reign, Catholics introduced the labels "Zwinglian" and "Calvinist" as terms of opprobrium for their religious adversaries: "The clear implication was that pure English Tudor and Catholic theology had been polluted from abroad by these foreign notions."[54] One Catholic author asserted that Edward VI's advisers, "seeking for new Evangelists in forraine countries, founde Bucer, Martir, and others whoes fingers tickled to be working in the newe harvest, who coming into the countrye and finding the people generally inclined to libertie easily made their entrance into change of Religion, and so in a shorte tyme under the plausible title of reforming abuses in the Church, they introduced a forme of Religion never heard of in England."[55]

For Mary and her Catholic supporters, then, the threat from the heretical new religion—something never before heard of in England—was far greater than any harm Mary's marriage to a Spaniard could inflict on the realm. Mary's Spanish match, after all, far from being an unsettling innovation in the body politic represented a return to traditional strategies of dynastic alliance. In marrying Philip, Mary was reconnecting England to the community of European Catholic nations that the country had abandoned after Henry VIII's divorce from Katherine of Aragon—the last Spanish-born ruler of England. For centuries before this, the monarchs of Catholic England had sought dynastic unions with other Catholic powers as a way of consolidating national security and prestige.

Marian Protestants responded to the Spanish match by conceptualizing England as a self-sufficient and inward-looking island nation. Once England turned officially "Protestant," in the next reign, this topos became even more central to Elizabethan Protestant rhetoric because it offered the vision of an embattled island nation surround by hostile Catholic powers. The topos had less appeal to Catholics, however, whose idea of England had to accommodate the country's separate identity with its place in the international structures of the Catholic Church. As we shall see in later chapters, the degree to which the Catholic subjects of Elizabeth and James saw England as closed or open to the

---

[54] *The Boy King: Edward VI and the Protestant Reformation* (New York: Palgrave, 1999), 171.

[55] *The Conviction of Novelty* (1632), 5 (*ERL* 138); also see Loades, "The Origins of English Protestant Nationalism," 299–300. Catholics spoke of Luther as a "foreign interloper whose followers had taken over the English church" (Margaret Sena, "William Blundell and the Networks of Catholic Dissent in Post-Reformation England," in Alexandra Shepard and Phil Withington (eds.), *Communities in Early Modern England: Networks, Place, and Rhetoric* (Manchester: Manchester University Press, 2000), 66).

outside world would be repeatedly tested by questions of royal successions and dynastic alliances.

PHILIP OF SPAIN

Even if committed Marian Catholics felt that a robust Englishness had nothing to fear from welcoming Spanishness into its midst, they nevertheless needed to dispel (popular) perceptions about Philip's alien otherness. Marian propaganda in fact fostered the impression that the new king was hardly a foreigner at all. Christopherson argued that Philip "is unto us no straunger, but one of the bloude royall of Englande, by reason that his father the emperours Majestie, that nowe is, both by hys father syde and mothers cometh of the kinges of Englande." To convince dubious readers "that this is of an undoubted trueth," Christopherson includes a folding genealogical chart setting out "the lineall discent" of both Mary and Philip from Edward III.[56] Readers of this simplified family tree could trace Philip back through his parents to two of Gaunt's daughters: Katherine and Philippa. Philip's legitimate if distant claim to the English crown makes his arrival in England no "invasion" but a sort of homecoming in which the offshoot of "the royall bloude of Englande ... at lengthe is called home, as it were to hys natyve countrey."[57]

Philip's Lancastrian/Plantagenet ancestry also played an important part in the pageantry staged by the City of London for the ceremonial entry of the newly married couple on August 18, 1554. John Elder, the chronicler of the day's events, describes the series of *tableaux vivants* along the route that hailed Philip variously as "sole hope of Cesars side" and as greater than the four Philips of antiquity.[58] The sequence culminated with the "most excellent pageant of al" at the west end of Cheapside, the ceremonial heart of the city, "Wherein was contained, declared, and shewed their moste noble Geneology from kinge Edward the third, which Geneologie was most excellently, and moste ingeniously set out, with a great Arbore or tree, under the roote whereof was an olde man liinge on his left side, with a long white beard, a close croune on his head, and a sceptour in his ryght hand and a ball Imperial in his lefte. Which olde man signified kinge Edward the third, of whom both their majesties are linially descended." The pageant's genealogy, a variation of the Biblical Tree of Jesse, was surmounted either side with the figures of Philip and Mary and "both their armes joined in one under one Crown emperial." The pageant's aim, John Edwards observes, "was to replace

---

[56] *An exhortation to all menne*, Mv^{r–v}, Mvi^r. Also see Edward J. Baskerville, *A Chronological Bibliography of Propaganda and Polemic Published in England between 1553 and 1558 from the Death of Edward VI to the Death of Mary I* (Philadelphia: The American Philosophical Society, 1979), 42.
[57] *An exhortation to all menne*, Mvi^v.
[58] John Elder, *The copie of a letter sent in to Scotlande* (1555), Bvi^r.

the Tudor myth of the reconciliation of the houses of York and Lancaster, after the Wars of the Roses, with one of a Lancastrian restoration which would also reconcile Spain and England."[59] According to one of the verses written for the wedding, "The Devil old enemy of mankind did not wish | That the English Queen Mary marry *English* Philip | And that the royal stock return to its source, | But God, the provident hope of the English, did wish it."[60]

For the wedding ceremony, Philip reinforced his claim to a reassuring Englishness by dressing as an Englishman. As Alexander Samson points out, Philip's "English-style clothing was crucial in paving the way towards his acceptance in England as Mary's consort and king of England. It was part of the process by which he identified himself with England and made himself available for appropriation by the foreign kingdom he was coming to rule by marriage."[61] To what extent Philip succeeded in this process, however, is open to doubt. Upon his arrival in England, he allegedly told his Spanish lords to embrace English customs in favor of Spanish ones. Then Philip asked for English beer to be served as a gesture of his assimilation to the local culture. Yet the fact that Philip would have made this appeal in the Spanish tongue (he never learned English), points up the limits to his ability to blend into his new surroundings.[62]

RECONCILIATION WITH ROME

Just as Marian Catholic nationalism found ways of incorporating the presence of a Spanish co-ruler into an ideology of Englishness, so it found ways of turning the country's reconciliation with the papacy into a vindication of English identity. In fact, Marian nationalists argued that outside of communion with Rome, England lacked its authentic identity. Only by returning to that communion and reassuming its pre-Reformation place within universal Christendom could England be true to itself once more. Before Mary's accession and reconciliation with Rome, "The bewtye of englande was banished clene," declared a ballad celebrating the queen's imagined pregnancy.[63]

---

[59] Ibid. Ci^v–Cii^r, Cii^v. John Edwards, "Introduction: Carranza in England," in *Reforming Catholicism in the England of Mary Tudor*, 14.

[60] Quoted in Alexander Samson, " 'Changing Places': The Marriage and Royal Entry of Philip, Prince of Austria and Mary Tudor, July–August 1554," *Sixteenth Century Journal* 36 (2005), 766.

[61] Samson, " 'Changing Places'," 765. Whereas Samson emphasizes "Philip's carefully staged identification with England," David Loades argues that "Philip made very little effort to project himself as king of England" ("Philip II and the Government of England," in Claire Cross, David Loades, and J. J. Scarisbrick (eds.), *Law and Government under the Tudors* (Cambridge: Cambridge University Press, 1988), 192).

[62] Quoted in Alison Plowden, *The House of Tudor* (Stein and Day: New York,1976), 173.

[63] "Nowe singe, nowe springe, oure care is exil'd, Oure vertuous Quene is quickned with child," in Hyder E. Rollins (ed.), *Old English Ballads 1553–1625* (Cambridge: Cambridge University Press, 1920), 20.

While most English people were happy to see the return of the Mass and Catholic ceremonies, they were far less enthusiastic about resubmitting to papal authority. Even among Marian conservatives, Henry VIII's vision of an independent England free of outside authority had proven remarkably appealing. Several generations of anti-papal polemic had made the pope a deeply suspect figure in England. Religious conservatives had benefited like many others in England from Henry VIII's distribution of church lands at the dissolution— lands they were now afraid would be reappropriated by the Church. Not surprisingly, the conservative authors who defended Mary's marriage to Philip and the new religious settlement side-stepped the question of papal supremacy or handled it in the most cautious terms by arguing that the pope's role as the guarantor of Church unity made him more of an administrative than a spiritual leader.[64]

The task of formally reconciling schismatical England to the Papal See was largely the responsibility of Cardinal Reginald Pole, who had spent over two decades in banishment for refusing to support Henry VIII's divorce or to acknowledge the royal supremacy.[65] Due to widespread suspicions in England about the papacy, Pole's return to England was delayed until the terms of his legatine mission were settled and an agreement reached on the crucial question of church lands.[66] When Pole finally arrived in November 1554, he was fully aware of the extent of anti-papal sentiment within the clergy and the nation as a whole. In his address to Parliament signaling formal reconciliation with Rome and absolving the English of their past schism and heresy, Pole stressed that the Apostolic See was not a threat to national autonomy, but a source of "manifold benefites," in time of need. To counter hostile views of the papacy as an alien institution, Pole reminded his audience that Englishmen themselves had occupied the Seat of Peter, including Pope Adrian IV. Adrian's more notable achievements included the conversion of Norway and the donation of dominion over Ireland to the kings of England. Pole also mentioned with patriotic pride the English scholar Alcuinus (Alcuin) who was induced by Carolus Magnus (Charlemagne) to bring learning to the newly established University of Paris and thus help spread the "light of religion."[67] In Pole's view, Britain had always

---

[64] For ambivalence toward the papacy among Marian writers, see Loades, "Relations between the Anglican and Roman Catholic Churches in the Sixteenth Century," in *Politics, Censorship,* 66–71; and Lucy E. C. Wooding, *Rethinking Catholicism in Reformation England* (Oxford: Clarendon Press, 2000), 127–34.

[65] See Thomas F. Mayer, *Reginald Pole: Prince and Prophet* (Cambridge: Cambridge University Press, 2000), ch. 6.

[66] Ibid. Loades, "The Enforcement of Reaction, 1553–8," in *Politics, Censorship,* 27–38.

[67] I quote from the version of Pole's address printed in John Elder, *The Copie of a letter,* Di^v– Eii^r. On the different manuscript and printed versions of the speech, see Thomas F. Mayer, *The Correspondence of Reginald Pole,* vol. 2: *A Calendar, 1547–1554: A Power in Rome* (Aldershot: Ashgate, 2003), 366–8.

functioned as a satellite to Rome in the Christianizing mission, and as a recipient as well as a purveyor of the Catholic faith.[68]

Pole and the other architects of the reconciliation with Rome made every effort to depict England as obedient rather than subservient to the papacy and as preserving an important degree of autonomy. Stephen Gardiner in a Paul's Cross sermon of 1554 referred ambiguously to England as both a "realm" and an "empire"—the latter, a term that recalled Henry VIII's famous declaration that "this realm of England is an empire."[69] "Empire," in this context, as David Starkey explains, meant "the *intensity* and *completeness* of royal rule over the particular territory of England" and not "the extent of rule over several states or territories."[70] Mary herself, it should also be noted, refused to give up the imperial title she inherited from her father as the appearance of the closed, imperial crown in the wedding pageantry indicates. Mary, in fact, as Lucy Wooding argues, "was often as defensive of the royal prerogative against Papal interference as her father."[71] When Gardiner and other Marian Catholics talked of "empire" they fused the Henrician idea of England as an independent sovereign territory with the idea that England was now part of an amalgamation of disparate states. In marriage, Philip and Mary became "King and Queen of England, France, Naples, Jerusalem, and Ireland; Defenders of the Faith; Princes of Spain and Sicily; Archdukes of Austria; Dukes of Milan, Burgundy, and Brabant; Counts of Hapsburg, Flanders and Tyrol." England, symbolically at least, was now part of an Anglo-Habsburg empire that also encompassed New Spain.[72]

Pole's "new Catholic nationalism," as Starkey calls it, stressed that the English owed a special obligation to Rome, not only because the Christian religion had first reached their Anglo-Saxon ancestors in Britain directly from Rome, but also because Britain had been chosen by Rome as the "first of all Ilandes [to receive] the light of Christes religion." This showed, claimed Pole, that

[68] As David Starkey observes, Pole realized that "to be welcome once more on English shores, the eternal verities of the Universal Church had to present themselves in terms of the particular national history of England" (*Elizabeth: The Struggle for the Throne* (London: Harper, 2001), 174).

[69] On Gardiner's sermon, see Mayer, *The Correspondence of Reginald Pole*, 2: 383; J. A. Muller, *Stephen Gardiner and the Tudor Reaction* (New York: Macmillan, 1926), 264–6, 384–5; Starkey, *Elizabeth*, 17, 31, 40, 174–5; John Gough Nichols (ed.), *The Chronicle of Queen Jane, and Two Years of Queen Mary* (London: Camden Society, 1850), 161–3.

[70] Starkey, *Elizabeth*, 173.

[71] "The Marian Restoration and the Language of Catholic Reform," in *Reforming Catholicism in the England of Mary Tudor*, 64.

[72] Paul L. Hughes and James F. Larkin (eds.), *Tudor Royal Proclamations: The Later Tudors (1553–1587)* (New Haven: Yale University Press, 1969), 2: 45–6. Also see David Loades, "Philip II and the Government of England," 179. In anticipation of Philip's marriage to Mary, his father, the Emperor Charles V, "resigned under his imperial seal the kingdoms of Naples and Jerusalem to his son Philip Prince of Spain whereby it might well appear to all men that the queen's highness was then married not only to a prince, but also unto a king." As part of the marriage treaty, the couple agreed to share all titles; Philip as king consort, however, enjoyed strictly limited powers in England. Philip did not become King of Spain until his father abdicated in 1556.

"The Sea Apostolike...hath a special respect to this Realme above al other" and "that god himselfe...hath geven this Realme prerogative of nobilitie above other."[73] Catholic narratives about Rome's conversion of Britain, whether the mission of Damian and Forganus sent by Pope Eleutherius, or the later and most famous mission of Augustine sent by Pope Gregory, formed a crucial part of the Catholic imagining of the nation well into the seventeenth century.[74] In the later sixteenth century, as we shall see in Chapters 3 and 4, Bede's *Ecclesiastical History* became an especially charged locus for competing visions of national identity both between Protestants and Catholics as well as among Catholics themselves.[75]

Once the "old religion" became a proscribed faith under Elizabeth, Catholics felt an even greater need to affirm their homeland's exceptional status in Roman Christendom. Pole's view about England's "prerogative of nobilitie above other" nations became a commonplace of Catholic nationalist rhetoric. Edmund Campion asserted at his trial, for example, that England was "the island of saints and the most devout child of the see of Peter."[76] According to William Allen, England, was "once mighty and noble, and certainly pre-eminent and glorious among those lands which gave their allegiance to Christ."[77] Catholic claims about England's religious exceptionalism indicate there was nothing innovative or unique about more familiar Protestant claims that England was as an "elect" nation, specially chosen by God as a new Israel. Indeed, as Krishan Kumar argues, the English idea of national election not only predates the Reformation— it is already present in Bede's *Ecclesiastical History*—but is borrowed from other cultures, in particular from thirteenth-century France.[78]

The Catholic subjects of Elizabeth and James also kept alive the idea of England's privileged place within Christendom through the tradition that England was "the Dowry of our Lady."[79] England was "so much devouted to the honour and service of our blessed Lady, above al other nations," wrote the author of *A treatise with a Kalendar*, "that it hath beene commonly called our Ladies Dowry."[80] This idea seems to derive from the most famous of the

---

[73] Starkey, *Elizabeth*, 327; Elder, *The Copie of a letter*, Di^v–Eii^r.

[74] Starkey, *Elizabeth*, 173.

[75] George Marshall, *A compendious treatise in metre declaring the firste originall of sacrifice, and the building of aultares and churches, and the firste receavinge of the Christen faith here in Englande* (1554), Biii^r.

[76] Quoted in Michael E. Williams, "Campion and the English Continental Seminaries," in Thomas M. McCoog (ed.), *The Reckoned Expense: Edmund Campion and the Early English Jesuits* (Woodbridge: Boydell Press, 1996), 294.

[77] *Letters of William Allen and Richard Barret, 1572–1598*, ed. P. Renold. Catholic Record Society, 58 (Oxford: Oxonian Press, 1967), 279.

[78] Kumar, *The Making of English National Identity*, 108.

[79] William Wizeman, "The Virgin Mary in the Reign of Mary Tudor," *Studies in Church History* 39 (2004), 239–48.

[80] *A treatise with a kalendar*, 35. See T. E. Bridgett, *Our Lady's Dowry: How England Gained that Title* (London: Burns and Oates, nd).

Medieval shrines of Our Lady at Walsingham in Lincolnshire that from the eleventh century was dedicated to the annunciation and Mary's saving grace. When Henry's minions destroyed this popular pilgrimage site during the Reformation, its memory lived on in Catholic circles as a symbol of England's glorious Catholic past and a metonymy of the present devastation of the faith. Although the outward signs of Marian devotion like shrines and statues were no longer publicly visible in England, the country remained under Mary's special protection.

This Marian tradition also flourished in the English Catholic colleges founded on the Continent beginning in the late 1560s to serve the needs of recusant youth. An account of the college at Seville in southern Spain, for example, observes that "schollers seme to shroude themselves very peculiarly under the protection of our blessed ladye the Queene of heaven, agaynst the persecution of your Queene of Ingland." The students at Seville as well as being devoted to the litanies of Our Lady had erected over one of the college gates a picture showing Mary flanked by two kneeling English scholars. Above the picture were the words "Anglia Dos Mariæ. Ingland is the Dowry of our ladye" "for so much as Britanie now called Inglande, was the first kingdome that wholy togeather gave it selfe and submitted her kingly scepter unto Christ Jesus the sonne and spouse of our lady; therfore by a certayne devout kinde of speach, ould Inglish authors did say Ingland to be the Dowry of our ladye."[81] The idea of the Virgin Mary as England's special guardian reflects the way her identity was reimagined by English Catholics under conditions of heresy. The medieval church had portrayed Mary as "meek," a model of female compliance, or as the "remote Queen of Heaven." But as critics have recently shown, Catholics in the later sixteenth century came to think of Mary as a militant warrior to whom they could directly appeal for saving grace and for protection against the forces of heresy. As part of this reinvention of Mary, English Catholics overhauled the traditional practice of the rosary, turning it into a powerful sacrament as well as a tool of resistance in an England shorn at the Reformation of Marian shrines, images, and other physical memorials to the Virgin Queen.[82]

The idea that England enjoyed the Virgin's special protection was particularly comforting to Catholics once they became an increasingly harassed religious minority under Elizabeth. But if they could agree that England was Mary's Dowry, they were more divided in other aspects of national imagining. Beneath a consensus Catholic view of English "exceptionalism," a factionalized Catholic

---

[81] Robert Persons, *Newes from Spayne and Holland* (Antwerp, 1593. *ERL* 365), 13ᵛ. See also Peter Davidson, "Recusant Catholic Spaces in Early Modern England," in Ronald Corthell, Frances E. Dolan, Christopher Highley, and Arthur F. Marotti (eds.), *Catholic Culture in Early Modern England* (Notre Dame, Ind.: University of Notre Dame Press, 2007), 25–7.

[82] McClain, *Lest we be Damned*, 81–107; Anne Dillon, "Praying by Number: The Confraternity of the Rosary and the English Catholic Community, c. 1580–1700," *History* 88 (2003), 451–71.

community both in exile and at home disagreed about what it meant to be English and Catholic. Should English Catholics make common religious cause with their Celtic neighbors? Should they look to the great Continental Catholic powers for royal heirs and material support? Must English Catholics obey the pope in secular as well as spiritual matters? Was English Catholicism something different from Roman Catholicism? As this study will show, just as different Catholic voices posed various answers to these questions, so there were alternative ways of being both English and Catholic in the early modern period.

2

First Wave: Exile and Catholic Identity 1558–1570

EARLY DIASPORA AND SITES OF EXILE

The accession of Elizabeth and the restoration of reformed religion through the Acts of Supremacy and Uniformity presented a dilemma to her religiously conservative subjects. Should they outwardly conform to the new state church, openly resist it, or leave the realm by going into overseas exile? The vast majority chose to accommodate themselves to the new religious requirements, occasionally attending Church of England services so as to avoid financial penalties. These so-called Church Papists remained Catholics at heart and whenever possible continued illicitly to practice the "old religion." As the first decade of the new reign unfolded, however, conforming Catholics came under increasing pressure from the papacy and clerics to separate themselves from Protestants, abandon reformed services, and instead embrace open recusancy.[1]

Only a tiny fraction of Catholics chose or were forced into exile. In a culture where most people stayed close to their place of birth, the decision to leave England without permission was an almost inconceivable one. Even travel to northwest Europe was expensive and risky; all travelers were required to have government-issued passports and ports were closely watched for religious dissidents attempting to slip out of the country undetected. The emigrant who had no support network at the journey's end, faced the prospect of a life of penury and insecurity. Moreover, the exile exposed himself and his family to serious legal repercussions, including attainder, the confiscation of land, wealth, and title. Leaving England could mean abandoning family, friends, and patrons, as well as the conventional markers of identity and good name. Still, some resolute Catholics—including academics, students, and other pious lay people, as well as priests and nuns—despite great risks and costs, either chose or were forced into exile during the early years of Elizabeth's reign.

---

[1] Alexandra Walsham, *Church Papists: Catholicism, Conformity, and Confessional Polemic in Early Modern* England. The Royal Historical Society (Boydell Press, 1993); Christopher Haigh, *English Reformations: Religion, Politics, and Society under the Tudors* (Oxford: Oxford University Press, 1993); Eamon Duffy, *The Stripping of the Altars: Traditional Religion in England, 1400–1580* (New Haven: Yale University Press, 1992).

Most scholarship on early modern religious culture has been drawn to martyrdom rather than exile because of martyrdom's obviously more sensational components of imprisonment, torture, and execution.[2] Moreover, Christian culture defined martyrdom as the ultimate form of witnessing, whereas exile contained little doctrinal advocacy. Unlike exile, the experience of martyrdom from an early period developed its own set of representational forms, including the martyrology and the saint's life or hagiography, thus providing critics with a well-defined set of narratives. Exile, on the other hand, in part because it lacked its own distinctive literary modes, has been overlooked both by early modern and contemporary observers as a less exalted calling than martyrdom—even as a strategy for avoiding the ultimate self-sacrifice. Yet, as a gesture of resistance to a dominant state-church, exile could also be construed not as an alternative *to*, but as an alternative *form of*, martyrdom. In this view, exiles were sometimes regarded as "white" or "bloodless" martyrs, unlike the "red" martyrs who died for their convictions.[3] Two prominent early Elizabethan exiles, Lady Hungerford and Jane Dormer, for example, are described as martyrs on account of the losses they suffered in leaving home and because of the sacrifices they made on behalf of less-fortunate exiles in Tommaso Bozio's *De Signis Ecclesiae Dei contra omnes hereses* (1591).[4]

This chapter will focus on the experiences and writings of one group within the emerging Catholic diaspora: the scholars and students who during the first decade of Elizabeth's reign settled in various parts of the Spanish Low Countries including especially Louvain and Antwerp.[5] Under the protection of Philip II,

[2] Recent studies include Brad S. Gregory, *Salvation at Stake: Christian Martyrdom in Early Modern Europe* (Cambridge: Harvard University Press, 1999); Anne Dillon, *The Construction of Martyrdom in the English Catholic Community, 1535–1603* (Aldershot: Ashgate, 2002); Susannah Brietz Monta, *Martyrdom and Literature in Early Modern England* (Cambridge: Cambridge University Press, 2005).
The major exception to the current preoccupation with martyrdom is Alison Shell's landmark book on *Catholicism, Controversy, and the English Literary Imagination, 1558–1660* (Cambridge: Cambridge University Press, 1999) which devotes two chapters to "The subject of exile." Shell's topics include Catholic manuscript verse and Jesuit drama.

[3] In early Christian teaching, confessors and martyrs were distinct categories of the faithful (see "Confessors" in the online version of *The Catholic Encyclopedia*, vol. 4 (New York: Robert Appleton Company, 1908) http://www.newadvent.org/cathen/04215a.htm). Jonathan Wright refers to exiles as being beneath martyrs in the Church's "Hierarchy of Confessors." "Marian Exiles and the Legitimacy of Flight from Persecution," *Journal of Ecclesiastical History* 52 (2001), 220–43. Also see Gregory, *Salvation at Stake*, 154–5; Frederick A. Norwood describes the "martyr as a cornered refugee" (*Strangers and Exiles: A History of Religious Refugees*. 2 vols. (New York: Abingdon Press, 1969), 1: 89–90). For Protestant examples of the exile-as-martyr, see Alexandra Walsham, *Charitable Hatred: Tolerance and Intolerance in England, 1500–1700* (Manchester: Manchester University Press, 2006), 185.

[4] Michael E. Williams, "Images of Martyrdom in Paintings at the English College Valladolid," in Margaret A. Rees (ed.), *Leeds Papers on Symbol and Image in Iberian Arts* (Leeds: Trinity and All Saints College, 1994), 69 n.12. A Protestant example of the exile-as- bloodless martyr would be the Duchess of Suffolk as described by John Foxe (John N. King (ed.), *Voices of the English Reformation: A Sourcebook* (Philadelphia: University of Pennsylvania Press, 2004), 292–9).

[5] Valuable earlier studies specifically devoted to this group of exiles include Peter Guilday, "The English Catholic Refugees at Louvain, 1559–1575," in *Mélanges d'histoire offerts à Charles Moeller* 2

the exiles formed a relatively stable and secure expatriate community that produced an impressive body of controversial and polemical literature. Between
1559 and 1570, the printing centers of Louvain and Antwerp issued over fifty
titles that were then smuggled into England for a Catholic readership. Post-
Reformation Catholics, as Alexandra Walsham reminds us, were just as willing
as reformers to embrace the printing press as a key instrument of ideological
warfare, for Catholicism as well as Protestantism was a religion of the printed
book.[6] These fugitive Catholic texts, I argue, helped fashion an English exile
identity from the beginning of the new reign to the early 1570s when the
Northern Rebellion and the excommunication of Elizabeth dramatically changed
the profile and politics of the diaspora.

For the first wave of Elizabethan Catholic exiles, Antwerp was one of several attractive destinations. Located in the southern Low Countries and thus
nominally under Habsburg control, the city was a relatively short journey from
London down the Thames estuary, across the North Sea, and up the River
Scheldt. In the first half of the sixteenth century, Antwerp was a haven for
religious refugees of various stripes. In the 1520s, the reformer William Tyndale
settled here, distributing the first English translation of the New Testament as
well as other Lutheran texts banned from England. During Mary Tudor's reign,
the city provided refuge to Protestant exiles. Antwerp's pragmatic magistrates
promoted their city's status as northwest Europe's preeminent trading center
by trying to maintain an open religious climate. During the second half of
the sixteenth century, however, the city was increasingly afflicted by religious
conflict making life especially difficult for its Catholic population.[7] Yet Antwerp's
reputation as a center of printing excellence with good lines of communication
to England continued to make it an attractive abode for English Catholics.[8]

(1914), 175–89; A. C. Southern, " 'The Best Wits out of England': University Men in Exile under
Elizabeth," *The Month* 7 (1952), 12–21; Leo Hicks, "The Catholic Exiles and the Elizabethan
Religious Settlement," *The Catholic Historical Review* 22 (1936), 129–48.

[6] Alexandra Walsham, " 'Domme Preachers'? Post-Reformation English Catholicism and the
Culture of Print," *Past and Present* 168 (2000), 72–123.

[7] In 1566 reformers unleashed a wave of iconoclastic "fury" in Antwerp, desecrating and
plundering Catholic churches of their riches. Philip II responded by sending the Duke of Alva
and his army to punish the ringleaders of the violence and restore order. The city changed hands
several times during the religious wars of the later sixteenth century; in 1576 it was brutally sacked
by mutinous Spanish soldiers venting their anger at lack of payment. Antwerp was finally seized
in 1585 by Spanish forces led by Alexander Farnese (the Duke of Parma), at which point "the
metropolis was transformed immediately from a bastion of Protestantism in the Netherlands and
revolution against Spain into a Spanish outpost in the struggle against rebellion and a bastion of
the Counter Reformation" (*Antwerp, Dissident Typographical Centre: The Role of Antwerp Printers in
the Religious Conflicts in England (16th century)* (Antwerp: The City of Antwerp Plantin-Moretus
Museum, 1994), 13–14).

[8] For a discussion of Antwerp's status as a cosmopolitan center of trade and printing, see the
chapters by F. de Nave and C. Coppens in *Antwerp, Dissident Typographical Centre*. Also see
Andrew G. Johnston and Jean-François Gilmont, "Printing and the Reformation in Antwerp," in
Jean-François Gilmont (ed.), *The Reformation and the Book* Eng. edn. and trans. by Karin Maag
(Aldershot: Ashgate, 1998), 188–213.

Some forty miles south of Antwerp was the city of Louvain—the major destination of the early Catholic exiles. Unlike Antwerp, Louvain was staunchly Catholic and orthodox during the sixteenth century. The city was a bishop's seat as well as the home of a major university, founded in 1425, whose conservative Faculty of Theology helped to formulate the edicts of the Council of Trent.[9] The Faculty had also been one of the first to publicly condemn Luther's teachings in 1519, while its refusal to support Henry VIII's divorce from Anne Boleyn gave the university "a reputation as a center of resistance to" the English king.[10]

During the reigns of Henry VIII and Edward VI, an earlier generation of English clerical and lay Catholics had taken refuge in Louvain.[11] Most notably, these earlier émigrés included relatives and clients of Sir Thomas More like John and Margaret Clement, William Rastell, and Thomas Roper, as well as friends of More like the London-based Italian merchant, Anthony Bonvisi, who supported many of the exiles in Louvain.[12] The More circle was dedicated to preserving the memory of this iconic Tudor martyr and to reshaping his image as a model of the Catholic recusant who placed his faith before his sovereign. Thomas Stapleton, a later admirer of More in Louvain, published the *Tres Thomae*—a triple hagiography that linked the lives of Thomas More, Thomas Beckett, and the Apostle Thomas.[13] The Louvain printer John Fowler, another key member of the More circle, married the daughter of one of More's

[9] See Lucy E. C. Wooding, *Rethinking Catholicism in Reformation England* (Oxford: Oxford University Press, 2000) on the reformist, Erasmian nature of the University of Louvain (183). For a contemporary account of the city and university, see Samuel Lewkenor, *A discourse not altogether unprofitable, nor unpleasant for such as are desirous to know the situation and customes of forraine cities without travelling to see them. Containing a discourse of all those citties wherein doe flourish at this day priviledged universities* (1600), 21^r–22^r.

[10] Peter Marshall, *Religious Identities in Henry VIII's England* (Aldershot: Ashgate, 2006), 247 n. 92. On the history of the university, see *Leuven University 1425–1985* (Leuven University Press, 1990). The Elizabethan Protestant firebrand, William Fulke, recalled "That Luther despised the universitie of Louaine, and called it a stable of Asses, stewes, and schoole of the divell, it was not for hatred of good learning; but in contempt of those Barbarous doltes, which in those daies opposed them selves against the light of the truth. (Erasmus whome all men knewe to have deserved verie well of good learning) writeth as hardlie of the universitie of Louaine in respect of the multitude of unlearned sophisters, which were in that time, as Luther: saying, there was no place for the muses there, where so manie hogges grunted, where so manie asses routed, so many Camells blattered, so many Jaies chattered, so many pies prattled" ("An Apologie against the Railing Declamation of Peter Frarine," in *A treatise against the Defense of the censure* (1586), 42).

[11] Marshall, *Religious Identities*, 256, 260–1. Marshall includes a useful appendix of Henrician Catholic exiles (263–76).

[12] James Kelsey McConica, *English Humanists and Reformation Politics Under Henry VIII and Edward VI* (Oxford: Clarendon Press, 1965), 269–71; Peter Guilday, *The English Catholic Refugees on the Continent, 1558–1795* (London, 1914), 10.

[13] *Antwerp, Dissident Typographical Centre*, 135–6; Gordon Albion, "An English Professor in Louvain: Thomas Stapleton (1535–1598)," *Miscellanea historica in honorem Alberta de Meyer* (Louvain and Brussels: University of Louvain, 1946), 895–913; Marvin R. O'Connell, *Thomas Stapleton and the Counter-reformation* (New Haven: Yale University Press, 1964).

secretaries and went on to issue editions of many of More's own works. These included his collected works in Latin (1565) as well as *A dialogue of cumfort against tribulation* (1573). More had composed the *Dialogue* in the Tower in 1534, and its message of consolation to those who suffered for the Old Faith now assumed renewed significance for England's Catholics. As Clark Hulse observes, these various texts about More, along with numerous portraits that circulated after his death, acted as substitute relics that helped "strengthen conviction, exorcise fear, and confirm the underground or exile communities" of Catholics.[14]

The new generation of Catholic exiles that arrived at Louvain in the years following Elizabeth's accession comprised mainly Oxford and Cambridge faculty and students who refused to reconcile themselves to the new Protestant reforms. The Protestant Bishop of Salisbury, John Jewel, reported in 1560 that "our universities, and more especially Oxford, are most sadly deserted; without learning, without lectures, without any regard to religion."[15] On the Catholic side, Edward Rishton observed that following the change of religion, "The very flower of the two universities, Oxford and Cambridge, was carried away, as it were, by a storm, and scattered in foreign lands. Some three hundred persons, of all conditions, went away at once into different parts of Europe, but especially to the Belgian universities."[16] Among the most prominent of the émigrés were Thomas Harding and Thomas Stapleton, both ex-fellows of New College, Oxford— the most conservative of all the Oxford colleges that provided the intellectual backbone of the English cohort in the Low Countries. Harding was appointed Doctor of Divinity at the University of Louvain while Stapleton became Professor of Sacred Scripture. In the first decade of Elizabeth's reign, thirty-three fellows of New College either resigned or were removed from their posts for religious reasons.[17]

[14]   Clark Hulse, "Dead Man's Treasure: The Cult of Thomas More," in David Lee Miller, Sharon O'Dair, and Harold Weber (eds.), *The Production of English Renaissance Culture* (Ithaca: Cornell University Press, 1994), 221. Also see James K. McConica, "The Recusant Reputation of Thomas More," in R. S. Sylvester and G. P. Marc'hadour (eds.), *Essential Articles for the Study of Thomas More* (Hamden, Conn.: Archon Books, 1977); and Michael Questier, "Catholicism, Kinship and the Public Memory of Sir Thomas More," *Journal of Ecclesiastical History* 53 (2002), 476–509. An earlier edition of More's Latin works printed at Basle in 1563 placed greater emphasis on More the humanist than on the saintly More of the Louvain edition.

[15]   *The Zurich Letters, comprising the correspondence of several English bishops and others, with some of the Helvetian reformers, during the early part of the reign of Queen Elizabeth. Translated from authenticated copies of the autographs preserved in the archives of Zurich*, Parker Society, ed. Revd. Hastings Robinson. 2 vols. (Cambridge: Cambridge University Press, 1842), 1: 77.

[16]   *The Rise and Growth of the Anglican Schism by the Rev. Nicolas Sander*, ed. and trans. David Lewis (London: Burns and Oates, 1877; Rockford, Ill.: Tan Books, 1988), 261.

[17]   Penry Williams, "Elizabethan Oxford: State, Church, and University," in James McConica (ed.), *The History of the University of Oxford*, vol. 3: *The Collegiate University* (Oxford: Oxford University Press, 1986), 407.

ATTACKING AND DEFENDING EXILE

The Louvain publishing project began as a response to Bishop Jewel's sermon preached at Paul's Cross and then at court in 1559–60 challenging the basic tenets of the Catholic faith. Jewel later developed and published his arguments as *An Apologie, or aunswer in defence of the Church of England* (1562, Latin and English) that defended to an international audience Elizabeth's claim to ecclesiastical supremacy while repudiating the power of popes and Church councils like Trent.[18] Jewel refuted Catholic charges that England was being torn apart by squabbling sects of reformers who would in time undermine the unity of Christendom. The "Gospellers," as Jewel called his fellow reformers, were not a new sect as Catholics alleged, but were restoring the original, pure faith of the first Christians. It was the Catholic Church, he claimed, with its invented traditions and bogus rituals that "rente in peces, kepe back, mayme, and burne the auncient Fathers workes."[19] Thomas Harding, once a fellow reformer and colleague of Jewel's at New College, issued the major Catholic rebuttal to Jewel's *Apologie* in *A confutation of a booke intituled An apologie of the Church of England* (1565), thus precipitating a series of responses and counter-responses that ended only with the deaths of Jewel and Harding in 1571 and 1572 respectively.[20]

Protestant and Catholic writers traded charges and counter-charges early in Elizabeth's reign, conscious that their respective confessional groupings had effectively switched places since the death of Mary Tudor only a few years ago. Under Mary, Protestants like Jewel had gone into exile overseas, while Catholics like Harding had held positions of influence at home. The "Louvainists" exploited this reversal of fortunes by pointing out that during Mary's reign many of the Protestant exiles had urged open resistance to her regime, even regicide. The Louvainist Richard Shacklock concluded his description of the "difference betwene the wryting of the Catholikes now, and the heretykes in Q. Maries dayes" with the words, "loke knoxes his bokes and others"—an allusion to John Knox, author of *The first blast of the trumpet against the monstrous regiment of women* (1558), a work composed in exile with the intention of discrediting female rulers and Mary in particular.[21] Unfortunately for Knox, his book was not published until after Mary's death; the newly-crowned Elizabeth, although no Catholic like her sister, was offended by Knox's anti-feminism and never forgave the Scotsman in spite of his apologies. The case of Knox's *Monstrous regiment* is raised repeatedly in the works of exiled Catholics as a touchstone

---

[18] Peter Milward, *Religious Controversies of the Elizabethan Age: A Survey of Printed Sources* (London: The Scolar Press, 1977), 1–6.

[19] *An apologie*, kiv[r].

[20] Gary W. Jenkins, *John Jewel and the English National Church: The Dilemmas of an Erastian Reformer* (Aldershot: Ashgate, 2006), esp. ch. 3 "The Catholic Reaction to Jewel."

[21] *A most excellent treatise of the begynnyng of heresyes in oure tyme* (Antwerp, 1565. *ERL* 24), A4[v].

for distinguishing their political loyalty from the subversive agenda of their Protestant counterparts. Thus Harding asked his Protestant readers: "What meant ye when ye layde your heads together being at Geneva in Quene Maries dayes, the faithfull brothers of England and Scotland, and devised a most seditious and traiterous booke against the most monstrous regiment of women? Mynded ye to blowe peace, tranquilitie, and good order to the realmes of England and Scotland, when ye sent abroade great numbers of those bookes printed in Geneva amongst the people, bearing name and title of the first and second blast of the trumpet?"[22] John Martiall echoed Harding's sentiments, asking all "indifferent" readers of his book defending use of the crucifix to compare the orderly writings of Catholics with the subversive discourses of Protestant exiles in the last reign: "there is no blast blown against the monstrous regiment of women," he protested, "There is no libel set forth for order of succession."[23]

The Louvainists, desperate to distinguish their identity as exiles from the Marian Protestant exiles before them, developed a self-justifying rhetoric that contrasted their loyalty to Elizabeth with the Marian Protestant's disloyalty to Mary. In the dedications and prefaces to their books, the Louvainists insisted they were the obedient subjects of the queen: Harding's *Confutation* of Jewel, for example, was dedicated to Elizabeth and ostentatiously displayed the royal arms and the motto "God save the Quene" on the verso of the title page.[24]

These gestures of loyalty by the Louvainists, however, were quickly impugned by their Protestant adversaries as empty rhetoric or coded insults. Jewel responded to the *Confutation*, accusing Harding of "fraudes... mockeries...[and] lothesome talke." "Thought you," asked Jewel, "by the weight of sutche reasons, to moove Mountaines, and to woorke woonders, and to force her Majestie to leave christe and his Gospel, and comme to Louaine to folowe you?"[25] Jewel's fellow Protestant James Calfhill upbraided the Louvainist John Martiall for the book he dedicated to the queen about her use of a crucifix in the royal chapel—evidence, Catholics believed, of Elizabeth's religious conservatism.[26] Calfhill accuses Martiall of only posing as the queen's devoted subject: "Thus trayterously ye seeke for defence at hir hands, whose person ye flee, whose doings ye impugne." According to Calfhill, the traitorous intentions

---

[22] Harding, *confutation*, 173ᵛ.

[23] *A replie to M. Calfhills blasphemous answer made against the Treatise of the crosse* (1566. *ERL* 203), **1ᵛ.

[24] Wooding, *Rethinking Catholicism*, 195; Harding's was one of four books by the exiles dedicated to Elizabeth (Peter Holmes, *Resistance and Compromise: The Political Thought of the Elizabethan Catholics* (Cambridge: Cambridge University Press, 1982), ch. 1, esp. 14). There is a sizable scholarly literature on the Marian Protestant exiles, bur see esp. C. H. Garret, *The Marian Exiles* (Cambridge: Cambridge University Press, 1938) and K. Bartlett, "The English Exile Community in Italy and the Political Opposition to Mary I," *Albion* 3 (1981), 223–41.

[25] *A defence of the Apologie of the Churche of Englande conteining an answeare to a certaine booke lately set foorthe by M. Hardinge, and entituled, A confutation of &c.*, (1567), Rrrᵛ.

[26] Milward, *Religious Controversies of the Elizabethan Age*, 17–18.

of the Catholics were apparent from their refusal to grant Elizabeth her full style and title as "Supreme Governor of the Church of England" on their title pages: "She to be Queene, and yet a subject to other: you to be Englishmen, and yet no subjectes to hir. In deede good cause you have with al the rable of your perverse confederates and outlawes." Elizabeth, Calfhill noted, had shown remarkable restraint in not pursuing and punishing the exiles as they deserved.[27]

For all their assertions of loyalty to Elizabeth, the Catholic exiles could not "escape" the fact that they had fled her territories for foreign realms. And this physical separation from home made them vulnerable to a host of charges—from being out of touch with events in England, to being fugitives and "unnatural and disordered subjects" who sought succor from foreign princes.[28] The most basic Protestant charge against the exiles was that by separating themselves from their homeland they were no longer qualified to discuss its affairs. Thus when Richard Shacklock published a translation of a letter by the Portuguese Bishop Osório da Fonseca imploring Elizabeth to return to Catholic orthodoxy, the Protestant Abraham Hartwell labeled Shacklock "a pryvate man, disneighboured from us by sea and lande, and in our affayres unacqueynted." Hartwell adopted a sardonic tone, asking Shacklock to

pardon mee, that I an Englishe man borne, one of the quenes majesties suppliauntes, and enfourmed in my countrie fashions, do make you aunswere, and use my penne somwhat franckely, not so muche upon an angry pange, or a bytter contentious harte, as to correcte this your mistaking of the englishe state, sponge of false surmises, and to restore the truethe unto them, whom peradventure this your letter hath perverted.

For Hartwell, the English-born Shacklock was just as much an alien as Osório who was unacquainted with England, "the most famous Isle in Christendome." Like Osório, Shacklock was accused of "grosse ignorance of our English customes," and of being "too busie a servitour in a forrein Realme, unadvisedly carpynge, where no man knoweth lesse then you."[29] Another translation by Shacklock of a work of the Prussian Cardinal Hosius provoked the Protestant John Barthlett to ask, "what hath Hosius being an alien, and ignoraunte of our Land, I pray you, to doe with" English affairs.[30] The exiles' Englishness was suspect in the eyes of Protestants not just because they had left England but also because they had tied their fortunes to foreigners who knew nothing about England.

The Louvainists responded to allegations that their flight abroad had compromised their Englishness by redefining the nature of exile. In his *A treatise*

---

[27] *An Answer to the Treatise of the Cross* (1565), A4[r–v].

[28] John Fowler trans. Peter Frarinus, *An oration against the unlawfull insurrections of the Protestantes of our time* (Antwerp, 1566. *ERL* 226), "The Translator to the Reader."

[29] *A sight of the Portugall pearle* (1565), Aii[v], Aiii[v]. For full details of the controversy, see Milward, *Religious Controversies of the Elizabethan Age*, 18–19.

[30] *The pedegrewe of heretiques* (1566), Ai[v].

intitled, Beware of M. Jewel (Antwerp, 1566), John Rastell insisted on a crucial distinction between physical and spiritual flight, external and internal exile. The Catholics, he argued, might have fled England but they had not "fled in hart or behaviour from the Catholike Faith of all christendome."[31] Similarly, Thomas Hide argued in his *Consolatorie Epistle to the afflicted Catholikes* (Louvain, 1580) that "the godly christian cannot be banished from Christ wherever he be, in Christ there is no banishment, and without Christ al is banishment."[32] Rastell, Hide, and their fellows saw their exile as categorically different from the biblical exiles imposed on Adam and Eve for disobeying God, and on Cain for slaying Abel. In both cases, physical exile constituted an outward sign of the sinner's spiritual separation from God. Cain, forced by God to wander "as a fugitive on the earth at the east side of Eden" was the negative archetype of the exile and one to which Protestant writers tried to assimilate Catholics whom, they alleged, "lie hid in the parts beyond sea, and are, as is reported, miserable vagabonds, as though they were accursed and fugitive Cains."[33] Protestant polemicist Matthew Sutcliffe called the Catholic exile and author Matthew Kellison, "a renegued fugitive Englishman, who hath surveyed divers other countries, and yet never found any settlement in his braine or habitation. Like *Caine* he hath bin long a vagrant fugitive fellow: *Vagus & profugus in terra:* and seeketh, if not to kill, yet to slander his countrimen and friends, imputing unto them most horrible opinions and crimes."[34] According to Catholics like Rastell and Hide, on the other hand, the real Cains were the Protestants who, even though they remained in England, had abandoned their spiritual home, the one true universal Church of Rome.

In his defense of the Louvainists, Rastell made another important distinction, this time concerning the respective distances that the Catholic exiles and the Marian Protestant exiles had put between themselves and England. "We [Catholics]," he proudly declared, "are not fled so far yet, as Geneva is." To Rastell, the flight of the Protestant fugitives under Mary was "far" both in terms of the physical distance between England and Geneva, and in terms of the spiritual gulf separating Calvinist Geneva from the Church of Rome. Unlike Geneva (as well as Basle, Frankfort, Strasborg, and Zurich), the Catholic centers of exile like Louvain and Antwerp were virtually on England's doorstep.[35] For Catholic

---

[31] *A treatise intitled, Beware of M. Jewel* (Antwerp, 1566. *ERL* 255), Av^r.

[32] *Consolatorie Epistle to the afflicted Catholikes* (Louvain, 1580. *ERL* 105), Evi^v.

[33] *The holie bible faithfully translated into English* (Douai, 1609. *ERL* 265), 14 (Genesis 4: 16); *Zurich Letters* 50: 248.

[34] *The blessings on Mount Gerizzim, and the curses on Mount Ebal. Or, The happie estate of Protestants compared with the miserable estate of papists under the Popes tyrannie* (1625), 364–5. After the accession of Elizabeth, the Marian persecutor, Dr John Story, reportedly "fled and lurked about in sundry corners, as did Cain when he had murdered his brother Abell" (*Declaration of the lyfe and death of John Story, late a Romish canonicall doctor by professyon* (1571), B1^r).

[35] *A treatise intitled, Beware of M. Jewel*, Av^r. Sander estimated that the journey from London to Antwerp took between two to three days ("Dr Nicholas Sander's Report to Cardinal Moroni on the Change of Religion in 1558–9 (1561)," in John H. Pollen, SJ, (ed.), *Miscellanea I*, Catholic Record Society 1 (London, 1905), 43).

exiles, the fact that they had found refuge so close to home was both spatially and symbolically significant in terms of how they saw themselves as Englishmen in exile. These destinations were not just a short journey from England, but also connected by historic ties to the exiles' homeland. This was especially true of the University of Louvain, one of northern Europe's great centers of learning, that had a long-standing tradition of educating humanist intellectuals and clerics from England. Since its beginnings, the university had welcomed scholars from Oxford and Cambridge who, after Erasmus and Busleiden established the *Collegium Trilinguae* (College of the Three Languages), were attracted by its reputation as an unrivalled center of language instruction.[36]

The city and University of Louvain, in other words, were places that Harding, Stapleton, and their fellows would have experienced as a home-away-from-home—part of a long-established intellectual community that encompassed Britain, Ireland, and northern Europe. A sense of shared Englishness among the exiles was sustained at Louvain by the way in which the scholars and students preserved their old collegiate identities by forming Oxford and Cambridge houses, a practice indebted to the university's medieval custom of grouping students by national origin.[37] The exiles' living arrangements further tightened their national bonds. In 1563, Stapleton, along with Martiall and Nicholas Sander are recorded sharing rooms in Louvain.[38]

The relative comfort of Catholic transplants in Louvain stemmed partly from the hospitality of the local people. When Cuthbert Scott, the deprived Bishop of Chester, died in the city in 1564, the writer of his epitaph, Richard Shacklock, apostrophized Scott's resting place as "lovely Louane [Louvain] happy towne in whom this corps dothe rest," and wished that Scott himself, "The Tullie of the Briton blood," were still alive to give thanks to Louvain for its support of the English Catholic cause. Shacklock continues:

> Behold how Louane doth lament and helpeth us to mourne,
> What meaneth this? Are we beguyled, was he in Louain borne?
> Nay nay as though he were in Louain borne and bred,
> With great renoune unto his grave, he is of Louain led.
> O kyndnes to be worshypped in every song of myne,
> O worthy to be sent to God in every vow of thyne.

---

[36] Henry de Vocht, *History of the Foundation and the Rise of the Collegium Trilingue Lovaniense, 1517–1550* (Louvain: Bibliotheque de l'Universite, Bureaux du Recueil, 1951–5), 4 vols.

[37] Christian Coppens, *Reading in Exile: The Libraries of John Ramridge (d. 1568), Thomas Harding (d. 1572) and Henry Joliffe (d. 1573), Recusants in Louvain* (Cambridge: LP Publications, 1993), 11–12.

[38] Jennifer Loach, "Reformation Controversies," in James McConica (ed.), *The History of the University of Oxford*, Vol. 3: *The Collegiate University* (Oxford: Oxford University Press, 1986), 386 n. 4.

Shacklock's delight at the recognition afforded his compatriot by Louvain's citizens suggests that the lot of the early Catholic exiles was not always characterized by alienation, dislocation, and nostalgia for a lost home.[39]

When it came to explaining and justifying their exile, Catholics shared with their Protestant counterparts a common set of authorities and arguments.[40] The Old and New testaments provided many texts and models that condoned flight, not least Christ's own words to the apostles in Matthew 10: 23: "And when they shal persecute you in this citie, flee into an other. Amen I say to you, you shal not finish al the cities of Israel, til the sonne of man come." The accompanying note to this verse in the Douai–Rheims Bible reads, "The Gospel up^o S. Athanasius day. Maij 2." St Athanasius, the Bishop of Alexandria, was the church father who offered the most cogent defense of flight: "to all men . . . is this law given, to flee when persecuted, and to hide when sought after, and not rashly tempt the Lord, but wait . . . until the appointed time of death arrive."[41] William Allen, who joined the exiles at Louvain in 1561, fused these various authorities in his claim that "we were constrained to flee and forsake our Countrie, parents, frendes, and what so ever by nature is there deere unto us, by the warrant and example of Christ, his Apostles, S. Athanasius, S. Hilarie, and other our forefathers in faith, in the like persecutions."[42]

Within the complex discourse of exile, voices approving flight jostled with others warning of its dangers and compromises. Like Protestants, Catholics faced conflicting advice about when (if ever) flight was an appropriate course of action, morally justifiable, and divinely sanctioned. Some commentators wondered if it were right for a person to flee when his co-religionists at home were suffering—a dilemma that was only heightened when the exile was a religious leader whose flock depended upon his guidance. Those who fled England might be accused of attempting to evade God's plan to test or punish them by exposing them to the dangers of heresy. On the other hand, Catholics often spoke of exile itself as a kind of suffering and as a harder punishment than any they might encounter back home. Thus, wrote Allen, "for our sinnes [we] . . . be constrained to spend either al or most of our serviceable yeres out of our natural Countrie."[43]

[39] Shacklock's epitaph was printed as part of a work by the Protestant Thomas Drant, *Impii cuiusdam epigrammatis quod edidit Richardus Shacklockus in mortem Cuthberti Scoti qnonda [sic] praesulis Cestrensis Apomaxis. Thomae Dranta Cantabrigiens authore. Also certayne of the speciall articles of the Epigramme, refuted in Englyshe by T. L.* (1565) di^v–diii^r. Drant framed Shacklock's epitaph for Scott with an anti-Catholic refutation.

[40] Wright, "Marian Exiles."   [41] Quoted ibid. 230.

[42] *An apologie and true declaration of the institution and endevours of the two English colleges, the one in Rome, the other now resident in Rhemes* (Rheims, 1581. *ERL* 67), 13^r; Martin Haile, *An Elizabethan Cardinal, William Allen* (London: I. Pitman, 1914), 31. On Athansius, see Alvyn Pettersen, " 'To Flee or Not to Flee': An Assessment of Athanasius's *De Fuga Sua*," in W. J. Sheils (ed.), *Persecution and Toleration* (London: Blackwell, 1984), 29–42.

[43] *An apologie . . . of the two English colleges*, 7^r.

If, as Allen suggests, exile was a form of divine punishment, it was also seen as a necessary condition if Catholics were to preserve their spiritual well-being. Allen explained in his defense of the English Catholic colleges that the main reason "so many of us are departed out of our natural Countrie, and do absent our selves so long from that place where we had our being, birth, and bringing up," was "the universal lacke . . . of the soveraine Sacrifice and Sacraments catholikely ministred, without which the soule of man dieth."[44] For the Catholic, salvation required regular participation in outward public rituals like confession and the sacrament of the altar. For Protestants, on the other hand, the doctrine of justification by faith alone meant that salvation was an essentially private and inward matter that was less dependent upon the institutional support of a church. The argument that flight was necessary to ensure salvation was thus far more compelling when lodged by Catholics.

Another Louvainist, Lewis Evans, also argued that "the Catholykes . . . doe but flye from the tyrannie of these caytyfes: they leave the realme to avoyde the rage of such Antichristes, and they departe from their country onely to be careful for the salvacion of theyr soules."[45] In justifying flight, Evans invoked the example of the apostle John who had urged Christians always to shun heretics. One day, when John was in a common bathhouse, he "leapt out immediatlie unwashed," after realizing that an arch-heretic, Cerinthus, was also bathing there. Thus, reasoned Evans, "we are admonished to avoyd yvel companie." The difficulty for the faithful, however, lay in deciding what form this avoidance should take: was it enough simply to stay away from heretics, their services and sermons, or was the ultimate act of temporal separation, flight to a foreign realm, necessary?[46]

Evans's appeal to the preservation of conscience as the main motivation for flight is also linked to a subsidiary justification of flight as escape from physical persecution.[47] Labeling the Protestants "tyrants" and "antichrists," Evans evokes the threat of bodily danger to Godly Catholics if they stay in England. In a similar move, Rastell cited Proverb twenty-eight to insist that the Catholic

---

[44] Ibid. 11^v–12^r.

[45] *Certaine tables . . . wherein is detected and made manifeste the doting dangerous doctrine, and haynous heresyes, of the rashe rabblement of heretikes* (Antwerp, 1565. *ERL* 52), Ev^v.

[46] Ibid. Avii^v. Lewis Evans was one of his age's more colorful serial-converts. Soon after completing *A brieve admonition to the nowe made ministers of Englande* he apostacized to the Protestant faith and in *The castle of christianitie* (1568) apologized to Elizabeth for having drunk of "the puddle of ignorancy." "This did I, this did all they, which fondly flee this your realm." Evans thanked Elizabeth for forgiving him and explained how he came to convert: "having passed over the seas moved with a vain zeal, to chunne it [reformed faith], and having at the length by translations and toys written against it, I returned privily (as occasion served me) into England again in that mind to depart thence as soon and secretly as I could" (A4^v, 7^r).

[47] On conscience, see two articles by Jonathan Wright: "Surviving the English Reformation: Commonsense, Conscience, and Circumstance," *Journal of Medieval and Early Modern Studies* 29 (1999), 381–402; and "The World's Worst Worm: Conscience and Conformity during the English Reformation," *Sixteenth Century Journal* 30 (1999), 113–33.

exiles were "not of that kinde [of fugitive], of the which it is wrytten *Fugit nemine persequente*, he fleeth when no man pursueth him."[48] Yet the problem with justifying exile as flight from persecution in 1565–6 was that Catholics in England were not yet suffering the kinds of physical and economic hardships that would later be inflicted by the Elizabethan regime. By 1581, when Allen published *An apologie ... of the two English colleges*, there was a lot more evidence of "the daily dangers, disgraces, vexations, feares, imprisonments, empoverishments, [and] despites" suffered by Catholics.[49] For the first decade of Elizabeth's reign at least, the authorities showed relative leniency toward Catholic subjects, rarely enforcing the recusancy statutes.[50] John Foxe, in the expanded second edition of his *Actes and Monuments* (1570), described this atmosphere of religious toleration. Some Catholics, wrote Foxe, "for their pleasure have slypt over the Seas, if their courage to see countreyes abroad did so allure them, who could let them? Yet this is certein, no dread there was of death that drave them. For what Papist have you sene in all this land to lose either life or lymme for Papistrye duryng all these xii yeares hetherto since this Queenes reigne?" Foxe admitted that a few recalcitrant Catholic clergy were "in custody: yet in that custody so shreudely are they hurt, that many a good Protestant in the Realme would be glad with al their hartes to chaunge rowmes and dyet with them, if they might."[51]

For Protestants, the contrast could hardly have been greater between the leniency with which they were now treating Catholics and the persecution they had suffered under Mary. During the first decade of Elizabeth's reign, the Protestants who had returned from exile under Mary kept the memory alive of their flight from the bonfires of Smithfield. Alexander Nowell, Elizabeth's Dean of St Paul's, recalled how young Protestant scholars under Mary were forced to flee England in fear of their lives: "Had wee [the Protestants under Mary] feared no woorse at your hands, then any of these [the Catholics under Elizabeth], whose case you so lament, doo suffer, wee woulde never have forsaken our naturall countrey, wandryng in farre more miserable dispersion, then you doo. Wee woulde in our countrey have bitterly lamented, the pitifull case of our countrey, then most miserably oppressed with popish superstition, and foraigne tyrannie."[52] According to another Protestant, Abraham Hartwell, the Catholic exiles in Louvain, were in some cases the same men who under Mary had "made those Antychristian fyers, you behelde the naked bodyes burning so long as the synewes wolde contein them."[53] From a Protestant perspective it was simply

---

[48] *A treatise intitled, Beware of M. Jewel*, Avi[r].

[49] *An apologie ... of the two English colleges*, 12[r].

[50] John J. La Rocca, SJ, "Time, Death, and the Next Generation: The Early Elizabethan Recusancy Policy, 1558–1574," *Albion* 14 (1982), 103–17.

[51] *Actes and Monuments* (1570), Preface "To all the professed frendes and folowers of the Popes procedynges," 13.

[52] *A reproufe written by Alexander Nowell* (1565), 11[r], 6[r].

[53] *A sight of the Portugall pearle*, Cii[v]. Hartwell knew that the Catholics would deny the charges that under Mary they had persecuted "good men," so to support his accusations he directed readers

absurd for the Louvain exiles to see themselves as refugees of religious persecution in England.

The religious exile of whatever persuasion, whether he fled from a society that physically persecuted him or only denied his religious freedoms, invariably felt the guilt of knowing that other fellow believers had stayed behind, possibly to face imprisonment and death. Under these circumstances, Catholic exiles might console themselves with the thought that the homeland they had left was a perversion of its true self and that in order to return it to its former identity, they needed temporarily to abandon it. John Leslie, the displaced Bishop of Ross in Scotland, whose fortunes were closely tied to the English exiles in the Low Countries, accused the Protestant cabal surrounding Elizabeth of filling the realm "with mo[re] then fortie thousand strangers...the very skom and froth of al Nations adjoyning that had abandoned their allegeance, and taken armes against their several Soveraignes...pyrates, thieves, murderers, Churche-Robbers and idle vagabunds."[54] Leslie repeated a trope that the banished Reginald Pole had used during Henry VIII's reign, of an England grown strange and unrecognizable to its true inhabitants. Since Mary Tudor's death, argued Leslie, the country had become "a new Land, a new Nation, [with] new Lawes, new customes, and manners, and plainly a new face and aspect of the people."[55] While England's Catholics were still modest, faithful, and sincere, heresy had produced "such a corruption of her people at home, as in shorte time threateneth plaine incivilitie and barbarous manners." Under the Protestant yoke, argued Leslie, England was no longer England and Catholics were no longer welcome or safe there.[56]

WRITING IN EXILE

The program of the early Catholic exiles, then, was to restore England to its ancient heritage by defending the orthodox tenets of the faith against the innovations of the heretics. From their temporary abodes in the Low Countries, the exiles saw themselves as in the ideal position to carry out this mission. Because the English at home, as Richard Shacklock averred, were so "blynded with the smoke

to Foxe's martyrology, "that notable cronicle (so lightly tearmed) such a monument as shall unto the worldes ende, not with wordes, but lively recordes of tormentes, imprisonment and horrible murther of good persons and vertuous refute all their lyppe labour."

[54] *A treatise of treasons against Q. Elizabeth, and the croune of England* (Louvain, 1572. ERL 254), 29[r], 47[v], 104[r].

[55] Ibid. 95[v].

[56] Ibid. 95[r]. Also on the trope of "the true England" in exile, see Peter Davidson, "Recusant Catholic Spaces in Early Modern England," in Ronald Corthell, Frances E. Dolan, Christopher Highley, and Arthur F. Marotti (eds.), *Catholic Culture in Early Modern England* (Notre Dame, Ind.: University of Notre Dame Press, 2007), 19–51.

of ignorance, that they themselves could not see the greate flames of heresies," it was the responsibility of outside observers in "farre countries," like the exiles, to warn them of impending catastrophe. The exiles were thus perfectly placed like "men which dwell on the hygh hylles of the Catholyke fayth, a farre of to descrye the flames which dayly consume England." Only from a vantage point beyond and above their homeland could the exiles see heresy for the insidious plague that it really was.[57]

United by a common cause, the exiles in Louvain formed a textual community (with tentacles in Antwerp and other Low Country centers) that produced a steady stream of theological, ecclesiological, and polemical works in the first dozen years of Elizabeth's reign. Shacklock notified Elizabeth of the volume and range of textual production undertaken by his fellow exiles, "your graces faythfull and learned subjectes on this syde of the sea"—"some to make nue workes never sene before, some to translate new bokes, which have bene made of other. Some to wryte in Latin, some in Englyshe, some in verse, and other some in prose."[58] Shacklock's own translations of Hosius and Osório were complemented by an edition of Lindanus by Lewis Evans as well as Thomas Stapleton's influential translation of Bede's *The history of the church of Englande*. Original works in Latin and English by Harding, Sander, Allen, Dorman, Rastell, Martiall, Harpsfield, and others defended the traditions of the Church, upheld the Latin Mass, the efficacy of images and confession, belief in purgatory and miracles, the power of priesthood, and the spiritual authority of the papacy.[59]

Louvainist books were conveyed secretly into England, finding their way to the universities as well as the Inns of Court and the royal court.[60] Some copies also reached a less privileged readership. According to James Pilkington, the Protestant Bishop of Durham, books by writers like Harding and others "now living in Louvain without license ... cause many times evil rumours to be spread and disquiet the people."[61] And in 1571 the Archbishop of York asked in his visitation injunctions

Whether there be anye person or persons, ecclesiasticall or temporall within your Parish, or else where, within this Dioces, that of late have retayned, or kept in theyr custodie, or that read, sell, utter, disperse, cary, or deliver to others anye Englishe bookes, set forth of late yeares at Louai, or in any other place beyonde the seas, by Harding, Dorman, Allen, Saunders, Stapleton, Marshall, or any of them, or by any other Englishe Papist,

[57] *An epistle of the reverend father in God Hieronimus Osorius* (Antwerp, 1565. *ERL* 329), 2[v]–3[r].
[58] *A most excellent treatise of the begynnyng of heresyes*, A4[r–v].
[59] See "The Works of the English Catholic Refugees," in *Antwerp, Dissident Typographical Centre*, 107–55; on the new centrality of the papacy to English Catholic thought in the 1560s, see Wooding, *Rethinking Catholicism*, ch. 6.
[60] Loach, "Reformation Controversies," and Penry Williams, "Elizabethan Oxford," in *The History of the University of Oxford*, 3: 363–440.
[61] Quoted in Philip Caraman, *The Other Face: Catholic Life under Elizabeth I* (NewYork: Sheed and Ward, 1960), 155.

eyther agaynst the Quéenes Maiesties Supremacie in matters ecclesiasticall, or agaynst true religion, and catholicke Doctrine now receyved, and established by common authoritie within thys Realme, and what their names and surnames are?[62]

The virulent anti-Catholic pamphleteer Thomas Norton also inveighed against the dangers of the Louvainists' "seditious" books spreading unchecked among the populace. There is, he noted sarcastically, a "companie of good sure men at home, [who] receive these goodly bookes, sprede them abroade, rede them in audiences and corners, commend them, defend them, geve them great praises for learning and substantialnesse as matters unanswerable."[63] The Elizabethan authorities regarded the Louvain books as serious threats to the precarious authority of the newly reestablished Church of England and after the mid-1560s took increasingly stringent measures to prosecute anyone involved in writing, reading, or distributing them.[64]

Protestants were especially dismayed by the sheer volume of Catholic material being produced in the Low Countries and brought to England. John Foxe felt obliged to issue a revised second edition of his *Actes and Monuments* (1570) partly to refute the many attacks upon the first edition from the Low Country presses. There was "Such blustryng and styrring," he complained, "against that poore booke through all quarters of England, even to the gates of Louaine: so that no English Papist almost in all the Realme thought him selfe a perfect Catholicke, unlesse he had cast out some word or other, to geve that booke a blow." Foxe was targeted in the works of Harding and Stapleton as well as in Book 5 of Nicholas Harpsfield's *Dialogi Sex* (1566). Composed in Fleet prison by the former Marian archdeacon, the manuscript was smuggled to the Continent where it was printed under a pseudonym by Christopher Plantin in Antwerp.[65]

Protestant polemic responded to the publishing project of the Louvain exiles in the most negative terms. "I mervayle," wrote Abraham Hartwell in a scathing attack, "who is mayster of the workes in Louayne, that suffreth every pratyng

---

[62] *Injunctions given by the most reverende father in Christ, Edmonde by the providence of God, Archbishop of Yorke primate of England, and Metropolitane, in his Metropoliticall visitation of the province of Yorke, aswell to the clergie, as to the laytie of the same province. Anno do. 1571*, Biii[r]. On the presence of Louvainist books in Sussex, see Roger B. Manning, *Religion and Society in Elizabethan Sussex* (Leicester University Press, 1969), 44–5. "As early as April 1565 Guzman de Silva, the Spanish Ambassador to England, writing to Philip II, stated that books shipped from Louvain had done incalculable service in spreading the faith" (Leona Rostenberg, *The Minority Press and the English Crown: A Study in Repression 1558–1625* (Nieuwkoop: B. De Graaf, 1971), 31).

[63] *A Warning against the dangerous practices of papistes* (1569), G1[r]. Also see K. J. Kesselring, " 'A Cold Pye for the Papitses': Constructing and Containing the Northern Rising of 1569," *Journal of British Studies* 43 (2004), 437.

[64] Matthew Racine, "*A Pearle for a Prynce*: Jerónimo Osório and Early Elizabethan Catholics," *Catholic Historical Review* 87 (2001), 418–19.

[65] John Foxe, *Actes and Monuments* (1570), Preface "To the right vertuous, most excellent and noble Princesse Quene Elizabeth," 7. On the Catholic response to *Actes and Monuments*, see John N. King, *John Foxe's* Book of Martyrs *and Early Modern Print Culture* (Cambridge: Cambridge University Press, 2006), 253–67.

pioner and inferior labourer to use his tongue for a pytcheforke, and to bestowe such durty dealynges upon men of renowmed learning and worthy authority."[66] Shacklock's dystopian vision imagines the Louvainists' project as an anarchy of social transgression and category confusions: Catholic men of no status presume to argue with their Protestant betters in rank and intellect, while dirty hands clutch pens instead of pitchforks. Other Protestants saw the Louvainists as nurturing a polemical "hydra" whose many heads had to be cut off by counter-argument. John Jewel envisaged his adversaries as cowering, subhuman enemies: "our fugitives at Louvaine began during the last year to be in violent commotion," he observed in 1566, "and to write with the greatest asperity against us all … they began to bark in their holes and corners, and to call me an impudent, bold, insolent, and frantic boaster."[67] The exiles were "monsters" in Jewel's view who assailed him with "abuse [and] contumely." Jewel's fellow Protestant, Abraham Hartwell, similarly described the exiles as wild animals incapable of rational discourse who emitted only meaningless noises. In response to the exiles' recent writings, Hartwell imagines the Catholic polemicists as a version of Spenser's slanderous Blatant Beast, ordering them: "Avaunt with this your barkynge after your bloudye bittes, you monstruous howlyng wolves."[68] The Louvainists' textual project left an impression on an early episode of *The Faerie Queene* (1590). Red Cross Knight, protector of the Protestant faith embodied in Lady Una, battles the monster Error—Spenser's figure of a feminized Catholic Church and its erroneous doctrines. When Red Cross finally strangles Error, "she spewed out of her filthie maw | A floud of poyson horrible and blacke | … | Her vomit full of bookes and papers was | With loathly frogs and toades, which eyes did lacke" (1.1.20). As commentators have recognized, Spenser alludes in part to Louvainist "bookes and papers," regurgitated in a grotesque parody of Counter-Reformation book production.[69]

The voluminous output of Catholic books was seen by Protestant critics as a sign of the exiles' excessive leisure: "There is none of all these [exiles]," wrote James Calfhill, "but may with more ease make xv suche bookes as they cumber the Printers of Antwerp withal, than answere xv leaves of sound doctrine." "This advauntage ye have … that ye have nothing else to do, but commit to writing your pievish fansies, and send them into England to set us a worke withal." Calfhill contrasts the perceived "ease" and "leisure" of the exiles with the work ethic of Godly Protestants: "We our selves are occupied otherwise," he writes, "(as friends to the flock of christ which we have in charge) than that we can or will attempre our doings, to the lewd desert of our contemned enimies." Protestants,

---

[66] *A sighte of the Portugall pearle*, Aiii[r].   [67] *Zurich Letters* 50: 147–8.

[68] *A sighte of the Portugall pearle*, Cii[v].

[69] Lawrene F. Rhu, "Romancing the Word: Pre-Texts and Contexts for the Errour Episode," *Spenser Studies* 11 (1994 for 1990): 101–9; "Error," in A. C. Hamilton et al. (eds.), *The Spenser Encyclopedia* (Toronto: University of Toronto Press, 1990).

Calfhill insisted, had too much "real" work to do to be bothered with the printed attacks of the exiles.[70]

Catholics naturally rejected suggestions that their exile was a form of holiday—a pastoral escape from the "real" world—or that their works were idle scribblings, composed collectively by groups of uneducated hacks. The Louvain authors saw nothing about their situation that remotely resembled the fantasy of exile played out by Shakespeare's characters in *As You Like It* in a locale whose very name evokes the landscape of the Catholic émigrés around Ardennes in Flanders and northeast France.[71]

In the prefaces, dedications, and introductions to their books, the exiled Catholic authors attest repeatedly to the fact that even though exile provided a space from which to write, translate, and publish, the material conditions of banishment hindered every stage of the process. In the first place, displaced writers could not easily find out what their adversaries were saying about them and thus what arguments they needed to answer. Living in Louvain, John Rastell was only able to get a copy of Jewel's first tome by splitting the high cost of the book with a friend. When the work finally arrived two months after its publication in England, Rastell divided the unbound volume in the middle, keeping one half for himself and giving the other to his friend. The two of them had planned to eventually exchange parts, but when the time came Rastell decided he had already read quite enough of Jewell.[72] The exiles also complained that they lacked access to the sources and research materials they needed. Thomas Stapleton, for instance, wished he could have "ben at home, and travailed the countre" when preparing his translation of Bede's *The history of the church of Englande*. In particular, he lacked the "speciall intelligence of eche shere and Countie as to that purpose was requisit."[73] Lewis Evans concluded his edition of Lindanus by explaining that the absence of his own library—"for lacke of my bokes to looke on"—had made the work of translation especially difficult and the result less than satisfactory.[74] Distance from events in England imposed limitations on Catholic writers' knowledge; as a result, Thomas Stapleton felt the need to defer to his English readers' "daily experience which you may see better at home then we which are abrode."[75] The translators of the Catholic Old Testament surely spoke for many of their fellow exiles when they explained how their "poore estate in banishment" had continually delayed their editorial project.

---

[70] *An Answer to the Treatise of the Cross*, A3[r–v].

[71] Carol Enos, "Catholic Exiles in Flanders and *As You Like It*," in Richard Dutton, Alison Findlay, and Richard Wilson (eds.), *Theatre and Religion: Lancastrian Shakespeare* (Manchester: Manchester University Press, 2003), 130–42.

[72] *A treatise intitled, Beware of M. Jewel*, A2 [r–v].

[73] Bede, *The history of the church of Englande* (1565), 9[v].   [74] *Certaine tables*, E8[v].

[75] *The apologie of Fridericus Staphylus* (Antwerp, 1565. *ERL* 268), 8[v].

Though begun in 1569, the Catholic Old Testament did not appear for another forty years.[76]

The difficulties faced by the exiles with research were compounded by problems of printing and distributing their completed texts. John Martiall, the "Corrector" of Harding's *An answere to Maister Juelles Chalenge*, complained in the work's preface: "I wishe oure loving countriemen to consider how harde it is for aliantes [aliens] to print English truly, who nieither understand, nor can pronounce the tonge rightly...Were there here an Englishman who had skill in setting a print, and knewe the right Orthographie of oure speach, then mightest thou reader looke for bookes more correctly set forth...I praye thee in this distresse beare with my litle oversigth...Farewel, at Antwerpe 12 Januarii 1565."[77] Martiall's wish was fulfilled later in the year when John Fowler received a printer's license from the University of Louvain. Before his death in 1579, Fowler printed over fifty Catholic texts as well as working as an editor and translator.[78] Martiall also remarked, in response to Protestant jibes, that his fellow Catholics gained nothing financially from what they wrote; all revenue raised by the books, he insisted, went either to the printers or to whoever would "convey [the books] into the realm."[79]

Despite the obstacles to writing, translating, and printing in exile, textual labor offered Catholic activists a way of reconnecting with their homeland and of coping with the trauma of their displacement. Exile, in fact, could come to represent, as it had for earlier Protestant exile writers like John Bale, a kind of "literary as well as a divine vocation."[80] Thomas Harding describes discovering this vocation as public author upon arriving in Louvain. He writes in the preface to *An answere to Maister Juelles Chalenge* that

Horace sayeth, they that runne over the sea, chaunge the ayer not the mynde, yet is it so reader, that I passing over the sea out of England into Brabant, have in some parte chaunged also my mynde. For where as being there, I mynded to send this treatise but to one frend, who required it for his private instruction, and never to set any thing abroade, now being arrived here in Louaine, I have thought good, by putting it in printe, to make it common to many.

Exile obliges Harding to speak in "defence of the Catholike faith, in these most perilouse times," requiring him to ignore the "stigma of print" by circulating his

[76] *The holie bible*, †2r.

[77] *An answere to Maister Juelles Chalenge* (Louvain, 1564. *ERL* 229), A3ᵛ.

[78] On Fowler, see Coppens, *Reading in Exile*, 18–20. John Heigham, an English Catholic publisher working in Flanders in the early 17th century, blamed errors and delays in printing on the "continuall warres in this countrey and the manifolde difficulties which all those that live here about doe feele." Quoted in Rostenberg, *The Minority Press*, 127.

[79] *A Replie to M. Calfhills blasphemous answer*, 1.

[80] Jane Kingsley-Smith, *Shakespeare's Drama of Exile* (New York: Palgrave Macmillan, 2003), 20.

work beyond a private audience, and to boldly embrace the role of author and public intellectual.[81]

The years in which Harding's *Answere* appeared were ones of intense textual activity among the exiles, including a concerted translation program of ten important works—five in 1565 alone. In that year, the Protestant Hartwell quipped sarcastically, "No lattin wryter a Papyst but shalbe Englished shortlye, no Englishe wryter a protestant but shalbe confuted."[82] As Hartwell implies, Catholics had developed a two-pronged strategy in which translations of carefully selected attacks on heresy by contemporary writers in Latin and European vernaculars complemented the original polemics defending key elements of Catholic faith in the wake of Jewel's challenge. The works to be translated were carefully chosen in order to have the greatest impact on an English audience. Thomas Stapleton's translation of *The apologie of Fridericus Staphylus*, for example, deftly exploited Staphylus's reputation "as the first convert from Protestantism to Catholicism" in the Reformation. Staphylus, once a student of Luther at Wittenberg, had until his recent death been Councilor to the Catholic Emperor Ferdinand.[83] Another translation by Stapleton, Bede's *The history of the church of Englande* (as we shall see in Chapter 4) was an attempt to capture for the Catholic cause a writer on the English past admired across the religious spectrum.

Translation was an attractive literary option for many of the exiles because it generally required neither the time nor the talent of original composition. Some authors were quite self-conscious about this situation—Richard Shacklock admitting, for instance, that he lacked the "strengthe, to bryng any principall beames, any corner stones, by wrytyng newe workes of myne owne invention." Thinking of the Louvainists' collective textual endeavors as akin to rebuilding the Temple in Jerusalem, Shacklock continues:

[Yet] rather then I would be an ydle loker on, I thought it my part to be an inferior laborer . . . by translatyng some worthy worke of some other wryter . . . there were many workes in Latten, which beyng translated in to Englyshe, might helpe to rayse up the ruynous walles of Christ hys churche in England.

Shacklock explained that he chose to translate Osório da Fonseca's, *An epistle of the reverend father in God Hieronimus Osorius* (commonly known as *A Pearle for a Prynce*) (Antwerp, 1565) because "this one semed to me to conteine moste spedy remedie and reparation."[84] Shacklock also translated *A most excellent treatise of the*

---

[81] *An answere to Maister Juelles Chalenge*, A4[r]. Like Harding, the anonymous translator of Lindanus presents his initial Englishing of the text as a purely personal act of devotion, undertaken as a kind self-healing. Only later is he persuaded to print the work for a wider audience after his friend discovers part of the manuscript in his chamber.

[82] *A sight of the Portugall pearle*, Av[v].

[83] *The Apologie*, 10[r]–11[r], 252[v]–254[r]; Ute Lotz-Heumann, "Tolerance and Intolerance in the Protestant and Catholic Reformations in Germany," in Vincent P. Carey (ed.), *Voices for Tolerance in an Age of Persecution* (Seattle: University of Washington Press, 2004), 38.

[84] *An epistle of the reverend father*, A2[r–v].

begynnyng of heresyes in oure tyme by Stanislaus Hosius, whose international reputation as a defender of papal authority and the Counter-Reformation was already
well established by his numerous publications. Shacklock's edition increased its
appeal to readers by including a visually arresting title page depicting the Polish
Bishop hacking with his axe at the tree of heresy on which grow branches of
bloodshed, apples of atheism, and leaves of lies.[85] In his left hand, Hosius displays
a copy of the Latin version of the book, *De Origine Haeresium nostri Temporis*.
First published in Louvain in 1559 just as the exiles were beginning to arrive
there from England, *De Origine* offered a coherent literary model for repudiating
the dangers of heresy (see Fig. 1).

Translation, then, allowed lesser-luminaries like Shacklock to participate in
the Louvainist project and to experience the consolations that writing in exile
afforded by contributing to the fight against heresy. The exiles' texts, focus-
ing mainly on the frustrations of writing outside England, have little to say
about these small and unexpected consolations, although they are hinted at
briefly by the anonymous English exile translator of Peter Canisius's *Certayne
necessarie principles of religion*. The translator says that he first encounters Canisius's book at an especially difficult time in his life when he is forced to
leave his home and take to the road between Artois and Paris because of
religious unrest in Flanders. Reading Canisius in Latin has a transformative
effect upon him by "appeas[ing] the sorowes" caused by his displacement.
The act of translating Canisius's book into English, though, has an even more
profound effect by "mitigat[ing]" "both the tediousnes whiche chaunced to me
in travayling, and my greefes which troubled me otherwise."[86]

Like all the activities of the Catholic exiles, translation as an act of
religio-political resistance drew hostile commentary from the Protestant camp.
Protestants belittled translation as an inferior literary practice: Catholics were
"*but* translaters of other mens travayles" (my emphasis), "seely translators."[87]
Protestant Alexander Nowell argued that to avoid the stigma of publishing
mere translations, Catholics pretended that they wrote "but lightly for a private
friende or twaine" and were prevailed upon by those friends to let the book
"come abroade"—a tactic attested to by the anonymous translator of Lindanus.
Alternatively, critics accused some Catholic translators of hiding their identity by
attributing their own paltry translations to one of their less esteemed brothers in
exile. In a reversal of this tactic, Protestants charged, Catholic translators would

---

[85] *Antwerp, Dissident Typographical Centre*, 115–16; Luc Racaut, *Hatred in Print: Catholic
Propaganda and Protestant Identity during the French Wars of Religion* (Aldershot: Ashgate, 2002),
58–9.

[86] *Certayne necessarie principles of religion* (London, secret press, 1578–9. *ERL* 2), "The Transla-
tour to the Reader."

[87] Barthlett, *The pedegrewe of heretiques* (1566), 1ᵛ; Nowell, *A reproufe written by Alexander
Nowell* (1565), A2ʳ.

Fig. 1. Stanislaus Hosius, *A most excellent treatise of the begynnyng of heresyes in oure tyme*, trans. Richard Shacklock (Antwerp, 1565). STC 13888.

also try to pass off others' work as their own, thus making them "borowers of those bookes, whose first authors they would appeare to be."[88]

Further, Protestant John Barthlett accused Catholic translators of "controlling," or distorting, the original "host" texts. Barthlett claimed, for example, that in the act of translating Hosius, Shacklock switched the root cause of heresy from covetousness to railing. In Barthlett's view, Shacklock was not a translator, but "a corrupter, an abuser, and a marrer of Hosius." Unconscionably, the most flagrant act of appropriation, however, was replacing the original staid titles of works with sensational attention-seeking ones.[89] Lewis Evans retitled *Certaine tables . . . wherein is detected and made manifeste the doting dangerous doctrine, and haynous heresyes, of the rashe rabblement of heretikes*, "the betraying of the beastlinesse of Heretiques." Shacklock renamed Hosius's *A most excellent treatise of the begynnyng of heresyes in oure tyme*, the "Hatchet of Heretiques."[90] For Protestant critics, this devious manipulation of works' titles, like the Louvain translation project as a whole, was a synecdoche for what they saw as the inherently fraudulent Catholic cause.

In spite of Protestant carping, the Louvainists regarded their "Englishing" of foreign texts as an expression of their unwavering Englishness and of concern for their stay-at-home brethren. Stapleton informed readers of his translation of *The apologie of Fridericus Staphylus* that "I have thought good to translate the whole in to our mother tongue, trusting in almighty God to profit hereby many a Christen soule of my dere deceived countremen which . . . was my only respect in this smal labour." Shacklock likewise undertook his translation of Hosius so that his "dearly beloved countremen" could profit from its lessons. As the translator of another work by Hosius, *Of the expresse worde of God* (Louvain, 1567. *ERL* 73), Stapleton thought it his duty "to imparte by the commodyte of our vulgar tongue to my unlerned countremen . . . some worthy worke of some other mannes." And John Fowler felt that his translation of Peter Frarinus was needed "to warne my dear countremen of [the heretics'] malice and cruelty."[91]

Through the use of the vernacular in both original and translated works, Catholic exiles were able to demonstrate their attachment to "our mother tongue" and to an emotionally resonant linguistic definition of Englishness.[92] In their prefaces and dedications, the translators expressed typical misgivings about the inferiority of the vernacular to Latin; English was a "rude utterance," a "base

---

[88] Nowell, *A reproufe*, A2[r–v].

[89] Barthlett, *The pedegrewe*, 1[v]–2[r]. Nowell noted how "simple and unlearned readers" often preferred books that were "more boldely then learnedly written" (*A reproufe*, B1[v]).

[90] Barthlett, *The pedegrewe*, 1[v].

[91] Stapleton, *The apologie of Fridericus Staphylus*, 5[r–v]; Shacklock, *A most excellent treatise of the begynnyng of heresyes*, avii[v]; Stapleton, *Of the expresse worde of God*, *ii[r–v]; Fowler, *An oration against the unlawfull insurrections*, A4[r].

[92] On the powerful appeal that could be made to "linguistic nationalism" at an earlier period in English history, see Adrian Hastings, *The Construction of Nationhood : Ethnicity, Religion, and Nationalism* (Cambridge: Cambridge University Press, 1997), 45–6.

tounge," and yet it remained our "natural and mother tounge be it never so bar-
barouse."[93] By self-consciously drawing attention to their use of the vernacular,
Catholic writers were effectively competing with Protestants for possession of the
"mother tongue" and for the symbolic capital it embodied. Protestants' sense of
ownership of the vernacular rested on their willingness to have church services
and scripture in the language of the common people.[94] For Catholics, on the
other hand, the question of rendering scripture and liturgy into the vernacular
was far more problematic. Indeed, several of the very works translated by the
Louvainists specifically objected to making sacred texts available in common
European tongues. Staphylus, for example, feared that the laity would "rashly
and roundely set upon [the vernacular scripture], as if it were Bevis of Hampton
or a tale of Robin hoode."[95] Stapleton also rejected divine service in the vulgar
tongue, arguing that auditors would be distracted from their "private devotions"
by trying to make sense of the English words. Even in the vernacular, the
scriptures were "hard." "The nations that have ever had their Service in the vulgar
tounge," he explained, "the people thereof have continued in Scismes, errours,
and certain Judaicall observances, so as they have not bene reakoned in the
number of the Catholike Churche. As the Christians of Moscovia, of Armenia,
of prester Joan his lande in Aethiopia."[96]

During the later 1560s some of the exiles themselves began to translate the
scriptures in spite of the statements of other exiles rejecting a vernacular bible,
as well as the prohibition of the Council of Trent in 1564 against the reading
of "sacred matters," in the "vulgar tongue." As Alexander Walsham remarks,
the exiles' realization that they needed their own version of the vernacular
scriptures to combat the growing influence of Protestant translations "dates
back to at least 1567, when Thomas Harding and Nicholas Sander wrote to
Cardinal Protector Morone that the evils arising from Protestant bibles might
be successfully counteracted by the preparation of a Catholic translation."[97] The
result was the Douai-Rheims New Testament of 1582 which, according to its
detractors, counteracted its own aims by adopting a strange Latinate style that
English readers could make little sense of.[98] Nevertheless, the exiles understood
that only by using the vernacular could they help ordinary readers in England

[93] Fowler, *An oration against the unlawfull insurrections* (Av^r); Shacklock, *An epistle of the reverend father*, 4^r; Shacklock, *A most excellent treatise of the begynnyng of heresyes*, av^r.

[94] On reformers' complex appropriation of and resistance to vernaculars, see Felicity Heal, "Mediating the Word: Language and Dialects in the British and Irish Reformations," *Journal of Ecclesiastical History* 56.2 (2005), 261–86.

[95] Stapleton, *The apologie of Fridericus Staphylus*, 65^v. Alexandra Walsham, "Unclasping the Book? Post-Reformation English Catholicism and the Vernacular Bible," *Journal of British Studies* 42 (2003), 155–7.

[96] *A returne of untruthes upon M. Jewelles Replie* (Antwerp, 1566. ERL 308), 123^r.

[97] "Unclasping the Book," 153. Wooding, *Rethinking Catholicism*, 183–6.

[98] Heal, "Mediating the Word," 273. Brett Foster, "Gregory Martin's 'Holy Latinate Jerusalem': Roman English, Romanist Values, and the *Rheims New Testament* (1582)," *Prose Studies* 28.2 (2006), 130–49.

"compelled to drink poison" by a heretical regime. For beleaguered Catholic readers in England, the exiles' books took on an especially vital role, acting in place of the priest "who is non-existent, or rare, far-away and ever-concealed."[99]

The translators' desire to reach ordinary English Catholics suggests that in the first decade of Elizabeth's reign, the exiles remained confident that the reconversion of their homeland could be accomplished by peaceful discursive means—by reaching out to the majority Catholic population that had allegedly been hoodwinked not by the queen herself but by her advisers and ministers. Before the end of the 1560s the exiles remained optimistic that their time abroad would be only temporary and could be ended by their own propaganda efforts. As one translator-in-exile remarked in 1567, he had not "laied downe al hope of the recoverie of the whole: no, I trust to see within these few daies such an alteration of things, that the verie remembrance of this most pestilent plague shalbe utterlie abolished."[100] Thomas Dorman, meanwhile, looked forward to when God "shall appointe the time and . . . move the harte of oure prince to call us home."[101] The hopes of the English exiles were boosted in 1568 by events in France when the young king Charles IX (1560–74) escaped a kidnap attempt by Huguenot leaders. Incensed by this outrage, Charles and his mother Catherine d' Medici moved decisively against the Protestants. Across the border in Louvain, the English Catholics quickly translated and printed the resulting anti-Huguenot legislation as *An Edict or Ordonance of the French King, conteining a Prohibition and Interdiction of al preaching and assembling, and exercise of any other Religion, then of the Catholique, the Apostolique, and the Romaine Religion* [and] *an other Edict of the same king, removing al Protestants from bearing any Office under the king, in the Realme of France* (Louvain, 1568. *ERL* 97). Events in France offered a stark warning to Elizabeth of the dangers that might befall her if she continued to countenance "the ministers of the newe opinion" and their backers among the aristocracy.[102]

REBELLION, EXCOMMUNICATION, AND BEYOND

The first stage of the Catholic exile experience under Elizabeth effectively concluded during the watershed years of 1568–70 when Louvain lost its centrality

[99] Quoted in Wooding, *Rethinking Catholicism*, 184; see also A. C. Southern, *Elizabethan Recusant Prose 1559–1582* (London, 1950), 231–62.

[100] Osório da Fonseca, *A learned and very eloquent treatie* (Louvain, 1568) trans. John Fen (*ERL* 318), BB3[r–v].

[101] *A disproufe of M. Nowelles reprouf*, *3[v].

[102] *An Edict or Ordonance of the French King*, Aii[v]. The failed kidnap attempt resulted in deteriorating relations between Charles and Catherine and their Huguenot subjects that led inexorably to the St Bartholomew's Day massacre of 1572 (Diarmaid MacCulloch, *The Reformation: A History* (New York: Penguin, 2004), 297, 327–9).

for English émigrés. In 1568, Louvain's importance was eclipsed by the establishment of the first English seminary at Douai in the Spanish Low Countries (Brabant) close to the French border. William Allen's institution was expressly designed for training English missionary priests who would be sent back to England to tend to the spiritual needs of Catholics and ultimately to help bring about the reconversion of their homeland.[103] In Allen's words, Douai was "this College for English theologians . . . this refuge of exiles, this residence and home of Catholics, this place held in just esteem by those from the schismatical Samaria, and who have the countenances of men going up to Jerusalem."[104] The seminary was designed to inculcate "regiment, discipline, and education most agreable to our Countrimens natures, and for prevention of al disorders that youth and companies of scholers (namely in banishment) are subject unto."[105] Several students and professors at Louvain migrated to Douai which was also the seat of a new university established by Philip II and the pope as a bulwark against the spread of heresy in the Low Countries.[106]

The foundation of the Douai seminay was quickly followed by the rising of the Catholic northern earls in 1569 and the excommunication of the queen by Pius V the following year—events that Protestants saw as being partly inspired by the opening of Allen's new seminary.[107] The events of 1568–70 were part of a series of related happenings both at home and abroad that English Protestants seized on as evidence of a growing Catholic menace. In 1568 the newly deposed Mary Stuart fled from Scotland into England where she sought Elizabeth's protection. The presence of Elizabeth's presumptive heir on English soil provided a dangerous rallying point for disaffected Catholics, a threat that was only heightened by schemes to marry Mary to the Catholic Duke of Norfolk without Elizabeth's consent. Norfolk was executed in 1572 while Mary remained in the custody of Elizabeth's most trusted Protestant servants.[108] The situation outside the British

[103] Wooding, *Rethinking Catholicism*, 225; Jenkins, *John Jewel and the English National Church*, 121.

[104] *Letters of William Allen and Richard Barret, 1572–1598* ed. P. Renold. Vol. 58 (Catholic Record Society, 1967), 6. "The Samaritans were Schismatikes from the Jewes." Gloss in Douai-Rheims Bible to Luke 9: 52–3. Also see Eamon Duffy's discussion in "William, Cardinal Allen, 1532–1594," *Recusant History* 22 (1995), 265–90.

[105] *An apologie . . . of the two English colleges*, 19ʳ.

[106] J. Andreas Löwe, "Richard Smyth and the Foundation of the University of Douai," *Nederlandsch Archief voor Kerkgeschiede* 79 (1999), 142–69.

[107] Thomas McCoog, SJ, *The Society of Jesus in Ireland, Scotland, and England, 1541–1588: "Our Way of Proceeding?"* (New York: Brill, 1996), 78. The bull *Regnans in Excelsis* called Elizabeth "the pretended queen of England and the servant of crime," absolved her subjects of any oaths they had taken to her, and "command[ed] all and singular the nobles, subjects, peoples and others . . . that they do not dare obey her orders, mandates and laws." A copy of the bull was pinned up at the Bishop of London's palace in St Paul's churchyard by John Felton who suffered a traitor's death as a result. However, its contents may have received greater publicity in Protestant refutations than via the circulation of the bull itself (G. R. Elton, *The Tudor Constitution: Documents and Commentary*, 2nd edn. (Cambridge: Cambridge University Press, 1982), 425–8).

[108] Wooding, *Rethinking Catholicism*, 224.

Isles seemed just as threatening to English Protestants. Anglo-Spanish relations were deteriorating while in France and the Low Countries religious violence continued to menace reformed rulers and movements.

Protestant propagandists were quick to see the hand of the English exiles in the planning and execution of the Northern Rebellion and the excommunication of the queen. Bishop Pilkington told Henry Bullinger that "Our Louvaine friends obtained bulls from the pope, that they might absolve the people from the allegiance due to the queen's majesty."[109] "Our Louanistes," Thomas Norton observed in 1570, "for a good while have written no more. What is the cause? They take them to other weapons, they hang upon expectation of the success of the rebellion or some like mischiefe, which by their former bookes they have travailed to stirre up and geve occasion."[110] In another tract, Norton claimed that the Louvainists, "in hope of the success of thys Bull...have stayed their handes from writing, and stand in suspense (better it were they did hang in suspense) and expectation what will become of these mischieves whereof them selves have bene the proctors."[111] Norton implicated Thomas Harding (d.1572) as the leading English "traitor" who had helped procure the bulls of excommunication against the queen.[112] The reputation that Harding had carefully cultivated in exile of being a Catholic loyal to Elizabeth in secular affairs was further damaged when one of the leaders of the Northern Rebellion, Thomas Percy, Earl of Northumberland, confessed in 1572 "that he had been very much impressed by writings of Harding, Stapleton, and others"[113] Whatever Harding had intended his writings to achieve, they had resulted in stirring up rebellion.

Norton was not the only Protestant to observe around 1570 that the exiles at Louvain had temporarily stopped producing books. John Jewel informed Bullinger in March 1571 that "Our friends at Louvaine have not written any thing for two years."[114] In *The scholemaster* (1570), Elizabeth's old tutor Roger Ascham referred in the past tense to the dangers posed by the "earnest books of Louvain": "when the busy and open papists abroad could not by their contentious books turn men in England fast enough from truth and right judgment in

---

[109] *Zurich Letters* 50: 222–3. A delegation of English exiles from Louvain petitioned to have Elizabeth excommunicated at the Council of Trent before it finally closed in 1563. Their efforts were blocked by Philip II who feared its implementation would result in the persecution of Catholics. See Rishton's remarks in Sander, *Rise and Growth of the Anglican Schism*, 293.

[110] "A bull graunted by the Pope to Doctor Harding and other, by reconcilement and assoyling of English Papistes, to undermyne faith and allegeance to the Quene. With a true declaration of the intention and frutes thereof, and a warnyng of periles therby imminent, not to be neglected," Biv[r]. See Kesselring, " 'A Cold Pye for the Papistes'," on Norton's status as an official government propagandist.

[111] "A disclosing of the great bull" (1570), Aii[v]–Aiv[r].

[112] "An addition declaratorie to the bulles, with a searching of the maze" (1570), Aii[r]–Aiii[r].

[113] *Calendar of State Papers Domestic Addenda 1566–79*, ed. Mary Anne Everett Green (London: Longman, 1871), 414. Also see Daniela Busse, "Anti-Catholic Polemical Writing on the 'Rising in the North' (1569) and the Catholic Reaction," *Recusant History* 27 (2005), 23–4.

[114] *Zurich Letters* 50: 239.

doctrine, then the subtle and secret papists at home procured bawdy books to be translated out of the Italian tongue."[115] In fact, 1570 saw the publication of only one Catholic book in English by the Louvainists, down from three in 1569 and from twenty-one and nine in 1565 and 1566 respectively.[116] In the years immediately following the rebellion of the northern earls, the publication of vernacular Catholic works by the exiles all but dried up. After 1570, the exiles generally wrote in Latin rather than English. This change of approach, as Daniela Busse suggests, was perhaps a miscalculation on the part of the exiles who, by turning away from the vernacular toward "long and elaborate Latin tracts ... lost the opportunity to influence the English people who should have been their main concern."[117] But the turn to Latin also suggests that after the Northern Rebellion and the publication of the bull excommunicating Elizabeth, the exiles realized that England could no longer be won back to the Old Faith through a vernacular publishing strategy aimed at ordinary English readers. Increasingly, the exiles turned their efforts to winning the support of an educated pan-European audience that had to be addressed in the *lingua franca* of Latin.

Events of 1568–70 dramatically changed the political landscape and hardened confessional divisions. The English parliament of 1571, incensed by the rebellion and excommunication, passed a series of anti-Catholic measures including the "acte agaynst fugitives over the Seas" that sought to curtail unlicensed foreign travel and prevent Catholics from sending financial support to the exiles. Anyone helping the exiles now risked "arrest and examination by the council."[118] The same parliament also extended the treason legislation of Henry VIII to encompass anyone either in or out of England who dared to "compasse, imagine, invent, devise or intende the death, or destruction, or anye bodylye harme tendyng to death, destruction, mayme, or wounding of the royall person of the same our Soveraigne Ladye Queene Elizabeth."[119] Beyond actual threats, attacking the

---

[115] Roger Ascham, *The Schoolmaster*, ed. Lawrence V. Ryan (Folger Shakespeare Library: University of Virginia Press, 1967), 68. The complaint was a familiar one. Stephen Gosson exclaimed in *Playes confuted in five actions* (1582) that the devil had "sente over many wanton Italian bookes, which being translated into english, have poysoned the olde maners of our Country with foreine delights, they have so hardned the readers harts that severer writers are trode under foote, none are so pleasunte or plausible as they, that sound some kinde of libertie in our eares" (B6r).

Ascham had visited Louvain during a mission to Europe in 1551 but had deliberately avoided the Catholic exiles, who, he wrote, "to see a mass freely in Flanders, are content to forsake, like slaves, their country." Cited in McConica, *English Humanists*, 271.

[116] These figures are based on AR. Also see the figures in Racine, "*A Pearle for a Prynce*," 418–19.

[117] "Anti-Catholic Polemical Writing," 27; Wooding, *Rethinking Catholicism*, 226–7; Holmes, *Resistance and Compromise*, 23–4.

[118] La Rocca, "Time, Death, and the Next Generation," 114; for a narrative of the 1571 parliament, see J. E. Neale, *Elizabeth I and her Parliaments 1559–1581* (New York, 1958), 1: 177–240.

[119] "At the Parliament begunne and holden at Westminster the second of Apryll, in the xiii yere of ... Lady Elizabeth" (1571), Aiir.

queen's authority by denying any of her titles or accusing her of heresy were now also acts of high treason.

As this new anti-Catholic legislation suggests, the aftermath of the rebellion and excommunication witnessed a sharp ratcheting up in Protestant rhetoric about the exiles. The "Acte agaynst fugitives over the seas" accused the exiles of practicing "trayterous, rebellious, seditious, and slaunderous thynges, as well by wrytyng as otherwyse."[120] A proclamation issued against Catholic books immediately before the rebellion in March 1569 refers only to "seditious books" and "malicious persons," whereas a similar proclamation issued in the aftermath of the rebellion and excommunication in July 1570 speaks of "the traitorous boldness of certain wicked and seditious persons" and of "high treasons against the estate and royal dignity of her majesty."[121] This change in official vocabulary suggests that, in the eyes of the government, the Catholic exiles had lost whatever potential they may have once had for rehabilitation and for being considered true Englishmen again.

Even as their Protestant antagonists redefined the Low Country exiles as inherently treasonous and unEnglish, the exiles themselves were forced to reassess their communal identity in response to the arrival of a new wave of refugees from England after the failure of the Northern Rebellion. John Jewel reported how some of the defeated "rebels" had "fled over into Flanders, where they are now remaining with the duke of Alva, and are making all the disturbance in their power."[122] The presence in the Low Countries of declared "rebels" now made it easier for the government to stigmatize *all* the exiles there as traitors, despite the fact that the earlier generation of scholars and students in Louvain appears not to have welcomed the lay newcomers under the leadership of the fugitive Earl of Westmorland. "Those who were at Louvaine for religion, before the rebels came, used not to come in their company," reported one Henry Simpson. One long-term resident at Louvain, the exile Sir Francis Englefield (a Privy Councilor under Mary), "refuse[d] to meet or speak with the Earl in the street, whereat the Earl was much offended." Perhaps by keeping their distance from the "rebels," the Louvainists were attempting to preserve their reputation as politically disengaged Catholic loyalists. Nevertheless, as Simpson also reported, some bonding among the various Catholic groups seems to have taken place, because "every Thursday all the English in Louvaine went to Church to hear mass and pray for England."[123]

---

[120] Ibid. Bi^v.

[121] See Kesselring, " 'Cold Pye'," 437–41. *Tudor Royal Proclamations: The Later Tudors (1553–1587)*, ed. Paul L. Hughes and James F. Larkin (New Haven: Yale University Press, 1969), 2: 312–13, 341–3.

[122] *Zurich Letters* 50: 228–9.

[123] *Calendar of State Papers Domestic Addenda 1566–79*, 368; also see Albert J. Loomie, SJ, *The Spanish Elizabethans: The English Exiles at the Court of Philip II* (New York: Fordham University Press, 1963), 20–1, 35, 95; Adrian Morey, *The Catholic Subjects of Elizabeth I* (Totowa, NJ: Rowman and Littlefield, 1978), 96; Guilday, *English Catholic Refugees on the Continent*, 11.

Whatever the political and theological differences among the established exiles and the newcomers in the Low Countries, the "English" Catholics all made their Englishness and their attachment to home central to their identities. Thomas Hoghton, another exile to arrive in the Low Countries after the Northern Rebellion, fled his Lancashire home and family in order to protect his conscience before his death in 1580. The ballad, "The Blessed Conscience," which may have been written by Hoghton or by one of his servants in exile, records a profound longing for "my soe deare coontrie."[124] As the speaker of the ballad, Thomas aches to return to a "merrie Englande" and especially to his "bower" at "Hoghton hygh"—the stately tower he had added to the family residence shortly before fleeing. But the song tells how his hopes of returning, of acquiring a license from the queen, and of reclaiming his lands and property while keeping his conscience clean are all thwarted by unscrupulous relatives who plot against him. As a result, Tomas never achieves his goal of rewarding his loyal retainers and of presiding as the benevolent master of a house and estate that would "open be to all."

About the same time as Thomas Hoghton's flight from England and not far from Antwerp, another Catholic exile of a different background, the Carthusian monk Dom Maurice Chauncy, formerly of the London Charterhouse, also longed for a return home. "We poor men," he wrote,

have remained at Bruges ever since we were expelled from England, silently awaiting God's mercy, hoping for blessings, for the peace of our country, for the dawn of a joyful return after the darkness of exile. We believe that not many years hence we shall see the blessings of the Lord in our land. The comfort of that hope makes exile lighter and more bearable for us, although, to tell the truth, the grievance of exile is not so great—a brave man is at home on any soil—as our distress at the ruin of our country.[125]

"A brave man is at home on any soil": How representative of the early Catholic exiles was Chauncy's stoicism? Did it matter to faithful Catholics where they made their home? Wasn't the true believer supposed to be at home anywhere in God's creation?[126] Chauncy's comment is very much a reflection of his order's eremetical religious life that stressed silent prayer and contemplation. The Carthusian monk lived a largely solitary existence in his individual cell, effectively shut off from the outside world. Moreover, as part of a trans-European fraternity, the Carthusian should be equally at home in any of the similarly designed charterhouses scattered across the Continent. Yet for most non regular and lay

---

[124] I quote the ballad from Joseph Gillow (ed.), *The Haydock Papers: A Glimpse into English Catholic Life under the Shade of Persecution and in the Dawn of Freedom* (London: Burns and Oates, 1888), 10–15. On Hoghton, also see E. A. J. Honigmann, *Shakespeare: The "Lost Years."* 2nd edn. (Manchester: Manchester University Press, 1998), 8–12.

[125] *The Passion and Martyrdom of the Holy English Carthusian Fathers: A Short Narration*, ed. G. W. S. Curtis (London: The Church Historical Society, 1935), 159. The text is dated 1570. Containing an account of the Carthusian martyrs under Henry VIII, Chauncy's *Historia martyrum Angliae* (1573) was reprinted several times in the 16th and 17th centuries.

[126] Wright, "Marian Exiles," 241.

Catholics displaced from England under Elizabeth, it mattered a great deal that they had had to leave their ancestral home. Contrary to hegemonic historical narratives that have made Englishness and Protestantism all but synonymous, post-Reformation Catholics were fully committed to resuturing the concepts of Englishness and Catholicism that reformist propaganda was working to unstitch. The Catholics at Louvain, Antwerp, and throughout the Low Countries certainly saw themselves as the true Englishmen and their "old religion" as a defining element of a lost national identity.

3

Turks, Northerners, and the Barbarous Heretic

Even as English Catholics living overseas thought that exile had intensified or heightened their Englishness, so they claimed that their Protestant antagonists' Englishness back home had withered under conditions of heresy. The Jesuit Robert Persons lamented how, under Protestant rule, the English as a people had degenerated from a "race whose rare nobility, even prior to receiving the Christian faith, is extolled as having always won praise for a certain humanity such as nature herself demands, and as having shrunk from all the barbarous cruelty of tyrants as from some kind of disease."[1] Before the arrival of Protestantism, he observed elsewhere, "no people instructed with Christian lawes and customes was ever eyther better framed to courtesie and humanitie...than this English people and nation." But heresy had changed this happy condition, "harden[ing] the hart" and "infecting [the English people] with deadlie poysons of malice."[2] Heresy was a toxin, a pestilential infection that targeted the heart and other vital organs of the individual as well as the collective body of the nation.[3]

Metaphors of illness, madness, and moral degeneration were widely used by Catholics to describe the negative changes wrought by heresy upon an English race imagined as once upright, noble, and humane. An equally popular trope in anti-Protestant discourse imagined heresy as effectively transforming Englishmen into another race, nation, or people. At the time of England's schism from Rome, the exiled Reginald Pole imagined that if the Carthusian priests imprisoned by Henry VIII for resisting his religious policies were suddenly set free, "they would have doubted whether the Englishmen had been driven out and some new nation from distant shores of the earth had occupied the realm, as once the Angles had done when they drove out the Britons...For they [the priests] always knew Englishmen as a most religious people." Likewise, other monks ejected from their monasteries and incarcerated by Henry could be forgiven for thinking that the world had changed, and that the Turks now ruled in England. In Pole's eyes, Henry's irreligious behavior had turned him into a type of the Great Turk, only

---

[1] *Letters and Memorials of Father Robert Persons, SJ*, vol. I *(to 1588)*, ed. L. Hicks, SJ, Catholic Record Society 39 (London, 1942), 36.

[2] *An epistle of the persecution of Catholickes in Englande* (Douai, 1582), 136–7 (*ERL* 125).

[3] Christine M. Boeckl, "Plague Imagery as Metaphor for Heresy in Rubens' *The Miracles of Saint Francis Xavier*," *Sixteenth Century Journal* 27 (1996), 979–95.

without the Turk's surprising tolerance for religious pluralism.[4] A generation after Pole, John Leslie employed a similar conceit, observing that under Edward VI the Protestant dukes had brought into England "infidelity, Barbarisme, and Turkish slavery . . . as Afrik, Grece, Bohemia and Hungary have tasted and do testifie." According to Leslie, the contamination of England by "a Religion so plainely Turkish and heathen" had brought about both the economic and moral collapse of the country.[5]

In anti-Protestant polemic, the Turks were one of several stigmatized out-groups repeatedly associated with English heretics. The Jews were another. James Shapiro observes that "Catholic propagandists were quick to seize upon the Judaizing propensities of the English Reformation as early as the 1550s." In the reign of Edward VI, rumors spread abroad that the king, "his council and kingdom had all become Jews and were waiting for the coming of the Messiah."[6] Catholics also developed analogies between heretics and New World Indians. These can be seen in a painting at the English College in Valladolid, Spain, that depicts "the proto-martyr of England, S Alban, killed by figures apparently Amerindian." This image, as Michael E. Williams points out, was "part of the metaphorical equation of the Protestant English with peoples then perceived as savage which formed a distinct part of Valladolid rhetoric."[7] This conflation of religious and ethnic categories whereby heretics were viewed in terms of Turks, Jews, or Indians was part of a discursive maneuver in which, to quote Ania Loomba, "the differences between Catholic and Protestant [were] complexly mapped onto notions of ethnic, national, [geographical], and religious difference."[8] The formulation and articulation of religious identities, in other words, did not occur only in narrowly religious terms, but across a wide range of overlapping discursive domains.[9] In examining Catholic representations of heresy, this chapter will first look at the ways in which English writers and

---

[4] Pole's "*Defence of the Unity of the Church*," trans. Joseph G. Dwyer (Westminster: Maryland, 1965), 212–17, 247. See also Peter Donaldson, "Machiavelli, Antichrist, and the Reformation: Prophetic Typology in Reginald Pole's *De Unitate* and *Apologia ad Carolum Quintum*," in Richard L. DeMolen (ed.), *Leaders of the Reformation* (Selinsgrove, Pa: Susquehanna University Press, 1984), 211–46.

[5] *A treatise of treasons against Q. Elizabeth, and the croune of England* (Louvain, 1572. *ERL* 254), 86ʳ, 148ʳ.

[6] *Shakespeare and the Jews* (New York: Columbia University Press, 2005), 21.

[7] Summary of a paper delivered at the Downside conference, "Recusant Archives and Remains from the Three Kingdoms, 1560–1789. Catholics in Exile at Home and Abroad." Downside Abbey, June 23–24, 2004. The conference proceedings are available at: http://www.catholic-heritage.net/recusant/.

[8] "'Delicious Traffick': Alterity and Exchange on Early Modern Stages," *Shakespeare Survey* 52 (1999), 206 n. 24.

[9] Samuel Chew, *The Crescent and the Rose: Islam and England during the Renaissance* (Oxford: Oxford University press, 1937), 101. Recent studies of polemic include Jesse Lander, *Inventing Polemic: Religion, Print, and Literary Culture in Early Modern England* (Cambridge: Cambridge University Press, 2006), and Luc Racaut, *Hatred in Print: Catholic Propaganda and Protestant Identity during the French Wars of Religion* (Ashgate, 2002).

publishers exploited religious, national, and ethnic categories to forge provocative connections between the Protestant heretic and Muslim Turk.[10] The second part of the chapter will then show how these discursive operations could be extended to take advantage of geographical and ethnographical factors in explaining the presence of Protestant heresy in the British Isles, Ireland, and other northern regions.

In the texts I examine, the label "Turk" is a flexible signifier that in different contexts can take on different religious, ethnic, or national valencies; it is a term, moreover, that is more or less interchangeable in early modern texts with various other terms, including Mohammedan, Ottoman, Saracen, Moroccan, and Moor.[11] Recent scholarship on the trope of the "Turk" in the period's confessional discourse has focused largely on its use by Protestants, while underestimating its prevalence in the counter-discourses of Catholic apologists.[12] This Protestant-centrism is partly a function of Luther's influential role in deploying the Turk as an ideological weapon on the reformed side of confessional battles. Luther's Bible notoriously linked the Great Turk and the pope in a woodcut illustration. Luther's German Catholic opponents, however, were just as quick to turn the discourse of the Turk against him. In 1529, Luther's arch-antagonist, the Catholic controversialist Johannes Cochlaeus produced a pamphlet in German and Latin that featured a monstrous seven-headed Luther on its title page. One of the heads attached to Luther's body wears a Turban, marking him as a Turkish infidel.[13]

In English reformed circles, Luther's equation of pope and Turk was explored most thoroughly in the second edition of John Foxe's *Actes and Monuments* (1570). Foxe includes a new history of the Turks, *The Turkes Storye*, and ponders the relationship between the Turk and the papacy as persecutors of the Godly. For Foxe, the Turk represented the latest in a long line of groups and figures, including the Old Testament Syrians and a corrupt papacy, that could be identified with

---

[10] Polemical writers used an array of loose designations to describe the peoples of the eastern Mediterranean and Arab worlds. These terms could have various levels of religious, geographical, and ethnic connotations: Turk, Mohammedan, Moslem, infidel, moor, Ottoman, Saracen. Other kinds of texts in the period developed a more coherent ethnographic discourse about the Turk and were more discriminating in their terminology.

[11] Ania Loomba, *Shakespeare, Race, and Colonialism* (Oxford: Oxford University Press, 2002), 71 and Chapter 4. On the indeterminacy of terms like "moor" and "Turk," also see Michael Neill, " 'Mulattos,' 'Blacks,' and 'Indian Moors': *Othello* and Early Modern Constructions of Difference," *Shakespeare Quarterly* 49 (1998), 364–5, and 366 n. 20.

[12] Important studies include Nabil Matar, *Turks, Moors and Englishmen in the Age of Discovery* (New York: Columbia University Press, 1999); Daniel Vitkus, *Turning Turk: English Theater and the Multicultural Mediterranean, 1570–1630* (New York: Palgrave Macmillan, 2003). Matthew Dimmock gives more attention than other studies to the Catholic appropriation of the Turk trope. See *New Turkes: Dramatizing Islam and the Ottomans in Early Modern England* (Aldershot: Ashgate, 2005).

[13] *Sieben Kopffe Mertini Luthers* (Leipzig: V. Schumann, 1529); see R. W. Scribner, *For the Sake of Simple Folk: Popular Propaganda for the German Reformation* (Oxford: Oxford University Press, 1994), 232–3.

the Antichrist of an apocalyptic history.[14] The damaging equation of England's enemies with the Turk was made repeatedly in the Protestant regime's propaganda organs. William Cecil, the queen's chief minister, allegedly attempted to make Philip of Spain "odious unto the people, [by permitting] certaine players . . . to scof and jest at him, upon their common stages. And the lyke was used in contempt of his religion; first, to make it no better than Turkishe, by annexing unto the very psalmes of David (as thoughe the prophet himself had bene the author thereof) this ensuing meeter:

> Preserve us lord by thy deere woord,
> From Turck and Pope defend us lord,
> That bothe would thrust out of his throne,
> Our lord Jesus Christ, thy deere sonne."[15]

The powerful ideological charge represented by the "Turk" was not one that Catholics could allow their adversaries to monopolize in the religious war of ideas. Among the English exiles in the Low Countries, John Fowler—the pro-lific translator, editor, printer, and publisher of recusant books—masterfully exploited the polemical potential of the interconnections between the Turks and Protestant heretics.[16] In 1566 Fowler published his translation of the German Peter Frarinus's *An oration against the unlawful insurrections of the Protestantes of our time* (Antwerp, 1566. *ERL* 226).[17] Although the text was ostensibly about the plight of Germany, Fowler's edition invited English readers to apply its lessons to their homeland. *An oration* pursued its central claim that heresy led inevitably to the subversion of all secular and religious authority, while showing how Luther endangered the security not only of Germany but of the whole of Christendom by forbidding Christians from opposing the Turk and by conspiring with Soliman.[18] Even though the Turks had eventually been beaten back from the borders of Germany, they still occupied Hungary—"no

---

[14] Stephan Schmuck, "The 'Turk' as Antichrist in John Foxe's *Acts and Monuments*," *Reformation* 10 (2005), 21–44. Foxe does not ultimately single out either the papacy or the Turk as the "greater Antichrist."

[15] Richard Verstegan, *A declaration of the true causes of the great troubles, presupposed to be intended against the realme of England* (Antwerp, 1592), 20–1 (*ERL* 360).

[16] On Fowler, see *Antwerp, Dissident Typographical Centre: The Role of Antwerp Printers in the Religious Conflicts in England (16th century)* (Antwerp: The City of Antwerp Plantin-Moretus Museum, 1994), 160–1; Christian Coppens, *Reading in Exile: The Libraries of John Ramridge (d.1568), Thomas Harding (d.1572), and Henry Joliffe (d.1573): Recusants in Louvain* (Cambridge: LP Publications, 1993), 18–20. William Allen called Fowler "that most Catholic and most learned printer of books" (A. C. Southern, " 'The Best Wits out of England': University Men in Exile under Elizabeth," *The Month* 7 (1952), 17).

[17] Frarinus (or Frarin) was a jurist and scholar of Antwerp. Frarinus's work was answered by the Protestant commentator, William Fulke, in his *Treatise against the Defense of the Censure given . . . against the Railing declamation of P. Frarine* (1586). See also Peter Milward, *Religious Controversies of the Elizabethan Age: a Survey of Printed Sources* (London: Scolar Press, 1977), 21; and *Antwerp, Dissident Typographical Centre*, 160.

[18] Frarinus, *An oration against the unlawful insurrections*, Dviii^v, Eiv^v.

The Turke againſt Chꝛiſten,by Chꝛi=
ſtēn is calde in,
with moꝛe then Turkiſhe treaſon and
moſt hoꝛrible ſyn,

Fig. 2. Peter Frarinus, *An oration against the unlawful insurrections of the Protestantes of our time*, trans. John Fowler (Antwerp, 1566). STC 11333 (copy 1), p. Eiii Fiii.

smal portion of Christendome"—thanks to the "rebellion and sedition of these heretical sectes."[19] Fowler ensured that Frarinus's text would have an impact on the widest possible English audience by adding to the original Latin version a set of crude woodcuts (each with an accompanying rhyme in English). Along with the gruesome images of the violence perpetrated against Catholics throughout Europe by the self-styled "Gospellers," was a woodcut showing Luther and a turbaned Turk approaching each other in a show of friendship. The message was designed to be obvious even to those who "cannot reade."[20]

Texts that Fowler only printed, and thus presumably influenced less, also highlight the Turk–Protestant connection. Produced by Fowler in 1568, John Fen's translation of Osório da Fonseca's *A learned and very eloquent treatie* accused

[19] Ibid. Fviii[v]

[20] Ibid. Kiv[r]. See Richard Williams, " 'Libels and Payntinges': Elizabethan Catholics and the International Campaign of Visual Propaganda," in Christopher Highley and John N. King (eds.), *John Foxe and his World* (Aldershot: Ashgate, 2002), 199. The *Oration's* "infamous picture" is attacked by William Fulke in *An Apologie against the railing declamation of Peter Frarine* (33). The *Apologie* is part of Fulke's *A treatise against the Defense of the censure* (1586). On the Catholic tradition of cheap didactic illustrations, see Kirstin Noreen, "*Ecclesiae Militantis Triumphi*: Jesuit Iconography and the Counter-Reformation," *Sixteenth Century Journal* 29 (1998), 689–714.

Luther of responsibility for the death of the king of Hungary and the subsequent victory of the Turks that had "laied open a gap into Christendom."[21] The actions of Lutheran heretics had not only sown dissension within the Catholic world but had helped breach the boundary of Christendom itself by letting in a Turkish enemy that might yet conquer western Europe.

The Turkish occupation of Hungary and its implications for Catholic representations of heresy were also at the heart of the edition of Thomas More's *A dialogue of cumfort against tribulation* that Fowler brought out in 1573 (Antwerp. *ERL* 25).[22] Originally written by More during his incarceration in the Tower in 1534, *A dialogue* was the only stand-alone work of More's to be published in English by the Louvain exiles, whose investment in promoting More as a recusant hero also lies behind their publication of his Latin *Opera* in 1565.[23] *A dialogue* is set against the backdrop of the Turkish invasion of Hungary in the 1520s with the two speakers, Antonie and Vincent, discussing the possibility of spiritual consolation in the face of a mounting Turkish threat.

Although critics have been reluctant to claim that More originally intended the Turks' attack on Hungary to be read as an allegory of heretical attacks on the English Church under Henry VIII, this is precisely how a later generation of English Catholic readers—in the wake of the Elizabethan religious settlement—interpreted *A dialogue*. More's Elizabethan biographer, Thomas Stapleton, claimed in the *Tres Thomae*, that *A dialogue*'s

references to Henry's cruelty, to the disturbances in England, to the fear and expectation of the spread of heresy there, to what comfort the good may have in view of such evils, present or to come, are all disguised cleverly and naturally in the person of a Hungarian who speaks of the cruelty of the Turkish Emperor, the unrest in Hungary, and the fear of future evils, so that you would be convinced that a Hungarian is speaking of his own land and not More of England . . . *He speaks of the carrying into Hungary of the blasphemies of Mahomet, but in reality he is referring to the coming into England of the doctrines of the Lutherans, Sacramentarians, and other heretics or schismatics.*[24] (my italics)

Stapleton, when preparing this life of More, would naturally have consulted Fowler's edition of *A dialogue* which, as Paul Voss has shown, helped consolidate More's heroic reputation with the recusant community at home and in exile. *A*

---

[21] John Fen (trans.). Osório da Fonseca, *A learned and very eloquent treatie* (Louvain, 1568. *ERL* 318), 51ᵛ.

[22] Earlier in the 16th century, several of More's works had helped establish what Matthew Dimmock calls the "satirical metaphor" of the Turk in confessional debates. Dimmock also discusses the circumstances surrounding the first printing of More's *Dialogue* in 1553 ("*New Turkes*," 26–35, 53–4).

[23] James K. McConica, "The Recusant Reputation of Thomas More," in R. S. Sylvester and G. P. Marc'hadour (eds.), *Essential Articles for the Study Sir Thomas More* (Hamden, Conn.: Archon Books, 1977), 137–49.

[24] [Stapleton], *Thomas Stapleton: The Life and Illustrious Martyrdom of Sir Thomas More*, trans. Philip E. Hallett (London: Burns Oates and Washbourne, 1928), 66, 126. For discussion, see Romuald I. Lakowski, "Thomas More, Protestants, and Turks: Persecution and Martyrdom in *A Dialogue of Comfort*," *Ben Jonson Journal* 7 (2000), 199–223.

dialogue likely acted as "a silent teacher and source of comfort" to the Catholic faithful in England because of the scarcity of priests.[25]

Fowler's preface to his edition of *A dialogue* resists a specific topical application of More's allegory, instead extending the text's message of comfort to all men: "under this particular case of Turks persecution [More] generally comprehendeth all kinds of afflictions and persecutions both of body and mind, that may any way be sufered, either by sicknes or health ... [including] Miscreants and Turks, and the very fiends and divels of hel also."[26] The preface's ecumenical, noncontroversial tone may, as Voss suggests, have been a device for making the book palatable to Protestant authorities (although the appearance of More's portrait immediately after the preface—a dangerous image to be sure—complicates this assumption).

Yet Fowler's marginal glosses to More's text work against the nonsectarian tone of the preface by insistently linking the acts of the Turks to those of contemporary heretics. "To this persecution of the Turkes may wel be resembeld the whole practice of heretikes in any place where they can prevaile." "All that is sayd of the Turke is in a parable meant of heretikes and Schismatikes."[27] When one of the speakers in *A dialogue* recalls the complacency of his Hungarian countrymen toward the Turkish threat, Fowler inserts in the margin: "How true is this proved by the breaking out of heresie from out of Germany into other Cuntries." And in another gloss, Fowler identifies "Turkish treacherie" with "Protestants practises and proceedings."[28] Fowler insists that if the Turks are still physically distant from England, they have already infiltrated the realm symbolically: "Blessed be God, that the Turkes themselves, though they have over-runne already almost al Hungarie and thereto wonne Cypres of late, are farre ynough of from us yet: and would God al their Turkish fashions and persecutions were as farre of from us to, and that Christian Charitie did raigne more truly and plentifully in the hartes of al that beare the name of Christians in Christendome."[29]

The English Catholic strategy of discrediting heretics through association with the Turks received its fullest exposition in 1597 with the appearance of William Rainolds's voluminous *Calvino-Turcismus id est, Calvinisticae perfidiae, cum Mahumetana collatio, et dilucida utriusque sectae confutation* (a title Robert Persons translated as "of Calvyns Religion leading to Turcisme, or a comparison of Turkish Religion with Calvinisme").[30] The work, over a thousand pages long and divided into four books, was published in Antwerp after being completed by William Gifford following Rainolds's death in 1595.[31] *Calvino-Turcismus* was answered with remarkable swiftness by the Protestant Matthew Sutcliffe in his slightly less monumental *De Turcopapismo* (1599) which spent only 605 pages

---

[25] Paul J. Voss, "The Making of a Saint: John Fowler and Thomas More, 1573," *Journal of English and Germanic Philology* 99 (2000), 510.

[26] Voss, "Making of a Saint," 509 n. 62; Lakowski, "Thomas More," 204.

[27] More, *A dialogue of cumfort,* 3ᵛ, 4ᵛ.   [28] Ibid. 4ʳ, 132ᵛ.   [29] Ibid. viᵛ.

[30] Robert Persons, *A relation of the triall made before the King of France, upon the yeare 1600. betweene the Bishop of Eureux, and the L. Plessis Mornay* (St Omers, 1604. *ERL* 305), 47.

[31] The British Library copy is 1,038 pages. A second edition was published at Cologne in 1603.

substituting Rainolds's coupling of Protestant and Turk with the alternative coupling of Catholic and Turk.[32] The Rainolds–Sutcliffe exchange became widely known. In 1607, for example, Robert Persons remarked that *Calvino-Turcismus* "is held by strangers to be one of the most learned [books] that has byn written of this kinde of controversy in our age, and M. Sutcliffe hath made himself ridiculous by attempting to answere the same."[33]

Protestant writers responded vociferously to *Calvino-Turcismus*, and even years after its appearance continued to engage with it polemically. In 1606 George Abbot declared, in response to the "slanders" of *Calvino-Turcismus*, that Protestants "from the bottome of our heartes detest Turcisme and Mahumetisme, and know that Mahomet was a false Prophet."[34] In 1613 John Boys included the *Calvino-Turcismus* in a mock canon of Catholic "Pasquils and invective libels" along with Richard Verstegan's "Theatrum Crudelitatum, the relations of Caietan annexed to Genebrards Chronologie, Stapletons tres Thomae . . . [and] the seditious pamphlets of Allen, Sanders, Campian, Bristo, Rob. Parsons; all which are not onely hyperbolici, but . . . hyperdiabolici."[35] Henry King, in 1621, counted the *Calvino-Turcismus* along with the "three Conversions, the life of Saint Francis, the story of Garnets strawe, and of our Lady of Loretto . . . and . . . the Golden Legend" as among the most notable Catholic libels.[36]

The formula of yoking together the religion of one's Christian adversary and the Turkish infidel in the titles of *Calvino-Turcismus* and *De Turcopapismo* also proved popular. An English translation of Cardinal Peron's *Luthers Alcoran* detailed in sixty points how "Lutheranisme agreeth with Mahumetisme, or Turcisme." Lutheranism is here used as a catch-all phrase to include other varieties of Christian heresy like Zwinglianism and Calvinism.[37] Originally written in French by Peron to combat Huguenot belief, the English version redirected the work's invective against English Puritan extremists.[38] In another variation on the title formula, Oliver Ormerod appended to his *The Picture of a Papist* (1606) a treatise called *Pagano-papismus*, that sought to show "by irrefragable

[32] For more on the controversy, see Milward, *Religious Controversies of the Elizabethan Age*, 146.

[33] *A treatise tending to mitigation towardes Catholicke-subjectes in England* (St Omers, 1608. ERL 340), 56–7. Also see Persons, *A relation of the triall*, 46–8.

[34] *The reasons which Doctour Hill hath brought, for the upholding of papistry* (1604), 23–4.

[35] *The autumne part from the twelfth Sundy after Trinitie, to the last in the whole yeere dedicated unto the much honoured and most worthy Doctor John Overal* (1613), 71.

[36] *A sermon preached at Pauls Crosse, the. 25. of November. 1621 Upon occasion of that false and scandalous report (lately printed) touching the supposed apostasie of the right Reverend Father in God, John King, late Lord Bishop of London* (1621), 57. The "three Conversions" is Robert Persons's *A treatise of three conversions of England from paganisme to Christian religion* (1603–4); "The life of Saint Francis" is probably Anthony Maria Browne's translation of Bonaventure's life of St Francis (1610); "the story of Garnets strawe" refers to the Catholic claim that a tiny image of Garnet's face appeared on a blood spattered piece of straw retrieved from his place of execution; "our Lady of Loretto" could refer to any number of texts about the Italian shrine famous for the house where Mary had been conceived and where the annunciation had occurred. The house had allegedly been transported by angels from its original site in Nazareth.

[37] Peron, *Luthers Alcoran* (np, 1645), 2, 19. [38] Ibid. 3–6, 21.

demonstrations, that Papisme is flat Paganisme: and that the Papists doe resemble the very Pagans."[39]

For Catholics, an especially damning similarity between the Protestant heretic and infidel Turk was the Deuteronomical prohibition they shared against the use of religious images. One Catholic account of Protestant iconoclasm told of how the heretics "broke and burned the crosse, and mocked at it everie where as the Turkes did sometyme at Constantinople."[40] Catholics could find evidence of this mockery in Foxe's treatment in the *Actes and Monuments* of the Turks' desecration of this same crucifix in Constantinople's "highe temple of Sophia." The Protestant Foxe, instead of denouncing the desecration, attacks Catholics for giving such "occasion of sclaunder and offence ... unto the barbarous infideles by this our ungodly superstition in having Images in our temples, contrary unto the expresse commaundement of God."[41] Catholics, insisted Foxe, were to blame for allowing images in churches in the first place, not Turks for destroying them. Reformers like Foxe also defended English alliances with Muslim powers against Catholic Spain by arguing that Protestants and Muslims could unite around a shared horror of idolatry.

Catholics saw Turkish and Protestant acts of iconoclasm as indicative of more fundamental linkages between infidels and heretics. The Church maintained, in fact, that at its roots the religion of Islam was a Christian heresy. "All historiographers that write of the first beginning of Turkes," claimed Stapleton's translation of Staphylus, "affirm with one assent, that the lawe of Mahomet writen in the Alcoran, was compiled by one Sergius an Arrian, and John a Nestorian, bothe auncient heretiques, and of a certain Jewe of the Talmudistes."[42] The beliefs of the Arian Sergius and of Nestorius were denounced as heresies at the fourth-century Council of Nicea and the fifth-century Council of Ephesus respectively. Sergius is certainly the better known of the two heretics: as an apostate monk, he allegedly shared his heretical beliefs with Mohammed who incorporated them into his doctrines. For later Catholic writers, Sergius's status as an apostate monk made him an obvious forerunner to Luther, another lapsed monk and breeder of schism in the Church.[43] The view that "the lawe of Mahomet" was indebted to heretics (Arians and Nestorians), and that Islam was thus the sum or "sink of all heresies" was most influentially stated by Peter the Venerable in the twelfth century. As well as writing *Summa totius haeresis Saracenorum* (*The Summary of the Entire Heresy of the Saracens*) and *Liber contra sectam sive haeresim Saracenorum* (*The Refutation of the Sect of the Saracens*), Peter also sponsored the first translations into Latin of key Islamic religious works, including the Koran, not to

---

[39] Ormerod, *The Picture of a Papist*, Title Page.

[40] Frarinus, *An oration against the unlawfull insurrections*, Hiii[r].

[41] Foxe, *Actes and Monuments* (1570), Book 6: 880. Also see Robert E. Scully, " 'In the Confident Hope of a Miracle': The Spanish Armada and Religious Mentalities in the Late Sixteenth Century," *Catholic Historical Review* 89 (2003), 654–5.

[42] *The apologie of Fridericus Staphylus* (Antwerp, 1565. ERL 268), 19[r].

[43] *Luther's Alcoran*, 27.

foster a better understanding of Islam but to discredit and spread misconceptions about it.[44]

Peter the Venerable's account of the origins of infidelity helps to explain how early modern Catholics could imagine new heresies like Lutheranism and Calvinism morphing into "the cursed infidelite of Mahomet." If the Turkish infidel was a mutation of the Christian heretic, then the Christian heretic could easily be imagined collapsing back into the Turkish infidel. As Staphylus had argued, "This fifte ghospell of Luther prepareth and fortifieth the waie for Mahomets Alcoran to come in to Germany."[45] Indeed, the slippage from Christian heresy to the infidelity of Islam was seen by Catholics as teleologically inevitable: "The divell therefore hath so directed allwaies and trayned all contentions and variaunces in religion, that all heresies ende in the Alcoran Mahomets lawe."[46] The Catholic convert, William Alabaster, thought that the *Calvino-Turcismus* "sheweth by evident arguments that the Doctrine of Calvin leadeth to Turcisme, nor can defend itself agaynst Turkishe reasons, except by help of the Catholique Church."[47] Nicholas Sander emphasized the force of the telos leading from heretic to Turk when he imagined the relationship in genealogical terms: "Of this rase [the Saracens/Turks] cometh John Wiclef, to Wiclef Joannes Hus succeded, to him Luther, to him Calvin, to him Germanus."[48]

Catholic fears that Protestant heresy would ultimately result in full-blown adherence to Islam are given immediate relevance in the fates of specific individuals mentioned by John Copinger in *The theatre of Catholique and Protestant religion*. Copinger names several influential Europeans—"Paulus, minister of the church of Cracovia . . . Gonesius and Gribaldus and Franciscus Davidis, for this last was superintendent of Hungarie . . . Adam Nimser the cheefe superintendent of Hedelberge in Palatyne of Rhene,"

who of Calvinistes, became Turckes and went to Constantinople, where they made open profession thereof, and protested that the religion of Calvinistes, tended directly to Turcisme, and before these people went out of Palatyne, they subverted many great preachers, who by their meanes became Turckes and taught publickly the Alcoran in Germanie.[49]

[44] Neil Elliot, " 'The Heresy of the Saracens' to 'The War against the Turk': A study of later medieval understandings of Islam from Peter the Venerable to Martin Luther." Centre for the Study of Islam and Christian-Muslim Relations, Department of Theology, University of Birmingham. Occasional papers, No. 9, September 2001. www.theology.bham.ac.uk/research/CSICPapers/Elliott1.htm; see also R. W. Southern, *Western Views of Islam in the Middle Ages* (Harvard University Press, 1962), 38; James Kritzeck, *Peter the Venerable and Islam* (Princeton: Princeton University Press, 1964). I am grateful to James Lenaghan for discussions about this material.

[45] *The apologie of Fridericus Staphylus*, 113ᵛ. Luther's enemies mockingly referred to him as the fifth evangelist—the author of the fifth gospel—in mockery of his pretensions to follow in the footsteps of Matthew, Mark, Luke, and John.

[46] Ibid. 18ᵛ.

[47] *Unpublished Works by William Alabaster (1568–1640)*, ed. Dana F. Sutton (Salzburg University, 1997), 116–17.

[48] *A treatise of the images of Christ, and of his saints* (Louvain, 1567. *ERL* 282), 36ʳ.

[49] Copinger, *The theatre of Catholique and Protestant religion* (St Omers, 1620), 81 (*ERL* 191).

From Copinger's perspective, it was a short step from the doctrines of Calvin and Beza to the Turk's rejection of the Trinity, the divinity of Christ, and the veneration of saints. Copinger is more specific about the stages of Adam Nimser's (Newser's) degeneration, "who from a Zvinglian, became an Arian, and afterwardes a Turcke." These three "sectes" of "Calvinisme, Arianisme, and Mahometisme" are "three briches of one cloathe."[50] Readers who wanted more details about Protestant apostates who had turned Turk are referred by Copinger to the authoritative "Calvini Turcismo."[51] Similarly, in *The converted Jew*, a Catholic dialogue by Roger Anderton (alias John Clare), readers are pointed to "that elaborate and mother-booke... *Calvino Turcismus*" for further examples of Protestants who had embraced Turkish Islam.[52]

For Catholics, the alleged resemblance between the doctrines of Turks and Protestants helped explain Protestants' unwillingness to cooperate in a general war against the Turks and their corresponding goal of profiting from conflict between Catholic forces and Islam. This point is made forcefully in a Catholic news pamphlet printed after the Turk's ejection from Malta by Spanish forces in August 1565, and hailing in its title *the goodly vyctorie, wyche the Christenmen by the favor of God have ther latlye obtayned*. The work was translated for an English audience from a French original and printed at Ghent—another refuge and printing center for English Catholic exiles in the Spanish Low Countries. This short, anonymous work highlights Protestant England's shameful "neutrality" in the recent military action.[53] The pamphlet explains how the English government had turned down Philip II's request to help fight the Turks. Even without English backing, Philip still scores a great victory that is heralded as protecting all of western Christendom from the threat of infidel aggression. By issuing the work in English, the anonymous translator of *Good nues* was no doubt seeking to embarrass the Elizabethan regime—shaming it into rejoining the family of European Christian nations.[54] John Jewel was no doubt referring to this same pamphlet when he complained sardonically of the "pretie Pamflettes" that Thomas

---

[50] Ibid. 73.

[51] Copinger, *The theatre of Catholique and Protestant religion*, 75. Also see Thomas H. Clancy, SJ, *Papist Pamphleteers: The Allen-Persons Party and the Political Thought of the Counter-Reformation in England, 1572–1615* (Chicago: Loyola University Press, 1964), 19.

[52] Anderton, *The converted Jew* (np, 1630), Part 2: 103–4 (*ERL* 206). Shapiro, *Shakespeare and the Jews*, 138–9, 268–9 n. 37.

[53] *Certayn and tru good nues, from the syege of the isle [of] Malta, wyith the goodly vyctorie, wyche the Christenmen...have ther latlye obtayned, agaynst the Turks* (1565. *ERL* 170). Although the work is not explicitly pro-Catholic, its publication in Ghent suggests it is the work of an exiled English Catholic. For further details, see A. C. Southern, *Elizabethan Recusant Prose, 1559–1582: A Historical and Critical Account of the Books of the Catholic Refugees Printed and Published Abroad and at Secret Presses in England together with an annotated Bibliography of the same* (London: Sands, 1950), 331–3.

[54] Samuel Chew points out that in England the government ordered thanksgiving prayers to be said on the occasion of the Turks' defeat at Malta (*The Crescent and the Rose*, 123–4).

Harding had "lately printed togeather, and joined with the Turkish Newes of Malta."[55]

Another conflict between Turks and Christians at which English Protestants remained bystanders despite the appeals for help from Catholic powers was the famous naval Battle of Lepanto in 1571. "The king of Spaine," noted the Catholic exile Richard Verstegan, "for the more repose and tranquilitie of Christendome joyned in league against the Turk with the Pope, and the Venetians, whereof followed the great victory, obtained by Don John de Austria his Generall at Lepanto."[56] English Protestant observers were deeply ambivalent about this Catholic victory over growing Turkish influence in the Mediterranean. As Samuel Chew observes, "At moments of crisis . . . anti-Muslim sentiments [in Britain] developed into an anxious sympathy with the Catholic powers which were struggling, alone or in various combinations, with the Turks."[57] "Anxious sympathy" toward a Catholic-led anti-Muslim crusade nicely captures the tone of the poem composed (years later) by James VI of Scotland to commemorate the Lepanto victory.[58] While the poem distinguishes between Catholic and reformed Christians, it places more emphasis on the differences between "the baptiz'd race" of Christians and the "circumcised Turband Turkes." Philip II and Don John of Austria may follow the false doctrine of Rome, but for James they also embody an admirable Christian heroism.[59]

English Catholics, lamenting their country's refusal to help defend Christendom against the Turk, also claimed that the Elizabethan regime was giving military support—"powder, shot, artillery, and other munition[s]"—to Philip II's enemies, including "the Moores that inhabited the kingdome of Granada," and had contracted alliances with "the great Turk, the Kinges of Fesse, Marocco, and Algiers, or other Mahometains and Moores of Barbarie, all professed enemies of Christ."[60] According to Verstegan, the chief actor in these shameless dealings was William Cecil, Elizabeth's chief minister. Indeed, from the late 1570s, and in defiance of canon law, the Elizabethan regime sold arms to the Turks for their wars against the Saracens. But Elizabeth not only peddled weaponry to the infidels, she exported raw materials like lead and iron that the Turks could convert into munitions. Catholics were outraged at this commerce, but their objections were exacerbated by the fact that the "raw materials" were not in fact

[55] *A replie unto M. Hardinges Answeare* (1565). "Preface to the Christian Reader," ¶3ʳ⁻ᵛ.

[56] *A declaration of the true causes*, 34–5.   [57] *The Crescent and the Rose*, 104.

[58] "The Lepanto of James the Sixt, King of Scotland," appeared in *His Majesties Poeticall Exercises at Vacant Hours* (Edinburgh, 1591). For a modern edition, see James Craigie (ed.), *The Poems of James VI of Scotland*, vol. 1 of 2. (1955). Also see Sandra Bell, "Writing the Monarch: King James VI and *Lepanto*," in Helen Ostovich, Mary V. Silcox, and Graham Roebuck (eds.), *Other Voices, Other Views: Expanding the Canon in English Renaissance Studies* (Newark: University of Delaware Press, 1999), 193–208.

[59] See Barbara Fuchs, "Conquering Islands: Contextualizing *The Tempest*", *Shakespeare Quarterly* 48 (1997), 56; and Matar, *Turks, Moors and Englishmen*, 143.

[60] Verstegan, *A declaration of the true causes*, 21, 48.

"raw" but prized articles of the Catholic Church. Protestants were recycling old church furnishings and melting down once sanctified Catholic objects like saints' statues and bells that the reformers deemed idolatrous.[61]

Elizabeth, fearing the response of even her own Protestant subjects, as well as of other European powers, to news of an Anglo-Turkish rapprochement, ordered ambassadorial missions and arms trading to be kept secret.[62] Catholic authors, however, were quick to spread rumors and publicize links between the Protestant regime in England and Muslim powers. William Allen on the eve of the Armada proclaimed that Elizabeth had "dealte with the cruel and dreadfull tirante and enemie of our faithe the Great Turke himself (againste whom our noble kinges have in olde time so valiantly foughte)." In betraying the heroic legacy of her Catholic forefathers in opposing the Turk, Elizabeth had made herself the enemy of "all true Englishmen."[63] Allen's colleague, Robert Persons, reprinted in *Newes from Spayne and Holland* what purports to be a verbatim transcript of a letter sent from "the Turk himselfe" (the Ottoman Sultan) to Elizabeth soon after the defeat of the Spanish Armada. The letter reveals that Elizabeth had approached the Turks about a strategic alliance against Philip II in order to help thwart Hapsburg aspirations for global dominance. It was an invitation the Turk could not resist.[64] To Persons, Elizabeth's overtures to the Turk reeked of "the highest infamy," a betrayal of Christendom, and a sure way to supplant Christianity with Mohammedanism in England itself.[65] Other Catholics also broadcast Elizabeth's shameful Turkish alliances. Some of the surviving copies of Thomas Stapleton's *Apologia pro Rege Catholico Philippo II* (Antwerp, 1592) contain "the text of a letter to Elizabeth from the Sultan of Turkey," confirming their unholy alliance.[66]

If the young King James and other reformed observers of the Turks felt a guilty fascination with the battle of Lepanto and similar Christian–Muslim conflicts—attempting to compensate for their lack of involvement by acts of textual commemoration—Catholic Englishmen saw the absence of Elizabeth's Protestant forces from Lepanto as confirmation of England's rogue status— one confirmed only the year before by the excommunication of the queen. As we saw in the last chapter, the papal bull of 1570 declaring Elizabeth "the pretended queen of England," marked the beginning of an intensification in her regime's anti-Catholic rhetoric along with legislation that sought to forge an even closer bond between the reformed religion and "true" Englishness. Elizabeth's government became ever more hostile to Rome and the "old religion,"

---

[61] Jonathan Burton, "Anglo-Ottoman Relations and the Image of the Turk in *Tamburlaine*," *Journal of Medieval and Early Modern Studies* 30 (2000), 131–2.

[62] However outrageous this Anglo-Turkish alliance appeared to Catholic observers, Elizabeth had sound strategic and economic reasons for pursuing it. See Burton, "Anglo-Ottoman," 1–8.

[63] *An Admonition to the people and nobility of England and Ireland concerninge the present warres* (np, 1588. *ERL* 74), xxiiii, viii.

[64] Persons, *Newes from Spayne and Holland* (Antwerp, 1593. *ERL* 365), 16ᵛ–19ᵛ.

[65] Ibid. 18ᵛ–19ᵛ.   [66] AR 1: 155–6.

targeting recusants at home and the soon-to-arrive missionary priests from over-seas with harsher penalties in the form of fines, imprisonment, banishment, and execution.[67]

Under these pressures, English Catholic writers themselves escalated the rhetorical identification of Protestant heretic and infidel Turk into a way of talking about the lamentable condition of their homeland. Richard Verstegan's works are especially notable for their nightmarish fantasy of an England turned into Turkey. In one of his tracts he moves seamlessly from a discussion of Turkish affairs to events in "England, which next unto Turkey I may speak of," as if the two lands were logically connected.[68] By 1592, after more than a decade of the highly publicized Protestant persecution of Catholics in England, Verstegan claimed that government surveillance and control were so pervasive that "to all the world [it] must needes seeme extreame barbarous, and to the very protestants themselves at home intolerable. who must needs also be sought, & examined as well as others, excepte they alwayes cary their pasportes with them in their pock-etts, & ride up & downe Ingland, as they would passe thorough Turky."[69] In the same vein, William Allen asserted that England was no less dangerous to Catholic missionary priests than more outlandish destinations like "the Indes ... any part of Turky or Hetheanesse."[70] In fact, the missionaries could expect even harsher treatment in England than "in Heathen Countries, where there were no such exquisite lawes against religion as in the Countries revolted."[71] From the perspec-tive of English Catholics, the cruelty of their Protestant countrymen far exceeded that of the Turks.

While condemning the "Turkish" ruthlessness of the Protestants, English Catholic writers nevertheless exploited a different perspective on the Turks that emphasized the surprising degree of religious toleration they showed to conquered Christians. John Fowler's edition of More's *A dialogue of cumfort* disseminated a widely credited view that

even in the mids of their owne Countreies [the Turks] suffer many Christen folke to dwel, paying certaine tributes and taxes for their safegard and sufferance to live there. And in other Countreies also which they newly subdue and win from the Christians, they do not so dispeople the whole lands ... but that they let many thousands dwel there stil professing openly and freely their faith, with Churches and Chappels allowed for them: this only provided, that they agnise [recognize] the Turke to be lord of the land, and themselves to live in quiet and civil subjection under him.[72]

Robert Persons also reached for the Turkish example when explaining why English Catholics could not in good conscience attend Protestant services and

[67] The first priests trained in Allen's Continental seminaries arrived in England in 1574.
[68] *A declaration of the true causes*, 49.
[69] *An advertisement written to a secretarie of my L. Treasurers of Ingland, by an Inglishe intelligencer as he passed throughe Germanie towardes Italie* (Antwerp, 1592. *ERL* 166), 22.
[70] *An apologie and true declaration of the institution and endevours of the two English colleges, the one in Rome, the other now resident in Rhemes* (Rheims, 1581. *ERL* 67), 82^v.
[71] Ibid. 84^{r-v}. [72] More, *A dialogue of cumfort*, vi^{r-v}.

when warning Church Papists of the dangers they faced by practicing occasional conformity in the Church of England. Persons finds examples from around the world in order to highlight the unprecedented nature of the penalties imposed by the Protestant authorities on English recusants:

Al Princes also, and Potentates of the world, have abstayned from the beginninge . . . from enforcinge men to actes against their conscience, especially in religion: as the histories both before Christ and since, doe declare. And amongest the very Turkes at this day, no man is compelled to any act of their religion, excepte he renounce firste his owne. And in the Indies and other farre partes of the worlde where infinite Infidels are under the governement of Christian Princes, it was never yet practized, nor ever thought lawful by the Catholicke Church, that such men should be enforced to anye one acte of our religion.[73]

By the early seventeenth century, Persons's approach had come full circle: from asking Elizabeth to grant her Catholic subjects freedom of conscience, to calling on Catholics to depose Elizabeth, to persuading James that Catholics and Protestants could live peacefully together in one commonwealth. In support of the last position, Persons asked rhetorically: "how doe Christians and Turkes live togeather under the Turkish Emperour of Constantinople, as also under the Persian without persecution for their Religion?" New anti-Catholic laws, Persons asserted, threatened to make the condition of Catholics in England "more miserable and intolerable, then that of the Jewes under any sorte of Christian Princes, or that of the Grecians, or other Christians under the Turke, or Persian."[74]

While some Catholic propagandists used Muslim tolerance of Christians as a way of vilifying Protestant intolerance of Catholics, others regretted Muslim liberality when it interfered with Catholics' desire for martyrdom. Thus, an anonymous Carmelite acknowledges his mission's success in "Preaching, Teaching, and Baptizing Mahometans," but laments that it "hath gone on too favourably, and hath not beene accompanied with tortures, torments, Imprisonments, and effusion of our Blood for the Gospell of Christ."[75] The problem is that "the King heere though a Mahometan, hath heretofore alwayes shewed towards us, so great signes of affection and love, that for our sakes he has not molested any Christian, under the name and title of a Christian."[76] When the king and his viceroy unexpectedly turn against their newly converted Christian subjects, however, the narrator finally finds cause for celebration.[77] The king, under pressure from the Mulaz—"the Doctors of Mahomets law"—and afraid of rebellion and usurpation, assents to the persecution of Muslim converts to

---

[73] *A brief discours contayning certayne reasons why Catholques refuse to goe to church* (Douai, 1580. *ERL* 84), Ttiii[v].

[74] *A treatise tending to mitigation* (1607), 35, 15.

[75] *A briefe relation of the late martyrdrome of the five Persians converted to the Catholique faith* (Douai, 1623. *ERL* 67), A3[r–v].

[76] Ibid. A3[v].   [77] Ibid. A4[r–v].

Christianity.[78] Even as he orders his own subjects stoned to death, however, he preserves the Carmelites, who—much to the narrator's frustration—are denied the glorious deaths of martyrs. Tellingly, the Islamic converts to Christianity are first betrayed to the king's tyrannical viceroy by "an English-man, whereof some are resident in Persia, to trafficke with the King for Silk."[79] Catholic readers would likely have interpreted this "Englishman" as a Protestant interloper who is led into Islamic lands by mercenary rather than pious motives. The Muslim authorities and the heretical English merchant eventually become partners in crime, co-conspirators against the true religion of the Carmelites.

In the vacillations of the king of Persia between befriending and persecuting Christians, *A briefe relation* captures the contradictory English view of the Islamic world as capable of both remarkable toleration and extreme cruelty toward Christian outsiders—a view that Protestant and Catholic observers generally shared. The Turks, along with the heathen Roman emperors of the early Christian era, the "heathen Saxons" at the time of Augustine's mission to Britain, and the "infidels of the Indies," were widely viewed as the cruelest persecutors of God's elect.[80] Protestant as well as Catholic works describe the sheer imaginative perversity of the torments inflicted by the Turks on their victims. At the sack of Constantinople in 1453, for example, John Foxe describes how Turkish soldiers, competing with one another to "devise most strange kinds of new torments and punishments," turned a city that was once the center of eastern Christendom into "a slaughter house or shambles of Christian mens bodies."[81] Stereotypes about the cruel Turk reached a wider English audience through plays like Shakespeare's *The Merchant of Venice*. In the play's courtroom scene, the Duke of Venice tries to shame Shylock into showing mercy to Antonio by saying that "stubborn Turks and Tartars never train'd | To offices of tender courtesy" would take pity on him (4.1.32–3). Even Jews, the Duke implies, do not want to be thought of as crueler than Turks.

In anti-Protestant polemic throughout Europe, the Turk's reputation for unparalleled cruelty was seen as paling in comparison to the atrocities perpetrated by contemporary heretics. Thus, John Fowler's translation of Frarinus's *An oration against the unlawfull insurrections of the Protestantes of our time* (Antwerp, 1566. *ERL* 226) refers to the heretics' "more then Turkysh crueltie." Protestant acts of sacrilege, iconoclasm, and murder were "far surpassing the Turk's tyranny." Even

---

[78] Ibid. B3ʳ.   [79] Ibid. A5ᵛ.

[80] Robert Persons, "Of the Life and Martyrdom of Father Edmond Campian," *Letters and Notices* 11 (1877), 329. Unless otherwise indicated, I use the term "Britain" to refer to the entire island encompassing the kingdoms of England, Wales, and Scotland. For a discussion of the perils of "British" terminology, see two essays by Alan MacColl: "The Meaning of 'Britain' in Medieval and Early Modern England," *Journal of British Studies* 45 (2006), 248–69; "The Construction of England as a Protestant 'British' Nation in the Sixteenth Century," *Renaissance Studies* 18 (2004), 582–608, esp. 599–602.

[81] Foxe, *Actes and Monuments* (1583), Book 6: 743.

"Soliman the great Turke himself never suffred Virgines and professed Nunnes to be so filthylie deflowred and forced by rape."[82]

For Catholic controversialists, only one other group came close to the Turks, and thus to modern heretics, in their capacity for cruelty. This was the legendary Scythians. Of the now infamous Protestant ritual of hanging, drawing, and quartering Catholic victims, Verstegan writes: "There was never Scythian, nor savage Tartar, that could use more inhumaine cruelty then to rip up the bodies of innocent men, being perfectly alive, to teare out their entrailes, to be consumed with fyre."[83] The practice of cutting down Catholic "traitors" from the gallows and disemboweling them while still semi-conscious is one of the gruesome acts depicted in Verstegan's Latin martyrology, *Theatrum crudelitatum haereticorum nostri temporis* (*Theatre of the Cruelties of the Heretics in our own Times*) (Antwerp, 1587).[84] Featuring twenty-eight harrowing engravings depicting the abuse, imprisonment, torture, and killing of Catholics at the hands of "enraged" heretics in various European settings, Verstegan's work sets the Scythian alongside the modern heretic to underscore the unprecedented viciousness of the latter: "The Scythian race, the savage which inhabits the rocks of the Caucasus, nor the savage empire of the Etruscan king, who joined dead bodies to the living, bears such savagery in its barbaric breast, as your tyranny, Calvin; nor so many monstrosities as your ministers construct." Of all modern heretics, Verstegan insists, "the worst and most hateful is that of Calvin's sect."[85]

By aligning modern heretics with archetypal persecutors like the Turks and Scythians, the *Theatrum* helped shape a Catholic "black legend" about the inhuman cruelty of north European heretics and, especially British, Protestants.[86] This "black legend," first developed by Catholics in response to Henry VIII's schism with Rome and subsequent attacks on the Church, functioned as a counterweight to the notorious Protestant "black legend" about the alleged atrocities of the Spanish, particularly in the New World.[87] As part of the Catholic

---

[82] Frarinus, *An oration*, Jiii^v, Ji^v, Jv^v.   [83] *A declaration of the true causes*, 45, 48–9.

[84] For a fascinating contemporary account of the semiotics of the public execution, see Ormerod, *The Picture of a Papist*, 268–9.

[85] Quotations from the *Theatrum* are from the translations provided by Anne Dillon in her Cambridge Ph.D. thesis, "The Construction of Martyrdom in the English Catholic Community to 1603" (1998), Appendix F, 224, 172. Parts of this translation appear in Dillon's subsequent book, *The Construction of Martyrdom in the English Catholic Community, 1553–1603* (Aldershot: Ashgate, 2002), 243–76. Also see Persons, *An epistle of the persecution*, 84.

[86] Verstegan reserves the term "Protestant" for English or British heretics. He observes that the "name ... fits the facts well, for they do one thing and protest another." For example, they claim to punish Catholics for political reasons when they actually do so for religious ones (Dillon, "Construction of Martyrdom," Appendix F, 151–3). Paul Arblaster argues that Verstegan singles out Calvinists as the most inhumane of contemporary heretics (*Antwerp and the World: Richard Verstegan and the International Culture of Catholic Reformation* (Leuven, Belgium: Leuven University Press, 2004), 204–5, 197–201.

[87] Alexandra Walsham, " 'Domme Preachers'? Post-Reformation English Catholicism and the Culture of Print," *Past and Present* 168 (2000), 99; Peter Marshall, "The Other Black Legend: The Henrician Reformation and the Spanish People." *English Historical Review* 116 (2001),

Fig. 3. Richard Verstegan, *Theatrum crudelitatum haereticorum nostri temporis* (*Theatre of the Cruelties of the Heretics in our own Times*) (Antwerp, 1592), p. 83.

counter-legend, Verstegan's *Theatrum* aims to provoke international Catholic outrage at heretics' atrocities and thus build support for a crusade against "that cruel parracide" Elizabeth, who had recently put to death Mary Stuart, the "most serene Queen of Scots [and] rightful heir to the crown of England."[88] Verstegan's engravings sought to achieve this aim by depicting the Catholic victims of Calvinist, Huguenot, and Protestant violence not as heroic martyr figures who might help console readers or inspire contemplation or emulation, but as brutalized and helpless figures surrounded by frantically animated persecutors.[89] The images cry out to readers to take immediate action against the further bloodletting of innocent Catholics. These politically incendiary engravings represent

31–49; William S. Maltby, *The Black Legend in England: the Development of anti-Spanish Sentiment, 1558–1660* (Durham, NC: Duke University Press, 1971).

[88] Dillon, "Construction of Martyrdom," Appendix F, 244. In her book, Dillon shows how Verstegan uses canine images in his engravings to suggest the figure of the irrational and unbridled Calvinist rebel (*Construction of Martyrdom*, 139–41, 261, 275–6).

[89] See my "Richard Verstegan's Book of Martyrs," in Christopher Highley and John N. King (eds.), *John Foxe and his World* (Aldershot: Ashgate, 2002), 183–97; Dillon, *Construction of Martyrdom*, 255, 260.

an affront to the ethical basis of Elizabeth's Protestant state and to the pretence that Catholic priests were executed, not as religious trouble-makers, but as dangerous traitors. Verstegan's images, although designed for a Continental Catholic audience, apparently circulated in England. At least they were familiar enough to English audiences at the end of the sixteenth century for the preacher Thomas Holland in a Paul's Cross sermon to number them, together with Rainolds's *Calvino-Turcismus*, among the most reprehensible books of the day.[90]

The association of Turks and Scythians in the popular imagination of early modern Europe (and it was an association that could be exploited on both sides of the confessional divide) went deeper than their shared reputation for cruelty. It had its basis, in fact, in classical and early modern ethnological classifications. One widely circulated theory of the Turks' origins traced them back to the "bloud and brood of the auncient Scythians." The Turks were "a branch of the Scythians."[91] In *The generall historie of the Turkes* (1603), Richard Knolles argued "That this barbarous nation [of Turks] which hath of late brought such fatall mutations upon so great a part, not of Christendom onely, but even of the whole world, tooke their first beginning out of the cold and bare countrey of SCYTHIA." Knolles offered in evidence of his claim the "antient testimonies of reverend antiquitie", but also asked his reader to take into account

the manners and conditions of the Turks, their antient attire, their gesture, their gate, their weapons, and manner of riding, and fight, their language and dialect, so well agreeing with the Scythians [that] a man shall find matter enough sufficient to persuade him in reason, that the Turks have undoubtedly taken their beginning from the Scythes; whom they in so many things resemble, and with whom of all other nations they best agree.[92]

Jean Bodin, the French political theorist, historian, and ethnographer whose works were widely available in English translation, considered the Turks, like the Scythians, to be in their geographical origins a "Northerne and warlike Nation"—"a Northerne nation" that lived "a barbarous and savage life."[93] The Scythians' status as a northern people was familiar to contemporaries: in *A View of the State of Ireland*, Edmund Spenser describes the Scythians as one of the "Northerne Nations [that had] overflowed all Christendome," and as the first

---

[90] *Paneguris D. Elizabethae, Dei gratiâ Angliae, Franciae, & Hiberniae Reginae* (Oxford, 1601), F4ᵛ.

[91] *The policy of the Turkish empire* (London, 1597), 7ʳ; *Method for the Easy Comprehension of History by John Bodin*, trans. Beatrice Reynolds (New York: Columbia University Press, 1945), 126.

[92] Knolles, *The generall historie of the Turkes*, 2. Also see Andrew Moore's *A compendious history of the Turks: containing an exact account of the originall of that people* (1659), 2.

[93] *The Six Books of a Commonweal: A Facsimile Reprint of the English Translation of 1606 Corrected and Supplemented in the Light of a New Comparison with the French and Latin Texts*, ed. Kenneth Douglas McRae (Cambridge, Mass.: Harvard University Press, 1962), 7ᵛ, 550; Knolles, *The generall historie of the Turkes* ("To the High and Mightie Prince James").

to populate Ireland.[94] For us, the Turks' association with the north is more surprising given modern views of the Turks as an eastern people. But through their
connections with the Scythians, the Turks were also regarded in the early modern
period as originally "a Northerne nation" that had spread south, "extend[ing]
the greatnesse of their empire to the goodliest regions of Asia, Affrica, and
Europe, having in a manner subdued all the ilands of the Mediterrannean sea."[95]
Commentators disagreed on quite when and why "the Turks (to the trouble of
the world) [had] left their naturall seats in the cold countrey of SCYTHIA, to seeke
themselves others in more pleasant and temperat countries more Southerly."[96] It
was this migration of the Turks from their primordial northern home to southern
regions that led Philip du Plessy Mornay to point out that "the word Turk in
Hebrewe, signifieth banished men, and is taken in way of reproche."[97]

THE NORTH: TURKS, SCYTHIANS, AND HERETICS

The recognition that Turks and Scythians were primordial *northern* peoples could
help early modern Catholics make sense of how it was possible that Protestant
heresy had managed to take root on British soil and in British hearts. Just as the
north had once bred cruel Scythian and Turkish infidels, so it now bred cruel
British heretics. Northerners, wrote Bodin, were "those who inhabit the land
from the fiftieth parallel to the sixtieth." They included the people of "Britain,
Ireland, Denmark, part of Gothland, Lower Germany from the Main and the
Bug River even to farthest Scythia and Tartary, which cover a good part of Europe
and Greater Asia."[98] The idea that heresy, barbarism, and cruelty emerged naturally out of a northern landscape is suggested in Verstegan's *Theatrum* where he
writes of the persecution of Catholics in Ireland, a country

separated from England by icy foaming waters and the sea washes between their severed
shores. But as the region is so close to Britain in region and in wildness, the same savagery
ravages her borders. The same impiety walks abroad against men who are holy with piety,
it exerts the same madness.[99]

Verstegan's evocation of persecution in the remote and wild northern latitudes
of the Atlantic archipelago gestures towards ancient theories of geohumoralism

[94]   *Edmund Spenser: A View of the State of Ireland*, ed. Andrew Hadfield and Willy Maley (Oxford:
Blackwell, 1997), 44.
[95]   Bodin, *Six Books*, 550.   [96]   Knolles, *The generall historie of the Turkes*, 2.
[97]   Philippe de Mornay, seigneur du Plessis-Marly, *A woorke concerning the trewnesse of the
Christian religion, written in French: against atheists, Epicures, Paynims, Jewes, Mahumetists, and other
infidels. By Philip of Mornay Lord of Plessie Marlie. Begunne to be translated into English by Sir Philip
Sidney Knight, and at his request finished by Arthur Golding* (1587), 472.
[98]   *Method for the Easy Comprehension of History*, 96.
[99]   Dillon, "Construction of Martyrdom," Appendix F, 240.

that explained the dominant physical and psychological characteristics of a people in terms of environmental forces like geography and climate. At a deep level, then, when English Catholics likened Protestant heretics to Turks they were thinking in more than metaphorical terms. As northern peoples, Turks, Scythians, and Britons were the product of the same environment and thus shared certain fundamental traits and propensities.

In geohumoral theories, the body of the northerner compensated for the cold climate by generating excessive heat that in turn produced "hot and viscous" blood, an intemperate disposition, and a tendency to be violent and cruel.[100] Geohumoral ideas may also lie behind Robert Persons's remark (cited earlier) that heresy had hardened Englishmen's hearts, since "hardness," like brute physical strength, was a characteristic also attributed to northerners.[101] Using the same imagery, Verstegan speaks of the need to "soften the hearts of the persecutors" by imploring God's help through the "intercession of the Blessed Virgin and all the Saints."[102]

Most importantly for our purposes, the overheated humoral bodies of northerners were prone to what one Catholic writer called the "unnatural heat of heresies."[103] Catholic visitors and newcomers to Britain from southern regions frequently commented on this quality in the British. For example, one of the Spaniards accompanying Philip II to England in 1554 described the islanders as "a barbarous and heretical race, with no fear of God or his saints," while another called his hosts "white, pink, and quarrelsome."[104] Other Catholic outsiders believed that the northern Briton's environmentally determined temperament

---

[100] Bodin, *Six Books*, 548–9. Levinus Lemnius wrote in *The touchstone of complexions* (Englished by Thomas Newton in 1576) that "they that dwell Northward and in cold regions, by reason of grosse bloud and thicke Spyrites, are seene to be bolde and full of venturous courage, rude, unmanerlye, terrible, cruell, fierce, and such as wyth very threatening countenaunce and manacinge wordes, make others to stande in feare of them" (13ʳ). In 1581, English traveler Stephen Powle wrote that "The Northern people be strong of body, and apt to be cruel, yet very faithful and secret, of wit dull and lumpish, therefore they must be governed by force." Quoted in Michael G. Brennan, "English Contact with Europe," in Andrew Hadfield and Paul Hammond (eds.), *Shakespeare and Renaissance Europe* (London: Thomson, 2005), 57.

[101] Bodin, *Six Books*, 551.

[102] *Descriptiones quaedam illius inhumanae et multiplicis persecutionis, quam in Anglia propter fidem sustinent Catholice Christiani* (*Several Illustrations of that Inhuman and Manifold Persecution which the Catholic Christians are Suffering in England for the Sake of their Faith*. Rome, 1584). Translated in Dillon, "Construction of Martyrdom," Appendix D, 48. Verstegan slides in this text and the *Theatrum* between references to England and Britain.

[103] What "impelled [Luther] to imbrace this madde mynde and onnaturall heate of heresies" was "filthie desire." Lewis Evans (trans.), Lindanus, *Certaine tables . . . wherein is detected and made manifeste the doting dangerous doctrine, and haynous heresyes, of the rashe rabblement of heretikes* (Antwerp, 1565. *ERL* 52), Aᵛʳ.

[104] Cited in David Loades, *The Chronicles of the Tudor Queens* (Stroud, Gloucestershire: Sutton, 2002), 46, and John Edwards, "Carranza in England," in John Edwards and Ronald Truman (eds.), *Reforming Catholicism in the England of Mary Tudor: The Achievement of Friar Bartolomeé Carranza* (Aldershot: Ashgate, 2005), 13. The reports of Italian, Venetian, and Spanish ambassadors to England contain many similar observations.

made him "fierce and unruly and given to novelties." Religious error, according to some observers, was the novelty the British people found most irresistible.[105]

Within the dominant Catholic humanist paradigm of geo-humoralism developed by writers like Bodin, the north's propensity to heresy and cruelty was set against the south's inclination to religious enlightenment.[106] Bodin observed that "all religions have in a manner taken their beginning from the people of the South, and from thence have been dispersed over the whole earth." Southerners, because of their humoral makeup, were widely viewed as more temperamentally inclined than northerners toward religiosity: "The more we draw towards the South, the more devout we find men, and the more firme and constant in their religion, as in Spaine, and more in Affricke [where] in one citie of Fez there are seaven hundred temples."[107] Northerners by contrast were temperamentally inclined to be fickle in matters of religion. "Bohemians and Saxons," observed Bodin, "were the first to desert the Roman rites . . . immediately all Saxony fell away, the Baltic cities, Denmark, Norway, Gothic Sweden . . . soon even Britain and Scotland."[108] For some commentators, the fact that the British were also an island people, surrounded by water and subject to strong lunar influences, made their disposition even more susceptible to change and religious innovation.[109]

As a theory of identity formation, geohumoralism was flexible enough to accommodate different agendas and perspectives. The same environmental factors that in Bodin's view made northerners hot and moist, in the view of other commentators made them open, plain-spoken, transparent, and honest (in contrast to subtle and cunning southerners). Thus when the Protestant traveler Fynes Moryson referred proudly to "our Northern Luther," it was precisely these qualities of plainness and honesty that the term "northern" was supposed to summon up. "Northern men," wrote Moryson, "are soone drawn with the love of Religion, the outside whereof the Southerne men can skilfully paint over." "Our Northern Iland England . . . [was] allwayes Religiously affected," even before the Reformation. To support this claim, Moryson pointed to the "Temples, Monasteries, Bels, and other older ornaments or religious vestures."[110]

[105] Sarah Warneke, "A Taste for Newfangledness: The Destructive Potential of Novelty in Early Modern England," *Sixteenth Century Journal* 26 (1995), 889. I owe this reference to Mary Floyd-Wilson.

[106] "Jean Bodin," in *Stanford Encyclopedia of Philosophy* http://plato.stanford.edu/entries/bodin/

[107] *Six Books*, 560.

[108] *Method for the Easy Comprehension of History*, 126–7. Bodin's distinction between Britain and Scotland suggests he is using the term "Britain" as a synonym for England—a usage that continues in England today (MacColl, "The Meaning of 'Britain'," 253–9).

[109] Warneke, "A Taste for Newfangledness": "Catholic commentators found it easy to blame the English Reformation on the English people's nature, while Protestant commentators feared such nature would lead the English people into such moral turpitude they would turn their faces from God completely" (890).

[110] Bodin, *Six Books*, 554; Moryson, quoted in Helga Quadflieg, "Approved Civilities and the Fruits of Peregrination: Elizabethan and Jacobean Travellers and the Making of Englishness," in Hartmut Berghoff, Barbara Korte, Ralf Schneider, and Christopher Harvie (eds.), *The Making of*

Even English Catholic observers might avail themselves of more positive views of northern character when it was strategically useful to do so. The Catholic priest Thomas Wright, for example, who composed *The Passions of the Minde in Generall* (1601) while imprisoned for his faith, claimed that northerners have "a naturall inclination to Vertue and honestie . . . a judgement disliking of evil." Southerners, on the contrary, were crafty and wary, unwilling to open themselves up.[111] The exiled Catholic leader, William Allen, perhaps attempting to counteract negative Italian views of the northern English, assured Pope Gregory XIII on behalf of his fellow exiles, that "we who have well known and investigated the humours of our own people, their minds, the inclinations of their souls, their endeavours and desires," had no doubt that heresy was incompatible with Englishmen's nature ("inmost desires").[112] Other Catholics, both inside and outside Britain, however, were less confident about the temperamental ability of these island northerners to resist heresy.

Underpinning these less sanguine views of the north as an environment conducive to the spread of heresy were ancient prejudices about the region as a benighted cultural zone, the seat of a pre-Christian underworld as well as the location of Hell and Satan.[113] In fact, Satan's biblical rebellion begins when he establishes his own monarchy in the north. Satan boasts in Isaiah 14: 12–13, that he will ascend to heaven and "sitte in the mount of the testament, in the sides of the North."[114] The Book of Isaiah was one of several Old Testament texts identifying the north with ominous danger. As Bodin writes, "God did threaten his peoples by the oracles of his prophets with the nations of the North, foretelling that warre, murder, and the ruine of Commonweales should come from thence." Bodin's marginal gloss to this passage reads, "Esai. 14: 41. Ezec. 16.51. Dan. 8.48. Zach. 11," but excludes the important reference in Jeremiah 1: 14 where God reveals that "From the North shal evil be opened upon al the inhabitantes of the land."[115] The prophets' view of the North was institutionalized in Catholic liturgy when the priest, "reading the gospel at mass," faced north, speaking as it were to the unconverted heathen masses.[116]

Modern Tourism: The Cultural History of the British Experience, 1600–2000 (New York: Palgrave, 2002), 36.

[111] *The Passions of the Mind in Generall. A Reprint Based on the 1604 Edition*, ed. Thomas O. Sloan (Urbana: University of Illinois Press, 1971), 1vii–1xiii.

[112] *Letters of William Allen and Richard Barret, 1572–1598*, ed. P. Renold. Catholic Record Society, 58 (Oxford: Oxonian Press, 1967), 281.

[113] Peter Davidson, *The Idea of North* (London: Reaktion Books, 2005).

[114] Facsimile of the Douai-Rheims Bible, *ERL* 266: 471.

[115] Ibid. 548–9. Bodin, *Six Books*, 550.

[116] Arthur H. Williamson, "Scots, Indians, and Empire: The Scottish Politics of Civilization 1519–1609," *Past and Present* 150 (1996), 46–83, esp. 46–52. Williamson points out that negative assumptions about the north "in no way lessened with the Reformation, for such geopolitical prejudice obviously worked to the disadvantage of northern (and Protestant) princes—as Roman Catholic controversialists quickly recognized" (50). Williamson identifies Olaus Magnus's *Historia gentibus septentrionalibus* (1555) as "the authoritative work on the northern regions" for early

Alluding to Jeremiah's prophecy, the anonymous Catholic author of a life of the Scottish Franciscan, Father Archangel, wondered "whether there can anie good come from the North whereas it is written: *Ab Aquilone pandetur omne malum*. All evill shall proceede from the North. But the infinite goodnesse of God hath not excluded the people of the North from the benefit of his holie vocation, but hath vouchsafed to call them to his heavenlie kingdome."[117] Father Archangel was one northerner who had been "called" to serve his country. Similar assumptions about the north appear in *The Mirror of the Peregrinations of the English Nuns of the Order of Saint Bridget* (early 1620s). The writer emphasizes St Bridget's origins in "the far distant and remote Kingdom of Sweden." God had chosen Bridget—"a strong woman from the furthest ends and capes of the world"—in order to show the world "that some good should come also from the North."[118]

In the prophecy of Ezekiel, northern evil is embodied in the mysterious figure of Gog, the leader of marauding northern tribes that will one day sweep down to attack God's chosen but wayward people (chs. 38–9). In biblical texts and commentaries, Gog—as the archetypal enemy of the True Church—was related to and sometimes conflated with Magog, a figure usually associated not with the north but the east. Thus the narrator of Thomas Stapleton's translation of *The apologie of Fridericus Staphylus* refers to the figures of Gog and Magog when blaming his German compatriots for failing to fight back Turkish attacks on Hungary. Their failure, he claimed, had virtually guaranteed "That the Northe shall rule over the Southe, and the Easte over the Weste. And so Magog from the Easte and Gog from the Northe shall come and destroie the Romain Empire, whiche yet though weake and almost spent, hangeth by a weake threde in the hande of us Germans."[119] For Catholic readers of these accounts, Gog's location in the north would likely have suggested the heretical Germanic lands, Britain, and Scandinavia. Protestant readers, on the other hand, wishing to protect the reputation of their own northern territories, would need to resituate Gog. The Protestant zealot John Bale took the initiative in the geographical re-imagining of Gog, moving him southwards into Catholic territory by arguing that the land

---

modern European readers (47). Magnus was an exiled Swedish bishop living in Rome at the time the book was published. It was first translated into English in 1658 as *A compendious history of the Goths, Swedes, & Vandals, and other northern nations written by Olaus Magnus.*

[117] *The life of the reverend Fa. Angel of Joyeuse, Capucin preacher... Together with the lives of the reverend fathers, Father Bennet Englishman, and Father Archangell Scotchman* (Douai, 1623. *ERL* 70), 1–2. (The Scottish Archangel's life is paginated separately).

[118] Christopher De Hamel, *Syon Abbey: The Library of the Bridgettine Nuns and their Peregrinations after the Reformation* (London: Roxburghe Club, 1991), 26–7.

[119] *The apologie of Fridericus Staphylus*, 128ᵛ–29ʳ. The prophecy is attributed to the 4th-century Church Father Lactantius and "divers other writers." On changing interpretations of Gog and Magog, see Victor I. Scherb, "Assimilating Giants: the Appropriation of Gog and Magog in Medieval and Early Modern England." *Journal of Medieval and Early Modern Studies*, 32:1 (2002), 59–84.

ruled by Gog in Ezekiel was in fact contemporary Italy. By this logic, Gog could be made to stand for the "Romish Pope."[120]

If Bale and his Catholic opponents disagreed about where to place Gog, they tended to agree that Magog's place was in the east. Bale went further, offering an alternative to the theory that the Scythians/Turks originated in the north, when he argued that Magog was "the first beginner of the Magogytes, whome the Grekes called the Scitheanes, and wee now the Tartareanes. And al the chiefe wryters specyfieth the Turkes of them to have taken their first originall." Just as Protestant polemic identified Gog with the pope, so it identified Magog with Mohammed; for reformers, the equation between "Romes Gog, and Turkish Magog" became proverbial.[121]

In both Protestant and Catholic commentary, though, the meanings attached to Gog and Magog remained fluid. Not all Catholics agreed that Magog was to the east what Gog was to the north. In a notable departure from the view of Bale and Stapleton that Magog was an eastern figure, the editors of the Douai–Rheims Bible describe "Gog and Magog . . . [as] the king, and people of Scithia, in the North part of the world, a barbarous, savage, and cruel nation" (annotations to Ezekiel 38). Instead of bifurcating the threat to the Church in a conventional way between north and east, the biblical editors conflate the two, imagining a single unified threat from the north that reasserts the Scythians/Turks' identity as a distinctively northern people. For the Douai–Rheims editors, the north subsumes the east as the source of all evil: Christian heretics, as well as the infidel Scythians and Turks originate there.

Both Protestants and Catholics interpreted the passage from Ezekiel as a typological prefiguration of the apocalyptic events in the Book of Revelation (or "The Apocalypse of John the Apostle" as the Catholic Bible calls it) where Gog and Magog make their final appearance as the enigmatic enemies of the True Church (20:8). As Victor Scherb observes: "the nations of Gog and Magog in Revelation literally surround the chosen people, evil and threatening, very much embodiments of the 'common fate' that awaits God's saints."[122] For British Catholics of the later sixteenth and early seventeenth centuries, their persecution at the hands of heretics could be seen as portending the imminent arrival of the "latter days" and the final reckoning between Christ and the Anti-Christ—events shadowed in Revelation's symbols of Gog, Magog, and the fall of Babylon, that quintessential seat of wickedness. In defiance of the standard

---

[120] *The image of both Churches after the most wonderfull and heavenly Revelation of sainct John the Evangelist* (1570), Hhhvi[r–v]. Also see Paul Christianson, *Reformers and Babylon: English Apocalyptic Visions from the Reformation to the Eve of the Civil War* (Toronto: University of Toronto Press, 1978), 15–19, 28.

[121] Bale, *Image of both Churches*, Hhhvi[v]; Robert Pricket, *The Jesuits miracles, or new popish wonders. Containing the straw, the crowne, and the wondrous child, with the confutation of them and their follies* (1607), E1[v]. "Of Magog came the S[cy]thians, and of them the Turks," claimed Thomas Heywood in *Troia Britanica: or, Great Britaines Troy* (1609), A5[r].

[122] "Assimilating Giants," 61.

Protestant identification of Babylon with Rome, Richard Verstegan offered a radical Catholic counter-view. He proposed "how Albion [i.e. Britain], might by transposing the letters, seme to be Babilon." Verstegan also reveals that he is considering writing a book called "The second confusion of Babilon," or alternatively, "The Confusion of Albion." And the book's preface would "touch briefly how the one name conteyneth the very same letters of the other."[123] Yet many recusant Catholics must already have felt that their homeland at this time had become another Babylon, or perhaps another Turkey. In the face of escalating persecution, they may have pondered the legends, stories, and theories associating the north with heresy and evil. Perhaps they believed the more zealous of their Protestant neighbors were unleashing those northern, Scythian/Turkish impulses of barbarity and cruelty that had for so long remained dormant, kept in check by the civilizing influences of a southern religion brought from Rome originally by Augustine and his missionaries. Without those influences, a people once "so religious, generous and faithful," had become "impious, faithless and degenerate." A "savage madness," lamented Verstegan, now reigned in England.[124]

[123] *The Letters and Despatches of Richard Verstegan, c.1550–1640*, ed. A. G. Petti, Catholic Record Society, 52 (1959), 142. As far as we know, Verstegan never wrote this book with its provocative appropriation of Protestant apocalyptic allegory. For other references by Verstegan to the Anti-Christ, see Arblaster, *Antwerp and the World*, 201.

[124] *Descriptiones quaedam illius inhumanae et multiplicis persecutionis.* Translated in Dillon, "Construction of Martyrdom", Appendix D, 58.

4

'The lost British lamb': Religion and National Identity among English, Welsh, and Scottish Catholics[1]

"THE PECULIARITY OF EXILES"

In October 1608, as part of the Counter-Reformation publishing campaign, the press at St Omers Jesuit college near Calais printed a Catholic martyrology to compete with Protestant examples of the genre like Foxe's *Actes and Monuments*. This work, compiled by John Wilson—an exiled English priest and "supervisor" of the press—was *The English martyrologe conteyning a summary of the lives of the glorious and renowned saintes of the three Kingdomes, England, Scotland, and Ireland*. One of the book's aims was to prevent English Catholics from losing touch with their religious heritage: "I have heere gathered togeather, and restored unto yow againe," wrote the work's editor, "that which the injury of tymes had violently taken from yow, and sought to abolish all memory therof."[2] Although the title is *The English martyrologe*, the calendar's subjects are drawn from not only the three kingdoms of England, Scotland, and Ireland, but from Wales too. Saints commemorated in the month of January, for example, include: "S. Meliorus Martyr" of Cornwall, "S. Croniacke Confessor" of Scotland, "S. Beno Priest and Confessor" of North Wales, and "S. Eoglodius Monke and Confessour" of Ireland. Wilson organizes the text by chronology rather than geography,

---

[1] The phrase, "The lost British lamb," is taken from one of Cardinal Allen's letters as quoted in Thomas McCoog, SJ, *The Society of Jesus in Ireland, Scotland, and England, 1541–1588: "Our Way of Proceeding?"* (New York: Brill, 1996), 124.

[2] *The English martyrologe*, *2ᵛ (*ERL* 232). J. T. Rhodes, "English Books of Martyrs and Saints of the Late Sixteenth and Early Seventeenth Centuries," *Recusant History* 22 (1994), 10–11. In November 1608, the government informer William Udall told Sir Julius Caesar that copies of Wilson's book had been smuggled into England from Dunkirk and Calais: "*The Lyves and Deaths of English, Irish and Scotish Saynts and martirs*, amongst which some of those which were executed for the Powder Treason are inserted, as Garnett, Oldcorne, etc." The next year Caesar noted that "many" copies of this book had been discovered with other illegal Catholic materials in the cellars of the Venetian embassy in London. Quoted in P. R. Harris, "The Reports of William Udall, Informer, 1605–1612," *Recusant History* 8 (1966), 238, 204, 245. Also see A. F. C. Beales, *Education under Penalty: English Catholic Education from the Reformation to the Fall of James II 1547–1689* (London: The Athlone Press, 1963), 189–90.

mingling saints of different regions on the same page, and thus offering a vision of an encompassing Catholicism that brings together the multiple kingdoms, nations, and peoples of the Atlantic archipelago. This idea of a Catholicism that transcends traditional national, ethnic, geographical, and linguistic boundaries is reinforced in many of the individual saints' stories that tell how, out of love for their "neighbour-Countreyes," the saints have left their homeland to preach the word of God.[3]

The boundary-crossing impulse in these stories can be found in other martyrologies, of which Jerome Porter's Life of Saint Patrick provides an exemplary case. Patrick, "borne of the race of auncient Britans, in that part of Wales now called Pembrookshire," first arrives "among the inhabitants of Ireland, who then were called Scotts," after being captured and taken there as a slave. Patrick's ensuing career is one of constant physical mobility, thus making him a culturally hybrid, boundary-blurring figure, one "skilfull, and readie in fower distinct languages, the Welch, the Irish, the French, and the Latin." After his early captivity, he escapes back to Wales, gains an education in France, and is ordained in Rome, before commencing his long-term itinerant ministry in Ireland.[4]

If Porter's Life of Patrick and Wilson's *English martyrologe* help to break down rigid ideas of nationhood by imagining a free-flowing, transnational Catholicism, they also betray a nagging uncertainty about how to characterize "our little Dominions" and the relationships among their constituent parts.[5] Wilson's unstable terminology speaks in both imperial, centralizing terms of "our *Great-Britany*, and . . . the Ilands belonging thereunto," and in more separatist, parochial terms of "our three Kingdomes, *England, Scotland & Ireland*."[6] Placing England first in the latter list bestows a priority upon it vis-à-vis its neighbors that is further underscored in Wilson's epigraphs from Matthew Paris and the Venerable Bede. England, described by Paris as "An Iland so shining with Martyrs, Confessours, and holy Virgins," effectively absorbs two kingdoms and a plurality of cultures.[7] Wilson's use of shifting labels for his homeland connects his work to what has come to be known in recent scholarship as the "the problem of Britain"—the question of the complex historical relations among the multiple territories, cultures, peoples, and nations of the Atlantic archipelago.[8]

---

[3] For a defense of the term "Atlantic Archipelago," see J. G. A. Pocock, "The Atlantic Archipelago and the War of the Three Kingdoms," in Brendan Bradshaw and John Morrill (eds.), *The British Problem, c.1534–1707: State Formation in the Atlantic Archipelago* (New York: St Martin's Press, 1996), 172–91.

[4] *The flowers of the lives of the most renowned saincts of the three kingdoms England Scotland, and Ireland Written and Collected out of the best authours and manuscripts of our nation, and distributed according to their feasts in the calendar* (Douai, 1632. ERL 239), 270–91. Quotations at 270, 287.

[5] *The English martyrologe*, *8ʳ.   [6] Ibid. *7ᵛ–*8ʳ.   [7] Ibid. *1ᵛ.

[8] On the various meanings of the word "nation" in this period, see David J. Baker, *Between Nations: Shakespeare, Spenser, Marvell and the Question of Britain* (Stanford: Stanford University Press, 1997), 5–6. Baker's introduction provides a useful overview on the "British problem" and its relevance for early modern literary studies.

For exiled Catholic Englishmen like Wilson and Porter, the problem of Britain was central to the task of reimagining a collective identity that had been thrown into crisis by the exigencies of geographical and social displacement. What did "home" mean to these exiles? What were its territorial boundaries and cultural coordinates? What peoples and cultures did it include and exclude? Was Britain a meaningful term in their lexicon? Recent historical scholarship by Jane Dawson, Roger A. Mason, Arthur H. Williamson, and others, has established the emergence of Britain as a resonant imaginative construct in English and Scottish Reformation ideology. Interest in Britain as a single territorial, political, and cultural entity of course existed long before the Reformation, most notably in the legendary British empire of King Arthur. But after Henry VIII's break with Rome, and especially during the reign of Edward VI, English and Scottish Protestants alike seized upon the idea of Britain as home to a unified Protestant monarchy, a bulwark against the encroachments of a hostile Catholic Europe.[9]

Even as the new historiography of the British Isles and Ireland exposes the limitations of previous Anglo-centric perspectives by taking into account the rich multicultural fabric of the early modern Atlantic archipelago, it remains constrained by the contours of a mainly Protestant narrative. This chapter and the next aim to reorient the current discussion by asking how the "British problem" was perceived from the other side of the confessional divide and from outside the archipelago among Catholic exiles during the reigns of Elizabeth and James. John Wilson's evocation in his *English Martyrologe* of a time before the Reformation when Britain and Ireland were imagined as sharing a unifying Catholic faith is, of course, the nostalgic fantasy of an exile. What the fantasy suppresses are the pressures exerted by alternative affiliations centered on national and ethnic identities, affiliations that sometimes conflicted with religious loyalties, and that complicated efforts by exiled Catholics from across the Atlantic archipelago to reconvert their particular homelands.[10] The Catholic diaspora was a heterogeneous assortment of lay people and religious: students, scholars, clerics,

---

[9] See Jane Dawson, "Anglo-Scottish Protestant Culture and Integration in Sixteenth-Century Britain," in Steven G. Ellis and Sarah Barber (eds.), *Conquest and Union: Fashioning a British State, 1485–1725* (London: Longman, 1995), 87–114; Roger A. Mason, "The Scottish Reformation and the Origins of Anglo-British Imperialism," in id. (ed.), *Scots and Britons: Scottish Political Thought and the Union of 1603* (Cambridge: Cambridge University Press, 1994), 161–86; Arthur H. Williamson, "Scotland, Antichrist and the Invention of Great Britain," in John Dwyer, Roger A. Mason, and Alexander Murdoch (eds.), *New Perspectives on the Politics and Culture of Early Modern Scotland* (Edinburgh: John Donald, 1982), 34–58, and "Patterns of British Identity: 'Britain' and its Rivals in the Sixteenth and Seventeenth Centuries," in Glenn Burgess (ed.), *The New British History: Founding a Modern State, 1603–1715* (London: I. B. Tauris, 1999), 138–72.

[10] As Albert J. Loomie, remarks, "The word 'Catholic' does not promise solidarity of action among the faithful of England, Scotland, and Ireland. The word can prove in many respects to be a 'portmanteau' term. The Elizabethan Catholic refugees retained many of their accustomed attitudes and prejudices. They made no serious effort at *rapprochement* with Irish or Scottish exiles; on the contrary, there were sparks of rivalry and hostility." *The Spanish Elizabethans: The English Exiles at the Court of Philip II* (New York: Fordham University Press, 1963), 231.

and ordinary men and women who refused to live under heresy. Although loosely held together by the desire to restore the Catholic faith to their homelands, the members of the diaspora never formed a unified community. If anything, the diaspora was the epitome of disunity. Robert Persons tellingly titled his memoir of the struggle to restore Catholicism in England, *A Storie of Domesticall Difficulties which the Englishe Catholike cause and promoters therof, have had in defending the same, not onely against the violence, and persecution of heretikes, but also by sundry other impediments among themselves, of faction, emulation, sedition, and division, since the chaunge of Religion in England.*[11] These self-inflicted "difficulties" included disagreements over discipline—could Catholics in England legitimately attend Protestant services?—and strategy—should missionary priests concentrate their efforts on the Catholic gentry or on the common people? Should the mission to England be essentially pastoral or political in nature? Like their stay-at-home co-religionists, the exiles were embroiled in "stirs" that pitted secular priests against Jesuits and supporters of a Scottish succession against backers of the king of Spain. William Allen, nominal head of the English exiles by 1582, found their condition mirrored in the plight of the Children of Israel in the Book of Numbers (verse 16):

I know for certain and from experience that it would be easier to guide to salvation a thousand souls in England than a hundred in this exile, which of itself breeds murmurings, complainings, contradictions and discontent. When Moses leads the people through the desert, he suffers much. Even at the very time that God rains down manna and quails and brings water from the rock they are not satisfied, but their soul is with the flesh-pots of Egypt, Core conspires, Dathan rises in revolt, Abiron is unruly, and they collect round them many partners. This is the peculiarity of exiles.[12]

Allen's friend and co-leader, Robert Persons, also likened "the English grumblers" to the behavior of "the children of Israel, who murmured continually against God and His servants." Murmuring, Persons assured the Jesuit Father Agazzari, was not "a national vice, as some would have it," but a result "of their being in exile and of the hardships that accompany that state."[13] The Mosaic model of exile was a cautionary one in several ways, helping to illuminate not just the plight of exiles but of stay-at-home Catholics too: in the editors' notes to Numbers 16 in the Douai–Rheims Bible (1609), Core, Dathan, and Abiron are held up as a warning to the faithful in England not to mingle with heretics by attending Protestant church services or sermons.[14]

---

[11] "The Memoirs of Father Robert Persons," ed. J. H. Pollen, SJ, in *Miscellanea II*, Catholic Record Society 2 (London, 1906), 48.

[12] Thomas Francis Knox (ed.), *The First and Second Diaries of the English College, Douay* (London: David Nutt, 1878), lxxvii.

[13] *Letters and Memorials of Father Robert Persons, S.J.: Volume I (to 1588)*, ed. L. Hicks, SJ, Catholic Record Society 39 (London, 1942), 198.

[14] *The holie bible faithfully translated into English* (Douai, 1609. *ERL* 265), 358–9.

The universities, seminaries, courts, and other settings across Europe in which uprooted Catholics from the British Isles sought refuge, may have offered them freedom from heresy back home, but they were also strange and sometimes hostile places, inducing nostalgia for an ancestral "home." The English exiles, "outsiders" both in England and abroad—like their co-religionists from Wales, Scotland, and Ireland—invariably coalesced into nations in exile, intensely conscious of their country of origin and jealous of the claims of these other "neighbor" nations with whom the English saw themselves in competition for the limited assistance of popes, princes, and other benefactors.[15] The expatriate cultures of England, Wales, Scotland, and Ireland, bound together by a shared religious heritage and political cause, had every opportunity and incentive to make common cause, inventing a collective archipelagic identity. Instead, the diverse expatriate communities, as I show in this chapter, cohered tenaciously along national and ethnic rather than confessional lines.

THE VENERABLE BEDE AND NARRATIVES OF ORIGIN

In order to grasp the attitudes of English exiles toward their Welsh, Scots, and Irish co-religionists, I want to focus on a text that had a profound role in shaping English assumptions and prejudices. *The history of the church of Englande* (Antwerp, 1565. *ERL* 162) by the Venerable Bede not only provided Catholics with the canonical narrative of early British history, but also set forth an assessment of Englishness in relation to the other constituent identities of the Atlantic archipelago. Composed originally in the eighth-century, Bede's history was translated into English for the first time by Thomas Stapleton in 1565 as part of the Louvainists' running controversy with the Jewel camp about the history and identity of the True Church. That Catholics thought of Bede's ecclesiastical history as a contribution to a polemical religious agenda, is evident from the fact that in some printed copies it is bound together with Stapleton's vigorous defense of the Church, *A fortresse of the faith first planted amonge us englishmen* (Antwerp, 1565. *ERL* 163).[16]

Bede's narrative was most valuable to Catholics for its account of how in the late sixth century Pope Gregory had dispatched Augustine to Britain to convert the heathen Saxons.[17] This offered crucial confirmation of the Roman origins of the Catholic Church in Britain, a church—Stapleton and others argued—whose traditions and authority had continued without interruption until the time of

---

[15] Grainne Henry, "The Emerging Identity of an Irish Military Group in the Spanish Netherlands, 1586–1610," in R. V. Comerford, Mary Cullen, Jacqueline R. Hill, and Colm Lennon (eds.), *Religion, Conflict, and Coexistence in Ireland* (Dublin: Gill and Macmillan, 1990), 53–77.

[16] AR 2: 145.

[17] On Gregory the Great, see Eamon Duffy, *Saints and Sinners: A History of the Popes* (New Haven: Yale University Press, 1997), 45–57, esp. 54–7.

Cranmer and the Protestant schism. Stapleton and other Catholics asserted that Augustine's mission to Britain was in fact the third and decisive conversion effort launched from Rome. As Robert Persons later explained in *A treatise of three conversions of England from paganisme to Christian religion* (St Omers, 1605. *ERL* 304–6), Augustine's mission followed *The First under the Apostles, in the first age after Christ* [and] *the second under Pope Eleutherius and K. Lucius, in the second age* (1605). Catholics did not all agree about who participated in the first conversion, but St Peter, the Apostle Simon, and Joseph of Arimathea were all candidates. What really mattered, of course, was that Britain had at an early point in its history received the faith directly from Rome.

Stapleton's edition of Bede's *history* was widely circulated in Catholic communities both at home and abroad. Numerous copies of what one government informer called "the most pestilential book ever published" by the Catholics, were distributed secretly in England.[18] William Allen recommended that the work be read by English students training to be seminary priests: when the students were later dispatched on the English mission, they could use *The history* as a polemical and pedagogical tool "to show our countrymen ... that our nation did not receive in the beginning any other than the catholic faith which we profess ... This is a very telling argument with the more sober sort."[19] Some of these young priests-to-be who entered the English college in Rome, noted in the admissions register (the *Responsa Scholarum*) that their conversion and politicization had been brought about specifically as a result of reading Stapleton's translation of Bede's *history*.[20]

As the standard Catholic authority on the British past, Stapleton's edition of Bede's *history* became a valuable weapon in polemics against Protestant historians like Foxe, Bale, and Jewel whom Stapleton derided for remaining adherents of "the vaine fabler Galfride" [Geoffrey of Monmouth] and the (legendary) British history contained in Geoffrey's *Historia regum Britanniae* (*History of the Kings of Britain*).[21] Persons's *A treatise of three conversions*, which draws extensively

---

[18] Leona Rostenberg, *The Minority Press and the English Crown: A Study in Repression 1558–1625* (Nieuwkoop: B. De Graaf, 1971; New York, 1971), 44. Stapleton's Bede was one of the many Catholic books found by government searchers in the library of John Stowe. See A. C. Southern, *Elizabethan Recusant Prose, 1559–1582* (London: Sands, 1950), 39.

[19] Knox (ed.), *The First and Second Diaries of the English College*, xlii. Also see Marvin R. O'Connell, *Thomas Stapleton and the Counter Reformation* (New Haven: Yale University Press, 1964), 55–6.

[20] Ethan Shagan, "Introduction: English Catholic History in Context," in id. (ed.), *Catholics and the "Protestant Nation": Religious Politics and Identity in Early Modern England* (Manchester: Manchester University Press, 2005), 12.

[21] Stapleton, *A counterblast to M. Hornes vayne blaste against M. Fekenham* (Louvain, 1567), 314ʳ (*ERL* 311). Also see Donna Hamilton, "Catholic Use of Anglo-Saxon Precedents, 1565–1625," *Recusant History* 26 (2003), 537–55. European Catholics scorned English Protestant writers for believing in "Geoffrey of Monmouth as a purveyor of absurd fables about Arthur and Merlin." In his *Chronographiae libri quatuor* (Paris, 1580), the Archbishop of Aix, Gilbert Génébrard, mocks the stories of "Galfridus et Balaeus" [i.e. John Bale]. Quoted in Alan MacColl, "The Construction of England as a Protestant 'British' Nation in the Sixteenth Century," *Renaissance Studies*, 18:4 (2004), 588 n. 20.

Fig. 4. The Venerable Bede, *The history of the church of Englande*, trans. Thomas Stapleton (Antwerp, 1565). STC 1778 (copy 1), p. 31^r (sig. H3^r).

on Stapleton's translation of Bede, also seeks to discredit Protestant writers by characterizing them as advocates not of the "approved" Bede but of Geoffrey's legendary British history.[22] Persons thought that Protestants favored Geoffrey because "he sheweth himselfe to favour the old Britans against S. Augustine that came from Rome."[23] Geoffrey explains towards the end of his work how the British monks and bishops at Bangor reject Augustine's Roman Christianity in favor of their own brand and subsequently refuse to help Augustine convert the Saxons.[24] As John Curran observes, "The Galfridian tradition" "glorified Britain"

through its eternal adversarial stance toward Rome. The nation's own story told of its origin from the same roots as Rome (Brutus), its defeat and sack of Rome (Belinus and Brennus), its defiance and nearly successful repulse of Roman invasion (Cassivellaunus versus Julius Caesar), its proud maintenance in the first century A.D. of national dignity even amidst Roman conquest (Guiderius and Arviragus), its retriumph over Rome (Arthur), and its final destruction as a fortress of pure Christianity by barbarians empowered and inspired by Rome.[25]

Given the anti-Roman animus in much of Geoffrey's *Historia*, it is understandable why, in a Catholic-owned copy of a book about the ancient history of Britain (*Rerum Britannicarum*), the selections from Geoffrey's text are heavily expurgated. As Michael E. Williams remarks, "The main alteration was the crossing out and mutilation of the chapter . . . relating to the prophecy of Merlin [which] can be explained as a defence against those protestant controversialists who made use of parts of the Arthurian legend, such as the visit of Joseph of Arimathea to Britain, to undermine the papal and Roman claim to be the originator of Christianity in these islands." Another text in the Galfridian tradition, "Arthurus Britannicus," was placed on the Spanish Index of forbidden books as "a condemned author."[26]

The dependence of Protestant historians like Foxe, Bale, and Jewel upon Geoffrey of Monmouth's anti-Roman narrative drew from Persons the taunt that they were "brutish rather then British" historians. In the loaded word "brutish," Persons evokes Geoffrey's claim that Brutus (or Brut), a refugee after the fall of

---

[22] "Approved" is Stapleton's epithet in *A counterblast* (314ʳ).

[23] Persons, *A treatise of three conversions of England from paganisme to Christian religion*, 3 vols. (St Omers, 1603–4. *ERL* 304–6), 304: 38. Persons accuses Protestants of fudging the dates of Bede and Geoffrey out "of envy, desyring to preferre Geffrey, that seemeth to favour them some tymes in his narracions about Saint Augustine, and to putt backe S. Bede, that is every where and wholy against them" (39). Persons describes Geoffrey as "much esteemed and alleged by our adversaries" (192).

[24] Pope Gregory's sending Augustine to the Saxons is mentioned briefly in the final chapter of Geoffrey's *Historia*. See Geoffrey of Monmouth, *The History of the Kings of Britain*, trans. Lewis Thorpe (Harmondsworth: Penguin, 1987), 265–6.

[25] John E. Curran, Jr., *Roman Invasions: The British History, Protestant Anti-Romanism, and the Historical Imagination in England, 1530–1660* (Newark: University of Delaware Press, 2002), 18.

[26] Michael E. Williams, "The Library of Saint Alban's English College Valladolid: Censorship and Acquisitions," *Recusant History* 26 (2002), 155–6.

Troy and nephew of Aeneas, was the eponymous founder of Britain. Persons thus exploits widespread skepticism in contemporary intellectual circles with the British history while at the same time associating Protestants with a narrative of national origins that connected the arrival of "civilization" in Britain not with the glories of Catholic Rome but with the failed empire of Troy.[27]

Despite Catholic attempts to lay exclusive ideological claim to Bede by forcing Protestants into the opposing historiographical camp of Geoffrey of Monmouth, reformers were unwilling to surrender *The history* to their opponents. John Bale, for example, celebrated Bede "as the spiritual successor to Joseph [of Arimathea] [with] quasi-patristic authority equivalent to that of Augustine of Hippo, Jerome, and Chrysostom."[28] In addition, Stapleton's Catholic translation of *The history* was closely related to the Basle edition of Bede's collected works that the reformed printer John Herwagen issued in 1563. Stapleton even advertised the fact in his own edition that the Protestants had "most diligently and with much commendation published [Bede's] workes" "in eight tomes contayning four great volumes . . . This worke is entituled *Collectanae Bedae*."[29] Critic Peter Jackson argues that part of Herwagen's motivation in undertaking his edition was the presence in Basle of a community of English Protestant refugees. Jackson speculates that one of these refugees was Bale himself, for whom "Bede was a kind of proto-Protestant who had maintained the faith free of Roman contamination."[30] Bale may even have supplied Herwagen with important Bedean manuscripts. So what is the religious orientation of the Basle edition of Bede in terms of contemporary confessional alignments? On the one hand, Herwagen's own reformist sympathies and his connections with Bale give the Basle edition a distinctly Protestant pedigree; on the other hand, though, this pedigree is offset by the fact that Herwagen and his editorial assistant dedicated the edition to the *Catholic* Bishop of Speyer. As Jackson observes, "the combination of two Reformed editors and a Catholic dedicatee was meant to ensure that [this edition of Bede] would appeal to partisans on both sides, and [help] to maintain 'the confessional neutrality' for which the Basle press was deservedly famous."[31] This episode illustrates how discourses of the national and religious past were always available for appropriation and re-appropriation by different ideological factions. No single group could ever claim exclusive "ownership" of figures like Bede or Geoffrey. Indeed, for polemicists on both sides, upholding ideological consistency was often less

[27] *A treatise of three conversions*, 304: 74. In Geoffrey, while Brut ends up in "Albion" after fleeing Troy, his Trojan relatives end up founding Rome.

[28] John N. King, *English Reformation Literature: The Tudor Origins of the Protestant Tradition* (Princeton: Princeton University Press, 1982), 70.

[29] *The history of the church of Englande*, A4ᵛ, A1ʳ, A2ʳ.

[30] See Peter Jackson, "Herwagen's Lost Manuscript of the *Collectanea*," in Martha Bayless and Michael Lapidge (eds.), *Collectanea Pseudo-Bedae* (Dublin, 1998), 116–17. I owe this reference to my colleague, Drew Jones.

[31] Ibid. 104.

important than marshalling the best evidence in a particular argument.[32] Thus, while Persons scoffed at the use of Galfridian history, other Catholics were only too happy to enlist Geoffrey to their cause.[33]

If Bede's *history* was an ongoing site of competition and rapprochement between Catholics and Protestants, it was also influential in conditioning English Catholic exiles' perceptions of their archipelagic neighbors: the "nations in exile" of Welsh, Scots, and Irish. In narrating the construction of a collective English and Christian identity among the Germanic tribes that had settled in "Brittany" and adjacent islands (the *gens Anglorum*), *The history* ranges widely over the entire archipelago. Yet despite this broad geographical canvas, Bede's story is decidedly Anglo-centric in orientation.[34] While this Anglo-centrism was intrinsic to Bede's original design, Stapleton amplified it in his edition's paratexts. He refers, for instance, to "this history of the church of England (our dere countre) containing in it beside the historical narration of the coming in of us englishmen into this lande," and he avers that the "hope and charitie [of oure forefathers the firste Christen englishmen] so wrought, that our dere countre of England hath ben more enriched with places erected to Gods honour, and to the fre maintenaunce of good lerning, then any one countre in all Christendome beside." Furthermore, Stapleton repeatedly reminds his readers that Bede is an Englishman, "a country-man of ours."[35]

In Bede's account of the English as God's people, the other inhabitants of the islands—the Britons, Scots, Picts, and Irish—sometimes embrace the

---

[32] On Bale's greater concern "with immediate effect [rather] than with overall consistency" in the way he constructs arguments, see Rainer Pineas as quoted in Andrew Hadfield, "Translating the Reformation: John Bale's Irish *Vocacyon*," in Brendan Bradshaw, Andrew Hadfield, and Willy Maley (eds.), *Representing Ireland: Literature and the Origins of Conflict, 1534–1660* (Cambridge: Cambridge University Press, 1993), 50.

[33] The most notable English Catholic attempt to appropriate the Galfridian narrative of the British past for a Counter-Reformation agenda was undertaken by the Douai exile Richard White. On White's *Historiarum Britanniae* (Arras and Douai, 1597–1602), see MacColl, "The Construction of England," 605–7, and "Richard White and the Legendary History of Britain," *Humanistica Lovaniensia* 51 (2002), 245–57. MacColl sees White's Catholic intervention in the British History as a failure: by the 1590s, "the reconstruction of the British history as a Protestant and indeed anti-Catholic text was now unshakably established" ("The Construction of England," 607).
For more on the confessional struggles over Bede (and by extension the Anglo-Saxon past), see Allen J. Frantzen, "Bede and Bawdy Bale: Gregory the Great, Angels, and the 'Angli'," in Allen J. Frantzen and John D. Niles (eds.), *Anglo-Saxonism and the Construction of Social Identity* (University of Florida Press, 1997), 17–39, and *Desire for Origins: New Language, Old English, and Teaching the Tradition* (New Brunswick: Rutgers University Press, 1990), 35–50, 136–7, and esp. 152–3; Benedict Scott Robinson, "John Foxe and the Anglo-Saxons," in Christopher Highley and John N. King (eds.), *John Foxe and His World* (Aldershot: Ashgate, 2001), 54–72.

[34] On Bede's construction of Englishness, see T. M. Charles Edwards, "Bede, the Irish, and the Britons," *Celtica* 15 (1983), 42–52; N. J. Higham, *An English Empire: Bede and the Early Anglo-Saxon Kings* (Manchester University Press, 1995); H. E. J Cowdrey, "Bede and the 'English People,'" *Journal of Religious History* 11 (1981), 501–23; Patrick Wormald, "Bede, the *Bretwaldas* and the Origins of the *Gens Anglorum*" in id. (ed.), *Ideal and Reality in Frankish and Anglo-Saxon Society* (Oxford: Oxford University Press, 1983), 99–129.

[35] *The history of the church of Englande*, B2^{r-v}, A3^{r-v}.

Christianity brought by Augustine from Rome and sometimes resist it, but they always play a secondary role to the "chosen" nation of the English. The Englishmen's main antagonists, the Britons, prove the most recalcitrant in accepting Christianity: "unto this daye the Britons maner, and custome is, to set light by the faithe and religion of English men," writes Bede, and he concludes *The history* by claiming that while the Picts and Scots/Irish have accepted English rule, the Britons continue to resist the English and Catholic Church.[36] The Britons— already partially Christianized when the Saxons first arrive—refuse to preach to and convert the heathen newcomers, and later "swarve" from the customs of Rome. And yet, writes Bede, "the goodnes of God did not so forsake his people, whom he foreknew to be saved. But provided for the sayd nation of the English much more worthy preachers, by whome they might be brought unto his fayth."[37] Only the English are deserving of Augustine and his missionaries from Rome. The "olde Brittons" meanwhile, as Stapleton recognizes elsewhere, are punished by God for their ingratitude, "being driven to the straightes, which they yet kepe."[38] Once a great race that dominated the whole island, the Britons eventually become the Welsh people, suffering a divinely imposed exile in the narrow confines of Wales.

For English Catholics of the later sixteenth century, Stapleton's edition of Bede acted as a prism through which perceptions of past and present Anglo-Welsh relations were filtered. Thus, in 1583 the prefect of studies at the Rheims seminary, Richard Barret, wrote to the rector of the English College in Rome, Agazzari, about the impending arrival of several Welsh students. Their irascibility, he remarked, was as "natural to them as it was in the time of the Venerabile Bede. In things of that manner they always follow the predilection of their own race like cattle."[39] Many Welsh Catholics, however, continued to imagine themselves as the direct descendants of Bede's Britons but without accepting the Anglo-centric prejudices implicit in the Bedean narrative. One prominent Welsh exile in Rome, Maurice Clenock, explicitly rejected that narrative when he proposed Wales as the best place to land an invading Catholic army in the 1570s. Clenock maintained that the Welsh were the "original stock of that island," and the upholders of "the ancient, the ancestral Catholic faith." As the "most devoted to the Catholic faith" of any people on the islands, the Welsh most deserved to welcome a "liberating" army. "The Welsh," he continued, "are the ancient and indigenous inhabitants of that island, and still distinct from the English by reason of their language... There, from times beyond the memory of any man, certain songs and rhymes are repeated in the mouths of all, in their own native tongue, in which they promise themselves that their liberation and all good things will

---

[36] Ibid. 74ᵛ, 191.   [37] Ibid. 29ʳ⁻ᵛ.

[38] *A returne of untruthes upon M. Jewelles Replie* (Antwerp, 1566), 19ᵛ (*ERL* 308). Hamilton, "Catholic Use of Anglo-Saxon Precedents," 537–55.

[39] Knox (ed.), *The First and Second Diaries of the English College*, 325. Translated from the Latin by Christopher Brown.

come from the city of Rome, and by means of a fleet which shall be sent to those regions from the city."[40]

Clenock's vision of Welsh greatness restored from Rome was directly inspired by the Galfridic narrative: at the conclusion of the *Historia regum Britanniae*, Geoffrey explains how the Britons, except for a few inhabitants of Wales, flee their ancestral land after their sins are punished by God with plague and famine. Cadwallader, the last king of the Britons, goes to Brittany where he is told by an "Angelic Voice" to forget about returning home and instead to go on pilgrimage to Rome. Cadwallader obeys with the understanding that "the British people would occupy the island again at some time in the future [but not] before the relics which once belonged to the Britons had been taken over again and they had transported them from Rome to Britain."[41] Geoffrey's *Historia* thus appealed to Welsh Catholics with its promise of future restoration and revival. Moreover, for Welsh exiles like Clenock the *Historia*'s concluding image of the British/Welsh as a banished people living in European diaspora had irresistible parallels to their own exilic condition. Like Cadwallader, Clenock and other Welsh had gone to Rome; like Cadwallader, they looked forward to a time when Rome would intervene to re-establish the ancient birthright of their people.[42] That propitious moment appeared to have arrived to many Welsh in Rome in the late 1570s when a tomb in St Peter's was uncovered that they claimed was Cadwallader's grave. The tomb quickly became a flash-point in Anglo-Welsh relations in the city. English exiles in Rome disputed Welsh claims about the tombstone, which carried the inscription "Caedwalla," by arguing that the name referred not to Cadwallader but to a Saxon king of Wessex who, like his British/Welsh namesake, had died in Rome at the end of the seventh century.[43]

TROUBLE AT ROME

Maurice Clenock was in Rome as the "the Governor [or Rector] Perpetual" of the English Hospice where pilgrims and visitors from England, Wales, and Scotland had for generations found a place to stay.[44] At the end of the 1570s, the Hospice continued to discharge its traditional duties while at the same

[40] J. M. Cleary, "Dr. Morys Clynnog's Invasion Projects of 1575–1576," *Recusant History* 8.6 (1966), 305–7.

[41] Geoffrey of Monmouth, *The History of the Kings of Britain*, 280–4.

[42] In 1597 the Welsh Catholic "Sîon Dafydd Rhys wrote a treatise (Peniarth MS 118D) criticizing Polydore Vergil's condemnation of Geoffrey of Monmouth's *Historia Regum Britanniae*." Geraint Bowen, *Welsh Recusant Writings* (Cardiff: University of Wales Press, 1999), 56.

[43] Jason A. Nice, "Being 'British' in Rome: The Welsh at the English College, 1578–1584," *The Catholic Historical Review* 92 (2006), 1–24.

[44] *The Letters and Memorials of William Cardinal Allen (1532–1594)*, ed. Thomas Francis Knox (London, 1882), 78–84.

time becoming a college for training young English and Welsh students for the priesthood.[45] The first batch of students who transferred to Rome from William Allen's overcrowded seminary at Rheims soon found themselves in conflict with their Welsh superiors, Clenock and Owen Lewis. Eventually, more than thirty English students accused Clenock and Lewis of providing inadequate leadership and of having a different conception of the college's mission than their own. While the students were determined to return to England as missionary priests after finishing their training, Clenock and Lewis saw the college's main task as training priests for positions in Rome and other hospitable locations.[46] According to their vision, the priests would only return home once England had reconverted to the Old Faith. The students, on top of this disagreement about the college's mission and constitution, also alleged that Clenock and Lewis showed favoritism to the "7 or 8" Welsh students who now rallied behind their superiors in a "nationall quarrell." Recalling similar tensions in the past between English and Welsh students at Oxford University, the quarrel soon drew in other Welsh and English Catholics in Rome and beyond.[47] According to Persons's version of events in *A Story of Domesticall Difficulties*, the English students complained they were not properly taken care of: for example, during the winter, while "all the Welchmen [were] double apareled," "the best borne Englishe went...with naked thighes and full of lice." Class privilege as well as national pride was at stake in the quarrel. The troubles in Rome reached a crisis point when the English students were expelled from the college, at which news the Welsh student Hugh Griffin "is said to have given a leape into the Colledge Hall sayinge 'Whoe now but a Welchman'."[48] The English students, on the verge of leaving Rome, secured an audience with Pope Gregory XIII who had "supposed the Welshe and Englishe, to be all as one," and who was unaware, in Persons's words, that the Welsh "would be Lords over the English men and use them according as they thought good." After persuading Gregory to transfer control

---

[45] Anthony Kenny, "From Hospice to College," in *The English Hospice in Rome*. The Venerabile Sexcentenary issue. May 1962. Vol. 21 (Exeter: Catholic Records Press), 218–73; Nice, "Being 'British' in Rome."

[46] Lewis Lewkenor, admittedly a hostile Protestant commentator, claimed that "the Welchmen [in Rome] pretended the first foundation of the Colledge to have bin by a British king, for the perpetuall behoofe of his Countrymen" (*The estate of the English fugitives under the king of Spaine and his ministers* (1595), G4ᵛ). The English students would no doubt have been irritated by Clenock and Lewis's tendency to refer to the newly instituted college as the "Seminarium Britannicum," or Welsh seminary. See Godfrey Anstruther, "Owen Lewis," in *The English Hospice in Rome*. The Venerabile Sexcentenary issue. May 1962. Vol. 21 (Exeter: Catholic Records Press), 277.

[47] "The Memoirs of Father Robert Persons," 86, 135–6. For a modern history of the college, see Michael E. Williams, *The Venerable English College Rome: A History 1579–1979* (London: Associated Catholic Publishers, 1979), ch. 1. Persons wrote to Allen in 1579: "who can stay young men or old eyther, once incensed on both sides by national contentions? You know what passeth in Oxford in like occasions" (*Letters and Memorials of William Cardinal Allen*, 74).

[48] "The Memoirs of Father Robert Persons," 144, 136.

of the college from Clenock and Lewis to the Jesuits, the students returned triumphant.[49]

Persons's account of the troubles in the college lays claim to a tone of dispassionate impartiality. Yet while pretending to be "voyde of all affection of both parties," he cannot conceal an underlying admiration for his fellow Englishmen.[50] Indeed, Persons is no detached observer of the unfolding events but a key participant in them: it is Persons, "lyving at that tyme in the Roman Colledge," who urges the English students to petition the pope for assistance.[51] He also uses the English students' response to their adversities in Rome as a way of affirming their fitness for the rigors of missionary work. As he points out, observers could only marvel that if the students used such "liberty of speech" and "stand thus immovable before such Princes in Rome, what will they do in England before the Heretiques."[52] Indeed, claims Persons, some observers likened the students to "a certayne company of Lawrences, Sebastians and the like intractable fellowes, who brought Emperours and princes to desperation to deal with them, for that they could neyther with giving or taking condescend to any one little poynt that they misliked."[53] In Persons's version of events, the students embody the best of English national traits, including an admirable resourcefulness and unity of purpose. The students, moreover, received alms and sympathy aplenty from all English expatriates in Rome who epitomized for Persons the ideal of a unified and self-supporting Catholic community in exile.[54]

Once the conflict at the college was resolved to the English students' satisfaction, they displayed, in Persons's view, characteristic generosity by requesting "that for the uniting better of the two Nations togethear and the better satisfaction of the [Welsh], that in the beginning of discipline all matters of burden and payne might be layd upon the Englishmen, and all prerogatives, both in

---

[49] Ibid. 86–7. Welsh expressions of national pride were not to be extinguished by their "defeat" in Rome. A Welsh student at the English College in Valladolid, Spain, described himself in the College Register as "sprung from the noble stock of the ancient Britons" (quoted in David Lunn, *The English Benedictines, 1540–1688: From Reformation to Revolution* (New York: Barnes and Noble, 1980), 30); another Welshman, Robert Gwyn, appears in the Douai College Register as "Robertus Guinus, Bangorensis...ex antiqourum Britonum natione" (quoted in Bowen, *Welsh Recusant Writings*, 28).

Tensions between Welsh and English interests in Rome may also have arisen over the allocation of resources for the printing and distribution of Catholic books in the respective vernaculars. Any expenditure on the translation and publication of works in Welsh could be seen by the English as detracting from their own propaganda efforts. Sometime in the 1570s, Owen Lewis penned a petition to Cardinal Sirleto, the Vatican librarian, asking for money to help print several edifying religious texts in Welsh. See Peter Guilday, "The English Catholic Refugees at Louvain, 1559–1575," in *Melanges d'histoire oferts a Charles Moeller* 2 (1914), 183 n. 2; and Andrew Breeze, "Welsh and Cornish at Valladolid, 1591–1600," *The Bulletin of the Board of Celtic Studies* 37 (1990), 108–11.

[50] "The Memoirs of Father Robert Persons," 142.   [51] Ibid. 87.

[52] Ibid. 147, 159–60.   [53] Ibid. 147.

[54] "Generally all the whole Nation [of English] was ready to spoyle themselves to furnishe [the students]" (ibid. 153).

apparell, bookes, chambers, and all other thing might be given to the [Welsh]."
The English students were "not only ready to pardon whatsoever the Welchmen
had done against them, or should do, but also were ready to kisse their feet,
and to serve them at table, and otherwise wherein soever they sould have neede,
upon the condition that they would be content to joyne in the procurement of
a good goverment and discipline." Persons gives the last word on the matter to
a witty "English Gentleman named Mr Pasquall [who] stept up and said that
he [agreed with this arrangement] in all things except in his portion of meate,
wherein he desired to be equall to any of the [Welsh], for that his appetite or
stomacke yelded to none of theirs."[55] "Pasquall"'s purported comments resonate
with contemporary notions about English masculinity that were closely bound
to ideas concerning an Englishman's proverbial appetite for meat—the "great
meals and iron and steel" that Shakespeare's French imagine the English soldiers
consuming in *Henry V* (3.7.135–6). The confrontation in the play between the
English common soldier, Pistol, and the Welsh captain Fluellen also replays in a
comic register the troubles at the English College Rome but ends up reversing the
outcome: instead of English students triumphing over their counterparts from
Wales, in *Henry V* the Welsh Fluellen routs the English Pistol.

The authorities at the Roman College also used representation to mediate and
defuse the ethnic tensions between English and Welsh. Anne Dillon observes
that one of the series of martyr murals painted for the college chapel in the early
1580s depicted the story of the virgin martyr Saint Winifred of Holywell in
Wales. Dillon speculates that Winifred's inclusion in the sequence of thirty-three
murals portraying the trials and triumphs of both ancient and contemporary
victims of persecution may "have been an attempt to thwart some of the more
xenophobic tendencies in the College," presumably by paying homage to a figure
beloved of its Welsh members.[56] The murals painted by Niccolò Circignani were
part of a Jesuit-inspired decorative program in the chapel that was organized
around Durante Alberti's "Martyrs' Picture" that hung over the Holy Trinity
altar. Alberti's altarpiece is a version of the familiar "Trinity with saints": God
the Father appears at the apex of this vertical composition supporting the wilting
and bleeding body of Christ by his arms. The wounds in Christ's body spray
blood onto an image of England beneath, which is flanked at the bottom of
the composition by the supporting figures of two English proto-martyrs, Saints

[55] Ibid. 152–3. The name Pasquall may well be a false one supplied by Persons to protect the
student's real identity. In the Renaissance, the name "Pasquil" was synonymous with wit, satire, and
jesting. See e.g., William Fennor, *Pasquils jestes mixed with Mother Bunches merriments. Whereunto
is added a bakers doozen of guiles. Very prettie and pleasant, to driue away the tediousnesse of a winters
evening* (1609).
[56] Anne Dillon, *The Construction of Martyrdom in the English Catholic Community, 1553–1603*
(Aldershot: Ashgate, 2002), ch. 4, esp.199. On the religious significance of Holywell, see Alexandra
Walsham, "Holywell: Contesting Sacred Space in Post-Reformation Wales," in Will Coster and
Andrew Spicer (eds.), *Sacred Space in Early Modern Europe* (Cambridge: Cambridge University Press,
2005), 211–36.

Thomas of Canterbury and King Edmund. Carol M. Richardson argues that
the painting's theme of the Trinity and its vision of God's all-encompassing love
presented "an ecclesial model of peaceful co-existence" that the college authorities
wished more than anything to promote in light of the disputes between the
English and Welsh in Rome.[57]

Alongside the "Many Memorialls, letters and other schrowles" recording the
tensions between English and Welsh in Rome there appeared a published account
in Anthony Munday's travelogue, *The English Roman Life* (1582).[58] Based on
Munday's actual visit to Rome, the first-person narrative recounts his desire to
see new countries and learn new languages; his dangerous journey across Catholic
Europe in the company of his companion, Thomas Nowell; and his eventual stay
in Rome. Munday's text is a tissue of scandalous revelations and strategic evasions
in which he names some fugitive English Catholics but withholds the identities
of others for fear of compromising their security. The tone throughout is anxious
and ambiguous. Munday is nervous that his presence in Rome will arouse suspicions with some English Protestants no matter how much he protests his loyalty
to Elizabeth. Yet the text itself seems to provoke rather than allay uncertainty
about its author's intentions and sympathies by sending mixed messages about
the nature of his trip, the English exiles, and Roman Catholicism.[59] Denun-
ciations of fake relics and the impious speeches of Catholic exiles against the
queen sit uneasily with descriptions of the orderliness of college life and the pious
generosity of Rome's citizens. Munday's narrative voice is constantly changing
tone, one moment dispassionately recording observations and remaining morally
detached, the next, becoming vituperative and polemically enraged. For example,
when Munday witnesses a self-inflicted Jesuit flogging, a marginal gloss exclaims
in outrage, "Egregious impudency," but the narrator's own response is more
complex, torn between admiration ("I was not endued with that strength and
fortitude as to abide and suffer the pains he did"), and pity ("I left him in his
chamber . . . lamenting to see a spectacle of so great folly").[60]

[57] Carol M. Richardson, "Durante Alberti, the *Martyrs' Picture* and the Venerable English
College, Rome," *Papers of the British School at Rome* 73 (2005), 223–63, esp. 250. On Alberti's
painting, also see Jason A. Nice, "Cross-Confessional Features of English Identity: The Ditchley
Portrait of Queen Elizabeth I and the High Altarpiece of the English College in Rome," in Philip
M. Soergel (ed.), *Studies in Medieval and Renaissance History: Nation, Ethnicity, and Identity in
Medieval and Renaissance Europe* 3rd ser. vol. 3 (New York: AMS Press, 2006), 185–209; and Peter
Davidson, "Recusant Catholic Spaces in Early Modern England," in Ronald Corthell, Frances E.
Dolan, Christopher Highley, and Arthur F. Marotti (eds.), *Catholic Culture in Early Modern England*
(Notre Dame, Ind.: University of Notre Dame Press, 2007), 19–51.
[58] "The Memoirs of Father Robert Persons," 87. Anthony Munday, *The English Roman Life*,
ed. Philip J. Ayres (Oxford: Clarendon Press, 1980). On Munday's actual presence in Rome, see
Anthony Kenny, "Anthony Munday in Rome," *Recusant History* 6 (1962), 158–62.
[59] For the intriguing claim that in *The English Roman Life* Munday reveals an ambivalent attitude
toward the Catholic community indicative of someone with Catholic sympathies but with political
loyalties to the Elizabethan regime, see Donna Hamilton, *Anthony Munday and the Catholics 1560–
1633* (Aldershot: Ashgate, 2005).
[60] *The English Roman Life*, 40.

The "conflicted self-presentation in *The English Roman Life*" of Munday's narrative persona is evident again in his account of "the dissension in the English College between the Englishmen and the Welshmen."[61] Like Persons, Munday is no mere observer of the English–Welsh stirs but a central player in them. When Maurice Clenock takes a sudden dislike to Munday and tries to kick him out of the college, the English students come to Munday's rescue, accusing Clenock of wanting to make the college "all Welshmen," and threatening to leave *en masse*.[62] The English students, even the ones who "made least account of" him, rally to Munday's side despite the fact that during his time with them he has been only a lukewarm participant in their rituals and has been frequently punished for violating college rules and for refusing to speak un-reverently about the queen and her council.[63]

Munday, as author of *The English Roman Life*, foregrounds the tenacity of ethnic and national bonds and the way they supersede religious ones. The students, in their disrespect for Elizabeth and their submission to foreign Jesuits, may not be loyal Englishmen but they are still English enough to take the side of a fellow ex-patriate (no matter how religiously suspect) against a Welshman. As narrator, Munday flaunts his role in exposing the ethnic faultlines that threaten to incapacitate Britain's Catholic exiles. The troubles in Rome that he broadcasts for the first time to an audience in England would have confirmed the hopes of some Protestants that the various political and national factions among Catholic exiles "wolde if they colde sucke upe each others blude."[64] Munday could lay claim to both exposing and perpetuating these factions because in *The English Roman Life* it is the sight of his mistreatment by Clenock that leads the students to request a new Jesuit rector from the pope.[65] Thus, Munday could imagine himself as indirectly responsible for the Jesuit takeover of the college and for laying the basis of the conflict between Jesuits and seculars that would afflict the college for years to come.

The participants in the quarrels at Rome were operating with assumptions about ethnic identity that focused not on the physical or cultural differences among peoples but on the historical and geographical origins of each particular *gens*. Persons explained the differences between Welsh and English through analogy to the "difference betwene the Biscayans and Castilians in Spaine, where the first are the reliques of the ould inhabitante Spaniards, and the second are more new, coming of the Gothes that conquered the country." Other observers adapted this Iberian model by representing the Welsh as equivalent not to the

[61] Melanie Ord, "Representing Rome and the Self in Anthony Munday's *The English Roman Life*," in Mike Pincombe (ed.), *Travels and Translations in the Sixteenth Century* (Aldershot: Ashgate, 2004), 50.

[62] Ibid. 79–81.   [63] Ibid. 37–8, 65–6.

[64] Quoted in Michael C. Questier, "What Happened to English Catholicism after the English Reformation?" *The Historical Journal* (2000), 40.

[65] *The English Roman Life*, 81–2.

Biscayans but to the Moors, even though "the Moores are later in Spayne than the Castilians."[66] Despite the historical incoherence of the analogy, it was picked up on by English malcontents in the Roman college. "It is naturally as impossible," they told the pope, "for a Welshman to treat well Englishmen subjected to him, as it is for a Moor to love a Spaniard."[67]

This habit of thinking about a *gens* in terms of its origins and its connections to other related *gens* prompted fears among Catholics that the English–Welsh conflict in Rome might escalate into broader Anglo-Celtic alliances and divisions. Persons reported that some English Catholics in the city were spreading rumors that Clenock was planning to replace the disruptive English students with Irishmen and Scotsmen.[68] Clenock was allegedly seeking to admit, "Welch, Irish, and Scottishe schollers in the College and they three joyning togeather against the Englishe (as easily they are wonte) they might the better hould downe the other." This plan was supposedly Clenock's way of exacting revenge against the English students who had succeeded through the intervention of the pope in wresting control away from him and Lewis into the hands of foreign Jesuits.[69] In another gesture of anti-English solidarity, Clenock's compatriot in Rome, Owen Lewis, reportedly urged the Scotsman John Leslie, Bishop of Ross: "let us stick together, for we are the old and true inhabiters and owners of the isle of Britanny; these others [the English] be but usurpers and mere possessors."[70] According to Jason Nice, the comments of Clenock and Lewis were inspired by the ancient *Armes Prydein* or "Prophecy of Britain"—the prediction that the Saxon usurpers in Britain would be overthrown by their united Celtic neighbors. With the supposed discovery by the Welsh of Cadwallader's tomb in St Peters, the terms of the prophecy seemed almost complete; as Merlin had foretold, "the Brytons shulde not recover this lande tyll the relykes of Cadwaladyr wyth other of holy saintes, were brought hyther [i.e. Wales] out of Rome." Welsh prophetic fantasies were dashed, however, when the Vatican ruled the tomb to be that of the Anglo-Saxon king Caedwalla.[71]

In retrospect, Persons saw this original quarrel between English and Welsh exiles at Rome as representing "the very first roote . . . of the greate differences that have fallen out since that tyme among Catholikes of our Nation"—differences that eventually resulted in the formation of two opposed groups: one strongly

---

[66] "The Memoirs of Father Robert Persons," 154.

[67] Quoted in Kenny, "From Hospice to College," 260.

[68] "The Memoirs of Father Robert Persons," 154.

[69] Ibid. 128–30. Persons reported another rumor that "the Scottishe nation had given up a Memoriall that they myght be admitted also to the participation of this new Colledge, and the like was doubtfull of the Irishe."

[70] *Letters and Memorials of William Cardinal Allen*, 82. Quoted in John Bossy, "Catholicity and Nationality in the Northern Counter-Reformation," in Stuart Mews (ed.), *Religion and National Identity* (Oxford: Blackwell, 1982), 294. Also see Thomas M. McCoog, SJ, "The Society of Jesus in Wales, The Welsh in the Society of Jesus," *The Journal of Welsh Religious History* 5 (1997), 1–27; Nice, "Being 'British' in Rome," 15–16.

[71] Nice, "Being 'British' in Rome," 16–24.

pro-Jesuit and pro-Spanish (with Persons himself at its head), the other anti-
Jesuit and dedicated to a Stuart succession to the English throne.[72] Opposition
to the policies of Persons and the Spanish–Jesuit agenda was eventually led by
Thomas Morgan and Charles Paget, former intriguers on behalf of Mary Stuart.
Persons accused these two of enlisting support from any exiled Catholics "given
to faction and nationality between English, Welsh, Irish or Scots."[73]

SCOTLAND AND THE SUCCESSION

Persons's success in parlaying an apparent disaster for the fledgling college in
Rome into a vindication of "Englishmens natures," reveals an underlying preoccupation with ethnic identities—a "racialism," to adapt John Bossy's view, that is
also apparent in Persons's curious description of Clenock as "an Englishman,
but sprung from that part of England which had once been the refuge of
the ancient Britons when they were conquered by the English, and was called
Wales . . . between these Welshmen and *true Englishmen* dissensions easily arise
from memory of their ancient rivalry, they being of the stock of different peoples."[74] Persons's comments both recognize and elide the status of Wales as a
separate geopolitical entity from England, independent of, and yet subsumed
within, a greater England. In the same way, Clenock both is and is not seen
as English; while recognizably similar to Persons (in faith and language), he is
different enough to be an inferior, "untrue" Englishman.[75]

    This "racialism," I propose, can also be found in other works by Persons
and a faction of English Catholic writers. It informs, for instance, one of the
most notorious Catholic texts of the Elizabethan era, *A conference about the next
succession to the crowne of Ingland*, on which Persons probably collaborated with
"Cardinal Allen, Sir Frauncis Inglefeld, and other principal men of our nation,"

[72] "The Memoirs of Father Robert Persons," 89; also see "Father Persons' Memoirs (concluded) . . . Punti per la Missione d'Inghilterra," ed. and trans. J. H. Pollen, SJ, as "Notes Concerning
the English Mission," in *Miscellanea IV*, Catholic Record Society 4 (London, 1907), 65–9. For a
hostile account of Catholic factions, see Sir Lewis Lewkenor, *A discourse of the usage of the English
fugitives by the Spaniards* (1595), D3ʳ–D4ᵛ. See also John Bossy, *The English Catholic Community
1570–1850* (London, 1975), 25.

[73] "The Memoirs of Father Robert Persons," 35, 31. For Persons's view of the providentially
engineered downfalls of Morgan, Paget, and their adherents, see "An Observation of Certayne
Aparent Judgments of Almightye God, againste suche as have beene Seditious in the Englishe
Catholique Cause" (1598), in "The Memoirs of Father Robert Persons," 202–11.

[74] Ibid. 159, 97; my emphasis; also see 136, 156–7. Bossy, "Catholicity and Nationality,"
293.

[75] Persons's attitude to the Welsh in Rome is even more intriguingly complex if, as has been
claimed, he was himself of Welsh stock. It has also been argued that on one occasion Persons adopted
the pseudonym "Jodocus Skarnhert": Skarhert meaning "broken-hearted," Jodocus alluding to St
Iodoc, "a Welsh exiled prince." See Jos Simons, *Robert Persons, S.J. Cartamen Ecclesiae Anglicanae: A
Study of an Unpublished Manuscript* (Assen, Netherlands: Van Gorcum, 1965), 304.

and that appeared in 1595 under the pseudonym "R. Doleman."[76] In the early 1580s, Persons and his associates had backed to succeed Elizabeth, first Mary Queen of Scots and later her son James, who they hoped at that time could be converted to his mother's faith. However, after Mary's execution, and once it became clear that James would remain a "heretic," they looked elsewhere for a Catholic candidate to the English throne.[77] Contributing to this search, *A conference* sets out the rights of various candidates to the English throne and considers the criteria for adjudicating their claims. An English civil lawyer, one of the main participants in the dialogue, argues that lineal succession and propinquity of blood, while relevant, are finally less important than the election of a ruler by the commonwealth. Then in the book's second part, a temporal lawyer analyzes the strengths and weaknesses of each candidate, but without, he insists, "stand[ing] upon the justification or impugning of any one title."[78] Indeed, he criticizes previous commentators on the succession who have pressed the claim of a single candidate for ignoring "the wonderful ambiguity and doubtfulnes which in this most important affair is to be founde."[79] *A conference*'s dialogical structure, tone of scholarly impartiality, and basis in genealogical research, lacks the kind of polemical advocacy characteristic of other treatments of the succession issue.[80] And yet, of the "Five Principal Houses or Linages" that are seen as having a valid claim to the crown—Scotland, Suffolk, Clarence, Britanny, and Portugal—it is the House of Portugal, bearing the claim of the Spanish Habsburgs, that *A conference* clearly favors. Philip II and his family are shown to have a primary claim to the English throne through their descent from the king of Portugal's marriage to Phillipa, the eldest daughter of John of Gaunt and his first wife Blanche, Duchess of Lancaster. This so-called Lancastrian claim is reinforced by several secondary claims that connect the Habsburgs to other branches of the dynasty established in England by William the Conqueror.[81] Improbably enough, *A conference* concludes by implicitly endorsing as Elizabeth's successor, Philip II's daughter, the Infanta Isabella of Spain, the "one forrayne prince . . . likest to beare it away."[82]

---

[76] Persons, *A briefe apologie, or defence of the Catholike ecclesiastical hierarchie* (Antwerp, 1601. *ERL* 273), 187[v]. Also see Leo Hicks, "Father Robert Persons S.J. and *The Book of Succession*," *Recusant History* 4 (1957–8), 104–37; Peter Holmes, "The Authorship and Early Reception of *A Conference about the Next Succession to the Crown of England*," *Historical Journal* 23 (1980), 415–29; and Victor Houliston, "The Hare and the Drum: Robert Persons's Writings on the English Succession, 1593–6," *Renaissance Studies* 14 (2000), 234–50.

[77] On Persons relationship with James, see Thomas M. McCoog, SJ, "Harmony Disrupted: Robert Parsons, S.J., William Crichton, S.J., and the Question of Queen Elizabeth's Successor, 1581–1603," *Archivum Historicum Societatis Jesu* 73 (2004), 149–220.

[78] *A conference about the next succession to the crowne*, Q5[r].   [79] Ibid. 2: 10–11.

[80] Henry Constable's, *A discoverye of a counterfecte conference* (Paris, 1600. *ERL* 6), shows how *A conference*'s apparent indifference in the matter of the succession is actually a rhetorical cover for promoting the claim of one candidate (44–6).

[81] *A conference about the next succession to the crowne*, 2: 107, 6–9, 160–93, 18, 24–6, 30–1.

[82] Ibid. 2: 263.

In 1595 when *A conference* was written, Persons and his co-authors' willingness to air, if not openly advocate, the claim of the Infanta was connected to the fact that Mary Queen of Scots was dead and Philip of Spain had demonstrated his interest in England by taking military action against Elizabeth. Before these events, Persons's own preference for a Habsburg candidate had been more circumspect. In March 1587 he wrote to Cardinal Farnese of the need to keep their backing of Philip a secret from the pope as well as from "other Catholic Christian princes," including Mary Stuart and her supporters. In *A conference*, Persons still had to worry that his favoring of Philip's claim would stoke fears that "Spain wanted to dominate the whole of Europe." The nomination of the Infanta instead of her father may have been a way of trying, in a small way, to calm these fears.[83]

A conference establishes Isabella's claim by disallowing others, and especially that of Elizabeth's most likely successor in 1595, James VI of Scotland. Despite the authors' claim that the book says "nothing . . . against him except on the score of his being a heretic," *A conference* presents the candidacy of James Stuart as undesirable on several counts.[84] Some opponents of James's title argued that he was disqualified from the succession because he was born outside England. Yet *A conference* avoids this argument because by the same criterion the Infanta would also be disqualified. In fact, in a chapter on the respective merits of home-born and foreign-born rulers, *A conference* argues that England might be better served by a foreign-born prince or his proxy who would assume the monarchy unencumbered by domestic rivalries and special interests.[85] As an example of this type of arrangement, the authors point to Spanish rule in the Low Countries where, until the recent revolts, peace and prosperity have allegedly flourished.[86] A young unmarried foreign candidate like the Infanta, *A conference* claims, far from imposing alien ways on the English, would be readily assimilated into English culture.[87] This argument about the benefits to England (and to all countries) of rule by a stranger prince is implicitly tied to a defense of the pope's right to intervene in the domestic affairs of nations.

A conference, however, does not countenance all forms of foreign rule—James's candidacy to the throne of England being a case in point. The problem with James's claim arises first from the proximity of his new to his old realm, where he "hath forces at hand to woorke his wil," and second from ethnic enmity: "the aversion and natural alienation of [the Scots] from the English, and their ancient inclination to joyne with the French and Irish against us."[88] Should James gain

---

[83] *Letters and Memorials of Father Robert Persons*, 292–4. In 1587 Persons wrote that if Mary Stuart survived an invasion of England by Philip, she could be "bestowed in marriage by His Majesty" and used to help establish "negotiations for the succession of His Majesty and the claim of the House of Lancaster—which existed both before and after the union of the two houses made in the person of King Henry VII" (294). Also see 299–303, 308.

[84] Quoted in Hicks, "Father Robert Persons S.J. and *The Book of Succession*," 112.

[85] *A conference about the next succession to the crowne*, 2: 193–233.   [86] Ibid. 2: 209–13.

[87] Ibid. 2: 224.   [88] Ibid. 2: 227, 118.

the crown, the authors assert, he would inevitably fill the realm with Scots, favoring them over the English, "as we reade that William Conqueror did his Normannes...to the incredible calamity of the English nation."[89] *A conference* predicts that James's accession would bring about a "violent union of nations, that are by nature so disunited and opposite, as are the English, Scotish, Irishe, Danishe, Frenche, and other on them depending, which by this meanes must needs be planted together in England."[90] Of the different kinds of foreign rule, *A conference* concludes ominously, "the kinge of Scottes case, is to be only feared."[91]

Once James became king of England in 1603, Persons scrambled to rethink his public approach to the Stuart regime. In a dedication Persons added at the last minute to his *A treatise of three conversions* (1603) "upon the newes of the Queens death; and succession of the King of Scotland," he likened James to the Emperor Constantine.[92] This appropriation of a favorite figure from Protestant iconography allowed Persons to point out how both James and Constantine were notable for their pious mothers (Mary Stuart and Helena respectively) and how both exercised dominion over "the whole *Ilande of Britany*". Moreover, Constantine's conversion to Christianity after becoming emperor provided a precedent for James's still hoped-for conversion to Catholicism. And perhaps, just as Constantine supposedly had "donated" temporal and ecclesiastical control of Britain and Ireland to the papacy, so James would once again restore religious control back to Rome.[93]

Yet even as Persons proclaimed his hope that James would show more tolerance to his Catholic subjects than had "the olde persecutor" Elizabeth, he remained deeply suspicious of a Scottish succession and the prospect of Anglo-Scottish union. In a letter of July 1603, Persons again likened the arrival of James's Scottish entourage in England to the coming of the Normans in 1066. He advised his correspondent to consult "the storie of the Abbot [Ingulph] of Croyland...who was secretarie to Duke William before he was King of England, and saw the suppression of his nation by the Normanes." It was a story, claimed Persons, that presented "a patterne of the tyme to come."[94] When news of Elizabeth's death reached Persons in Rome, he observed ominously that the Scots in the city, anticipating their countryman's accession, "do begin already to exasperate too much in speeches everywhere against the English."[95]

[89] Ibid. 2: 120.   [90] Ibid. 2: 121.   [91] Ibid. 2: 228.

[92] As I show in Ch. 6, Persons also applied the figure of Constantine to Philip II.

[93] *A treatise of three conversions*, 304: *2ʳ. The Protestant Matthew Sutcliffe observed of Persons's comparison of James to Constantine in *A treatise of three conversions*, that "not many yeares since, in his most trayterous booke of titles [i.e. *A conference*]...[Persons] sought to deprive this Constantine of the crowne of England, and to convey the same to the Infanta of Spaine." *The subversion of Robert Parsons his confused and worthlesse worke, entituled, A treatise of three conversions of England from paganisme to Christian religion* (1606), A6ʳ.

[94] "The Memoirs of Father Robert Persons," 216.

[95] Quoted in Francis Edwards, SJ, *Robert Persons: The Biography of an Elizabethan Jesuit 1546–1610* (St Louis, Missouri: Institute of Jesuit Sources, 1995), 284.

The Scotsmen whom Persons thought were gloating in Rome at the prospect of James's succession were part of a broad coalition of Catholics and Protestants in England, Scotland, and on the Continent that backed James and the union of the kingdoms. Among Scottish Catholics, even Jesuits generally preferred James to the Infanta. The Scottish Jesuit, Alexander MacQuhirrie, for example, supported James, and though he thought the union project "very difficult of execution," he favored it on the grounds that English law (which he assumed would become the law of a united realm) was less severe toward Catholics than Scottish law.[96] Another Scottish Jesuit, William Crichton, also defied Persons by backing James. Crichton objected strenuously to the publication of *A conference*, arguing that it would only make life more difficult for Catholics.[97] As Arthur Williamson points out, among Scottish Catholics there was "no Scottish Robert Parsons; even Catholic-led opposition [to union] soon conceded the principle and concentrated on the best terms for Scotland."[98]

Crichton and other Catholic Scots had good reasons to oppose Persons's pro-Spanish agenda: Crichton was aggrieved, for example, that the king of Spain had helped establish "a seminary [at St Omers] for poor and undistinguised boys from England," while ignoring "boys from Scotland of noble lineage." Crichton's explanation of this iniquity conflated ethnic and class stereotypes: "the English were more persistent and went begging far and wide, while the Scots were of a more reserved and aristocratic temperament unsullied by this vulgar trait."[99] Scottish Catholics also alleged that Persons had tried to persuade Philip "to refuse to support the founding of a Scots seminary in Flanders, since the Scots preferred their own King to succeed to the throne of England."[100]

Many Protestant discussions of *A conference* assumed that it represented the views of *all* Catholics despite efforts by James's Catholic supporters like the secular priests Henry Constable, William Watson, and William Clarke to prove otherwise.[101] The Scottish Protestant jurist, Sir Thomas Craig, for example, who "outed" Persons as the author of *A conference* from behind the pseudonym of "Doleman," argued that the idea of Anglo-Scottish union was anathema to what

[96] Quoted in William Forbes-Leith, SJ (ed.), *Narratives of Scottish Catholics Under Mary Stuart and James VI* (Edinburgh: William Paterson, 1885), 277.

[97] McCoog, "Harmony Disrupted," 165–9.   [98] "Scotland, Antichrist," 45.

[99] Quoted in Edwards, *Robert Persons*, 170. Persons thought Crichton's plans "for curing the ills of Scotland... were not well-founded and, indeed, impracticable," 171. Also see McCoog, "Harmony Disrupted," 171.

[100] Michael E. Williams, *St Alban's College Valladolid: Four Centuries of English Catholic Presence in Spain* (New York: St Martin's Press, 1988), 15 n. 5. Also see Hubert Chadwick, "The Scots College, Douai, 1580–1613," *The English Historical Review* 56.224 (1941), 571–85; Brian M. Halloran, *The Scots College in Paris, 1603–1792* (Edinburgh: John Donald, 1997).

[101] Constable, *A discoverye of a counterfecte conference* (1600); Watson, *A decacordon of ten quodlibeticall questions* (np, 1602. *ERL* 197); Clarke, *A Replie unto a certaine libell* (np, 1603. *ERL* 115). These writers attacked *A conference* as part of a universal Jesuit plot. On Constable, see Alison Shell, *Catholicism, Controversy, and the English Literary Imagination, 1558–1660* (Cambridge: Cambridge University Press, 1999), 122–3.

he imagined to be a monolithic and unified Catholic community. Craig claimed that Persons, in "working to secure for the Pope the recovery of this famous island," had "spared no pains in his writings to combat the proposed union of the kingdoms."[102] Craig denied Persons's charges that a union would be detrimental to England because the Scots were an impoverished people, "turbulent, uncivilized, and animated by bitter hatred towards Englishmen."[103] For Craig and other Protestant unionists, Anglo-Scottish integration promised—even without the formal unification of their national churches—to create an island bastion of reform, an anti-Catholic super-state.

One enterprising group of Protestant Englishmen, as a way of exposing what they considered all Catholics' opposition to Anglo-Scottish union, took a Catholic pamphlet appealing for toleration from the new king and reissued it as *The Supplication of certaine Masse-Priests falsely called Catholikes* (1604). The work's Protestant editors reframed the original text with their own title pages, prefaces, marginal annotations, and commentary that denounced the putative authors for political disloyalty, including their alleged hindrance of the king's union scheme. "It is very improbable," the new editors wrote, "that the uniting of these two Kingdomes of *England* and *Scotland* under one King could please [the Catholic petitioners]. For the stronger this Kingdome is, the lesse hope have Masse-priests to prevaile ... [W]ho can imagine, that the Popes vassals can joy hartily in the strength of his Majesties Empire, that dependeth not on their Lord the Pope."[104]

The opposition of some Catholics like Persons to Anglo-Scottish union may have owed something to an ingrained "Scottophobia" or "racialism," but it also had a sound basis in religio-political realities. English Catholics were fearfully aware that recusancy laws were harsher in Scotland than in England (witness Father MacQuhirrie's comments) and that Scotland was home to a radical anti-episcopal brand of Protestantism that, they predicted, would infiltrate England in the event of closer ties between the countries.[105] The authors of *A conference* warily observed that James was a favorite candidate of the Puritan party in England and that in Scotland he already "standeth in awe of this exorbitant and populer power of his ministers"; even "moderate" Protestants like Sir Henry Spelman warned about the danger to England of "those fiery spirited ministers that in the fury of the[ir] zeale have not only perverted the stable goverment of [the Scottish] church but even wounded the very kingdome

---

[102] *De Unione Regnorum Britanniae Tractatus*, ed. and trans. C. Sanford Terry (Edinburgh: Scottish History Society, 1909), 411–12. Persons later wrote to James that the pseudonym "Doleman" was chosen because of its "allusion to vir dolorum, therby to insinuate the griefe, and sorrow [the authors] fealt" at James's failure to convert to Catholicism (McCoog, "Harmony Disrupted," 197).

[103] Ibid. 426.   [104] *The Supplication of certaine Masse-Priestes*, C2ᵛ.

[105] See Brian P. Levack, *The Formation of the British State: England, Scotland and the Union, 1603–1707* (Oxford: Clarendon Press, 1987), 112.

itselfe."[106] It was English Catholics, though, who had the most to fear from Scottish Presbyterians intent on promoting their radical religious agenda south of the border through a "unioun of these kingdoms under one God and Christ, one king, one faith, one law."[107]

For some English Catholics, these fears appeared to have been realized in the first years of James's reign when greater toleration and the relaxation of penal laws they had expected from the new king failed to materialize. In this context of dashed hopes and Catholic resentment against the Scots, the Gunpowder plot took shape in 1605: had Guy Fawkes and his fellow plotters succeeded in their violent scheme, they would allegedly "have blown [all the Scots] back into Scotland" and immediately issued a proclamation against Anglo-Scottish union. Fawkes and his allies were also ready to replace James with one of his daughters who was still young enough to be raised an Anglicized Catholic.[108]

Persons, writing a few years earlier to the Scottish Earl of Angus, expressed a wish "to see both our realms united together under one Catholick governor and prince of our owne bloud."[109] Yet in the past when Persons and other English Catholics might have promoted the idea of a unified Catholic Britain they remained instead parochially Anglo-centric in outlook. For example, when advancing the claim to the English throne of Mary Stuart and James in the early 1580s, Persons and his allies could have exploited an available rhetoric of Britishness; yet English Catholics apparently did not conceive the claims of these Scottish princes in terms of a larger vision of Anglo-Scottish or British unity. Likewise, in *The Jesuit's memorial for the intended reformation of England*, Persons's blueprint for a future Catholic realm written in 1596, the emphasis is exclusively on the English nation.[110] Although Persons states in the preface that "what is

---

[106] *A conference about the next succession to the crowne*, 2: 123, 243. Spelman, "Of the Union," in Bruce R. Galloway and Brian P. Levack (eds.), *The Jacobean Union: Six Tracts of 1604* (Edinburgh: Scottish History Society, 1985), 176–7, lxviii–lxx. Also see Levack, *Formation of the British State*, 118–19.

[107] Quoted in Arthur H. Williamson, "From the Invention of Great Britain to the Creation of British History: A New Historiography," *Journal of British Studies* 29 (1990), 273. Williamson's source is David Calderwood, ed. *The History of the Kirk of Scotland* (Edinburgh, 1845), 6: 523.

[108] Jenny Wormald, "Gunpowder, Treason and Scots," *Journal of British Studies* 24 (1985), 161–2. Also see Bruce Galloway, *The Union of England and Scotland, 1603–1608* (Edinburgh: John Donald, 1986), 80; and Albert J. Loomie, SJ, *Guy Fawkes in Spain: The "Spanish Treason" in Spanish Documents* (Bulletin of the Institute of Historical Research, Special Supplement No. 9. Nov. 1971).

[109] Quoted in McCoog, "Harmony Disrupted," 207. Also see Michael E. Carrafiello, *Robert Persons and English Catholicism, 1580–1610* (London: Associated University Presses, 1998), 110.

[110] I quote from the first printed edition of the work issued by the Protestant Edward Gee with the title *The Jesuit's memorial for the intended reformation of England* in 1690 after the Catholic James II had been deposed. For further discussion, see J. J. Scarisbrick, "Robert Persons's Plans for the 'true' Reformation of England," in Neil McKendrick (ed.), *Historical Perspectives: Studies in English Thought and Society* (London: Europa Publications, 1974), 19–42; Carrafiello, *Robert Persons*, chs. 4–5; and Ronald Corthell, "Robert Persons and the Writer's Mission," in Arthur

said in this Treatise for the Kingdom of England, is meant also for Ireland, so far as it may do good," he actually pays scant attention to England's relations with Ireland or to the special problems of governing what historically was England's most intractable neighbor.[111] Likewise, Scotland is neither included in Persons's plans nor seen as having any special connection to England. Instead, the northern kingdom figures only as one among many "of our Neighbours oppressed or infected with Heresie, as namely, Denmark, divers parts near to us, of Germany, Poland, Gothland, Sweedland, Scotland, Muscovy, and the Isles of Zeland."[112] Finally, in an extraordinary elision of Celtic Catholicity, Persons ignores the lives and sufferings of Irish and Scottish recusants, mentioning only the "Executions of English Catholick Priests" sent to Scotland and Ireland—a sign, he believes, that God has chosen England to be a "Light and a Lantern to other Nations near unto it."[113] John Bossy, discussing these and other works of Persons, sees in them a "Greater English" theory of Catholic nationhood in which England alone was destined to lead the northern Counter-Reformation.[114]

During the lifetime of Mary Stuart some Scottish Catholics did appeal to the idea of a united Catholic Britain. John Leslie, the Scottish Bishop of Ross and Mary's roving ambassador on the Continent, first published his *A treatise touching the right, title, and interest of the most excellent princesse Marie, Queene of Scotland, and of the most noble King James, her graces sonne, to the succession of the croune of England* in 1569 after Mary's flight into England. When the book was republished in 1584, Leslie added "an exhortation to the English and Scottish nations, for uniting of themselves in a true league of Amitie." The title page also included the motto, "All Britain Yle (dissensions over past) in peace and faith, will growe to one at last," as well as a woodcut illustration depicting the figure

F. Marotti (ed.), *Catholicism and Anti-Catholicism in Early Modern English Texts* (New York: St Martin's Press, 1999), 48–56. Victor Houliston observes that much of *The Jesuit's memorial* is reprinted in Persons's *A manifestation of the great folly and bad spirit of certayne in England calling themselves secular priestes* (Antwerp, 1602. *ERL* 169), a work meant to reassure readers of its author's Englishness ("The Polemical Gravitas of Robert Persons," *Recusant History* 22 (1995), 294).

[111] *The Jesuit's memorial*, A3ʳ.
[112] Ibid. 150. In 1605, Persons prepared a report for the Holy See on the state of religion in Northern Europe generally. Persons appealed for papal intervention to help the "remote and much afflicted regions" that included England, Scotland, and Ireland, as well as Scandinavia, Muscovy, Germany, and Belgium. Persons left the method of converting these territories up to the pope, but suggested reviving "the Congregation of the Propagation of the Faith." Oskar Garstein, *Rome and the Counter-Reformation in Scandinavia*, vol. 2: *1583–1622* (Oslo: Universitetsforlaget, 1980), 263–4.
[113] *The Jesuit's memorial*, 3.
[114] "Catholicity and Nationality," 293. My argument is indebted throughout to Bossy's fascinating article. Bossy distinguishes between the "Greater-Englanders" like Persons and Richard Verstegan, and "Little-Englanders" like the secular Appellant priests whose defensive Englishness was accompanied by suspicion of the world beyond England (295).
English Jesuits like Persons may have been encouraged to formulate a specifically English vision, instead of developing an ideology of Catholicism that integrated the different parts of the Atlantic archipelago, by the Jesuit organization of its missions, vice-provinces, and provinces along parochial national lines. Thus the Vatican established Cardinal Protectors to look after the affairs of England, Scotland, and Ireland, but not to oversee British affairs as a whole.

Fig. 5. John Leslie, *A treatise towching the right, title, and interest of the most excel-lent princesse Mare, Queene of Scotland, and of the most noble King James, her graces sonne, to the succession of the croune of England* (np, 1584). STC 15507. Detail of title page.

of concord with English and Scottish soldiers shaking hands. Leslie generally plays down the idea that his version of a unified Britain would be Catholic in religion. In fact, only on the final page does he make it clear "that this dispersed people may be called together, under the regiment of one rightfull Prince, and Catholique religion of their auncestors."[115]

Leslie's harnessing of a discourse of union for a Catholic agenda does little to change the fact that by the later sixteenth century the language and imagery of Britain had become irrevocably linked with the Protestant cause in both England and Scotland. As Jane Dawson has shown, the discourse of British imperial union was first effectively appropriated for religious purposes by English and Scottish Protestant supporters of a marriage alliance between Edward VI and the young Mary Stuart—the so-called "Rough Wooing." When political initiatives like this failed, ideas of union and British identity were taken up by an unofficial Anglo-Scottish Protestant culture—one based upon a shared vernacular and the circulation of common religious texts including, preeminently, the Geneva Bible. At the imaginative center of that culture was the island of Britain, itself a political construct. God, so Protestants argued, had purposefully placed the Scots and English together on an island protected from Catholic Europe by a sea wall.[116] It was this myth of Britain as a self-enclosed world, a sanctuary for beleaguered Protestantism, that ran contrary to everything for which Persons and his supporters worked. Their objective was to reinscribe England—a country not self-contained but "situated almost out of the world"—on a map whose center

[115] *A treatise towching the right*, Title Page, 62–71, 71ʳ.
[116] Dawson, "Anglo-Scottish Protestant Culture," esp. 103–10. On the so-called "Rough Woo-ing" of Mary and Edward, see Mason, "The Scottish Reformation," 169–70.

was at Rome.[117] For Persons and many English exiles, the only union worth pursuing was the alternative "union of the general and universal Catholic Church and faith."[118]

Even as they privileged England over larger archipelagic concerns, English Catholics realized that their country's conversion required a strategy that included the broader Anglo-Celtic frontier.[119] In the decade before the execution of Mary Queen of Scots, militant English Catholics planned a "Celtic strategy" for the liberation of their homeland. Persons identified several regions that "as time went on would be best able to further our cause." These included "Wales, a region of wide and ample spaces, which was not so hostile to the Catholic religion but yet, owing to the lack of labourers, had sunk into a state of dense ignorance." Persons also mentioned Cambridgeshire and the Anglo-Scottish borders, but the crucial region was Scotland itself, "on which country depends the conversion not only of England but of all the lands in the North."[120] Throughout the 1580s, Persons and Allen focused their attention on Scotland: promoting the claim of Mary Queen of Scots to the English throne, converting her son, James Stuart, to Catholicism, and planning a military expedition that would pass from Spain to England via Scotland.[121] A Scottish enterprise was close to realization in 1582, when a group led by Persons and Allen met in Paris to coordinate plans with the Duke of Guise (leader of the militant French Catholic League). The ringleaders drafted a memorial asking the pope and the king of Spain for "eight thousand infantrymen" and money to support an army for six to eight months, supposedly long enough to pass through Scotland to London and to overthrow a queen who they claimed "has come to be hated by everybody."[122] The memorial's appraisal of possible opposition was very much the fantasy of exiles grown out-of-touch with political realities: Scots and English would overwhelmingly rally to the Catholic side (the English population was supposedly two-thirds Catholic), while "large and wealthy cities on the route, such as Newcastle, [and] York ... will surrender to the army without drawing the sword." In an ironic fusion of the circumstances surrounding the advent of Tudor rule in England with that same dynasty's supposed imminent demise, the petitioners claimed that their scheme

---

[117] John Wilson, *English martyrologe*, *1ᵛ.

[118] Quoted in Carrafiello, *Robert Persons*, 110. Also see Persons's, *A treatise of three conversions*, 304: 217. Willy Maley describes the "British project" as articulated by Bacon and other early 17th-century Protestants, as "on one level, an alternative to the continent, an attempt to establish 'another Europe'" ("'Another Britain'?: Bacon's *Certain Considerations Touching the Plantation in Ireland* (1609)," *Prose Studies* 18 (1995), 10.

[119] On the formation of the English mission and its anomalous status within the Jesuit organizational structure, see Thomas M. McCoog, SJ, "Establishment of the English Province of the Society of Jesus," *Recusant History* 17 (1984), 121–39.

[120] Persons, *Letters and Memorials*, 108–9.

[121] See McCoog, *The Society of Jesus*, ch. 5, "On the Conversion of Scotland," 178–223.

[122] Persons, *Letters and Memorials*, 163, 161; "The Memoirs of Father Robert Persons," 30–2 for an account of the meeting. Also see McCoog, *The Society of Jesus*, 187.

would approximate "the victory won by Henry, Earl of Richmond ... who with a very small band of men got possession of the kingdom through having a little inside information."[123]

Although centered on Scotland, the confederacy's enterprise had a broader transnational dimension. Persons wanted Owen Lewis, Maurice Clenock's former assistant at the English College, Rome, and now Archdeacon of Cambray, to accompany the enterprise in order to encourage "the Welsh, his countrymen. [Lewis] will be able to give considerable assistance in this affair ... on account of the great love [the Welsh] bear to the Catholic faith." Others urged that rebellion should also be stirred in Ireland.[124] Yet possibilities of an encompassing archipelagic Catholic solidarity were again threatened by endemic national and ethnic rivalries. According to Persons, a major obstacle facing the mission in late 1582 was "a natural jealousy between the two nations of Scotland and England." To offset this distrust, Persons urged "that whenever orders or other things come from his Holiness the two nations are treated as being exactly on the same footing; and this will be the case if the English see that Mr. Allen, or some such other Englishman ... is associated as representing England, with the most Reverend Archbishop of Glasgow as representing Scotland."[125] By 1584, however, Allen altogether rejected the idea of landing a force in Scotland, fearful that a Catholic army descending upon England from north of the border would be mistaken by potentially sympathetic English Catholics as a hostile Scottish force bent on "subjecting the English to the Scottish rule. And if once this doubt is injected, it is to be feared that the invading army will not only have the heretics for enemies, but also the catholics who will suspect everything from an army marching on them from Scotland."[126] Once again, national allegiances were seen as more powerful than religious solidarities.

BEYOND 1603: RICHARD VERSTEGAN'S *A RESTITUTION OF DECAYED INTELLIGENCE: IN ANTIQUITIES* AND ALTERNATIVE CATHOLIC UNIONS

Catholics uneasy with a Scottish succession and the idea of Anglo-Scottish union produced various kinds of texts both before and after James's accession.

[123] Persons, *Letters and Memorials*, 163, 162.
[124] Ibid. *Letters and Memorials of William Cardinal Allen*, xxxvi.
[125] Persons, *Letters and Memorials*, 147–8. Sanders had earlier foreseen such rivalries, and urged that "The honourable Nuncio should be an Italian, lest Englishmen might be indignant at an Irishman being preferred before them, or *vice versa*, and the same reasoning applies also to the Scots" ("Some Letters and Papers of Nicolas Sander 1562–80," in *Miscellanea XIII*, Catholic Record Society 26 (London, 1926), 17).
[126] *Letters and Memorials of William Cardinal Allen*, lxvi.

In Antwerp, Richard Stanihurst, an Old English Catholic exile from Ireland, collaborated on a now lost work, *Beware of the Northern Gate* (1598), that his adversaries called a " 'Brickbat' against James's title."[127] Another anonymous Catholic work, the Latin *Prurit-anus* (1609) described James's Scottish courtiers "as a barbarous people . . . and likened [them] to the locusts who devoured everything in Pharoah's Egypt."[128] Other Catholic writers registered their misgivings in more oblique ways and in less polemical genres, including the discourse of antiquarianism that in the early modern period was complexly implicated in Reformation and Counter-Reformation political culture.[129]

A landmark contribution to this discourse was Richard Verstegan's *A restitution of decayed intelligence: in antiquities* (1605), a work "Printed at Antwerp by Robert Bruney . . . And to be sold at London in Paules-Churchyeard, by John Norton and John Bill."[130] Verstegan, the English-born grandson of Dutch immigrants, was educated at Oxford where he rejected the Elizabethan religious settlement. After his illegal Catholic press was discovered by the authorities, he fled the country, spending time in Paris and Rome before settling in Antwerp in 1586–7 where he established himself until his death in 1640 as a producer and disseminator of Catholic literature and news.[131] *A restitution* seemed to signal a change of course in the career of its zealous Catholic author whose publications under Elizabeth had included illustrated Catholic martyrologies and polemical pamphlet attacks on the English government; Verstegan had also played an important role in the planning and editing of *A conference about the next succession*.[132] Verstegan's latest tome, however, far from abandoning the

---

[127]   Albert J. Loomie, SJ, "Richard Stanyhurst in Spain: Two Unknown Letters of August 1593," *Huntington Library Quarterly* 28 (1969) 149–50; Colm Lennon, *Richard Stanihurst the Dubliner 1547–1618* (Dublin: Irish Academic Press, 1981), 50–1.

[128]   Harris, "The Reports of William Udall," 203, 243. AR 1: 44–5.

[129]   Anthony Low, "Recent Studies in the English Renaissance," *Studies in English Literature 1500–1900* 37 (1997), 218. Also, Joseph M. Levine observes that "almost all [early modern] antiquarian study was ancillary to some other purpose: either to classical imitation or to religion and politics" (*Humanism and History: Origins of Modern English Historiography* (Ithaca, NY: Cornell University Press, 1987), 99).

[130]   *A restitution*, Title Page (*ERL* 323).

[131]   Christopher Highley, "Richard Verstegan's Book of Martyrs," in Highley and King (eds.), *John Foxe and his World*, 183–97.

[132]   For a comprehensive study of Verstegan's life and career, see Paul Arblaster, *Antwerp and the World: Richard Verstegan and the International Culture of Catholic Reformation* (Leuven University Press, 2004). On Verstegan's contributions to *A conference*, also see A. G. Petti, "A Bibliography of the Writings of Richard Verstegan (c.1550–1641)," *Recusant History* 7 (1963), 96; Southern, *Elizabethan Recusant Prose*, 351; Joel Hurstfield, "The Succession Struggle in Late Elizabethan England," in S. T. Bindoff, J. Hurstfield, and C. H. Williams (eds.), *Elizabethan Government and Society* (London: Athlone Press, 1961), 369–96. Anthony Petti thinks that Verstegan was also the joint author of a lost, "probably unpublished" pamphlet "against the nobles of the Scottish party" (1596) ("Bibliography," 98).

confessional agenda of these earlier works merely re-articulated it in a different, more indirect and abstruse, register.[133]

A restitution's thesis about national origins was simple, yet, at the time, startling: the English people were descended from the Germanic Saxons, and, contrary to frequent claims, were unrelated to the ancient Britons.[134] Although Bede and Polydore Vergil in his *Anglia Historia* (1534) had lodged similar arguments, for a work of 1605 to discard so thoroughly the alleged British heritage of the English must have seemed especially provocative given the aura of Britishness surrounding the new king. James's accession inspired a welter of genealogies, poems, and other tributes attesting to his British and Welsh blood and linking him to the Galfridian heroes Brut and Arthur.[135] The appearance of *A restitution* in these circumstances raises the same question that John Chamberlain had asked in 1599 of another perplexing work, John Hayward's *The first part of the life and raigne of King Henrie the IIII* (1599): "why such a storie shold come out at this time [?]"[136] In seeking answers, we should remember that antiquarian works are as much about the present as the past, and that like all texts their meanings are not fixed but contingent—as the cultural circumstances surrounding the production and reception of texts change, so texts accrue new meanings. Thus, whatever motives underlay Verstegan's original research for the project—which may have begun as early as the 1570s—in 1605 *A restitution*'s antiquarian arguments would have resonated in a cultural landscape dominated by a new Scottish king, by his plan for union, and by the resulting "speculation about the nature of England."[137]

Verstegan's fulsome dedication of the book to James, "King of Great Britain, France, and Ireland", hardly suggests an oppositional stance toward either the king or his cherished union scheme. Indeed, the work's dedication along with its seemingly apolitical subject matter were probably what allowed it to be legally imported and sold in England. Verstegan's dedicatory gesture of support for James is perhaps evidence of tentative confidence among Catholics before

---

[133] Donna Hamilton, "Richard Verstegan's *A Restitution of Decayed Intelligence* (1605): A Catholic Antiquarian Replies to John Foxe, Thomas Cooper, and Jean Bodin," *Prose Studies* 22 (1999), 1–38.

[134] On the tendency of English historians to conflate Britons and Saxons, see Mason, "The Scottish Reformation"; Hugh McDougall, *Racial Myth in English History: Trojans, Teutons, and Anglo-Saxons* (London: University Press of New England, 1982).

[135] Curtis Perry, *The Making of Jacobean Culture: James I and the Renegotiation of Elizabethan Literary Practice* (Cambridge: Cambridge University Press, 1997).

[136] *Letters of John Chamberlain*, ed. Norman McLure, 2 vols. (Philadelphia, 1939), 1: 70.

[137] Graham Parry suggests that Verstegan may have begun work on *A restitution* during his student days at Oxford in the early 1570s when Matthew Parker and other Protestants were busy collecting and studying Anglo-Saxon documents in order to lend historical legitimacy to the reformed faith (*The Trophies of Time: English Antiquarians of the Seventeenth Century* (Oxford: Oxford University Press, 1995), 51–2); Arblaster, *Antwerp and the World*, 85–93. On early Protestant scholarship about the Saxons, see Frantzen, *Desire for Origins*, 35–50; and T. D. Kendrick, *British Antiquity* (London: Methuen, 1950), 115–16.

the Gunpowder Plot of November 1605 that, while the new king might not return England to the Old Faith, he would at least relax the draconian anti-Catholic penal code of the late queen.[138] For Verstegan and his co-religionists, there was cause for cautious optimism in James's reverence for the memory of his "martyred" mother, Mary, whom the would-be king of Great Britain was planning to rebury in a grand new tomb in Westminster Abbey.[139]

If James had read beyond the work's dedication, however, he could hardly have been pleased by Verstegan's arguments. James's own pronouncements, along with the many propaganda pieces by his admirers and suitors, portrayed him predominantly in terms of the British, not the Saxon, past. Anthony Munday developed the conceit in his 1605 mayoral show, *The triumphes of re-united Britania*, that James's accession meant a reversal of the divisive legacy of the legendary Brut. As a result of James's "happye comming to the Crowne, *England*, *Wales*, and *Scotland*, by the first *Brute* severed and divided, . . . [are] reunited, and made one happy *Britania* again."[140]

With its Saxon-centered perspective, Verstegan's work virtually discards this British past and its heroes like Brut and King Arthur (another type for James in contemporary propaganda), whose twenty six-year reign receives one sentence in *A restitution*. As a Catholic, Verstegan's indifference to the British history, with its emphasis on a politically unified archipelago, reflects an awareness that by the early seventeenth century, as we have seen, the rhetoric of Britishness had been firmly claimed by Protestants. After the emergence of a common Anglo-Scottish Protestant culture during the reign of Edward VI—and its subsequent consolidation with the victory of the Congregation party in

---

[138] See Robert Peters, "Some Catholic Opinions of King James VI and I," *Recusant History* 10 (1970), 292–303. Also see, Hamilton, "Richard Verstegan's *A Restitution*," 24; Philip Caraman, *Henry Garnet, 1555–1606 and the Gunpowder Plot* (London: Longmans, 1964), 308. On James and the promised toleration of Catholics, also see Antonia Fraser, *Faith and Treason: The Story of the Gunpowder Plot* (New York: Doubleday, 1996), 88–9. On the history of recusancy legislation under James, see John J. La Rocca, " 'Who Can't Pray with Me, Can't Love Me': Toleration and the Early Jacobean Recusancy Policy," *Journal of British Studies* 23 (1984), 22–36.

[139] See Parry, *Trophies of Time*, 50. Verstegan regarded Mary as a Catholic martyr of singular importance (see Anthony G. Petti, "Richard Verstegan and Catholic Martyrologies of the Later Elizabethan Period," *Recusant History* 5 (1959), 78–81). On Mary Stuart's second resting place, see Julia M. Walker, *The Elizabeth Icon, 1603–2003* (London: MacMillan, 2004), 26–33. Verstegan described James as "a man lyke to condescend to any thing whereby he may please our state [i.e. the English government] or procure himself mony: a man irresolute in any thing, mutable in his favours, of no religion but for advantage" (*The Letters and Despatches of Richard Verstegan, c.1550–1640*, ed. A. G. Petti. Catholic Record Society, 52 (London, 1959), 164).

[140] *Pageants and Entertainments of Anthony Munday*, ed. David M. Bergeron (London: Garland, 1985), 7. James's accession was greeted enthusiastically by many Catholics in Ireland who constructed an Irish genealogy for him. The Irish bards derived one branch of his ancestors "from the Ulster King Fergus, the first Irish King of Scotland," and another branch from "Corc, the fifth-century king of Munster" (Breandán ó Buachalla, " 'James our True King': The Ideology of Irish Royalism in the Seventeenth Century," in D. George Boyce, Robert Eccleshall, and Vincent Geoghegan (eds.), *Political Thought in Ireland Since the Seventeenth Century* (London: Routledge, 1993), 11).

Scotland—Protestant writers on both sides of the border had seized on Britain's status as a self-contained island once inhabited by an ancient people to promote their vision of fuller integration between England and Scotland, including the formation of a Protestant British empire. In his unionist *Exhortation* (1547), Scotsman James Henrisoun argued the feasibility of a unified Protestant British empire on the basis of the racial identity of Scots and English—both peoples, he claimed, retaining in themselves "the bloud and generacion" of the original Britons.[141]

If, then, by 1605 Verstegan was prompted by the strong Protestant valencies of the British past to explore alternative genealogies for the English, his advocacy of a Saxon lineage was no innocent choice but one fully informed by a Counter-Reformation vision. In privileging the Saxon moment, Verstegan aligns *A restitution* with the work that English Catholics, as we have seen, considered the most significant account of their nation's past: Bede's *The history of the church of Englande*. Indeed, Bede is invoked throughout *A restitution* as a major authority, especially around the account of that seminal event in the history of English Catholicism: Augustine's "first bringing of the faith of Christ unto Englishmen"—an event that Catholics regarded as sealing an irrevocable connection between England and Rome and that Protestants saw as corrupting an earlier apostolic Christianity. Verstegan's book mirrors Stapleton's edition of Bede in underscoring the significance of the Augustinian moment by including a woodcut that shows the newly-arrived Augustine preaching to Ethelbert, King of Kent.[142]

Readers of *A restitution* who compared Verstegan's account of the English people's Saxon roots with the commonplace narratives of King James's British ancestry were no doubt struck by an ethnic divide separating the ruler from his new subjects. In the work's dedication, Verstegan partly negotiates this worrying disjunction by finding in James traces of English blood, the king having "descended of the chiefest blood royall of our ancient English-Saxon kings"—a claim also lodged by other antiquarian writers like Robert Cotton in his "A Discourse of ye Descent of the K's Mty from the Saxons."[143] Such genealogies helped to Anglicize James by subordinating all that was disturbingly Scottish and alien about him to his essential links with an English royal line. James had his own strategies for Anglicizing and thus authorizing his cultural identity to a suspicious public, including publishing at the beginning of his new reign an "Englished" version of his manual on kingship, *Basilikon doron*—a work that he had originally composed in middle Scots.[144]

---

[141] Quoted in Mason, "The Scottish Reformation," 171–2.

[142] Verstegan, *A restitution*, 143–4.

[143] Ibid. †2r; Kevin Sharpe, *Sir Robert Cotton 1586–1631: History and Politics in Early Modern England* (Oxford: Oxford University Press, 1979), 114–15.

[144] Jenny Wormald, "James VI and I, *Basilikon Doron* and *The Trew Law of Free Monarchies*: The Scottish Context and the English Translation," in Linda Levy Peck (ed.), *The Mental World of the*

Fig. 6. Richard Verstegan, *A restitution of decayed intelligence: In antiquities.: Concerning the most noble and renovvmed [sic] English nation* (Antwerp, 1634), p. 144.

But if Verstegan's work attempts in a minimal way to assimilate James as a nominal Saxon-Englishman, it is less committed to incorporating his Scottish subjects. Indeed, following the accession of James, English anxieties revolved not so much around a Scottish monarch *per se*, as around the coterie of Scots with which James surrounded himself in England. Neil Cuddy explains that when James planned his new court in 1603 he judiciously included an equal number

Jacobean Court (Cambridge: Cambridge University Press, 1991), 36–54. See also Patricia Fumerton, "Subdiscourse: Jonson Speaking Low," *English Literary Renaissance* 25 (1995), 76–7.

of English and Scottish courtiers in his Outer and Privy Chambers, as a sort
of emblem of his commitment to the "union of hearts and hands." "But here,"
observes Cuddy,

James drew the line. If the Outer and Privy Chambers were to be visible embodiments of
even-handed Union, James's new bedchamber...which now took over the whole of the
king's practical body service and turned the formerly important English Privy Chamber
into an outer reception room, was to be an entirely Scottish preserve. The Scots who
transferred from the Edinburgh Chamber to the London Bedchamber were all James's
trusted agents and familiar companions.[145]

English observers, as well as noting the Scottish monopoly of the bedchamber,
were aware of the intrusion of Scots "into the king's household, the cellar,
the buttery, the pantry, the larder, the bakehouse, [and] the kitchen," where
they received "'the like wages' to those of English yeomen and grooms and
serjeants."[146] Englishmen had even more to fear if James proved successful in
persuading parliament to endorse a "perfect union" that went beyond the simple
union of the crowns to include "unity in outward marks of government" and the
adoption of a new royal style. If union were pursued and achieved in the areas of
law, trade, offices, and religion, then the influx of large numbers of "naturalized"
Scots into England would be all but assured.

   By insisting upon the distinctive racial purity of the Saxons, Verstegan's *A
restitution* implicitly sets itself against the threat of Scottish immigration and
the feared pollution of English-Saxon racial stock. Tracing the emergence of the
Saxons to their Germanic forebears, Verstegan notes the remarkable success of
the Germanic people in protecting their racial integrity by resisting intermarriage
and conquest: "they were never subdued by any [,]... have ever kept themselves
unmixed with forrain people [,]...And for their further honor...they have not
only bin the ever keepers of their own countrey...but many moste warlyke
troops have gon out of Germanie, and taken possession in all the best countries
of Europe, where their offspring even to this day remaineth." Thus, the Saxons,
when they took possession of Britain, instead of marrying the indigenous people,
banished them to the western wilderness.[147]

   Verstegan asserts the continuity and homogeneity of Saxon racial identity by
arguing that the Danes and Normans who later mingled with the Saxons were not

---

[145] "Anglo-Scottish Union and the Court of James I, 1603–1625," *Transactions of the Royal
Historical Society* 5th ser. 39 (1989), 110.

[146] Jenny Wormald, "The Union of 1603," in Mason (ed.), *Scots and Britons*, 33. Also see Bruce
R. Galloway and Brian P. Levack (eds.), *The Jacobean Union: Six Tracts of 1603* (Edinburgh: Scottish
History Society, 1985), xiv. For details of anti-Scottish feelings in London, see Fraser, *Faith and
Treason*, 88.

[147] *A restitution*, 43.

racially Other but essentially the same, scions of an original Germanic whole.[148]
Yet when Verstegan turns to the origins of the Scottish people and their relation
to an original Germanic Ur-race, he expresses uncertainty:

The Scotishmen yf originally they came out of Scythia (as some of their own authors
affirme) and so take the name of Scottes or Scyttes . . . then in all lykelyhood was it from
the German Scythia, whereof some do accompt a parte of Denmark also to have bin, and
seeking new habitation might passe over to the Orcades, and coasting down southerly
along by the shore of Ireland, crosse over into Cantabria: and from thence (in some tyme
after) come into Ireland. This I say must bee presumed, yf rejecting the tale of Scota wee
accord unto such authors, as wil bring them from Scythia into Spaine, from whence it is
held they came into Ireland, and so into Scotland.

If Verstegan acknowledges an affinity between the Scots and the "English-Saxons"
in terms of their common territorial link to a German homeland ("the great &
spatious country of Germanie"), he notably fails to assert the same degree of
kinship and compatibility between the two peoples that he does between the
"English-Saxons" and the Normans or Danes.[149]
   Verstegan's ambiguous account of Scottish origins and his reluctance to posit
connections between the Scots and "English-Saxons" recalls arguments about
the antipathy between the two peoples in *A conference about the next succession to
the crowne of Ingland*. The authors of that work assert "the aversion and natural
alienation of [the Scots] from the Inglish," an alienation that was seen as deriving
in part from the perceived racial proximity of Scots and Irish.[150] Assertions of an
innate sympathy between Scots and Irish were again heard during the union
debate; the Protestant Englishman Sir Henry Spelman remarked, for instance,
that only limited English union with Scotland was possible because the Scots'
"manners and language, though in parte often resemble us, yet the greatest parte
concurres with the naturall Irishe, embracing their mariages and customes in that
respect and the unfitter also to be united."[151]

---

[148] "The Danes and the Normannes were once one same people with the Germans, as were also
the Saxons; & wee not to bee accompted mixed by having only some such joyned unto us againe,
as somtyme had one same language and one same originall with us" (*A restitution*, 187).
[149] Ibid. 114, 156.   [150] *A Conference about the next succession to the crowne*, 2: 118.
[151] "Of the Union," in Galloway and Levack (eds.), *The Jacobean Union*, 180–1. Even as Spelman
emphasizes the links between Scotland and Ireland, however, he recognizes that "the inhabitantes
of the lower parte of Scotland, which they calle Lawlandmen, to be discended of our auncestors
the Inglesh Saxones as well as ourselves, and from them to have received the semblance of language
which we and they doe now participate" (166). Verstegan likewise explains that after the Norman
invasion the royal family and nobility of England sought refuge with King Malcolm of Scotland,
where, eventually, "English became the language of all the south parte . . . the Irish before that having
bin the generall language of that whole countrey" (*A restitution*, 180).
  Far from alleviating anxieties about the racial Otherness of James and his Scottish followers
in 1603–4, however, such accounts of an 11th-century English influx into Scotland and of the
consequent transformation of the indigenous culture, may have highlighted the profound effects

Of all the groups that took an interest in the issue of Anglo-Scottish union, Verstegan and his fellow Catholics perhaps had the most to fear, especially from the prospect of closer religious ties between the two countries in the event of a "perfect union."[152] Catholics therefore needed to construct an alternative identity for England that looked backward in time to before the Reformation, and southward in space to the great Catholic powers of Europe and their collective center in Rome. Verstegan's Bedean account of Augustine's mission from Rome to convert the peoples of Britain does just this, but so too, albeit in a more oblique way, do Verstegan's geological speculations about the origin of the landmass he calls "Albion." Highlighting "the neernes of land betweene *England* and *France*," and the similar topography of their respective coastlines, Verstegan argues for "a conjunction in tyme long past, to have bin between these two countries; whereby men did passe on dry land from the one unto the other, as it were over a bridge or *Isthmus* of land." Verstegan's theory of continental drift displaces a modern union *within* Britain with a much grander historic union to the south in which "Albion" is seen as part of a now fragmented European whole—"the mayn continent of the world."[153] If this effort at reimagining England's religio-spatial coordinates seems like the fantasy of a Catholic exile wishing to reconceive his absent "home," we should remember that much of the energy of English Catholic exiles during this period was similarly devoted to the principle of reconnection—a reconnection being made, for example, in the steady circulation of Catholic books, devotional paraphernalia, and missionary priests between England and the Continent.

As King James promoted his vision of a Protestant empire of Great Britain that could dissolve ancient enmities between English, Scots, Welsh, and Irish, his Catholic adversaries clung to an alternative imperial ideal of a reunited Christendom. Ironically, James too on occasion appealed for the reunion of Christendom, an ideal he thought could be achieved via a holy war against the Turkish infidel. James was willing to reach out to "moderate" Catholic princes but

that strangers could have upon a dominant culture. Spelman has little doubt that in the event of a complete union, the Scots would overrun England, "interlac[ing]" themselves "with the English in all places." "The English ar our family; shall we then give awaye their breadde, which is their freedomes and libertyes, unto straungers? ... But our houses, our landes, our lyvinges shall by that meanes be boughte upp in all places. The citty and cuntry shal be replenisshed with Scottes. The Courte shall abounde with them not as passingers but as commorantes" (175–6).

[152] Spelman, "Of the Union," 176–7. Also see Levack, *Formation of the British State*, 118–19.

[153] *A restitution*, 97, 98. Also see Mark Netzloff, "The English Colleges and the English Nation: Allen, Persons, Verstegan, and Diasporic Nationalism," in Ronald Corthell, Frances E. Dolan, Christopher Highley, and Arthur F. Marotti (eds.), *Catholic Culture in Early Modern England* (Notre Dame, Ind.: University of Notre Dame Press, 2007), 258 n. 52. At the very least, Verstegan's theories of continental drift would have made it harder for English men and women to talk so confidently about the insular, autonomous nature of Britain, as if it were a world unto itself, specially set apart by God as the bastion of the reformed faith.

not to the pope or to militant Catholic orders like the Jesuits.[154] In this context, the "British problem" that confronted English Catholics was not just a matter of negotiating an identity for themselves amid pressures from their Welsh and Scottish co-religionists, but of figuring out how best to use emerging concepts of geo-political power to their advantage.

[154] W. B. Patterson, *King James VI and I and the Reunion of Christendom* (Cambridge: Cambridge University Press, 1997), 49–50, 96. Franklin L. Baumer, "England, the Turk, and the Common Corps of Christendom," *The American Historical Review* 50.1 (1944), 43–8.

5

English Catholics and Ireland

As we saw in the previous chapter, Thomas Stapleton's edition of Bede's *The history of the church of Englande* helped shape English Catholic perceptions of the various peoples of the Atlantic archipelago. Stapleton, I claimed, co-opted Bede to promote a deeply Anglocentric view of the past that depicted the Anglo-Saxons, the *gens Anglorum*, as God's chosen people—a view that involved an implicit rejection of Celtic Christian traditions. Whereas Bede singles out the Britons (Welsh) as especially resistant to the divinely ordained mission of the English, he shows the Irish (*Scotti*) playing a more positive role in the consolidation of a *gens Anglorum*. Bede describes Ireland as a mild and fertile place "rich in milk and hony," home to "a harmlesse seely people, which had ever bene great frinds to the english nation."[1] In particular, Bede commends the Irish for preaching the gospel to the English—something the Britons had conspicuously refused to do and for which they incur divine displeasure. Because of his positive vision of the Irish, Bede—who "had long been available in Irish translation"— was exempt from the kind of ire that later champions of Ireland's early history like Geoffrey Keating directed especially at Gerald of Wales's negative representations of their country.[2]

In fact, early modern Catholic writers from Ireland themselves drew upon Bede, a "holie sainct of the english nation," in narratives about their own country's religious identity. In *A mnemosynum or memoriall to the afflicted Catholickes in Irelande* (np, 1606. *ERL* 129), the Old English priest John Copinger relies heavily on Stapleton's version of Bede's *The history of the church of Englande* to illuminate Ireland's historical relationship to "mainland" Britain and in so

---

[1] Bede says this about the Irish people who are "miserably spoyled and destroyed" by the invading armies of Ecgfrith, King of Northumbria (*The history of the church of Englande* (Antwerp, 1565. *ERL*, 162), 14ᵛ, 145ʳ). See T. M. Charles Edwards, "Bede, the Irish, and the Britons," *Celtica* 15 (1983), 42–52.

[2] Bernadette Cunningham, *The World of Geoffrey Keating: History, Myth and Religion in Seventeenth-Century Ireland* (Dublin: Four Courts Press, 2000), 93. An Old Irish version of the *Ecclesiastical History* may have existed as early as Alfred's reign (H. E. J Cowdrey, "Bede and the 'English People,'" *Journal of Religious History* 11 (1981), 521). On Gerald's views of Ireland, see John Gillingham, "The English Invasion of Ireland," in Brendan Bradshaw, Andrew Hadfield, and Willy Maley (eds.), *Representing Ireland: Literature and the Origins of Conflict, 1534–1660* (Cambridge: Cambridge University Press, 1993), 24–42.

doing reverses the ideological thrust of Stapleton's project.[3] Copinger uses passages that in Stapleton's translation are subsumed within an overarching Anglocentric narrative to establish Ireland's religious preeminence over England. For example, Copinger relates that when "Finan and Colman were bishops" in Ireland, "many noble and meane people" came over from England "for obtaininge of divine knowledge and for embracing a continent life: some did enter into religion…others did labour to get and purchase knowledge, and science, for whom Irishmen most gladlie erected seminaries furnishing them with books, and all other necessaries for their purpose without money or rewarde."[4] Copinger uses Bede to construct Ireland as an isle of saints and scholars that welcomes immigrants from England desiring the life of piety or learning. Such hospitality, Copinger concludes, demonstrates "the charitie of Ireland towards Englishmen."[5]

Like Copinger, the Dublin-born Jesuit Henry Fitzsimon invokes Bede as a friendly source in his account of Ireland's past in *A Catholike confutation of M. John Riders clayme of antiquitie* (Dovai 1608. *ERL* 182). In the dedication addressed to his "Countrymen Catholicks," Fitzsimon refutes the charge of the Protestant Bishop of Dublin, John Rider, that Ireland's earliest Christianity had looked more Protestant than Catholic. Fitzsimon argues in response that the earliest Christian missionaries to Ireland had established a distinctively Catholic religion, with devotion to the cross, the erection of religious houses, and the prizing of virginity. Bede's testimony is essential to Fitzsimon's claims that the form of Christianity practiced in contemporary Ireland had not "degenerat[ed]" from its ancient original.[6] Fitzsimon cites Bede's account of the Irish missionaries who had spread "the truth" across Britain and Europe, evangelizing and establishing educational centers like the University of Paris.[7] Even as the Irish took religion to others, Fitzsimon claims, so Ireland became a destination for foreigners seeking education or the contemplative life. The Irish had even built a seminary in County Mayo especially for students from England.[8]

While Bede is an important authority in helping Fitzsimon to demonstrate Ireland's spiritual preeminence over England and surrounding countries, *The history of the church of Englande* has nothing to contribute to a central element in Fitzsimon's argument—the mission of St Patrick to Ireland.[9] Bede says nothing about Patrick, whose mission to Ireland predated Augustine's mission to the

---

[3] Copinger, *A mnemosynum*, 236. On Copinger see my "John Copinger and the Counter-Reformation: The Writings of a Forgotten Exile from Ireland," *Prose Studies*, 24 (2002), 1–14.

[4] Copinger, *A mnemosynum*, 258–60.   [5] Ibid. 260.

[6] *A Catholike confutation*, e2ᵛ, a3ᵛ.   [7] Ibid. e2ᵛ.   [8] Ibid. a4ᵛ.

[9] Ibid. e3ʳ. Fitzsimon refutes St Jerome's claim that Ireland was barbarous by quoting other authorities who say that Ireland "excelled all neighbour nations" in Christian devotion, even though it lacked the laws of other nations. In Ireland, religion and civil order are on different temporal tracks. And in Fitzsimon's view, even if there were barbarism , it did not diminish the piety of the Irish.

Britons by more than a century. For Fitzsimon, it is ultimately St Patrick's success in achieving the "universal conversion" of a "stiff-necked people" like the Irish that makes Ireland ("the Occidental Britanie") "a wonder . . . incomparable above all other nations."[10]

If Bede offered readers an image of the deep religiosity of the Irish people, he also offered a far more problematic portrait of the orthodoxy of the Irish Church. While Stapleton's edition of Bede advertised the extraordinary piety and charity of the people of Ireland, it also called into question the institutional legitimacy of the Irish Church, particularly in the account of the famous Synod of Whitby.[11] Presided over by Oswiu, king of the Northumbrians, the Synod adjudicates questions of ecclesiastical discipline, including the correct date of Easter and the proper form of tonsuring. The controversy pits representatives of the Irish Church who celebrate Easter according to one calculation against representatives of the "universal" Roman Church—newly embraced by the Anglo-Saxons—who celebrate it differently. After some testy exchanges between the spokesmen of the two camps, Colman and Wilfrid, King Oswiu condemns the Irish forms of Easter worship and tonsuring.[12] At one stroke, Ireland's religious traditions, as observed by the country's fathers like St Columba, are rejected. Most of the Irish clergy willingly renounce their "unperfectenesse" in favor of approved Catholic practices, thus signaling the demise of a semi-autonomous Irish Church with its own indigenous traditions. Ireland, this "smal corner of the uttermost ilond of the earth," becomes absorbed into the universal structures of Roman Christendom.[13]

From an early date, Irish intellectuals recognized that Bede's account of the Synod of Whitby damaged their religious self-image and so was best ignored. Thus when Bede's history was translated into Middle Irish some time between the ninth and tenth centuries, all references to the alleged heresies of the Irish Church were omitted.[14] But while later Catholics from Ireland like Copinger and Fitzsimon concentrated on what Bede had to say about the religiosity of the people of Ireland, English Catholics insisted on drawing attention to the outcome of the Synod of Whitby to show that a Roman, Anglo-Saxon Catholicity had ultimately triumphed over its Irish counterpart. Robert Persons, for instance, reminded readers of *A treatise of three conversions of England* that the Easter heresy had mostly infected the Irish.[15]

The ethnic tensions that simmer just beneath the surface of Bede's account of the Synod of Whitby are evident a few chapters later when Colman— the defeated representative of the Irish lobby—establishes a monastery off the

[10] Ibid. a2^v, a3^r.   [11] I owe this point to Nicholas Howe.

[12] Edward James, "Bede and the Tonsure Question," *Peritia* 3 (1984), 85–98.

[13] *The history of the church of Englande*, 102^v–106^v.

[14] Proinseas Ni Chathain, "Bede's Ecclesiastical History in Irish," *Peritia* 3 (1984), 115–30.

[15] *A treatise of three conversions of England from paganisme to Christian religion* (St Omers, 1605. ERL 304–6), 49, 52.

coast of Ireland designed to allow Irish and English monks to live together.[16] This attempt at ethnic rapprochement, however, is short lived because the two "nations" "cowld not agree together, for that the Scottes [i.e. Irish] in somer tyme when harvest was getting in, wold leave the monasteries and go wander abrode in places of their acquayntaunce, and then at winter wold come againe and require to enjoy in common such thinges as the english men had provided and layed up." Colman's solution to the "discord" caused by the different cultural habits of the English and Irish is to move the English monks off the island and into their own monastery.[17]

Bede's account of the separation of English and Irish monks foreshadows the segregation of Catholic students from early modern England and Ireland that usually occurred in Continental exile. Although exiles from Ireland found an early refuge in William Allen's English seminary in Douai, once the seminary moved to Rheims many of them went to Paris where they petitioned the pope for "a little house of their own" which finally opened in 1594.[18] Also in the early 1590s, Robert Persons, perhaps fearing a repetition of the Anglo-Celtic rivalry involving English and Welsh students in Rome, succeeded in excluding Irish students from the new English college in Valladolid, Spain.[19] Tensions between English and Irish exiles were already simmering in the early 1560s as Stapleton worked on his translation of Bede at the University of Louvain. Indeed, Stapleton's attitude toward Ireland's people and religion may have been influenced by the presence of Irish students at Louvain who "were more extreme than most in their views," and especially pro-Spanish. This group included Nicholas Comerford and James Archer who a decade later would be described by an English official as being like all "the students of Ireland that are in Louvain and come from thence": "the merest traitors and breeders of treachery that liveth."[20] Comerford and Archer's militant, anti-Elizabeth views would not have endeared them to Stapleton who, as a self-declared loyal subject of the queen in 1565, dedicated his translation of Bede to the "Quene of England, Fraunce, and *Ireland*," and reproduced the royal coat of arms on the verso of the title page.[21] Whereas Stapleton considered Elizabeth to be queen of Ireland, Comerford and Archer definitely did not.

Although Bede's original text had stressed the religiosity of the Irish, Stapleton's translation of *The history* may have clouded the picture because of its inconsistent

---

[16] *The history of the church of Englande*, 117^v–118^v.   [17] Ibid. 118^r.

[18] Helga Hammerstein, "Aspects of the Continental Education of Irish Students in the Reign of Queen Elizabeth I," *Historical Studies: Papers Read Before the Irish Conference of Historians* 8 (Dublin: Gill and MacMillan, 1971), 144–5. "Allen's great missionary schemes treated Ireland as a mere side line" (145).

[19] Thomas Morrissey, "The Irish Student Diaspora in the Sixteenth Century and the Early Years of the Irish College at Salamanca," *Recusant History* 14 (1978), 246.

[20] Ibid. 244–5. On Irish students at Louvain, see Brendan Jennings, "Irish Students in the University of Louvain," *Measgra I gcuimhne Mhichil Ui Chleirigh* (Dublin, 1944), 74–83.

[21] My italics.

identification of the Irish as Scottish. In Bede's Latin, the word "Scottia" refers not to the territory that we (like the Elizabethans) know as Scotland but to Ireland (which Bede also, though less frequently, calls "Hibernia").[22] Stapleton's translation potentially confuses readers, however, by sometimes translating "Scottia" and "Scotti" as "Scotland" and "Scottish," and sometimes as "Ireland" and "Irish."[23] Judging by the explanatory remarks deemed necessary by other Catholic writers from Ireland, not all readers would have immediately understood that Stapleton's "Scotland" referred to Ireland, not to the north parts of Britain. Henry Fitzsimon, for example, goes to great lengths in the dedicatory epistle to *A Catholike confutation* to make sure his readers understand that, before the destruction of the Picts, the terms "Scotland" and "Scots" meant only Ireland and its inhabitants.[24]

Fitzsimon's specificity was a way of refuting the claims of some Scottish Catholics that Ireland's ancient saints were in fact Scottish. The most notorious attempt at appropriating Ireland's religious heritage was made in the 1620s by the Scottish "hagioclept" Thomas Dempster, who, "exploit[ing] confusions surrounding the geographical term Scotia," argued that many Irish saints like Columbe and Brigdit were actually Scottish.[25] Fitzsimon, on the contrary, insists that "S. Bryde or Brigida wilbe an Irish Virgin ... S. Columbanus wilbe ane Irishman" so long as martyrologies and saints' lives by writers like Bede survive.[26] The same anxiety that "Scotia" might be mistakenly interpreted to mean "Scotland" rather than Ireland is also shared by the Franciscan translator of a collection of Irish saints lives who explains that "for the latin word *Scotia*, I have most commonly translated *Ireland*."[27]

While there is no external evidence to suggest that Stapleton deliberately set out when translating *The history of the church of Englande* to downplay the sometimes positive role played by Ireland in Bede's account of the transmission of Christianity to England, Stapleton's habit of sometimes rendering "Scotti" as "Scottish" instead of "Irish" reveals (a perhaps unconscious) desire to muddy

---

[22] Stapleton's translation says of Ireland, "This is properly the country of the Skottes, owt of the which they isshuing hath inhabited Britany being before possessed of the Britons and the Pictes" (14ᵛ).

[23] Stapleton does say that "concerning the proper names of places, as of cyties and monasteries mencioned in the history, we have many tymes kept the latin or rather Saxon names: where Polydore and other instructions coude not helpe us to call them by their present names they now beare" (9ʳ⁻ᵛ). And yet Stapleton would have known that the present name of "Scottia" was Ireland.

[24] *A Catholike confutation*, e3ᵛ–i3ʳ.

[25] Colin Kidd, *British Identities before Nationalism: Ethnicities and Nationhood in the Atlantic World, 1600–1800* (Cambridge: Cambridge University Press, 1999), 157. On Dempster, see Colm Lennon, "Political Thought of Irish Counter-Reformation Churchmen: The Testimony of the 'Analecta' of Bishop David Rothe," in Hiram Morgan (ed.), *Political Ideology in Ireland 1541–1641* (Dublin: Four Courts Press, 1999), 200; and Cunningham, *The World of Geoffrey Keating*, 86.

[26] *A Catholike confutation*, i2ᵛ.

[27] Robert Rochford (trans.), Jocelinus, *The life of the glorious bishop S. Patricke apostle and primate of Ireland* (1625. ERL 210), xviii.

belief in the value of Ireland's Catholic heritage.[28] For Stapleton, English (Anglo-Saxon) Christianity was ultimately superior to all competing versions; as he wrote to the pope in 1572, "the kingdom of England, once mighty and noble . . . [was] certainly pre-eminent and glorious among those lands which gave their allegiance to Christ."[29]

We might expect that Ireland's ancient reputation as a stronghold of Catholicism as well as its resistance to Protestant reforming efforts in the sixteenth century would represent an inspiration to the recusant Catholic community in England. Yet Stapleton's edition of Bede, in its ambivalent handling of Ireland and the Irish, suggests instead deep-seated uncertainties among English Catholics about the value of Celtic, and particularly Irish, Christianity. In order to explore these uncertainties further and to map the place of Ireland in the national imaginings of English Catholics, I turn now to examine several key figures from the later sixteenth and early seventeenth centuries who offer different perspectives on the vexed relationship between the Catholics of England and Ireland.

EDMUND CAMPION: JUGGLING MOUNTEBANK OR ADMIRER OF IRELAND?

I begin with the early career of the Jesuit proto-martyr Edmund Campion who, before arriving on the Continent and entering the Society of Jesus in 1573, spent a brief period in Ireland as the Dublin guest of Sir James Stanihurst and his family of loyalist Old English Catholics.[30] Campion had tutored James's son, Richard Stanihurst, at St John's College, Oxford—the religiously conservative college at which Campion held the position of Lecturer in Rhetoric.[31] At some point in 1570, it appears that Campion reached a religious crossroads, deciding to abandon his outward conformity to the Church of England and embrace Rome instead. Campion's sponsor at Oxford, the Company of Grocers, judged

---

[28] In their notes to the Latin text, Colgrave and Mynors write that " 'British' here means what we now call Welsh. The Irish language was afterwards taken by the *Scotti* to Scotland, but *Scotti* in Bede always means the Irish race whether in Scotland or Ireland. *Scotia* refers to Ireland alone though he uses *Hibernia* too, apparently using both terms indiscriminately as in the first paragraph of iv.26" (*Bede's Ecclesiastical History of the English People*, ed. Bertram Colgrave and R. A. B. Mynors (Oxford: Clarendon Press, 1969), 16).

[29] Thomas M. McCoog, SJ, *The Society of Jesus in Ireland, Scotland, and England, 1541–1588: "Our Way of Proceeding?"* (New York: Brill, 1996), 90. The memorial in which these lines appear was co-written with William Allen and Thomas Harding.

[30] Robert Persons, "Of the Life and Martyrdom of Father Edmund Campion," *Letters and Notices* 11 (1877), 230–1. However, Colm Lennon observes that James Stanihurst's religious affiliations are hard to pin down at a "time when the lines of religious demarcation were not clearly drawn" (*Richard Stanihurst the Dubliner 1547–1618* (Dublin: Irish Academic Press, 1981), 34).

[31] Gerard Kilroy, *Edmund Campion: Memory and Transcription* (Aldershot: Ashgate, 2005), 48; see also Michael A. R. Graves's *ODNB* entry on Campion.

in 1568 that their scholar was "suspected to be of no sound judgment in religion" because he had failed to deliver the public sermons expected of him.[32]

Sometime between 1566 and 1570, Campion also composed the Latin poem *Sancta salutiferi nascentia semina verbi* (*On the Birth of the Church*) that Gerard Kilroy has recently edited.[33] Campion dedicates this resounding affirmation of the transcendence of the See of Rome over the mutabililty of Rome's secular powers, to Anthony Browne, First Viscount Montague—a politically loyal member of the elite, as well as an outspoken defender of the Catholic faith. Thus, when Campion left Oxford on "a traveling fellowship" in 1570, his commitment to Rome and to the reconversion of his homeland was already secure, even though he had not been formally reconciled to the Roman faith. In *On the Birth of the Church*, Campion apostrophizes that homeland as the spiritually bereft seat of the "Britons": "hearts once so much praised: if your sacred rites had stood firm like that, if you had prayed and fasted like that (would that you had done so!) your sacred rites too would now have stood firm." In this reinvention of Virgilian epic Campion fuses the memory of Trojan decline with the heroism of the early Christians, mournfully imagining Britain as a latter-day Troy, a once-glorious place now leveled by the chaos of heresy.[34]

For a short time Campion was secure in Dublin, enjoying the protection of the Stanihursts and of other powerful figures like the Lord Deputy, Sir Henry Sidney, and the loyalist Old English Earl of Kildare. But following the excommunication of Elizabeth in 1570, the "hotter" Protestants in the colonial elite gained the upper hand. Campion became a wanted man and was forced to flee to the Continent via England in 1571.[35] Before leaving, he composed *A Historie of Ireland* that Richard Stanihurst would later incorporate into the first edition of Raphael Holinshed's *Chronicles of England, Scotlande, and Irelande* (1577). Campion's dedication of his work to the Earl of Leicester suggests Campion's eclectic religious and political affiliations at this time as well as the fluidity of confessional boundaries within a European humanist milieu. Leicester, like Sidney, was a Protestant—even a militant one—but he was also enough of a politique to patronize nonconformists like Campion.

---

[32] Ibid. 48. Campion himself was not officially Catholic at this time—"neither priest nor religious man," in Persons's words—yet zealous enough to debate "controversies against the heretics" (Persons, "Life and Martyrdom," 232–3). James V. Holleran thinks that "Campion's flight to Ireland rather than the Continent, where most Catholic exiles went, suggests that he had not yet formally returned to the Catholic Church" (*A Jesuit Challenge: Edmund Campion's Debates at the Tower of London in 1581* (New York: Fordham University Press, 1999), 18). Rudolph B. Gottfried argues that by 1570 "there can be little doubt that Campion is a Catholic," if not yet of the militant Counter-Reformation variety (*Edmund Campion, A Historie of Ireland (1571)* (New York: Scholars' Facsimiles and Reprints, 1940), iv).

[33] Kilroy, *Edmund Campion*, 149–93.   [34] Ibid. 53.

[35] Vincent P. Carey, "A 'Dubious Loyalty': Richard Stanihurst, the 'Wizard' Earl of Kildare, and English–Irish Identity," in Vincent P. Carey and Ute Lotz-Heumann (eds.), *Taking Sides: Colonial and Confessional Mentalites in Early Modernn Ireland. Essays in Honour of Karl S. Bottigheimer* (Dublin: Four Courts Press, 2003), 64–5.

Campion's *Historie of Ireland*, assembled out of "the most approved Chronicles," including Gerald of Wales and Jocelinus of Furness, presented Ireland as one of the last outposts in the Atlantic archipelago to be Christianized—a task undertaken singlehandedly by St Patrick, as though "the realm had been reserved for him."[36] Before Patrick's mission, writes Campion, "no country was more lamented then Ireland, which partly for distance from the heart of Christendome, partly for their infinite rudenesse, had yet received no fruit of true Religion."[37] Campion devotes a chapter to Patrick's conversion of Ireland and another to "The Irish Saints"—"Gods friends, more glorious to a Realme then all the victories and triumphs of the world."[38]

Yet unlike Bede, and even some early modern Protestant writers, Campion's account of early Christian Ireland is unenthused; unlike William Camden, for instance, he does not call Ireland "Sanctoram patria," "the native countrey of Saints," or describe Ireland as a center of learning sought out by neighboring peoples.[39] Campion certainly admires elements in Ireland's religious fabric, including the reluctance of the people to shed the blood of holy men and the fact that "Clarkes and Lay-men" when "vertuously bred up or reformed, are such mirrours of holinessse and austeritie that other Nations retaine but a shewe or shadow of devotion in comparison of them"[40] As Rudolf B. Gottfried argues in the introduction to his edition of *A Historie of Ireland*: "For [Campion] the story of mediaeval Ireland is largely the record of holy men and abbeys. He opens a chapter on the Irish saints by calling 'the memory of Gods friends, more glorious to a Realme then all the victories and triumphs of the world' . . . ; his account of the sufferings caused by the Scottish invasion gives precedence to those inflicted on the Church . . . ; and he laments the passing of the old religious benefactions of the Middle Ages."[41]

Overall, though, Campion disparages the attachment of the Irish people to Christianity: "since the time of Saint Patricke," he writes, "Christianitie was never extinct in Ireland, yet the governement being hayled into contrarie factions, the Nobilitie lawlesse, the multitude willfull, it came to passe that Religion waxed with the temporall common sort cold and feeble."[42] Campion sees the "uplandish" or Gaelic Irish as especially retrograde Christians because of their belief in "idle miracles and revelations," that include popular superstitions about St Patrick's purgatory, a subterranean cavern or "closet of stone" "in the north edge of Ulster" where pilgrims are reportedly granted visions of the afterlife and from which some visitors are said never to return. While Campion concedes that God may "reveale [to men] by miracles the vision of joyes and paines eternal,"

---

[36] Campion, *A Historie of Ireland*, 37.   [37] Ibid. 36.   [38] Ibid. 42
[39] William Camden, *Britain* (1637), 67–8. Similar sentiments about early Christianity in Ireland can be found in other Protestant works. See Colm Lennon, "Edmund Campion's *Histories of Ireland* and Reform in Tudor Ireland," in Thomas M. McCoog (ed.), *The Reckoned Expense: Edmund Campion and the Early English Jesuits* (Woodbridge: Boydell Press, 1996), 67–84.
[40] *A Historie of Ireland*, 13, 44.   [41] Ibid. iv.   [42] Ibid. 16.

he refuses to believe that St Patrick's Purgatory is in any way a conduit of divine revelation.[43] Campion notes, moreover, that the Patrick who establishes the Purgatory is more likely an Abbot of Ulster than the Apostle of Ireland himself.

Contrasting with Campion's skeptical rejection of St Patrick's Purgatory, is the view of Don John de Lacey—an Irishman living in exile in Lisbon—who presented the Spanish authorities with a plan in 1593 for the liberation of his homeland. De Lacey proposed establishing in Ireland a military order of St Patrick dedicated to driving the English heretics out of his country, just as the Spanish military order of Santiago had once helped rid Spain of the Moors.[44] This new Irish order was to be based in St Patrick's Purgatory at Lough Derg, Ulster, partly for tactical reasons—the north of Ireland being a stronghold of native resistance—and partly for symbolic reasons—St Patrick's Purgatory having acquired the reputation in the Iberian world as a transnational sacred site.[45] Campion, as a Catholic Englishman, shares none of De Lacey's enthusiasm for the militant potential of St Patrick and his Purgatory, an enthusiasm that was reflected in the new lives of Patrick written after the Council of Trent's decree enforcing higher scholarly standards in the construction of saints' lives.[46]

Campion's deeply conflicted perspective on Irish Catholicity was roundly criticized in the seventeenth century by the Old English Catholic Geoffrey Keating in his own history of Ireland, the *Foras Feasa ar Eirinn* ("Compendium of Wisdom about Ireland"). Even though by this time the "Blessed" Edmund Campion had become a revered figure in the pantheon of Counter-Reformation martyrs, Keating still included him in a list of English writers accused of defaming the Irish and their achievements.[47] Keating condemns Campion not just for a general hostility toward Gaelic culture, but specifically for his views about the gullible religiosity of the Irish:

Campion says ... that the Irish are so credulous that they deem whatever their superiors tell them to be true, however incredible it may appear to others. As a proof of this, he relates a very stupid fable, which I here repeat: "There was once," says he, "a certain licentious prelate in Ireland, who was able to impose anything upon his people. This

---

[43] Ibid. 14, 41–2.

[44] Enrique García Hernán, "Philip II's Forgotten Armada," in Hiram Morgan (ed.), *The Battle of Kinsale* (Bray, Ireland: Wordwell, 2004), 57. The implicit equation of the English heretics with pagan moors is striking.

[45] Micheline Kerney Walsh, "The Military Order of Saint Patrick, 1593," *Seanchas Ard Mhacha* 9 (1979), 277. Walsh prints a translation of De Lacey's proposal.

[46] See Bernadette Cunningham and Raymond Gillespie, "'The Most Adaptable of Saints': The Cult of Patrick in the Seventeenth Century," *Archivium Hibernicum; or, Irish Historical Records* 49 (1995), 82–104; and Salvador Ryan, "Steadfast Saints or Malleable Models: Seventeenth-Century Irish Hagiography Revisited," *Catholic Historical Review* 91 (2005), 251–2.

[47] Cunningham, *The World of Geoffrey Keating*, 86–7, 115; Scott Pilarz, "'Campion dead bites with his friends' teeth': Representations of an Early Modern Catholic Martyr," in Christopher Highley and John N. King (eds.), *John Foxe and His World* (Aldershot: Ashgate, 2002), 216–34.

prelate having but a scanty stock of ready money, and hoping to receive a supply from his flock, told them that, within a few years past, St Patrick and St Peter had had a quarrel about an Irish Galloglass [soldier], whom St Patrick wished to introduce into heaven, but that St Peter, enraged thereat, struck St Patrick on the head with the key of Heaven, and fractured his skull. In consequence of this story the prelate received the contribution that he required from the people." In reply to Campion, I must say that, in this place, he appears less in the character of the historian than of the juggling mountebank, vending ridiculous squibs from off a stage. For, how could any Irish Christian believe that St Patrick could get his skull broken, having died more than a thousand years ago . . . I do not consider any more of [Campion's] falsehoods worth taking up; he, himself, confesses, in the epistle prefixed to his work, that he had spent but ten weeks in writing the history of Ireland.[48]

Keating dismisses Campion's views on Ireland as the product of typical English prejudice and of a tight writing schedule that prevented Campion from conducting proper research. The "fable" from Campion that Keating analyzes, moreover, reveals more about Campion's deficiencies in logic and historical method than it does about the supposed vulnerability of the Irish to a priestly conman.

In spite of Campion's divided opinions about Irish Catholicism, his skepticism about Patrick's Purgatory, and his amused view of Irish foolishness, he appears to have remained captivated by St Patrick for the rest of his life. When he fled Ireland as a fugitive from the Protestant authorities, he dressed in the livery of the Earl of Kildare under the assumed name of Patrick.[49] Then, in 1580, when Campion set out from Rome on the inaugural Jesuit mission to England, he once more, as his traveling companion Persons attests,

took unto himself for his journey the name of his old protector in Ireland, by which he escaped before, which was of St Patrick apostle of that country, recommending himself most devoutly unto him; and so kept the same until he was ready to enter England, at what time he was persuaded to leave it in respect of the new troubles raised in that country by Dr. Sanders' arrival there, for which occasion he [Campion] might be suspected or called perhaps in question for an Irishman . . . whereupon he left it and called himself Edmonds in remembrance of St Edmond King and Martyr of England whom he desired to imitate.[50]

At one level, Campion's use of the name Patrick represents nothing more than the clerical custom of assuming a name in religion. But Alison Shell, commenting on Campion's acts of self-fashioning, also sees in his choice of pseudonym,

---

[48] Geoffrey Keating, *Foras Feasa ar Eiriun (The History of Ireland)*, trans. and ed. John O'Mahony (Kansas City: Irish Genealogical Foundation, 1983), 1: li. See also Raymond Gillespie, *Devoted People: Belief and Religion in Early Modern Ireland* (Manchester: Manchester University Press, 1997), 143, on the importation of Campion's books into Ireland in the 1580s.

[49] Carey, "A 'Dubious Loyalty'," 65 n. 14.

[50] Persons, "Of the Life and Martyrdom of Father Edmund Campion," *Letters and Notices*, vol. 12 (1878), 2, and vol. 11 (1877), 234–5; Richard Simpson, *Edmund Campion, A Biography* (London, 1896), 153.

"a means of sacralising the surface dishonesty of pretence."[51] What lay behind Campion's attraction to Patrick, though, is certainly more complex than at first appears. Campion was not identifying with Patrick's innate Irishness because, as Campion himself relates in *A Historie of Ireland*, Patrick was actually a native of the Anglo-Scottish marches who was captured by pirates and sold into serfdom in Ireland. *A Historie of Ireland* shows Patrick actively constructing himself as Irish by learning "their tongue perfectly," before leaving for the Continent from whence he returns decades later to convert Ireland. Perhaps it was Patrick's status as a fellow exile in Ireland that appealed to Campion, as well as the fact that Patrick's later career as a *peregrinus Christiani* in Europe provided a road-map to Campion's own aspirations as a missionary priest.[52] Either way, Patrick's status as a prototypical religious exile might also have attracted Richard Stanihurst who composed *De vita S. Patricii, Hiberniae apostoli* (Antwerp, 1587) after embracing a self-imposed religious exile on the Continent. Stanihurst, perhaps inspired by the martyrdom of Campion to pursue a militant Counter-Reformation agenda, dedicated his hagiography to Alexander Farnese, the Spanish governor of the Low Countries, and the potential commander of a future military operation to rid Ireland of heretical rule.[53] Stanihurst deployed St Patrick in the same way that Stapleton in his translation of Bede deployed St Augustine: as an argument for the antiquity and historical continuity of the Roman Catholic faith in their homelands, Ireland and England.[54]

As Campion's conflicted handling of Ireland's Christian heritage in *A Historie of Ireland* suggests, his gestures of self-fashioning represent something more complicated than a celebratory identification with Irish religious figures; rather, Campion selectively appropriates elements of Irish Christendom.[55] Thus if he could "become" St Patrick of Ireland, he could just as readily "become" St Edmund of England—the ninth century ruler of East Anglia, martyred by the heathen Vikings, whose name Campion shared. When Campion remarked to his Protestant captors that "In condemning us you condemn all your own ancestors. All the ancient priests, bishops and kings, all that was once the glory of England, the island of saints and the most devout child of the see of Peter,"

---

[51] Shell also mentions his "character-acting as an Irish servant" ("'We are Made a Spectacle': Campion's Dramas," in McCoog (ed.), *The Reckoned Expense*, 111).

[52] Campion, *A Historie of Ireland*, 37. On the Irish tradition of *peregrinato* or voluntary exile from Ireland, see Marie Theresa Flanagan, "The Contribution of Irish Missionaries and Scholars to Medieval Christianity," in Brendan Bradshaw and Daire Keogh (eds.), *Christianity in Ireland: Revisiting the Story* (Dublin: Columba Press, 2002), 35–43, and T. M. Charles Edwards, "The Social Background of Irish *Peregrinatio*," *Celtica* 11 (1976), 43–59.

[53] The choice of dedicatee "implicitly identified Patrick's mission with that of the Spanish campaign aimed at wiping out heresy that was currently active in the Low Countries" (Ryan, "Steadfast Saints or Malleable Models," 253).

[54] Lennon, *Richard Stanihurst the Dubliner*, 43–4; Cunningham and Gillespie, "'The Most Adaptable of Saints'," 82–104.

[55] Simpson, *Campion*, 447, 414.

he was claiming for England the kind of privileged status that Ireland's Catholics would have declared more applicable to their own country.[56]

Campion's examination of Ireland's past in *A Historie of Ireland* inevitably ran into the powerfully contested question of who "owned" the country. According to the terms of the widely circulated Donation of Constantine, the first Christian emperor had granted Pope Sylvester I temporal as well as spiritual dominion over all the islands of the western ocean, including Ireland. As late as 1555, Mary and Philip reaffirmed this arrangement when they acknowledged "The Holy See's special rights over Ireland...in their acceptance of the Bull of Paul IV."[57] And in the 1580s William Allen reminded readers that Ireland was a papal fief, "the Sea Apostolique [having] an olde claime unto the soveraintie of that Countrie."[58] However, the papal claim to Ireland was complicated by the fact that another pope, the Englishman Adrian IV, had allegedly issued a bull, *laudabiliter* (1155), granting the right to rule over Ireland to Henry II and all future English monarchs.[59] In *A Historie of Ireland* Campion adduces Adrian's bull in support of England's "invincible title" to the country. And he reinforces this claim by arguing that England has a prior claim to Ireland both on the basis of lawful conquest and in the submission of Irish princes to various ancient British rulers, including Arthur.[60] Indeed, claims Campion, "the Irish...were subjects to the Crowne of Brittaine before they set foote in Ireland" because, allegedly, the Iberian ancestors of the Irish had sworn allegiance to the British king Gurguntius during their sea passage from Spain to their new home. Campion stresses in a list of British/English "claimes to the Land of Ireland" that sovereignty over the territory had never reverted back to the pope: Pope Alexander III had "confirmed the gift of Adrian"; the papal legate Vivian had excommunicated those Irish who disobeyed the English crown; and the Irish clergy had twice "determined the conquest to be lawfull."[61] Campion further denied the canard that King John had surrendered sovereignty over England and Ireland to the pope, and received Ireland back again in exchange for an annual tribute of three hundred marks.[62] By promoting an English or British *imperium* instead of a papal and Roman one in Ireland, Campion was adopting the position

---

[56] Quoted in Michael E. Williams, "Campion and the English Continental Seminaries," in McCoog (ed.), *The Reckoned Expense*, 294.

[57] Morrissey, "The Irish Student Diaspora," 245, quoting Ludwig Freiherr Von Pastor, *The History of the Popes from the Close of the Middle Ages*, ed. Ralph Francis Kerr, vol. 34: *Clement VIII* (London: Kegan Paul, Trench, Trubner, 1933), 68–9.

[58] *A true, sincere, and modest defence, of English Catholiques* (np, 1584. *ERL* 68), 140.

[59] See "Donation of Constantine" and "Pope Adrian IV" in *The Catholic Encyclopedia* online at: http://www.newadvent.org/cathen/. "In the West, long after [the Donation's] authenticity was disputed in the fifteenth century, its validity was still upheld by the majority of canonists and jurists who continued throughout the sixteenth century to quote it as authentic. And though Baronius and later historians acknowledged it to be a forgery, they endeavoured to marshal other authorities in defence of its content, especially as regards the imperial donations" ("Donation of Constantine").

[60] *A Historie of Ireland*, 28–9, 69–72.   [61] Ibid. 71–2.

[62] Ibid. 75. Campion cites both Thomas More and John Bale in support of this point.

of the Old English families of the Pale like the Stanihursts who (until the 1580s) remained steadfastly loyal to the English crown while continuing to practice their Catholic faith.[63]

Campion's attachment to a notion of British imperial authority over Ireland was typical of many English Catholics who remained reluctant to support the struggles of their fellow Catholics in Ireland against English Protestant rule. William Allen's cagey discussion "Of the Late Warres in Ireland for Religion," in *A true, sincere, and modest defence, of English Catholiques* also reflects this reluctance. While Allen provides a theoretical defense of the pope's right to use the sword and wage just wars, he remains noncommittal on the rebellion in Ireland and makes no effort to depict the Irish as defenders of the True Church: "As for his Holines action in Ireland; we that are neither so wise, as to be worthie, nor so mallepert, as to chalenge to knowe his intentions council and disposition of thos matters: can nor wil nether defend nor condemne it."[64]

Yet Allen's evasive neutrality did not prevent Protestants from blaming him and other English Catholics of stirring up trouble in Ireland. Campion and his fellow Jesuits were an especially convenient target for these attacks: at his treason trial, Campion was accused of supporting the insurrection against the queen's forces in Ireland that coincided almost exactly with the arrival of the Jesuits in England. Protestant authorities saw little difference in the fact that Campion's Jesuit superiors had expressly forbidden his group from getting involved in political or military schemes, since even the suspicion of such meddling would endanger the irenic and pastoral goals officially sanctioned for the mission.[65] Furthermore, on the eve of the mission, Pope Gregory XIII issued an *explanatio* informing Elizabeth's subjects that the terms of her excommunication were suspended *rebus sic stantibus* (under present conditions). This decree, designed to calm government paranoia about the nefarious intentions of Catholics, had

[63] Later in the century Old English Catholics would question the foundation of England's claim to sovereignty over Ireland, rejecting *laudabiliter* or suggesting that it gave the English crown only limited and conditional dominion in Ireland. Philip O'Sullivan Beare offers a detailed refutation of English claims to Ireland, including the authority of *lauabiliter*, in his *Historiae Catholicae Iberniae Compendium* (*Compendium of the Catholic History of Ireland*) (Lisbon, 1621). See Hiram Morgan, "'Un Pueblo Unido...': The Politics of Philip O'Sullivan Beare," in Enrique García Hernán et al. (eds.), *Irlanda y la Monarquía Hispánica: Kinsale 1601–2001. Guerra, Política, Exilio y Religión* (Madrid: Universidad de Alcalá, 2002), 265–82. This article is also available online at the Center for Neo-Latin Studies, University College Cork http://www.ucc.ie/acad/classics/CNLS/lectures/Morgan_madrid.html

[64] *A true, sincere, and modest defence*, 136–7. See also Thomas Clancy, *Papist Pamphleteers: The Allen-Persons Party and the Political Thought of the Counter-Reformation in England 1572–1615* (Chicago: Loyola University Press, 1964): "Though [Allen, Persons et al.] sympathized with the sufferings of their fellow Catholics, their outlook on Ireland and the wars there was not notably different from that of other Englishmen of their day" (75).

[65] For a recent discussion of Persons and Campion's efforts to assert the "purity of their motives" in England, see Peter Lake and Michael Questier, "Puritans, Papists, and the 'Public Sphere' in Early Modern England: The Edmund Campion Affair in Context," *The Journal of Modern History* 27 (2000), 587–627.

the opposite effect by drawing attention to the fact that Catholics were only postponing their wish to depose the queen.[66] At trial, Campion denied any knowledge, let alone involvement, in the rebellion that would soon engulf much of Ireland. Eventually the rebellion drew in the Geraldine Desmonds of Munster, as well as dissident Catholic gentry of the Pale and their Gaelic allies led by James Eustace, Third Viscount Baltinglass. Baltinglass had imbibed the militant spirit of Counter-Reformation Catholicism during his sojourn in Rome in the 1570s; in the words of one Protestant observer, Baltinglass was now mixed up in "the most perilous [rebellion] that ever was begun in Ireland. Foreign help in multitudes is looked for presently."[67]

NICHOLAS SANDER: HONORARY IRISHMAN?

Unlike Campion, Nicholas Sander—another prominent English exile—played a major role in promoting rebellion in Ireland. Sander spent the early years of his exile from England as a theologian and polemicist at the University of Louvain, a magnet, as we have seen, for Catholic exiles from both England and Ireland.[68] His works of religious controversy included a defense of the Mass and of transubstantiation as well as an account of the cult of the saints and the privileges of the papacy. His *magnum opus*, the *De visibili monarchia Ecclesiae* (Louvain, 1571) responded to John Jewel's defense of the Church of England, *An Apologie, or aunswer in defence of the Church of England* (1562), eliciting in turn a string of Protestant refutations.[69]

In the late 1570s, Sander's chance to act on his militant anti-Protestant impulses came when he joined forces with James Fitzmaurice Fitzgerald, an Old English kinsman of the Earl of Desmond. Fitzgerald was already on the Continent seeking support from Catholic leaders for a crusade to end Elizabeth's rule in his homeland. After years of shuttling between France, Spain, Portugal, and Rome, Fitzgerald finally got the required backing. Sander was appointed as

---

[66] Michael L. Carrafiello, "*Rebus Sic Stantibus* and English Catholicism, 1606–1610," *Recusant History* 22 (1994), 29–40.

[67] William Palmer, *The Problem of Ireland in Tudor Foreign Policy 1485–1603* (Woodbridge, Suffolk: Boydell, 1994), 111; Christopher Maginn, "The Baltinglass Rebellion, 1580: English Dissent or a Gaelic Uprising?" *Historical Journal* 47:2 (2004), 205–32. Baltinglass escaped to Spain after the failure of the rebellion where he died in 1585.

[68] Sander, *The Rise and Growth of the Anglican Schism*, ed. and trans. David Lewis (London: Burns and Oates, 1877; Rockford, Ill.: Tan Books, 1988), xix.

[69] On these controversial writings, see Peter Milward, *Religious Controversies of the Elizabethan Age: A Survey of Printed Sources* (London: Scolar Press, 1977), 5, 12–14. The seventh book of the *De visibili* was thought too topical and inflammatory even by the Catholic censors (who wanted to mollify Elizabeth, not anger her, at this time). See Christian Coppens, *Reading in Exile: The Libraries of John Ramridge (d.1568), Thomas Harding (d.1572) and Henry Joliffe (d.1573), Recusants in Louvain* (Cambridge: LP Publications, 1993), 10–11.

the pope's representative on the mission, thus giving official sanction to what Vincent P. Carey calls "the first modern ideologically motivated rebellion in Irish history."[70] The religious inspiration for the rebellion was vividly in evidence as participants disembarked near Smerwick in July 1579:

Leading the procession were two Franciscans, bearing banners, one of which was the Papal Standard emblazoned with the emblem of the Holy Cross. A Bishop in mitre and crozier followed. Then came Fitzmaurice, Dr. Sander, priests and friars, the members of Fitzmaurice's family, fifty or sixty soldiers, the crews of the six vessels, and perhaps a number of prisoners captured on the voyage from Spain.[71]

Sander's cooperation with Fitzgerald—the Captain General of the pope's army in Ireland—represents one of the few well-documented occasions when a leading English Catholic crossed ethnic boundaries to work constructively with fellow Catholics from Ireland. In this, Sander took a dramatically different view from Campion of both the importance of Ireland to the reconversion of England and of the quality of Irish Catholic spirituality. In the *De visibili* Sander shows what for an Englishman was an unusual respect for Ireland's Catholics by including a discussion of Irish martyrs as part of his denunciation of Protestant sects and heresies.[72] Sander's rhetorical skills were indispensable in Ireland, where he and Fitzgerald issued proclamations explaining the purpose of the rebellion and calling on the Catholics of Ireland to unite. Sander also composed letters appealing for assistance from Rome and Spain, as well as a (now lost) treatise on the rebellion, *De Bello Hibernica* (1580).[73]

   The first proclamation issued by Sander and Fitzgerald claimed divine sanction for the deposition of the heretical Elizabeth—"the pretended Queen of England." God had placed the task of deposing her into the hands of Ireland's own inhabitants, thus avoiding the need for the intervention of foreign Catholic princes: "If we then dispossess her first, shall not the country of Ireland obtain the greatest glory that ever it had since it was an Ireland?" The pope had deliberately sent only a small number of foreign soldiers on the mission so that the people of Ireland could take credit for the impending victory over

---

[70]   " 'An Irishman can have no right or justice': The Pale Rebellion and the Conflict of Colonial Elites, 1578–83," in *Surviving the Tudors: The Wizard Earl of Kildare and English Rule in Ireland, 1537–1586* (Dublin: Four Courts Press, 2002), 179–211, quotation at 181; also see Thomas McNevin Veech, *Dr. Nicholas Sanders and The English Reformation, 1530–1585* (Louvain: Bureaux du Recueil, Bibliothèque de l'Université, 1935), 260.

[71]   Myles V. Ronan, *The Reformation in Ireland Under Elizabeth 1558–1580 (From Original Sources)* (London: Longmans, 1930), 612.

[72]   For a discussion of this 800-odd page Latin work, see Alan Ford, "Martyrdom, History, and Memory in Early Modern Ireland," in Ian McBride (ed.), *History and Memory in Modern Ireland* (Cambridge: Cambridge University Press, 2001), 47–8.
   Edward Rishton, the editor and continuator of Sander's *De origine ac progressu schismatis Anglicani* (1585) observed that "the people of that country [Ireland] are before all things Catholic" (269).

[73]   Veech, *Dr Nicholas Sanders*, 288 n. 2; Milward, *Religious Controversies of the Elizabethan Age*, 13–14.

the "she-tyrant." At the same time, the proclamation made clear that Fitzgerald
was "not at war against the legitimate and honourable crown of England," but
against only its Protestant usurper who, by assuming the headship of the Church,
"has deservedly forfeited her royal authority."[74] The proclamation's goal was to
secure a "common front" among the traditionally fractious Gaelic leaders and
members of the Old English Catholic elite. Fitzgerald invited his "noble and
valiant countrymen . . . the princes, leaders, and rulers of this our dear country,
to meet together with me," in order to "make a perpetual peace, league and
friendship, first to the utter destroying of all schism and heresy, and next to
the establishing of true love and amity amongst ourselves."[75] Fitzgerald was
appealing to what Hiram Morgan calls a faith and fatherland patriotism—one
that envisaged all of Ireland's Catholics, whatever their regional, ethnic, or family
affiliations, as forming a unified nation-wide religious body.[76]

Fitzgerald and Sander ultimately hoped to draw into their uprising sympa-
thizers not just from Ireland but from across Elizabeth's territories, including
"Wales, Chester, Lancashire and Cumberland, where the country people, the
best fitted to bear arms, were strongly Catholic in sympathy."[77] The mission,
although launched in Ireland, aimed—as Sander's surviving letters make clear—
to reestablish the Pontifical Faith throughout the Atlantic archipelago. To this
end, Sander urged the Holy See to include in the original party, "English,
Irish, and Scottish priests, two at least from each of these nations . . . For it is
scarcely possible but that upon the outbreak of war in any one of these islands,
it must soon be begun in another also, especially if the business be managed
with prudence and address." Sander took care to avoid conflict among these
various "nations" by making sure that the Nuncio Apostolic was an outsider to
the Atlantic archipelago, preferably an Italian, "lest offence should be taken by
the English, that an Irishman, or by the Irish, that an Englishman, should be
preferred to them; and the same reasoning holds equally good as to the Scots."[78]

Elizabeth's government was quick to demonize Sander given the dangerous precedent he set for the cooperation of militant Catholics from England

[74] Quoted in Ronan, *The Reformation in Ireland*, 613–15, 620. On the willingness of another
English exile in Spain, Lady Jane Dormer, to help Fitzmaurice, see ibid. 595–6. For further
discussion of the influential Dormer, see Albert J. Loomie, SJ, *The Spanish Elizabethans: The English
Exiles at the Court of Philip II* (New York: Fordham University Press, 1963), ch. 4.

[75] Quoted in Ronan, *The Reformation in Ireland*, 615.

[76] Hiram Morgan, "Faith and Fatherland in Sixteenth-Century Ireland," *History-Ireland* 2
(1995), 13–20. Also see Brendan Bradshaw, "The English Reformation and Identity Formation
in Ireland and Wales," in Bradshaw and Peter Roberts (eds.), *British Consciousness and Identity: The
Making of Britain 1533–1707* (Cambridge: Cambridge University Press, 1998), 64.

[77] Quoted in Veech, *Dr Nicholas Sanders*, 263. Also see Mícheál Mac Craith, "The Gaelic Reaction to the Reformation," in Steven Ellis and Sarah Barber (eds.), *Conquest and Union: Fashioning a
British State, 1485–1725* (London: Longman, 1995), 144–5, and John. J. Silke, "The Irish Abroad,
1534–1691," in T. W. Moody, F. X. Martin, and F. J. Byrne (eds.), *A New History of Ireland* (Oxford:
Clarendon Press, 1976), 3: 587–633, esp. 595–8.

[78] Quoted in Ronan, *The Reformation in Ireland*, 589.

and Ireland. A pamphlet by one "A.M." (possibly Anthony Munday) noted facetiously that "Our good countryman of the Devils owne dubbing, Doctor Saunders (an Apostata towards his Saviour, an Archtraytor to his Soveraigne) is there in [Ireland], but where, it is unknowen."[79] The Lord Justice of Munster, William Pelham, offered "the best reward" for the apprehension of "that unnatural, traitorous priest," while the Lord Deputy himself, Lord Grey de Wilton, informed the queen how he had offered to pardon the Earl of Desmond if he would hand over to the English, "quick or dead," his brother John of Desmond and Doctor Sander. The offer, Grey explained, had been to no avail because, even in desperate times, "these mercifull dealinges have ever lifted [the rebels] up to greater insolencies."[80] After Sander's death, William Cecil, one of the architects of Elizabethan policy in Ireland, described him as "a lewd scholar and subject of England, a fugitive and a principal companion and conspirator with the traitors and rebels at Rome...the Pope's firebrand in Ireland."[81]

The resistance to English rule in Ireland organized by Sander and Fitzgerald suffered a major setback when the latter was killed; for a time, Sander kept the confederacy alive with the help of the Earl of Desmond and his brothers, as well as the Old English Palesman, Viscount Baltinglass, whose uprising engulfed Dublin and its hinterlands in late 1580.[82] English fears of a nationwide revolt, however, proved unfounded, and when a newly arrived attachment of Italian mercenaries was massacred by English troops under Lord Grey at Smerwick, the rebellion was effectively ended.[83] Sander died shortly afterwards, in dignified conditions according to his friends, in horrible ones according to his enemies. Cecil imagined a fitting death for the outcast Sander: "wandering in the mountaines in Ireland without succour [where he] died raving in a phrensey," while later hostile obituaries claimed that his corpse was consumed by wolves.[84]

Whatever the circumstances of Sander's death, he immediately entered Catholic Ireland's cultural memory. In fact, Catholics from both England and Ireland revered him as a martyr-patriot. The Old English cleric Peter Lombard, for instance, calls Sander an "excellent man"—learned, pious, and zealous— who "had passed into Ireland from Spain about the beginning of this war to comfort and advise the Catholics engaged in it." Lombard sees Sander's arrival in Ireland as inspirational, causing "not only many of the Irish, but also some of the English Catholics then living in Ireland, to join the same war." Even when

---

[79] *The true reporte of the prosperous successe which God gave unto our English souldiours against the forraine bands of our Romaine enemies, lately arived... in Ireland* (1581), Aiiii[v].

[80] Quoted in Veech, *Dr Nicholas Sanders,* 279 n. 1; National Archives (PRO) SP 63/82/54. 26 April 1581. Transcription by Andrew Zurcher available at http://www.english.cam.ac.uk/ceres/haphazard/letters/63–82–54.pdf.

[81] Quoted in Veech, *Dr Nicholas Sanders,* 289 n. 1; Robert M. Kingdon (ed.), The Execution of Justice in England *by William Cecil and* A True, Sincere, and Modest Defence of English Catholics *by William Allen* (Ithaca, NY: Cornell University Press, 1965), 13, 15.

[82] Veech, *Dr Nicholas Sanders,* 271–84.   [83] Ibid. 284–6.

[84] Ibid. 289 n.1. See also Barnaby Rich, *A new Irish prognostication, or popish callender* (1624), 89.

defeat was imminent, claims Lombard, Sander "remained to the end," having planted the seeds of Ireland's future "liberation" from England.[85] Respect for Sander amongst Ireland's Catholics is also evident in an edition of Jocelinus's *The life of the glorious bishop S. Patricke apostle and primate of Ireland* produced by the Irish Franciscans at Louvain in 1625, in which Sander is credited with saying that "the people of [Ireland] are farre more Catholike, then many other Nations."[86] Just as Sander included Irish martyrs in his own printed martyr catalogues, so Ireland's Catholics like John Howlin returned the compliment by including Sander in his *Perbreve Compendium*, "the first early modern Irish martyrology"— an unusual honor indeed for an Englishman in an Irish-authored martyrology.[87] The fact that neither Sander's corpse nor his grave were ever identified may have inhibited the development of a focused cult of Sander the martyr in Ireland. As Clodagh Tait observes, martyr cults in early modern Ireland typically centered on the martyr's burial site that devotees associated with thaumaturgical powers.[88] Devotees also believed these miraculous powers to inhere in the martyr's relics that did not survive in the case of Sander. Sander's nemesis, William Cecil, however, seems to have taken special delight in acquiring as a kind of trophy the "firebrand"'s chalice and mass vestments—objects the English labeled Sander's "masking furniture," in a parodic mockery of the Catholic veneration of the martyr's sacred relics.[89]

Sander and Campion represent different positions on the spectrum of English Catholic attitudes toward early modern Ireland. While Campion exploited Ireland and its symbols in his acts of self-fashioning, he regarded the country as England's inferior in both religion and culture, and as an indispensable component of a British imperial design. Sander, on the other hand, was able to subordinate national prejudices and parochial rivalries to the daring vision of an archipelagic Catholic nationalism. As we might expect, these differences between Campion and Sander over Ireland were deliberately elided in hostile Protestant narratives that lumped the two men together as representatives of a monolithic

---

[85] Peter Lombard, *De Regno Hiberniae, Sanctorum Insula, Commentarius*, the final chapters of which have been translated in *The Irish War of Defence 1598–1600: Extracts from the* De Hibernia Insula Commentarius *of Peter Lombard, Archbishop of Armagh* ed. and trans. Matthew J. Byrne (Cork University Press, 1930), 13, 21. Not all English Catholics involved in schemes to liberate Ireland from Elizabeth received Lombard's approbation. Lombard dismissed the adventurer Thomas Stukeley, for example, as "an Englishman ... little acceptable on his own merits to the Irish nation" (9).

[86] *The life of the glorious bishop S. Patricke* (*ERL* 210), vi.

[87] Howlin's martyrology listed victims of persecution in Ireland during the 1570s and 1580s (Colm Lennon, "Taking Sides: The Emergence of Irish Catholic Ideology," in Carey and Lotz-Heumann (eds.), *Taking Sides*, 87–8). Also see Ford, "Martyrdom, History, and Memory," 52–3.

[88] "Adored for Saints: Catholic Martyrdom in Ireland *c.*1560–1655," *Journal of Early Modern History* 5 (2001), 150–1.

[89] Quoted in Veech, *Dr Nicholas Sanders*, 279–80. Sander, according to O'Sullivan Beare's *Compendium*, when he "knew he was terminally ill ... asked the bishop of Killaloe to administer last rites and he died at dawn the following day. He was buried in an unmarked grave near Clonlish by four Irish knights" (Thomas Mayer, *ODNB* entry on Sander).

threat to the Elizabethan state. The Protestant pamphlet *An advertisement and defence for trueth against her backbiters* (1581), for example, describes Sander as "an errant and detestable Traitour ... one of the saide Campions companions," and presented their two endeavors as closely intertwined.[90] Likewise, William Charke in *An answere to a seditious pamphlet lately caste abroad by a Jesuite, with a discoverie of that blasphemous sect* (1580) explicitly bracketed Sander's mission to Ireland with Campion and Persons's contemporaneous venture to England. The composer of a ballad account of the execution of Campion and his allies had no doubt "that they were Authors ... and styrrers, of late, in the Irysh Rebellion."[91] This alleged link was further strengthened in the popular imagination when, following Campion's arrest, the English authorities asked suspected seminary priests the so-called "Bloody Question" concerning their opinion of Sander's Irish expedition and of Sander's defense in *De visibili* of the papal deposing power.[92] Official Protestant constructions of Catholic intentions in Ireland refused to acknowledge any diversity; instead, all Catholics were adjudged guilty of supporting rebellion in Ireland against the queen.[93] Thus, the author of an anti-Catholic tract on the defeat of Fitzgerald's forces assumed a simple, bifurcated, response to his "happy newes": whereas the "true religious and obedient subject" would be overjoyed, the "supersticious disloyall recusant" [i.e. the English Catholic reader] would be dismayed and confused.[94] You are either "with us," or "against us."

Robert Persons, recalling the beginning of the Jesuit mission to England on which he accompanied Campion, regrets the ease with which the Protestant authorities were able to conflate the careers of Campion and Sander:

[90] *An Advertisement and defence*, Aii[v]. English authorities used the rebellion in Ireland as a pretext for cracking down on English Catholics. The Spanish ambassador noted in October 1580 that the queen "has ordered [four earls], five barons and three hundred gentlemen to be imprisoned ... in fear of the rising of Catholics here as well as in Ireland" (quoted in J. H. Pollen, SJ, "The Irish Expedition of 1579," *The Month* 101 (1903), 82).
[91] "A Triumph for True Subjects and a Terrour unto al Traitours" (1581) in Hyder E. Rollins (ed.), *Old English Ballads 1553–1625* (Cambridge, 1920), 64–9.
[92] Simpson, *Edmund Campion*, 144. Campion's fellow priest, William Filbee, answered the question about Sander in Ireland with an evasiveness for which the Jesuits were notorious: "if he had bene in Ireland, when Doctour Saunders was there, hee woulde have done as a priest should have done, that is, to pray that the right may have place" (*A particular declaration or testimony, of the undutifull and traiterous affection borne against her Majestie by Edmond Campion, Jesuite, and other condemned priestes* (1582), Di[v]–Dii[r], Cii[r–v]). The author of *An aduertisement and defence for trueth against her backbiters* (1581) explains that the captured Catholic priests were asked "to declare what they thought of the saide Popes Bull (by which her Majestie was in the Popes intention deprived of the Crowne) and of Doctor Sanders, and of Bristowes traiterous writings in maintenance of the saide Bull, and allowance of the Rebellion in the North, and of Saunders trayterous actions in Irelande" (Aiiii[r]).
[93] Carol Z. Wiener, "'The Beleagured Isle': A Study of Elizabethan and Early Jacobean Anti-Catholicism," *Past and Present* 51 (1971), 27–62.
[94] *The true report of the prosperous success which God gave unto our English soldiers against the foreign bands of our Roman enemies lately arrived ... in Ireland, in the year 1580*, Aii[v].

Dr. Allen also told us that he had heard from Spain that Dr. Sanders was just gone into Ireland ... to comfort and assist the Earl of Desmond, Viscount Ballinglas, and others that had taken arms in defense of their religion ... Though it belonged not to us to mislike this journey of Dr. Sanders ... yet were we heartily sorry, partly because we feared that which really happened, the destruction of so rare and worthy a man, and partly because we plainly foresaw that this would be laid against us and other priests, if we should be taken in England, as though we had been privy or partakers thereof, as in very truth we were not, nor ever heard or suspected the same until this day.[95]

Persons now lamented Sander's mission to Ireland, "wherein all good men do wish that he had never byn, considering the great good he might have done to all Christendome by his most learned books, yf his lyfe had not byn shortened that way."[96] If even a militant English Catholic like Persons regretted Sander's commitment to the Catholic cause in Ireland, then the prospects were limited for further cooperation between Catholics from the two sides of the Irish Sea. Sander's intervention in Ireland proved a remarkable if ill-fated initiative by a leading English exile to achieve an ecumenical, ethnically inclusive, British–Irish reconversion effort. Significantly, though, he was not the only English Catholic involved in that effort. During the late 1570s and early 1580s, other English Catholics, unimpressed with the claims of Elizabethan imperial ideology, went to Ireland either to help the rebels and/or to escape religious persecution at home. In 1580 the Venetian Ambassador described English Catholic activists who "have fled to Ireland, where they have joined the rebels."[97] In the same year, the Godly Protestant preacher, James Bisse, told his Paul's Cross audience of "the Foxes of England, that are now in Ireland" helping "the Irish coltes" against "an English Gray"—an allusion to the queen's Lord Deputy, Arthur Lord Grey de Wilton, under whose command the insurgency of Sander, Fitzgerald, and their allies was to be brutally suppressed.[98] In the tumultuous years of the later sixteenth century, the boundary between the Catholic communities of England and Ireland was more open and more traversed than we have perhaps realized.

ENGLISH CATHOLICS AND THE TYRONE REBELLION

With the subsequent intensification of conflict in Ireland during the 1590s and the emergence of Hugh O'Neill, Earl of Tyrone, as the self-styled leader

[95] Quoted in Simpson, *Edmund Campion*, 146.

[96] *A manifestation of the great folly and bad spirit of certayne in England calling themselves secular priestes*, 33[v]–34[r] (Antwerp, 1602. *ERL* 169). Other references to Ireland appear at 32[r], 91[v], 92[r], 40[v]. Persons points out that Sander was a secular priest, not a Jesuit as some had alleged.

[97] *Calendar of State Papers and Manuscripts Relating to English Affairs Existing in the Archives and Collections of Venice* 2 (1558–1580) ed. Rawdon Brown and G. Cavendish Bentinck (London, 1890; Kraus Reprint, 1970), 646. Also see Veech, *Dr Nicholas Sanders*, 283 n. 4.

[98] *Two Sermons Preached, the one at Paules Crosse the eight of Januarie 1580, The Other, at Christes Churche in London the same day in the afternoone* (London, 1581), D4[v]–D5[r].

of a Catholic confederacy, English Catholics both at home and in exile were confronted with a more pressing test of their loyalties.[99] What were they to do if sent to fight for the cause of a Protestant queen against fellow Catholics in Ireland? This was the question that a Catholic gentleman, "one of the principal officers in the Irish wars," posed to the seminary priest John Gerard:

When...he told me he was anxious to return to the Irish wars, I was doubtful whether this was lawful in conscience, so he promised that if the priests over there, to whom I referred him, decided it was unlawful (they were on the spot and in a better position to judge), then he would resign his commission and return to England. Soon after arriving in Ireland he was killed in battle by a musket ball...But he had consulted the priests (he told me this in a letter), and they had said that it was lawful to fight against the Catholic faction, because no one had seemed at all clear why they had taken up arms.[100]

English (and other) Catholics who remained confused about the motives of the "Catholic faction" in Ireland were offered clarification in 1603 when eighteen doctors of Theology and Canon Law at the Universities of Salamanca and Valladolid published a single broadsheet *in English* declaring it lawful for all Catholics to fight on behalf of "The moste noble Prince Hugh ONeill" against English heretics, "as if they should feight against the Turques."[101] Citing as authority a papal brief, the doctors promised indulgences to those who helped O'Neill, and threatened damnation to those Catholics who supported Elizabeth's unjust war. Yet the doctors also deemed "Indifferent allegiance" a legitimate option, one that would allow Catholics to refuse to get involved on either side. Indeed, the doctors' declaration was not a call to arms: Catholics in Ireland who wished to avoid trouble were even permitted by the pope to pay "ordinarie taxes" to the queen and her officers.[102]

[99] O'Neill's religious convictions and motives remain a matter of scholarly debate. Nicholas Canny, in a recent reappraisal of the character of O'Neill, concludes that the Irish chief was "a man committed to few causes other than his own survival" ("Taking Sides in Early Modern Ireland: The Case of Hugh O'Neill, Earl of Tyrone," in Carey and Lotz-Huemann (eds.), *Taking Sides*, 115). Thomas O'Connor, on the other hand, sees O'Neill undergoing "some sort of religious conversion in the mid-1590s," partly as a result of his own successes against the English in battle ("Hugh O'Neill: Free Spirit, Religious Chameleon or Ardent Catholic?," in *The Battle of Kinsale*, ed. Morgan, 71).

[100] *John Gerard: The Autobiography of an Elizabethan*, trans. Philip Caraman (Oxford: Family Publications, 2006), 175, 178.

[101] My emphasis. *An extract of the determinacion, and censure of the doctours of the universities of Salamanca and Valledolid touching the warres of Ireland, and declaracion of the poape his breve concerning the same warres* (np, 1603. *ERL* 200). A contemporary reference to this decision appears in John Hull, *The unmasking of the politike atheist* (1602), A4r–v. Also see Clancy, *Papist Pamphleteers*, 76 n. 63.

The Irish college at Salamanca, established by the Jesuit Thomas White in 1592, was "the most important of the Iberian colleges" for exiles from Ireland. See Patricia O'Connell, "The Early-Modern Irish College Network in Iberia, 1590–1800," in Thomas O'Connor (ed.), *The Irish in Europe, 1580–1815* (Dublin: Four Courts Press, 2001), 54.

[102] The doctors' verdict was republished in the 17th century by the militant Irish exile Philip O'Sullivan Beare as part of his *Compendium* (1621). See Morgan, "'Un Pueblo Unido...'," 267.

Protestant responses to the declaration took various forms. Richard Broughton attempted to undermine the legitimacy of the ruling by claiming that "Xistus quintus did rather allow, then approve their opinion," never having actually seen "the resolution of that schoole."[103] In *The anatomie of popish tyrannie* (1603), Thomas Bell, a zealous convert from Catholicism, interpreted the declaration— "hammered in Salamanca the seventh day of March, 1602"—as allowing "the Catholikes in England [to] favour Tyrone in his warres, and that with great merit, and hope of eternall reward, as though they warred against the Turkes." Bell taunted his arch-enemy Robert Persons with the doctors' judgment, demanding, "Now Father Parsons, speake out man, have any of your company beene prac-ticioners in the treasons of Ireland?"[104] English Catholics who remained loyal to Elizabeth also had no doubt that Jesuits like Persons were stoking the fires of rebellion in Ireland. Robert Charnock, a secular priest, claimed in 1602 that English Jesuits "of the Spanish faction" had "great hopes . . . of making England a Japonian island by conquest of Ireland, according to the old prophecie, *He that England will win, through Ireland he must come in.*"[105]

Notwithstanding the allegations of their opponents, English Catholics took various positions on O'Neill and the Nine Years' War in Ireland. Similarly, among Catholics from Ireland there was no consensus about the legitimacy of rebellion against English rule. Some Catholic priests in Ireland remained loyal to the English crown, even advancing the strange argument that Pius V's Bull excommunicating Elizabeth "had not deprived Elizabeth of Ireland but only of England."[106] Even the Catholics of Ireland who resented the erosion of their religious liberties were not unanimous in support of O'Neill, the self-declared Catholic champion of the rebellion against English Protestant rule. Their recal-citrance upset Florence Conry, a Franciscan exile from the west of Ireland and a committed supporter of O'Neill's confederacy, who complained to Philip III in 1602 that the governors at the Irish college in Salamanca not only admitted students from the provinces of Ireland "subject to the Queen, and consequently schismatical," but also taught the students to obey the queen, indoctrinating them "with so bad milke as is the obedience towards the Queene and the cordiall love towards all things to her." Conry was alarmed that students were being taught "that the queene may be obeyed and armes taken against your Majestie [i.e. Philip] and they confesse and absolve and do admit to mass and other offices

---

[103] *A just and moderate answer to a most injurious, and slaunderous pamphlet* (np, 1606. *ERL* 93), H2ʳ.

[104] *The anatomie of popish tyrannie*, 2: 73–4.

[105] *An answere made by one of our brethren, a secular priest* (np, 1602. *ERL* 112), Aiʳ⁻ᵛ. Charnock stages a dialogue between the narrator and his interlocutor: "What man, Ireland? Yea, I say Ireland. What, Ireland woon from her Majestie? Yea, and from Teron [Tyrone] too." The narrator claims that the English Jesuits "will never yeeld to the appellants . . . untill Ireland be wholly theirs."

[106] John J. Silke, *Kinsale: The Spanish Intervention in Ireland at the End of the Elizabethan Wars* (New York: Fordham University Press, 1970), 66.

such as do it."[107] Conry wanted the Irish colleges to be bastions of support for O'Neill, not breeding grounds of disaffection with his cause.

Conry, along with O'Neill's other supporters, took part in a European-wide debate about the Gaelic chief's motives and religious sincerity which his enemies were quick to call into question. Peter Lombard, O'Neill's agent in Rome from the later 1590s, reassured Pope Clement VIII in 1600 that O'Neill's struggle against the English occupation of Ireland was inspired by religious fervor and that O'Neill himself was an exemplary son of the Catholic Church.[108] In offering these reassurances, Lombard also warned of

persons scattered amongst foreign nations who, to lessen the fame and hopes which the successes of this war have aroused, keep dinning into the ears of many that they doubt if this Chief, its general, is a Catholic, at least if he is a real Catholic, and is really concerned for religion in this his rebellion, as they call it. Whether in this they are actuated by zeal for religion, as they desire to appear, or by some political jealousy, I will not take upon myself to say.[109]

"These devices [i.e. tricks]," Lombard continued, "and others of more questionable and wholesale character calculated to weaken the Irish Princes and people by calumniating and defaming them, were, I am sorry to say, employed abroad by *even Catholics of that nation* (i.e. of England), whom its heretics have to this day endeavored to oppress so severely at home."[110] In Lombard's view, even English Catholics persecuted for the faith, could not be trusted to assist the Catholic cause in Ireland.

Lombard's allegations about the hostility of émigré English Catholics towards the Irish fed suspicions between the two "nations" in exile. These suspicions, especially between English and Irish expatriates at the Spanish court, were noticed by the Catholic Englishman Thomas Fitzherbert, King Philip's Secretary of English Letters. Fitzherbert explained in *A defense of the catholyke cause* that

---

[107] Hammerstein, "Aspects of the Continental Education of Irish Students," 149–50. Hammerstein distinguishes between politicized Irish Franciscans like Florence Conry who cooperated with the Gaelic chiefs, and theoretically-minded, cautious Irish Jesuits (mainly Old English), who were suspicious of O'Neill's religious motives. Patricia O'Connell writes of the Irish College at Salamanca that "Its early years were marked by differences between the Jesuit administration and the exiled Gaelic aristocracy. They judged the Irish Jesuits hostile to Northern Gaelic students and indulgent towards Old English Leinster and Munster candidates ... [This was a sign of the] ... depth of divisions among migrant Irish Catholics." The Jesuits were mostly from Old English stock and were more ready to "maintain good relations with [the] Stuarts" (which is what Spain wanted), unlike the more militant Gaelic Irish ("The Early-Modern Irish College Network," 55).

[108] Hiram Morgan, *Tyrone's Rebellion: The Outbreak of the Nine Years War in Tudor Ireland* (Woodbridge, Suffolk, UK: Royal Historical Society, 1993), 4–5. Lombard was seeking papal backing for O'Neill when he offered a presentation manuscript of his *Commentarius* (1600) to the pontiff. Also see John J. Silke, "Hugh O'Neill, the Catholic Question, and the Papacy," *Irish Ecclesiastical Record*, 5th ser. 104 (1965), 65–79; Thomas O'Connor, "A Justification for Foreign Intervention in Early Modern Ireland: Peter Lombard's *Commentarius* (1600)," in id. and Mary Ann Lyons (eds.), *Irish Migrants in Europe after Kinsale, 1602–1820* (Dublin: Four Courts Press, 2003), 14–31.

[109] Byrne (ed.), *The Irish War of Defence*, 41.   [110] Ibid. 43; my emphasis.

the English exiles, contrary to rumor, had known nothing about O'Neill's latest military adventure. How could they, when the Irish exiles were so careful to keep O'Neill's plans secret? In fact, claimed Fitzherbert, the Irish exiles at court not only concealed their affairs from the English, but also "desyre[d] the Kings ministers not to communicate them with us." Fitzherbert advised the English authorities seeking confirmation that Irish exiles in Spain distrusted their English counterparts to interrogate Hugh Buy, a former agent of O'Neill's in Spain who now worked for Elizabeth's government. Mr. Buy could testify, claimed Fitzherbert, that English and Irish exiles never even "saluted one another" at Philip's court.[111] English and Irish exiles in Madrid, far from being allies, were rivals for the attention and resources of the Spanish courtly elite.

By 1606, relations between English and Irish exiles in Spain had became so strained that Philip III expressed the hope that O'Neill's arrival in Habsburg territories would help bring about the reconciliation of the two nations. Philip, seeking papal backing at this time for his plan to invade Ireland, instructed his ambassador at Rome to approach the Englishman "Father Personio [Persons], whose prudence and talents are known to you...Procure, as coming from you, that he raise this matter [the invasion] with the Pope and that he incline the Irish Earls to do the same." When O'Neill heard that Philip was getting Persons and the English exiles involved in plans to "liberate" Ireland, he warned the king not to trust the English. According to O'Neill, Persons might be "a very good and virtuous religious," but he was also

in correspondence with many English people whom he believes are honest [but who] are not all as good as he is. Among so many English people there is always a spy and one who will play with both hands. Although it is true that for our purpose it is necessary that we should find out from them the state of affairs in England, we cannot let them know what we plan to do in Ireland, for *under no circumstances do they wish to see the advancement of our country, and we know this with certitude through long experience.*[112]

Despite O'Neill's description of Persons as "a very good and virtuous religious," the Irishman may also have had doubts about Persons's own attitudes toward Ireland. After all, in *A conference about the next succession to the crowne of Ingland* (1595), Persons (and his co-authors) puts into the mouth of the civil lawyer a defense of government by strangers that takes Ireland as an exemplary case. Ireland is shown to benefit from English rule. As the lawyer asks rhetorically: "are not the favours and indulgences used towards the civil Irish that live in peace much more than to the Inglish themselves in Ingland? For first, their taxes...be much lesse...For matters of religion, they are pressed much lesse then

[111] *A defense of the catholyke cause* (np, 1602. *ERL* 146), 5ʳ⁻ᵛ. Also see Albert J. Loomie, SJ, *Spain and the Early Stuarts, 1585–1655* (Aldershot: Ashgate, 1996), 4: 219.
[112] Micheline Kerney Walsh, *Hugh O'Neill: an Exile of Ireland, Prince of Ulster* (Dublin: Four Courts Press, 1996), 84–5. My emphasis. In the same letter of 1608, Philip claimed that "Ireland belongs to the Apostolic See."

home-borne subjects, albeit their affections to the Roman religion, be knowne to be much more universal, then it is in Ingland." In this view, the inhabitants of Ireland (at least the Old English of the Pale) should be grateful that they are governed by a benevolent, if heretical, foreign ruler rather than "at the handes of their owne natural Princes" who are more likely to mistreat them.[113]

O'Neill's misgivings about English Catholic intentions toward Ireland were not always justifiable. As the case of Nicholas Sander shows, some high-profile English Catholics were willing to work with their co-religionists from Ireland. Another English Catholic in this group was the Elizabethan soldier Sir William Stanley. In 1587 Stanley defected to Spain, surrendering to Philip II the town of Daventer in the Low Countries, and taking with him a regiment that consisted overwhelmingly of Irish mercenaries whom he had originally recruited for the queen.[114] Later, Stanley worked with an "Irish militant circle on the continent" consisting mainly of Old English exiles, including Richard Stanihurst, Edmund Campion's friend and Dublin host. Stanihurst had emigrated from Ireland in 1580, embraced militant Catholicism, become a supporter of O'Neill, and revised his earlier negative views about Ireland's Gaelic population.[115] Whereas Stanihurst had once denigrated the Gaels as fickle, weak, and "of no great reputation in the world," he now came to appreciate them as members of an Ireland-wide confessional community that embraced all ethnic and national groupings. Although historian Grainne Henry argues that "relations between the Old Irish [i.e. Gaelic] and 'English' exile groups in general were not as close as might be perceived," the case of Stanihurst suggests that high levels of cooperation were possible among the various Catholic factions from England and Ireland.[116]

Other examples can be cited of individuals and groups of Catholics from Ireland and England mingling, sharing, and working together as part of transnational resistance to the ideological agendas of the English Protestant state. The prejudices engendered against Irish Catholicity by works like Campion's *Historie of Ireland* as well as by long-standing English stereotypes about Ireland, were never so pervasive as to turn Catholics from England and Ireland into monolithic hostile communities. Many English Catholics, in fact, saw Ireland as an attractive refuge in the sixteenth century from the increasingly repressive

---

[113] Persons et al., *A conference about the next succession*, 2: 209, 229.

[114] Grainne Henry, "The Emerging Identity of an Irish Military Group in the Spanish Netherlands, 1586–1610," in R. V. Comerford, Mary Cullen, Jacqueline R. Hill, and Colm Lennon (eds.), *Religion, Conflict, and Coexistence in Ireland* (Dublin: Gill and Macmillan, 1990), 54, 60–1, 66; Simon Adams, "A Patriot for Whom? Stanley, York and Elizabeth's Catholics," *History Today* 37 (1987), 46–50.

[115] Grainne Henry, *The Irish Military Community in Spanish Flanders, 1586–1621* (Dublin: Irish Academic Press, 1992), 120–1; Lennon, *Richard Stanihurst*, 42–4, 125–28; Albert J. Loomie, SJ, "Richard Stanyhurst in Spain: Two Unknown Letters of August 1593," *Huntington Library Quarterly* 28 (1965), 146, 149, 151.

[116] Henry, *Irish Military Community*, 121.

Elizabethan state. In Ireland throughout Elizabeth's reign, the pressures to conform to reformed religion, as well as the penalties for not doing so, were significantly less than in England. Campion was assured before he left England that in Ireland "he could more freely—anyway with less certain danger—practise the true religion."[117]

Other English recusants followed Campion across the Irish Sea. In the 1580s, the Munster plantation established after the defeat of the Sander/ Fitzgerald/Desmond rebellion attracted many English Catholics to southern Ireland in spite of the government's attempts to block their participation. Even some of the leaders or "undertakers" of the project had Catholic credentials. The State Papers for this period are full of complaints by New English Protestant officials in Ireland about "the perverse recusants that come out of England hither."[118] In the next decade, reports continued to be made of English Catholics going to Ireland, "where for the tyme they are at more quiet then yf they were in England."[119] Some of these émigrés included the children of wealthier recusant families in England who sent their sons and daughters across the Irish Sea as part of a strategy of religious survival.[120] These patterns of temporary or permanent emigration to Ireland continued into the seventeenth century. The Dublin-based English Protestant Barnaby Rich complained in *A new Irish prognostication, or Popish callender* (1624) that "there bee . . . perverse Papists that come daily creeping out of England to plant themselves in Ireland . . . and are more daungerous to his Majesties estate, then those that are naturally borne in Ireland." Moreover, bemoaned Rich, "Our English Recusants . . . have . . . so planted themselves through every part of Ireland, that they are more pernitious in their example, then the Irish themselves."[121]

Contrary to received opinion, the Nine Years war in Ireland also saw some English Catholics supporting what they considered O'Neill's religious crusade. Catholics in England offered passive resistance by refusing to pay the recusancy fines specifically levied to finance the crown's campaigns in Ireland; in 1598, when "the Privy Council directed officials in the provinces to collect payment from the kingdom's wealthiest recusants for the supply of the Queen's light horse regiments in Ireland," the officers delivering the news in Lancashire were attacked

[117]   Quoted in Kilroy, *Edmund Campion*, 54–5.
[118]   Quoted in Michael McCarthy-Morrogh, *The Munster Plantation: English Migration to Southern Ireland 1583–1641* (Oxford: Clarendon Press, 1986), 190–7, 199–203; quotation at 193.
[119]   *The Letters and Despatches of Richard Verstegan, c.1550–1640*, ed. A. G. Petti. Catholic Record Society 52 (London, 1959), 87.
[120]   Unpublished paper by James Lenaghan, Department of History, The Ohio State University. I am grateful to the author for sharing his work with me. Also see David Edwards, "A Haven of Popery: English Catholic Migration to Ireland in the Age of Plantations," in Alan Ford and John McCafferty (eds.), *The Origins of Sectarianism in Early Modern Ireland* (Cambridge: Cambridge University Press, 2005), 95–126. "Ireland swarms with English recusants," wrote a government official in the early seventeenth century, "for the laws [of Ireland] have no power to deal with them" (113).
[121]   *A new Irish prognostication*, 54, 93.

and the local recusants proved difficult to track down.[122] The recusant strong-hold of Lancashire offered more active resistance to Elizabeth's wars in Ireland when men impressed in the county allegedly refused to fight "against fellow Romanists, even if they were Irish."[123] Richard Vaughan, Bishop of Chester, one of the Protestant officials responsible for enforcing the recusancy laws in Lancashire, told Robert Cecil in 1600 "that the recusants in his diocese 'have been much encouraged by our ill success in Ireland.'" "Of late," Vaughan continued, the recusants "have grown very desperate, being doubtless fed with hopes by their priests and other factious firebrands who lurk in these parts and fill the peoples' ears with dangerous rumours and both here and in Ireland sow the seeds of rebellion."[124] Another informer from Lancashire told Cecil that he had apprehended a seminary priest who "I suppose . . . is a far traveller and hath spent some late time in Ireland with Tyrone and can reveal matter importing the state of that country."[125] After O'Neill's flight to the Continent in 1607, the government spy William Udall claimed that the Gaelic leader was about to return to Ireland to renew the insurrection. "The forerunners of this bellum ecclesie," Udall warned, "are the Jesuites, who daily come into England, but especially into Irelande, to prepare the consciences of subjectes for these exploites. Lancashire is a most daungerous countrey, and expectinge and provideinge for these attempts a long tyme, but never soe busy as nowe."[126] We will never know how many Catholics crossed the Irish Sea from Lancashire or elsewhere in England to support their co-religionists' struggle against the heretics, but around the same time that Udall was writing, the Earl of Thomond observed from Ireland that "There come many English recusants out of England who do much hurt here."[127] Some English Catholics evidently saw the defense of their faith as an international cause that meant sacrificing petty national chauvinism for the supranational ideals of the universal Catholic Church.[128] In Ireland, lay Catholics from England and Ireland were to prove far more compatible than many of the English, Irish, and Welsh

---

[122] Margaret Sena, "William Blundell and the Networks of Catholic Dissent in Post-Reformation England," in Alexandra Shepard and Phil Withington (eds.), *Communities in Early Modern England: Networks, Place, Rhetoric* (Manchester: Manchester University Press, 2002), 58; see also Donna Hamilton, "Richard Verstegan's *A Restitution of Decayed Intelligence* (1605): A Catholic Antiquarian Replies to John Foxe, Thomas Cooper, and Jean Bodin," *Prose Studies* 22 (1999), 15–16.

[123] Mark Charles Fissel, *English Warfare, 1511–1642* (New York: Routledge, 2001), 95.

[124] Quoted in John McGurk, *The Elizabethan Conquest of Ireland: The 1590s Crisis* (Manchester: Manchester University Press, 1997), 118.

[125] Quoted in J. Stanley Leatherbarrow, *The Lancashire Elizabethan Recusants* (Manchester: Chetham Society, 1947), 142.

[126] P. R. Harris, "The Reports of William Udall, Informer, 1605–1612," *Recusant History* 8 (1966), 231.

[127] *Calendar of the State Papers, relating to Ireland, of the Reign of James I*, vol. 2: *1606–8*, ed. C. W. Russell and John P. Prendergast (Nendeln/Liechtenstein: Kraus Reprint, 1974), 258.

[128] Marie B. Rowlands, "Hidden Peoples: Catholic Commoners, 1558–1625," in *English Catholics of Parish and Town 1558–1778* (London: Catholic Record Society, 1999), 10–35.

exiles on the Continent. As David Edwards observes, "For the best part of a century, from 1540 to 1640, English Catholics coming to Ireland seem to have felt they had less to fear from, and more in common with, Irish Catholics, than English Protestants." In Ireland, at least, religion trumped ethnicity in shaping the identity of the English Catholic diaspora.[129]

ENGLISH "CATHOLIC" WRITERS ON IRELAND: ANTHONY MUNDAY AND SIR JOHN HARINGTON

While English Catholics offered various kinds of practical help to their fellow papists in Ireland, some English "Catholic" writers also reworked orthodox Anglocentric Protestant discourses about Ireland in unexpected ways. Donna Hamilton has recently made a compelling case for seeing Anthony Munday as a covert Catholic who struggled to combine fidelity to the "old religion" with loyalty to the Elizabethan state.[130] Munday, an often savage critic of Spanish Catholicism and "Spaniolized" orders like the Jesuits, expressed the nostalgic wish to see England taking its place once more among the league of Christian nations loyal to Rome. Munday conveyed this ideology in the Iberian chivalric romances that he translated between the late sixteenth and early seventeenth century.[131] The most popular of these, *Palmerin of England, part 1* (multiple editions in 1596, 1602, 1609, and 1616), imagined an England that was supported rather than threatened by her European neighbors—neighbors that are represented by wayfaring knights like Palmerin himself who come to "Great Britain" to help free the ruler's son from the tyranny of the enchantress Eutropa. Members of the same knightly caste, especially the Knight of the Savage Man, also rescue Ireland from the misrule of usurping giants. *Palmerin of England* does not depict Ireland's giants as indigenous to Ireland or as allegorical projections of Spanish imperial power like Grantorto in Book 5 of Spenser's *Faerie Queene*. On the contrary, *Palmerin*'s giants are essentially English in nature. After Calfurnian is killed by the Knight of the Savage Man, his brother—"Camboldam of Mulzella, the Lord of Penebroque, one of the cruellest Tyrants in all the world"—sails from England to Ireland in search of "sharpe revenge" against his brother's killer. But he too is quickly dispatched, this time by the Knight of Fortune.[132] As Hamilton points out, Camboldam is a loosely disguised allegory of Richard de Clare, the Second Earl of Pembroke, one of the leaders of the Anglo-Norman "conquest" of

---

[129] Edwards, "A Haven of Popery," 126. See also 111–12.
[130] Donna B. Hamilton, *Anthony Munday and the Catholics, 1560–1633* (Aldershot: Ashgate, 2005).
[131] Ibid. 73–112, esp. 82–5.
[132] Munday, *Palmerin of England, part 1* (1596), ch. 27 and 32.

Ireland in the late twelfth century. Spenser and other Protestant writers indebted to Gerald of Wales's foundational narrative about this "conquest" revered Strongbow (as de Clare was known) as a quasi-legendary figure, a model of violent masculinity, and a culture hero for embattled New English colonists in the late sixteenth century. Spenser's Irenius recalls in *A View of the State of Ireland* how "the Earle Strangbowe, having conquered that land, delivered up the same into the hands of Henry the Second, then King."[133] Munday, then, by choosing not to change or delete the title "Lord of Penebroque" that appeared in the original Spanish text, and by figuring the earl as a monstrous giant, signals his rejection of the orthodox Protestant view of Strongbow. Instead, Munday makes it possible for his readers to think of Ireland as the victim of oppression from England.

Just as the translation of texts from a European Catholic literary tradition allowed Munday to smuggle culturally heterodox ideas into the mainstream of English culture, so John Harington also employed translation and other literary forms to express counter-cultural views of Ireland. Recent criticism has recognized in Harington an equivocal religious sensibility that longed for a pre-Reformation past typified by consensus rather than division. Harington, a comically self-styled "protesting Catholique Puritan," cleverly evaded prosecution for his religious views by expressing them in the limited circles of manuscript culture and often under a veneer of jocularity.[134] Gerard Kilroy's recent study of the surviving manuscripts of Harington's *Metamorphosis of Ajax* (1596), epigrams, and succession tract (1602), presents a writer deeply committed to religious toleration and debate, to the extrication of the state from matters of individual conscience, and to the proposition that Catholics have just as good a claim on the "Truth" as Protestants.[135] In the final chapter of Harington's succession tract titled "Of Religion," he debunks the Elizabethan myth of the Reformation: "the beginning of Reformation that K. Henrie the viiith made was not so sincere, but that it was myxed with private and politique respeces, of gayne, of revenge, of fancie; and finally that even in Protestantes opinions it was not worthie the name

---

[133] Edmund Spenser, *A View of the State of Ireland*, ed. Andrew Hadfield and Willy Maley (Oxford: Blackwell, 1997), 53.

[134] Donna Hamilton writes that Harington "normally kept his Catholicism out of public view," while Alison Shell describes Harington as "an author who favoured religious toleration and liked to keep his own confessional allegiance ambiguous." Hamilton, "The Persecution of Catholics in Renaissance England," in Vincent P. Carey (ed.), *Voices for Tolerance in an Age of Persecution* (Washington DC: The Folger Shakespeare Library, 2004), 116; Shell, *Catholicism, Controversy, and the English Literary Imagination, 1558–1660* (Cambridge: Cambridge University Press, 1999), 120.

[135] Kilroy, *Edmund Campion*, ch. 4. Also see Jason Scott-Warren's review of Kilroy's book in *Early Modern Literary Studies* 12.2 (2006), where he warns that a "New Catholicism" in early modern literary studies is often too quick to apply the term "Catholic" in an un-nuanced way to writers usually seen as religiously reformed. In his *ODNB* article on Harington, Scott-Warren states that Harington "had a strong leaning towards Catholicism."

of a Reformation; and I am sure the Papistes counte it a confusion, a destruction, and a deformation."[136]

But what of Harington's views on Ireland and particularly Irish religion? One place to look, as Clare Carroll has shown, is Harington's translation of the *Orlando Furioso* (1591), a work deeply influenced in its ideas, imagery, and language by one of the poet's several sojourns in Ireland.[137] In passages that feature Irish settings and figures, Harington eschews the typically derogatory New English view of the Gaelic Irish as "primitive and culturally barbaric."[138] The Irish knight Oberto is depicted, for example, as "a perfect chivalric hero" and a devoted servant to the lady he rescues.[139] The Gaelic soldiers that appear in Book 10 are described as having "valiant harts | And active limbs" and as following "The noble Earls of Ormond and Kildare."[140] And when in the same book, Rogero is carried on his winged horse across the "Irish seas ... [and] Saint *George* his channell" toward "the Irish Ile," the narrator is compelled to mention how

> Saint Patricke built a solitarie cave
> Into the which they that devoutly go
> By purging of their sinnes their soules may save
> Now whether this report be true or no
> I not affirme and yet I not deprave.

In the Historical Commentary appended by Harington at the end of the book, he (unlike Campion in *A Historie of Ireland*) refrains from mocking Ariosto's neutrality about St Patrick's Purgatory. Instead, Harington first directs readers to other authorities: "And whereas he speakes of *S. Patricke* the Irish saint, I would have them that would know the storie of him to looke in *Surius de vitis sanctorum*, and there they may see it at large." Then Harington shares with the reader his own experiences in Ireland, expressing his respect for Saint Patrick and keeping open rather than foreclosing the issue of Patrick's Purgatory: "for mine owne part at my being in Ireland, where I taried a few moneths, I was inquisitive of their opinion of this Saint, and I could learne nothing other then a reverent conceipt that they had of him as becomes all Christians to have of devout men and chiefly of those by whom they are firste instructed in the Christian faith: but for his purgatorie, I found neither any that affirmed it or beleeved it."[141]

---

[136] *A Tract on the Succession to the Crown (A.D. 1602) by Sir John Harington*, ed. Clements R. Markham (London: J. B. Nichols, 1880), 98–9. Also see Kilroy, *Edmund Campion*, 113.

[137] Clare Carroll, "Ajax in Ulster and Ariosto in Ireland: Translating the *Orlando Furioso*," in *Circe's Cup: Cultural Transformations in Early Modern Writing about Ireland* (Notre Dame, Ind.: University of Notre Dame Press, 2001), 69–90.

[138] Ibid. 70.

[139] Ibid. 71. *Orlando Furioso. Translated into English Heroical Verse by Sir John Harington*, ed. Robert McNulty (Oxford, Clarendon Press, 1972), Book 11.

[140] *Orlando Furioso*, ed. McNulty, 119.   [141] Ibid. 122.

Harington also mentions Saint Patrick's Purgatory in non-judgmental terms as part of a general discussion of Ireland's religious condition in an appeal he penned to Robert Cecil and the Earl of Devonshire in 1605. Given the title, "A Short View of the State of Ireland," by its nineteenth-century editor, the text represents Harington's (eventually unsuccessful) appeal to be appointed both Chancellor and Bishop of Ireland.[142] A remarkably ecumenical and irenic analysis of Ireland's past, as well as a plan for Ireland's future, the text has not received the scholarly attention it deserves. Harington's account of the different inhabitants of Ireland both testifies to their essential goodness and condemns their treatment by English colonists: "I never fownd in the remote sheers of England or Walls [Wales] eyther the gentry more kynde...or the marchawnts and townsmen and women more cyvill in behaveowr, or the mean sort and peasawnts more loving and servisable whear they are honestly used...but they are so seldome used to soch usage, and so grosly abused, somtyme by the soldyer in war, somtyme by the offycer in peace, that yt ys no wonder yf they take revenge."[143] Although Harington denies the charge of being a "Papist," his discussion of Ireland's Catholics and his proposals for religious reform must surely have raised the suspicions of his select audience.[144] Harington claims that attempts by Protestants to reform religious services in Ireland have proven so inept that he can hardly blame "the recusant Lords" for not cooperating.[145]

At every opportunity in "A Short View of the State of Ireland," Harington seeks common ground with Ireland's Catholics, diminishing rather than exaggerating the differences between their religious traditions and his own. He thus defends the proper use of religious images and condemns acts of iconoclasm in churches. Those who would "creep to [images] and are prostrate afore them as to deytyes," he writes, are just as culpable as "those that wold breake [images] and defase them with scorn." He approves the copes and vestments of Irish clerics; he endorses confession so long as it is freely performed; he condones "Fasting in Lent and other appointed days"; he is open-minded about the number of sacraments and the nature of "the Lord's Supper," and shares the queen's wish that "men wold leave disputing of yt and beleeve of yt evry one as God showld geve him grace." Finally, he agrees with Catholics that bishops are the rightful successors to the apostles, but insists "that this exoticall power claymed by one over all hath slender fowndacion in Scripture"—a remark suggesting Harington's adherence to a kind of *sotto voce* non-papal Catholicism. Harington's call for "myld conferences" and for an emphasis on charity in dealing with the inhabitants of Ireland represents a radical departure from the violent and

---

[142] Harington, "A Short View of the State of Ireland," in *Anecdota Bodleiana: Gleanings from Bodleian MSS*, ed. W. Dunn Macray (Oxford: James Parker, 1879), 17.

[143] Ibid. 9.   [144] Ibid. 14.   [145] Ibid. 16.

confrontational rhetoric of most New English officials and settlers in Ireland at this time.[146]

Some six years before Harington wrote this text on Ireland he paid a diplomatic visit with Sir William Warren to Hugh O'Neill at "the arch-rebel's" Ulster headquarters. Harington's epistolary account of the meeting suggests he was both surprised and mesmerized by what he witnessed. O'Neill turns out in fact to be no churlish "arch-rebel" but every bit an English earl who "used far greater respect to me than I expected."[147] The earl is self-deprecating, good-humored, and charming—the charismatic focus of a kind of Renaissance court in pastoral exile "under the stately canopy of heaven." As critics have noted, the account is highly literary, refracted through the fictional conventions of chivalric romance that Harington mastered in the *Orlando Furioso*. But the romanticized quality of the narrative does nothing to lessen the shock for the reader of O'Neill's "solemn protestation that he was not ambitious, but sought only safety of his life, and freedom of his conscience, without which he would not live, though the Queen would give him Ireland." O'Neill's demand for freedom of conscience for Ireland's Catholics is not ridiculed or rebutted by Harington in the way it had been by English officials when O'Neill had made the demand in the past. In fact, given Harington's repeated insistence that the ideal commonwealth could peacefully accommodate diverse religious viewpoints, he might well have looked favorably upon O'Neill's demand.[148]

Harington hoped that the accession of a wise and impartial King James would usher in this ideal commonwealth in which every subject "serve[d] God . . . praie[d] for the Prince, love[d] his neighbour, [and] lyve[d] in his vocation."[149] But this outcome was prevented by an influential holdover from Elizabeth's reign. Robert Cecil, unlike Harington, reacted to O'Neill's religious agenda with a patronizing gesture of dismissal, inscribing the word "Ewtopia" on the list of 22 demands that O'Neill "published" in 1599, and that included the far more provocative request "that the Catholic, Apostolic and Roman religion be openly preached and taught throughout all Ireland."[150] Harington, like others

---

[146] Ibid. 16–19.

[147] For Harington's account of his visit to O'Neill in 1599 and for modern discussions of it, see *The Letters and Epigrams of Sir John Harington*, ed., Norman Egbert McClure (Philadelphia: University of Pennsylvania Press, 1930), 76–79; Carroll, *Circe's Cup*, 74–6; David Gardiner, " 'These Are Not the Thinges Men Live by Now a Days': Sir John Harington's Visit to the O'Neill, 1599," *Cahiers Elisabéthains: Late Medieval and Renaissance Studies* 55 (1999), 1–15; Andrew Murphy, *"But the Irish Sea Betwixt Us": Ireland, Colonialism, and Renaissance Literature* (Lexington, KY: University Press of Kentucky, 1999), 105–9.

[148] In his tract on the succession, Harington argued that only James could bring about this religious accommodation through "a peaceble parley" of all sides (*A Tract on the Succession to the Crown*, ed. Markham, 109).

[149] Ibid. 107.

[150] The articles, along with hostile government responses to them, are reproduced in Hiram Morgan, "Faith and Fatherland or Queen and Country? An Unpublished Exchange between O'Neill

in England whose religious sympathies we can identify, however provisionally, with the broad and contested category of "Catholic," understood the religious aspirations of the people of Ireland. And despite the hostile suspicion of Cecil and other English leaders, he was confident that his vision of an Ireland at peace and religiously unified was no dreamlike "Eutopia" but an imminent possibility.[151]

and the State at the Height of the Nine Years War," *Du'iche Ne'ill: Journal of the O'Neill Country Historical Society* 9 (1994), 9–65, esp. 32–4.

[151] "A Short View of the State of Ireland," ed. Macray, 6. As Morgan reminds us, "the disputed term 'Catholic'... signified universal and encompassed all the followers of Jesus Christ dispersed over the face of the earth" ("Faith and Fatherland or Queen and Country?" 20).

6

Anglo-Spanish Relations and the Hispaniolized English Catholic

IRELAND, SPAIN, AND THE POLITICS OF ETHNICITY

The rebellion against English rule in Ireland led by Hugh O'Neill, Earl of Tyrone, effectively ended when his forces were defeated at the battle of Kinsale in December 1601. In the years after his defeat, O'Neill led a precarious existence in Ulster; although pardoned by King James, he continued to be harassed by New English officials in Ireland. When the government summoned O'Neill to London in 1607, he feared that he would either be executed or imprisoned in the Tower. In response, O'Neill hastily fled Ireland for the Continent along with other members of his confederacy, their families, and servants. O'Neill and his party traveled through France and the Spanish Low Countries before arriving in Rome, where he solicited help for his return to Ireland at the head of a Catholic army. Yet neither Philip III nor Pope Paul V, despite their initial hospitality, was keen to succor the exile leader. Philip, wary of jeopardizing his peace treaty with England, refused O'Neill permission to leave Rome for Madrid. Moreover, O'Neill and his Irish allies found themselves in competition with English exiles for the attentions of Spain and for the resources that were increasingly scarce in the overstretched and nearly bankrupt Habsburg empire of the early seventeenth century.[1]

Rivalries between these two groups from the Atlantic archipelago were exacerbated when the exiles from Ireland, in their bid for preferential treatment from the Spanish, resorted to an early modern identity politics by invoking the putative genealogical ties between the peoples of Spain and Ireland. O'Neill and his confederate ally O'Donnell had already exploited this tactic in an attempt to secure Spanish support during the Nine Years War.[2] Their case depended

---

[1] R. A. Stradling, *Europe and the Decline of Spain: A Study of the Spanish System, 1580–1720* (London, 1981), Introduction and ch. 1; Paul C. Allen, *Philip III and the Pax Hispanica, 1598–1621: The Failure of Grand Strategy* (New Haven: Yale University Press, 2000).

[2] Hiram Morgan, *Tyrone's Rebellion: The Outbreak of the Nine Years War in Tudor Ireland* (Woodbridge, Suffolk, UK: Royal Historical Society, 1993), 209; John Carey, "Did the Irish Come from Spain? The Legend of the Milesians," *History Ireland* 9.3 (2001), 8–11; Colin Kidd, *British Identities before Nationalism: Ethnicity and Nationhood in the Atlantic World, 1600–1800* (Cambridge: Cambridge University Press, 1999), 64–5, 146–58.

largely upon the medieval Irish chronicle, the *Leabhar Gabhala*, or The Book of Invasions, which detailed the waves of invaders and immigrants who had settled in Ireland from biblical times. O'Neill and O'Donnell distilled the arguments of the *Leabhar* in a memorial written to Philip in 1608 which offered "a brief account of their race and their descendence" from the ancient inhabitants of Spain. "The Earls," they said of themselves,

> are direct descendants of King Gathelo who was married to Scota, daughter of the Pharao King of Egypt. This Gathelo fled from the plagues with which God punished Egypt through the agency of Moses; he embarked with his people and his wife Scota and did not land until he reached Galicia [northwest Spain] and, having conquered Biscaya, Asturias and Galicia, he proclaimed himself king of the territory. One of his descendants, a king called Milesius, sent his sons with a fleet of sixty ships, which sailed from the port of La Coruña, to conquer and populate Ireland.

Like so many myths about the origins and prehistories of nations and peoples in the Renaissance, the so-called Milesian myth begins with a noble patriarch (Gathelo) and traces his heroic struggles and the struggles of his progeny (the sons of Milesius) to the promised land (Ireland).[3] The story of the sons of Milesius is an utterly specious bit of pseudo-history but an invaluable ideological fantasy for Irishmen like O'Neill and O'Donnell bent on proving their affinity with the Spanish.[4]

Other Irish exiles made similar, pointedly ideological, claims about the ancient consanguinity of the peoples of Ireland and Spain. The historian Philip O'Sullivan Beare, for example, hoped to gain special respect from his Spanish hosts for his own faction among the Irish exiles in the early seventeenth century by invoking the Milesian myth. Beare's writings creatively reinvent the categories for classifying the various peoples of Ireland. Beare distinguishes between two main groups: the Old or Ancient Irish, the "*veteres Iberni*"—descendants of the Gaels; and the New Irish, the "*novi Iberni*"—descendants of the Anglo-Normans. He further subdivides the New Irish into the English Irish and the Mixed Irish. Beare's approach is innovative because each group is defined not strictly on the basis of ethnic or racial factors, but also according to the religious, cultural, and political affiliations of its members. Thus Beare himself, although of Anglo-Norman descent and thus nominally an Old Englishman according to an alternative nomenclature, sees himself as one of the Mixed Irish whose religion, culture, language, and, most importantly, anti-English political allegiances, are

---

[3] Quoted in Micheline Kerney Walsh, *Hugh O'Neill: an Exile of Ireland, Prince of Ulster* (Dublin: Four Courts Press, 1996), 137–8, 77. Compare the Milesian myth of the founding of Britain by the Trojan exile Brutus as related most famously by Geoffrey of Monmouth. Roger A. Mason, "Scotching the Brut: Politics, History and National Myth in Sixteenth Century Britain," in id. (ed.), *Scotland and England 1286–1815* (Edinburgh: John Donald, 1987), 60–84. On Habsburg myths of origin, see Marie Tanner, *The Last Descendant of Aeneas: The Hapsburgs and the Mythic Image of the Emperor* (New Haven: Yale University Press, 1993).

[4] Ciaran O'Scea, "The Devotional World of the Irish Catholic Exile in Early Modern Galicia, 1598–1666," in Thomas O'Connor (ed.), *The Irish in Europe, 1580–1815* (Dublin: Four Courts Press, 2001), 27–31.

closely identified with those of the Ancient Irish. Beare's political agenda is to convince the Spaniards to place their trust in the united efforts of the Ancient Irish and the Mixed Irish exiles in Spain, rather than in the English Irish who have a tendency, O'Beare claims, to favor the English government. To help secure Spanish support for his own faction, Beare streses that

The Ancient Irish, as these are descended from the Spaniards, desire always to be governed by the kings of Spayne and his successors, and bear greater affection and love to the Spanish nation, contrarywise great hatred and enmity to his enemyes and in sharpness of wit and valour in warr are altogether like unto the Spaniard.[5]

Beare supplements this invocation of the Milesian myth in his *Historiae Catholicae Iberniae Compendium* (*Compendium of the Catholic History of Ireland*) (Lisbon, 1621) with other arguments designed to impress upon a Spanish readership (the work was dedicated to Philip IV) the ancient and abiding connections between Ireland and Spain. As Hiram Morgan shows, the *Compendium* refers to Ireland throughout not as "Hibernia" but as "Ibernia," suggests that Spain's patron saint James visited Ireland before the mission of Patrick, and documents the popularity with Spanish pilgrims of St Patrick's Purgatory.[6]

Philip O'Sullivan Beare made his home in northern Spain from an early age after leaving Ireland during the Nine Years War.[7] From the 1580s onwards he was joined in Spain's territories by countless numbers of his countrymen who took advantage of Ireland's well-established commercial and military ties with the Iberian Peninsula.[8] Irish expatriates made an especially significant contribution to the Habsburg military machine, most notably in the Low Countries. Grainne Henry has recently estimated that between 1586 and 1610 "roughly 20,000 Irish soldiers saw service in Flanders." The culmination of this influx of Irishmen into Spain's armies was the "consolidation of all Irish companies into a regiment under Colonel Henry O'Neill" (Hugh O'Neill's second son) in 1605.[9]

---

[5] Quoted in Clare Carroll, "Irish and Spanish Cultural and Political Relations in the Work of O'Sullivan Beare," in Hiram Morgan (ed.), *Political Ideology in Ireland: 1541–1641* (Dublin: Four Courts Press, 1999), 247.

[6] Hiram Morgan, "'Un Pueblo Unido...': The Politics of Philip O'Sullivan Beare," in Enrique García Hernán et al. (eds.), *Irlanda y la Monarquía Hispánica: Kinsale 1601–2001. Guerra, Política, Exilio y Religión* (Madrid: Universidad de Alcalá, 2002), 273–4. Article also available online at the Center for Neo-Latin Studies, University College Cork, http://www.ucc.ie/acad/classics/CNLS/lectures/Morgan_madrid.html

[7] O'Sullivan Beare refers in his own writings to the Fifteen Years War, dating the outbreak of hostilities to the defeat of the Spanish Armada in 1588.

[8] Thomas O'Connor, "Irish Migration to Spain, and the Formation of an Irish College Network, 1589–1800," in Luc François and Ann Katherine Isaacs (eds.), *The Sea in European History* (Pisa, Italy: Università di Pisa, 2001), 109–23.

[9] Grainne Henry, "The Emerging Identity of an Irish Military Group in the Spanish Netherlands," in R. V. Comerford, Mary Cullen, Jacqueline R. Hill, and Colm Lennon (eds.), *Religion, Conflict, and Coexistence in Ireland* (Dublin: Gill and MacMillan, 1990), 54–5; Jerrold Casway, "Henry O'Neill and the Formation of the Irish Regiment in the Netherlands, 1605," *Irish Historical Studies* 18 (1973), 481–8.

Through loyal service to the Spaniards, Irishmen of all backgrounds were able to win the recognition and trust of their hosts and to become assimilated to Spanish culture. "Unlike English subjects," as Henry notes, "the Irish in Spanish territories were accorded the same legal privileges as Spanish subjects."[10] Furthermore, in recognition of their services to Spain, Irish nobles and officers were granted the highest Spanish military honors. For example, Philip O'Sullivan Beare's uncle, Domnall Cam, who had fought with Hugh O'Neill in Ireland, was made a Knight of the Order of St James, and of the Order of Santiago, as well as Conde de Birhaven (Count of Berehaven) by Philip III.[11]

ENGLISH EXILES IN SPANISH TERRITORIES

In contrast to the many exiles from Ireland in Habsburg territories like the Beares and O'Neills who had little difficulty thinking of themselves as subjects of the Spanish monarch, English exiles in the same lands could neither claim to be descended from the Spanish nor to be entitled to the same legal privileges afforded Irish émigrés.

Despite these disadvantages, some English Catholics nevertheless left England with the intention of transferring their allegiance to Spain. John Story was one notorious English exile who fits this pattern. After fleeing England and settling in Louvain, he eventually ended up in Antwerp, where he was abducted by Elizabeth's agents and brought back to face trial. In his defense, Story claimed that he had been "freelye licensed" to leave England by the queen, and that as a "castawaye" he was no longer her subject but a latter-day Abraham, commanded by God to go forth from his country of origin. Story claimed unapologetically that he had renounced his allegiance to Elizabeth and sworn it instead to Philip II.[12] To the authorities questioning Story, however, his claim that he had shifted allegiance from one monarch to another was both treasonous and a theoretical impossibility. According to the logic of the Elizabethan state, subjecthood was inherent and inalienable. Story remained a subject of the sovereign in whose territory he was born and raised. In the words of Protestant preacher John Howson: "it is not flying into forraine countries that can deliver you from your alleagiance, or from punishment due for the violating of it. *Coelum non hominem mutant qui trans mare currant*, you may flie beyond the seas from the

---

[10] Henry, "The Emerging Identity of an Irish Military Group," 64 and n. 50; Micheline Kerney Walsh, "The Military Order of Saint Patrick, 1593," *Seanchas Ard Mhacha* 9 (1979), 280 n. 3.

[11] Walsh, *Hugh O'Neill: An Exile of Ireland*, 104–6, 119.

[12] *A Declaration of the lyfe and death of John Story, late a Romish canonicall doctor, by professyon* (1571), Ciii[v]. Another hostile account of Story can be found in *A copie of a letter lately sent by a gentleman, a student in the lawes of the realme, to a frende of his concernyng D. Story* (1571).

natural aire of your native country, but not from your selves, nor your natural alleagiance."[13]

Similar questions about the nature of exile subjecthood and the effects on the self of transferring political allegiances were central to contemporary discussions of English men and women who lived under Habsburg rule. Lewis Lewkenor's *The estate of English fugitives under the king of Spaine and his ministers* (1595) offers a Protestant perspective on these questions. As a convert from Catholicism and formerly a captain in the Spanish army in Flanders, Lewkenor writes with the characteristic enmity of the apostate and ex-insider who now seeks to expose the political system he once served.[14] Lewkenor purports to give an eyewitness account of the horrors awaiting unsuspecting Englishmen who leave home to seek preferment, wealth, or freedom of conscience under Philip. He claims that the English fugitives find the opposite, that they are exploited, refused wages, and finally cast off by their Spanish masters who bear "a rooted and ingrafted malice ... to our whole nation."[15]

Lewkenor parades before his reader a "miserable and discontented troupe of [English] Gentlemen," including "Lieutenants and Ensignes [who] ... go up and downe sickly and famished, begging their bread, covered onely with poore blankets and tikes of featherbeds."[16] Typifying the fate of the English captains who mistakenly place their loyalty in the Spanish is a man with the quintessentially English name of "Smith." Smith, writes Lewkenor, falls "thorough sicknesse and povertie into such extremitie of wantes, that of a Captaine hee was faine to become a victualler, and to buy butter and cheese, and by making sale thereof againe to helpe to relieve his poore estate. Withall, he fel into so strange and extreme a dropsie, that I scarcely believe the like was ever heard of ... either of his legs was swollen to that bignes of a mans middle, his face onely was bare of flesh and miserable, and his eies sunke into his head, in such sorte that I never remember to have beheld a more pittifull

---

[13] *A sermon preached at St Maries in Oxford, the 17. day of November, 1602. in defence of the festivities of the Church of England, and namely that of her Majesties coronation* (London, 1603), 25. Howson went on to say that God punished the Catholic exiles by either putting a hook in their nostrils and bringing them back to England "to suffer condigne punishment for these lewde and most unchristian practises," or by making sure that they "perish[ed] miserably like runagates and vagabonds, or exiled malefactours in a forraine countrey." Story's fate fit the former category.

[14] The text exists in two distinct versions. *The estate* is an expanded version of *A discourse of the usage of the English fugitives, by the Spaniard* (1595); Lewkenor claims in his preface to *The estate* that the earlier *Discourse* was published without his consent. See Albert J. Loomie, SJ, *The Spanish Elizabethans: The English Exiles at the Court of Philip II* (New York: Fordham University Press, 1963), 10–11. A play entitled "*English Fugitives*" in Henslowe's diary may be "an attempt to dramatize the 1596 *Discourse of the Usage of English Fugitives by the Spaniard*" (James Forse, "How 'Black' was the 'Black Legend' in Elizabethan England?," *Shakespeare and Renaissance Association of West Virginia Selected Papers* 25 (2002), 26).

For Richard Verstegan's alarm at the harm that Lewkenor's book might cause the exiles, see Anthony G. Petti (ed.), *The Letters and Despatches of Richard Verstegan (c.1550–1640)* Catholic Record Society 52 (London, 1959), 219.

[15] *The estate of English fugitives*, F2^r–F3, G1^{r-v}.   [16] Ibid. E4^r, B^r.

spectacle."[17] Smith's literal "infection" by Spanish humors results in the grotesque deformation of a wholesome English body (that Lewkenor elsewhere describes the Spaniards ridiculing for its stereotypical "big joynts and broad shoulders").[18] Moreover, Smith's fate bears out Lewkenor's warnings about the Circean powers of the Spaniards: "Fly therefore from the inchanted snares, you that will not bee transformed into monsters. Those that beheld the head of Medusa were only turned into stones, but these that are insorcered with these Spanish inchantments, are transformed into shapes much more horrible and monstrous."[19]

Lewkenor also describes a less grotesque if more notorious case of "degeneration" resulting from fraternization with the Spanish in the person of Sir William Stanley.[20] Stanley had become a *cause célèbre* to many English Catholics in 1587 when, as a colonel in Elizabeth's army, he surrendered the garrison town of Deventer in the Low Countries with his entire regiment to the Spanish. At first, Lewkenor notes, Stanley was rewarded by Philip and acknowledged by the pope, while his regiment became a "nurserie and seminarie of souldyers," an ironically styled "golden world" attracting priests and Catholic gentlemen. But in the end, Spanish scheming forced Stanley's regiments out of Deventer and alienated Stanley from his men, who were forced to seek pardon from Elizabeth.[21] Stanley, whose expertise in military affairs goes unappreciated by the Spanish, ends his days "sequestred . . . from the court, and coming discontented to Antwarp, there hired a house, where foure or five monthes hee lived full of melancholy and passion, making evident shew that his mind was utterly unable to beare the burthen of so great an indignitie."[22] Lewkenor shows that Stanley's misplaced trust in the Spaniards leads inexorably to his condition as a mentally disordered outcast.

Lewkenor's sensational account of his own alleged experiences in the Spanish Low Countries belongs to what has come to be called the Black Legend of Spanish mendacity and cruelty—a collection of negative images about the inhabitants of the Iberian Peninsula that developed in northern Europe in the later sixteenth century.[23] The crucial text in the formation of this legend, however, was neither

[17] Ibid. C4[r–v].   [18] Ibid. F4[v].   [19] Ibid. I4[v].
[20] Ibid. D1[r] ff.   [21] Ibid. D1[v].

[22] Ibid. F3[v]–F4[r]. For condemnations of Stanley's actions at Deventer, see Gerard Prouninck, *A short admonition or warning, upon the detestable treason wherewith Sir William Stanley and Rowland Yorke have betraied and delivered for monie unto the Spaniards, the town of Deventer, and the sconce of Zutphen* (1587). This is a translation from the Dutch. The author argues that because one or two Englishmen prove traitors, the Dutch should not distrust all the English. "Some say that in England manie traitors are punished, whose quarters are to be seene round about London in great number. But would to God there were in other places moe Londons, about the which might be seene the quarters of the traitors, which in other places escape their deserved punishment" (Aiiii[r]). Another attack on Stanley is the anonymous *A briefe discoverie of Dr Allens seditious drifts* (1588).

[23] See William S. Maltby, *The Black Legend in England: The Development of Anti-Spanish Sentiment 1558–1660* (Durham, NC: Duke University Press, 1971); for a qualification of Maltby's argument, see Forse, "How 'Black' was the 'Black Legend'."

north European nor Protestant in orientation, but Spanish, Catholic, and written by a priest. Bartolomé de Las Casas's, *Brevisima relación de la Destruycion de las Indias occidentales* (1552) was first published in English translation in 1583 as *The Spanish colonie, or Briefe chronicle of the acts and gestes of the Spaniardes in the West Indies, called the newe world*. Las Casas, a Spanish Dominican Friar, described in harrowing detail the "*cruelties and tyrannies*" inflicted by the Spanish Conquistadores upon the native peoples of the West Indian archipelago.[24] The Spanish, claimed Las Casas, had slaughtered "12, 15, or 20 millions of poore reasonable creatures," all in the pursuit of gold. For English readers of the 1583 translation, the eyewitness accounts of gruesome atrocities would have been deeply shocking. Perhaps just as alarming to an English reader, though, was the anonymous translator's explanation that the book was meant "to serve as a President and warning to the xii Provinces of the Lowe Countries." Dedicating the work "to all the Provinces of the lowe countreys," the translator of *The Spanish colonie* had no doubt that the violence inflicted by Spaniards on the peoples of the New World could just as easily be visited upon the Protestant peoples of northern Europe unless they mounted a concerted resistance.[25] Indeed, just a few years before the appearance of *The Spanish colonie*, Philip announced a more draconian approach to his rebellious provinces by appointing Alexander Farnese as the new governor of the Netherlands. Farnese's ruthless tactics included laying siege to the strategic port town of Antwerp, finally capturing it in August 1585 after starving the citizens into submission.[26]

The prejudice of the English toward the Spanish was equaled only by the English fear of becoming like the Spanish. As an element of a general Hispanophobia, fear of hispaniolization assumed renewed urgency in the later sixteenth century. In fact, the *OED* records the earliest appearance of the term "hispaniolization" in 1583 in Thomas Stocker's translation from the French of *A tragicall historie of the troubles and civile warres of the lowe Countries...together [with] the Barbarous crueltie and tyrannie of the Spaniard*. Along with its cognates—Spaniolized, Spagnolized, hispanized, and hispanated—the adjective "hispaniolized" denotes any non-Spaniard who serves or fraternizes with Spaniards. Thus Stocker's text refers to the "Hispaniolized low Countrey men" and the "trecherous hispaniolized Walloons" who support the Spanish occupation

---

[24] Andrew Hadfield notes that the first English translation conveniently omits Las Casas's defense of Amerindians' right to their land and resources. See Hadfield (ed.), *Amazons, Savages, and Machiavels: Travel and Colonial Writing in English, 1550–1630. An Anthology* (Oxford: Oxford University Press, 2002), 250.

[25] *The Spanish colonie*, "To the Reader."

[26] After its surrender, Antwerp "was transformed immediately from a bastion of Protestantism in the Netherlands and Revolution against Spain into a Spanish outpost in the struggle against rebellion and a bastion of the Counter Reformation". F. De Nave, "Antwerp, Dissident Typographical Centre in the 16th Century: General Synthesis," in *Antwerp, Dissident Typographical Centre: The Role of Antwerp Printers in the Religious Conflicts in England (16th century)* (Antwerp: Plantin-Moretus Museum, 1994), 16.

of Flanders.[27] As the case of Sir William Stanley suggests, though, hispaniolization also resulted in negative spiritual, mental, and bodily effects, deforming once stout and loyal English subjects. These dangers were especially acute when the English subject not only served Spanish interests but also ventured into the heart of the Spanish empire on the Iberian Peninsula.

Despite the novelty of the terminology, English fears of hispaniolization were nothing new in the 1580s, as the paranoia aroused in some quarters by Mary's marriage to Philip II earlier in the century indicates.[28] But in the 1580s, the anti-Catholic discourse of hispaniolization gained a new dimension with the opening of the first English Catholic colleges on the Iberian Peninsula. In previous decades, young Catholic exiles from England wanting to train for the priesthood had mostly congregated at the seminaries in the Low Countries, France, and Rome. With escalating political tensions in northern Europe and the inability of the seminaries to accommodate all the would-be entrants, the exile leaders were forced to seek openings elsewhere on friendlier ground. English seminaries were established at Valladolid in Castile, north central Spain, in 1589, and at Seville in southwestern Spain in 1592.[29] The Elizabethan regime reacted by accusing the students of not only betraying their country, their sovereign, and the True Religion, but of defecting to the nation's arch-enemy, the Habsburg tyrant, and his symbolic twin, the Papal Antichrist. Moreover, these unsuspecting English students had also left their natural environment for a strange southern land to which their constitution was inherently unsuited.

The Protestant ideologues who railed against these hispaniolized émigrés were assisted by various dissident Catholics, including exiled aristocrats like Charles Paget who worked in support of Mary Stuart's cause from exile in Paris and Brussels. Paget's anti-Spanish agenda was shared by members of the English Catholic secular clergy who in a series of published tracts denounced the Jesuit designs of Persons and his alliance with Spain.[30] Known as the "Appellants" for their appeals to the pope requesting that the Catholic mission to England be kept out of Jesuit control, these secular priests secretly collaborated with Elizabeth's

---

[27] *A tragicall historie*, Title Page, aii[r].

[28] For a representative anti-Spanish text of the 1550s, see the anonymous, *A warnyng for Englande conteynyng the horrible practises of the Kyng of Spayne, in the kyngdome of Naples* (Emden, 1555). On the idea that Englishness is a kind of property that can be corrupted or lost, see Frances E. Dolan, *Whores of Babylon: Catholicism, Gender, and Seventeenth-Century Print Culture* (Ithaca: Cornell University Press, 1999), 35–41.

[29] Leo Hicks, "Father Persons, S.J., and the Seminaries in Spain," *The Month* 157 (March 1931), 193–204, 410–17; Michael E. Williams, *St Alban's College Valladolid: Four Centuries of English Catholic Presence in Spain* (New York: St Martin's Press, 1988), ch. 1; A. C. F. Beales, *Education Under Penalty: English Catholic Education from the Reformation to the Fall of James II 1547–1689* (London: Athlone Press, 1963), 39–48, chs. 7 and 8.

[30] The *ODNB* entry for Paget states that "Although an enthusiastic supporter of the Spanish armada and a recipient of a Spanish pension, Paget became in the 1590s again a committed supporter of a Scottish solution to the English succession question, while Persons adopted the Spanish alternative."

government in securing presses and coordinating attacks on the Spanish faction among the English Jesuits.[31] In particular, the seculars urged the pope not to appoint George Blackwell as Archpriest over the English mission. Blackwell, they claimed, was a stooge of the Jesuits and their pro-Spanish agenda of assassination and armed invasion. The Appellants, styling themselves "the ancienter sort of secular Priests"—the upholders of indigenous Catholic traditions—and the loyal subjects of Elizabeth, fashioned their own hyperbolic Englishness in opposition to the hispaniolized tendencies of their Jesuit rivals.[32] While the Appellants claimed to be upholding the ancient and native forms of English Catholicism— "the old approved pathes of our forefathers"—they accused the Jesuits of bringing into England not only disloyalty and rebellion against the crown but an alien set of devotional practices.[33] Above all, Appellant texts were instrumental in forging the link for readers between the Jesuits and the Spanish. As the Appellant Thomas Bluet observed, however much the students in Spain protested their loyalty to England, they were now "altogether Hispaniated...the better to resemble and imitate their founder and father Ignatius Laiola a Spaniard."[34] Needless to say, Loyola was a figure repeatedly demonized in Appellant texts.

DULCIS ODOR PATRIAE: CLIMATE AND SELF

Protestant and Catholic authors alike imagined the hispaniolization of Englishmen on the Iberian Peninsula as having alarming physical consequences. The English body, shaped within a northern environment, was dangerously "out of place" in Spain's southern climes. In fact, the hot Spanish climate was supposed to present the same dangers for Englishmen as the intemperate conditions of North America.[35] Karen Kupperman explains that "People considering or promoting emigration [to the new world] feared effects extending beyond the initial period of adjustment, specifically the possibility that in leaving England they might be leaving their Englishness also, running the risk of becoming

---

[31] Gladys Jenkins, "The Archpriest Controversy and the Printers," *The Library* (1948) 180–7 ff.; Thomas Graves Law (ed.), *The Archpriest Controversy: Documents Relating to the Dissensions of the Roman Catholic Clergy, 1597–1602. Ed. from the Petyt Mss. of the Inner Temple* (Westminister: Camden society, 1896–8).

[32] Christopher Bagshaw, *A sparing discoverie of Our English Jesuits and of Fa. Persons proceedings under pretence of promoting the Catholicke faith in England* (London, 1601. *ERL* 39), 9; Thomas Bluet, *Important considerations which ought to move all true and sound-Catholikes...to acknowledge that the proceedings of her Majesty...have been both mild and mercifull* (np, 1601. *ERL* 31), 19–20.

[33] Bluet, *Important considerations*, 2.   [34] Ibid. 42.

[35] See Karen Ordahl Kupperman, "Fear of Hot Climates in the Anglo-American Colonial Experience," *William and Mary Quarterly*, 213–40, esp. 214, for an explanation of the humoral theory on which climatic determinism is based; also see Kupperman, "Climate and the Mastery of the Wilderness in Seventeenth-Century New England," *Seventeenth-Century New England* (Boston, 1988), 3–37.

more like the Spaniard, whom they perceived as choleric and untrustworthy."
Such arguments depended, of course, upon long-accepted theories of climactic
determinism and the idea that the body's humors, and hence the individual's
constitution and disposition, were largely a product of the climate to which he
was accustomed. For a person to move to a radically different climate meant
running the risk of unbalancing the body's humors and jeopardizing its health.
These fears were clearly on the mind of preacher William Crashaw when he
reassured members of the Virginia Company in 1609 that while central Virginia
shared the same approximate latitude as central Spain around Toledo, Virginia
was "not so hot as Spaine, but rather of the same temper with the south of France,
which is so temperate and indifferent, as if our owne were something neerer unto
it, we would be well content with it."[36]

Englishmen, accustomed to "temperate" conditions in the northern hemi-
sphere, would—observers feared—be exposed in Iberian towns like Valladolid,
Seville, and Lisbon to both enervating heat and dangerous unfamiliar "airs."[37]
The secular priest John Mush claimed that English students were "consumed
by the distemperat air of Spain, and die there." Mush considered the seminaries
in the Low Countries and northern France to be "regions more agreeable with our
English nature than Valle de Leith [i.e. Valladolid] or Civill," home to English
colleges since the late 1580s.[38] (If the proximity of northern Europe to the coast
of England made the colleges of Douai and Rheims more attractive to Mush
than their counterparts in Spain, so too did the fact that Douai and Rheims were
controlled by the seculars rather than the Jesuits). Edward Daunce in *A briefe
discourse of the Spanish state* (1590), offered a helpful physiological account of
why the English body "failed" in Spain when he wrote: "we being brought up
in a more temperat and colder clime than Spaine, have our naturall moisture
easilie exhausted by the heat of that country opening our poers in the sommer:
by which that quicke and subtill ayre named *Serena* entreth the vitall parts, and
sleyeth the bodie."[39]

Protestant traveler Lewis Owen also noted the deleterious effect of the Spanish
atmosphere upon English Freshmen at Valladolid, where "within a short time

---

[36] Kupperman, "Fear of Hot Climates," 215. Crashaw, "A sermon preached in London before the
right honourable the Lord Lawarre, Lord Governour and Captaine Generall of Virginia" (London,
1610), E2ʳ. I owe this reference to Jean Feerick.

[37] In classical typologies, England belonged in the northern zone. Early modern English writers,
however, tended to push the southern boundary of this "extreme" zone further northward, thus
placing their country in a moderate, temperate region. See Mary Floyd-Wilson, "Temperature,
Temperance, and Racial Difference in Ben Jonson's *The Masque of Blackness*," *English Literary
Renaissance* 28 (1998), 184–5. However, Thomas Wright argues that the Alps were the major
dividing line between zones, with the English on one side and the Spanish on the other (*The Passions
of the Minde in Generall. A Reprint Based on the 1604 Edition*, ed. Thomas O. Sloan (Urbana:
University of Illinois Press, 1971), lvii–lxiii).

[38] John Mush, *A dialogue betwixt a secular priest, and a lay gentleman* (Rheims, 1601. *ERL* 39),
113.

[39] *A briefe discourse of the Spanish state*, 31.

after their arrivall...[they] do fall sicke, and some of them dye, by reason of the unwholesomnesse of the ayre." English students in Spain who left Jesuit-controlled seminaries to join the Benedictine monastic order also became ill or died, claimed Owen, "like so many rotten sheepe," because of miasma or because "they did not like so well of the fashion and condition of the Spaniards, or of their dyet." As a remedy, the English monks were transferred to "some temperate part of the Country, which was best agreeing to their nature and complexion."[40] Thomas Robinson, author of *The anatomy of the English nunnery at Lisbon in Portugall*, related the story of Father Strange, "tenderly brought up in England, he fell very sick shortly after his profession, perhaps by reason of the unwholesomenesse of the aire, which neither at Rome nor Valladolid is very pleasant."[41] As Robinson's remark attests, the air at Rome, like Spanish air, was often described as notoriously bad for English visitors: "the city and suburbs of Rome are very unwholesome...especially the stifling aire of that part of Rome which is neere the Holy House, or Inquisition," observed the Protestant John Gee who also warned of the "bad ayre upon the bankes of Tyber."[42] Even in more northerly latitudes than Spain and Rome, however, Englishmen breathed air that their bodies were not naturally equipped to process. Thus when William Allen fell sick in the Low Countries in 1562, he risked arrest by returning to England in order to convalesce in the wholesome air of his native Lancashire.[43] Surely the Catholic layman, Sir Thomas Copley spoke for many of his reluctant fellow exiles when he informed Sir Francis Walsingham in anticipation of his journey to the coast of France: "I finde the saying so true *Dulcis odor patriae*, that alreadie me seemith, the ayer I shall breathe on the hills neere to Roan, looking towards Ingland, wil be sweeter than I can drawe from any other parte."[44]

COMPLEXION, SKIN COLOR, ETHNIC ORIGINS

Spanish "airs" could leave their mark both on the internal humors of the hispaniolized Englishman's body and on its external surfaces. When the Appellant priest

---

[40] *The running register: recording a true relation of the state of the English colledges, seminaries and cloysters in all forraine parts* (1626), 52, 88.

[41] *The anatomy of the English nunnery at Lisbon in Portugall: Dissected and laid open by one that was sometime a yonger brother of the convent* (1622), 20.

[42] *The foot out of the Snare: with a detection of sundry late practices and impostures of the priests and Jesuits in England* (1624). Quoted in David Lunn, *The English Benedictines, 1540–1688: From Reformation to Revolution* (New York: Barnes and Noble, 1980), 51; Gee, *New shreds of the old Snare* (1624), 48.

[43] Martin Haile, *An Elizabethan Cardinal, William Allen* (London: I. Pitman, 1914), 37.

[44] Sir Thomas Copley, *Letters of Sir Thomas Copley*, ed. Richard Copley Christie (London, 1897), 140.

Thomas Bluet described the "hote Spanish clime" as harming "the Angels faces" of English youth as well as the respectable visages of English matrons, he tapped into racialized assumptions about physical beauty that privileged pale skin over dark.[45] Bluet's allusion to his countrymen's Angel-like appearance also evokes the story in Bede's *The history of the church of Englande* (translated by Thomas Stapleton in 1565) of Pope Gregory's providential encounter in the Roman marketplace with a group of young male Anglo-Saxon slaves captured in Britain. Gregory, in awe of the youths' "white skinne and comly countenance," asks where they have come from and who they are. When the youths reply, "Angles, or english," Gregory exclaims, "Truely not without cause . . . they be called Angles for they have an Angels face. And it is mete suche men were partakeners, and inheretors with the Angels in heaven."[46] As a result of this encounter, Gregory vows to Christianize the Angles' homeland—a task he delegates to the missionary Augustine. In Bluet's allusive retelling of the incident, the darkening of the English students' "Angels-faces" under the Mediterranean sun implicitly reverses the significance of Bede's original story. The pale skin of Bede's youths makes them stand out from others, draws Gregory's attention, and leads inexorably to Augustine's Christianizing mission to Britain. For Bluet, on the other hand, the darkening of the skins of modern English youth under the Spanish sun signals the loss of the youths' innocent and elect identity.[47]

In early modern taxonomies of racial identity that used skin pigment as a form of classification, the fair complexions of the northern Anglo-Saxon people were often contrasted with the darker hues of Spaniards. The Spanish physician Juan Huarte, whose *Examination of mens wits* was translated into English in 1594, described his countrymen as being "somewhat browne [with] blacke haire," while characterizing the English and their northern neighbors as having "whitenesse of the face."[48] In the anti-Spanish Black Legend, however, Spain's hot southern climate alone could not account for the Spaniard's swarthy complexion. Another contributing factor was thought to be the interbreeding of earlier generations of inhabitants on the Iberian Peninsula with settlers from north Africa. In *A View of the State of Ireland* (*c*.1596), Edmund Spenser, no friend of Habsburg imperialism, recounts a widely credited theory about the successive waves of

---

[45] Bluet, *Important considerations*: "Never shall the Angels faces, the flower of Englands youth, the beauty of Britaines Ocean be appald, impaired, over-clouded, with a steepe downe shower of stormy sorrowes, by our unnaturall attempts, plots and devices" (A3ʳ). On the meanings of "race" in early modern England, see Kim F. Hall, *Things of Darkness: Economies of Race and Gender in Early Modern England* (Ithaca: Cornell University Press, 1995).

[46] *The history of the church of Englande* (Antwerp, 1565. ERL 162), 48ᵛ–49ʳ.

[47] On the Appellants' religio-political agenda at this time, see Michael C. Questier, *Catholicism and Community in Early Modern England: Politics, Aristocratic Patronage and Religion, c.1550–1640* (Cambridge: Cambridge University Press, 2006), 250–65.

[48] Quoted in Floyd-Wilson, "Temperature, Temperance, and Racial Difference," 185 n. 5, 187. Huarte is quoting Aristotle's theory of climatic determinism which places together the Flemish, Dutch, English, and French as inhabitants of the cold northern zone.

invaders who had settled in Spain. Irenius, one of the speakers in Spenser's dialogue, declares that

the Moores and the Barbarians, breaking over out of Africa, did finally possesse all Spaine, or the most part thereof, and did tread, under their heathenish feete, whatever little they found yet there standing. The which, though after they were beaten out by Ferdinando of Arragon and Elizabeth his wife, yet they were not so cleansed, but that through the marriages which they had made, and mixture with the people of the land, during their long continuance there, they had left no pure drop of Spanish blood, no more than of Roman or of Scythian. So that of all nations under heaven (I suppose) the Spaniard is the most mingled.[49]

Whereas in Spenser's nuanced account of ethnic identity formation, Spanish hybridity is not in itself bad, in the attacks by Catholic Appellant priests and their supporters on their hispaniolized co-religionists, hybridity was a kind of anathema.[50] Anthony Copley imagined, for example, that "this sweete plot" of England was the antithesis in every way of the "barren and desert soyle" of Spain, "a meere forreine and Morisco nation." The Spaniard, moreover, was a "stranger, and a demi-Moore . . . whose language we understand not, and whose humours and fashions we shall never be able to abide."[51] The Appellant party denounced those hispaniolized, "unnatural and degenerated Englishmen" who sought the destruction of their homeland—the "noblest of nations"—by "the most cruel nation that liveth, a nation not fully an hundred years since wholly they received Christianity, and as yet are in their hearts Pagans and Moors."[52] Another anti-Spanish observer alleged that "this semi-Morisco nation as touching its beginning is sprung from the filth and slime of Africa, the base Ottomans and the rejected Jews, and which is more infamous, a great part of Spain unchristened until an hundred years ago that Granada was conquered by Ferdinando and Isabella."[53]

Remarks like these held up for ridicule the pretensions of a Spanish society increasingly obsessed in the late sixteenth century with its purity of blood or *limpieza de sangre*. The introduction of new blood laws in Spain excluded Moors and *conversos* from public office in order to create what was supposed to be a racially pure political nation.[54] Readers in England became aware of these

<hr/>

[49] *Edmund Spenser: A View of the State of Ireland*, ed. Andrew Hadfield and Willy Maley (Oxford: Blackwell, 1997), 50.

[50] Paul McGinnis and Arthur H. Williamson, "Britain, Race, and the Iberian World Empire," in Allan I. Macinnes and Jane Ohlmeyer (eds.), *The Stuart Kingdoms in the Seventeenth Century: Awkward Neighbours* (Dublin: Four Courts Press, 2002), 88–9.

[51] *An answere to a letter of a Jesuited gentleman* (1601. ERL 31), 56; *Another letter of Mr. A. C. to his dis-jesuited kinseman* (1602. ERL 100), 11, 17.

[52] *An answere to a letter of a Jesuited gentleman*, 12.

[53] Quoted in John Stoye, *English Travellers Abroad, 1604–1667* (New Haven: Yale University Press, 1989), 233–4.

[54] M. J. Rodriguez-Salgado, "Christians, Civilized and Spanish: Multiple Identities in Sixteenth Century Spain," *Transactions of the Royal Historical Society* 8 (1998), 241. Spain's ruling elites

developments through works like *Newes from Spaine: The king of Spaines edict, for the expulsion & banishment of more then nine hundred thousand Moores out of his kingdome, which conspired and plotted to bring the kingdome of Spaine under the power and subjection of the Turkes and Saracens* (1611).

In a process that was the antithesis of Irish attempts to identify their heritage with the Spaniards, English Protestants deliberately distanced their own *gens* from all things Spanish. From the late 1580s onward, as Eric Griffin's recent work on Hispanophobia in early modern England has shown, Protestant anti-Spanish polemic shifted from a focus on "Spanish ambition" and "'pagan' Roman Catholic error" to "Spain's ethnic difference" from the English.[55] While Irish hispanophilic discourses posited a convergence between Irish and Spanish ethnicities, hostile English representations of the Spaniard's racial pedigree were designed to distance the "true-born" Englishman from the Spaniard, to deter English Catholics from visiting Iberia, and to demonize their compatriots already there.

The Englishman in Spain, as well as confronting the ethnic "otherness" of the Spanish and their alien climate, was subject to more contingent but no less hispaniolizing and thus deforming cultural forces.[56] Diet, as one of the most symbolically charged elements of a culture, figures prominently in contemporary discussions of hispaniolization like Lewis Owen's *The running register: recording a true relation of the state of the English colledges, seminaries and cloysters in all forraine parts* (1626). Purportedly the first comprehensive guide to the "receptacles" harboring English Catholic exiles across Europe from St Omers in northern France to Seville in southern Spain, *The running register* was a guide- and news-book—reporting gossip and naming English Catholics abroad—as well as an ethnography, especially in its attention to dietary codes and practices. Along with the local climate, argued Owen, the unfamiliar diet threatened to upset the English traveler's natural constitution. The Spanish, in terms of what they eat, "fare but meanely."[57] Staples of the English diet like "powdred Beefe" and

---

fought charges from "competing Christian powers [that] ... taunted and denigrated the Spaniards with references to their Jewish and Muslim past"; also see Bruce Taylor, "The Enemy Within and Without: An Anatomy of Fear on the Spanish Mediterranean Littoral," in William G. Naphy and Penny Roberts (eds.), *Fear in Early Modern Society* (Manchester: Manchester University Press, 1997), 78–99.

[55] Eric Griffin, "From Ethos to Ethnos: 'Hispanizing' the Spaniard in the Old World and the New," *CR : the new centennial review* 2:1 (2002), 69–116. Also see two other essays by Griffin: "The Specter of Spain in John Smith's Colonial Writing," in Robert Appelbaum and John Wood Sweet (eds.), *Envisioning an English Empire: Jamestown and the Making of the North Atlantic World* (Philadelphia: University of Pennsylvania Press, 2005), 111–34; "Un-Sainting James: Or, *Othello* and the 'Spanish Spirits' of Shakespeare's Globe," in Stephen Orgel and Sean Keilen (eds.), *Shakespeare and History* (New York: Garland, 1999), 278–320.

[56] Cultural identity in the late medieval and early modern world was generally regarded as the product of various immutable and contingent factors, including descent group, geography, climate, and diet. See Robert Bartlett, "Medieval and Modern Concepts of Race and Ethnicity," *Journal of Medieval and Early Modern Studies* 31 (2001), 39–56.

[57] *The running register*, 63.

"pickled-Oisters" are unknown in Spain, making it necessary for the exiles to import these and other staples like "Pilchers and English Butter, Cheese or Bacon," that make life bearable.[58] What the Spanish diet consists of, Owen never says; it is defined in this and other texts simply as an absence of nutritious English foodstuffs.

Issues of food and diet are raised repeatedly in English narratives about the events surrounding the Spanish Match of the early 1620s that warned James about the pitfalls of marrying his surviving son and heir, Charles, to Philip III's daughter, the Infanta Maria.[59] The most dramatic episode in the whole affair was Charles's clandestine mission to Spain in 1623 to woo the Infanta in person—an ill-conceived adventure that to many commentators seemed a sure way to turn the prince into a hispaniolized Englishman. The Protestant Thomas Scott's *The second part of vox populi, or Gondomar appearing in the likenes of Matchiavell* (1624) was one of many works written in the wake of the ultimately unsuccessful mission. As an index of the incommensurability of English and Spanish, Scott recounts the problems of feeding Charles's entourage. Scott notes a "great want of victual and provision" even at the center of the realm in Madrid. As a result, the English "were faine to send seaventeene miles off for a calfe, for his Highnesse dyet." Scott even makes Gondomar—the infamous Spanish ambassador at James's court and a chief proponent of the match—admit that "those places they call in England, East-cheape and Smith-field Barres, kills, and utters more Beefe and Mutton in a month, then all Spaine eats in seaven yeares." Scott presents his countrymen, not as gluttons, but as "the greatest feeders of the World"—their hearty appetites a metonomy for a capacious and vigorous national spirit. Spaniards who came to England, on the other hand, betrayed their weakly constitutions when, confronted with the plentiful English diet, they overeat, surfeit, and die.[60]

In the dire writings of Protestants and anti-Spanish Catholics, the homesickness of the Englishman exiled in Spanish territories is sometimes imagined as a kind of gastronomic longing. The Catholic apostate James Wadsworth, for example, author of the allegedly autobiographical *The English Spanish pilgrime. Or, a new discoverie of Spanishe popery and Jesuiticall stratagems* (1629) tells of Sir William Stanley's final years after his notorious hispaniolization which, as we have already seen, began with his surrender of Deventer to the Spanish. After years of being ignored or slighted by his Spanish masters, Stanley—writes Wadsworth—"laments now his misfortunes, and sayes he hath out-lived his friends, and in the yeere 1624 hee was constrained to goe to Spaine in his old age, having now seene 95 yeeres, and there to goe Cap in hand to all the Privy Counsellors, to crave his pension which had not beene paid him in six yeeres

---

[58] Ibid. 70.
[59] See Glyn Redworth, *The Prince and the Infanta: The Cultural Politics of the Spanish Match* (New Haven: Yale University Press, 2003).
[60] *The second part of vox populi*, 21–2.

before ... seeing himselfe thus cozened in his old age [he] turned Carthusian at Austend ... where I have heard him often complaine of the Jesuites ... and that if his Majesty of Great Britaine would grant him pardon, and leave to live the rest of his daies in Lancashire with beefe and bagge-pudding, hee should deeme himselfe one of the happiest in the world."[61] The *OED* identifies bag pudding, not very helpfully, as "a pudding boiled in a bag"; in Wadsworth's text it functions more as a kind of early-modern "comfort food" that English expatriates are thought naturally to crave.

ROBERT PERSONS, HISPANIOLIZATION, AND EXILE IDENTITY

In the texts of Protestants and anti-Spanish Catholics alike, the Jesuit leader Robert Persons was held up as the example *par excellence* of the hispaniolized Englishman: "the bastard Cowbucke, Spaines so leud Apostle," as the Appellant priest Anthony Copley called him.[62] Of all the rumors and charges that helped to demonize Persons in the English imagination—he was allegedly of obscure birth, a drunkard, his sister's rapist, and an ex-member of the Family of Love— none was repeated as often as his traitorous allegiance to Spain.[63] Persons secured this reputation after *A conference about the next succession to the crowne of Ingland* (1595) was widely if inaccurately credited solely to him. Not only did the treatise meddle publicly with the taboo subject of the queen's succession, it dared to suggest that Philip II's daughter, the Infanta Isabella Clara Eugenia, would be a suitable heir to the English throne. Reports circulated that Catholic students in the overseas seminaries were being coerced into consenting to the book's recommendations and forced to hear readings from it at meal times.[64]

Persons's reputation as the leading Hispanophile among the Catholic exiles was reinforced by other works he published in defense of the king of Spain like *A temperate ward-word, to the turbulent and seditious Wach-word of Sir Francis Hastings knight* (1599) and *A manifestation of the great folly and bad spirit of certayne in England calling themselves secular priestes* (1602).[65] Although he published these works either pseudonymously or anonymously, his enemies were quick to identify them with him.[66]

---

[61] *The English Spanish pilgrime*, 68–9.

[62] *Another letter of Mr. A. C. to his dis-jesuited kinseman*, 15.

[63] See e.g. ibid. 50–2, and Bagshaw, *A sparing discoverie*, 41–2.

[64] See Mush, *A dialogue*, 92–3; Bagshaw, *A sparing discoverie*, 57, 62–3; Bluet, *Important Considerations*, 4v, 34–5.

[65] The works are *ERL* 31 and 169 respectively.

[66] Thomas James, *The Jesuits downefall threatned against them by the secular priests for their wicked lives, accursed manners, hereticall doctrine, and more then Matchiavillian policie. Together with the*

In *A temperate ward-word*, especially, Persons offered a bold and cogent defense both of "the noble and renowned nation of Spanyardes, and their most Catholique, pious, wise, and potent king" Philip II, against the slanders of Protestant and Catholic critics alike.[67] Persons answered both major strands of hispanophobic discourse, countering religio-political allegations that the Spanish were proud, voluptuous, and tyrannical, as well as ethnically based slurs. The Spaniards, Persons argued, should not be smeared for their alleged consanguinity with moors and other swarthy pagans, but instead congratulated on "valiant delivering of themselves out of the handes and captivitie of the mores that invaded and oppressed their countrie." Contrary to the views of Spenser, Copley, and others that the Spanish were the most hybridized and impure of peoples, Persons praised them as God's chosen people.[68]

The Black Legend of Persons as the consummate hispaniolized Englishman stemmed both from his advocacy of the Spanish people and their Habsburg rulers as well as from his instrumental role in founding the network of seminaries on the Iberian Peninsula designed (in the minds of their critics) to transform other young Englishmen into the hispaniolized enemies of their rightful sovereign, Elizabeth. The first of these colleges opened in 1589 in northwest Spain in the city of Valladolid—the country's former capital and home to the Inquisition, a royal chancery, and an ancient university.[69] The college was established with the help of Philip and several Spanish noblemen, and proved immediately attractive to students from the increasingly crisis-ridden seminaries in northern Europe.[70] Despite a host of obstacles, including opposition from local residents, plague, poverty, internal dissension, and the defection of disaffected students, the college averaged between thirty to sixty residents annually, most of whom planned to return to England as missionary priests.[71]

---

life of Father Parsons an English Jesuite (Oxford, 1612), 58. On Persons's use of anonymity and pseudonymity in his publications, see Marcy L. North, "N. D. versus O. E.: Anonymity's Moral Ambiguity in Elizabethan Catholic Controversy," *Criticism: A Quarterly for Literature and the Arts* 40 (1998), 355–75.

[67] *A temperate ward-word*, 118. Also see Griffin, "From Ethos to Ethnos," 95.

[68] *A temperate ward-word*, 105–6.

[69] Valladolid was briefly restored as the national capital in 1600. According to Samuel Lewkenor, the University of Valladolid "was wont to be numbred among the seven most auncient universities of *Spaine*. It hath beene long drowned in obscuritie, even untill the dayes of king *Phillip* late deceased, who because he was there borne, did restore unto it the antique priviledges and prerogatives thereto belonging, and did his uttermost endevors to raise it to his former dignitie. He there hath lately erected a Colledge for the institution of yong English Gentlemen, which have abandoned their countrey." *A discourse not altogether unprofitable, nor unpleasant for such as are desirous to know the situation and customes of forraine cities without travelling to see them Containing a discourse of all those cities wherein doe flourish at this day priviledged universities* (1600), R3ᵛ.

[70] Michael E. Williams, *St Alban's College Valladolid: Four Centuries of English Catholic Presence in Spain* (New York: St Martin's Press, 1988), ch. 1. Also see A. C. F. Beales, *Education Under Penalty: English Catholic Education from the Reformation to the Fall of James II 1547–1689* (London: Athlone Press, 1963), 39–48, chs. 7 and 8.

[71] See Williams, *St Alban's College Valladolid*, chs. 1–2. The figures are at 22.

While still in its infancy, the English college at Valladolid became the focus of the exiles' most assured defense yet of the English Catholic experience in Spain and an attempt to demystify critics' paranoia about the threat of hispaniolization. Persons's treatise, *A relation of the King of Spaines receiving in Valliodolid*, recounts the visit of Philip II and his family to the English college in August, 1592. As the royal party passed through the city during a summer progress en route to Aragon, where Philip's 14-year-old son and heir was to "receive the othes of fidelitie of that kingdome," Persons seized the opportunity to refute English government propaganda about Philip's intentions toward England and about the life of the college students.[72] At the same time, Persons's used the king's visit as an occasion to publicize the college to potential recruits and donors.

The King of Spaines receiving in Valliodolid represents a multipurpose souvenir program of the sort often produced to commemorate royal spectacles such as Richard Mulcaster's account of Elizabeth's pre-coronation procession through London, *The quenes majesties passage through the citie of London* (1558). Apparently *The King of Spaines receiving in Valliodolid* found a ready market because nine years later the same Antwerp-based press of Arnout Conincx issued a kind of sequel describing the visit to the Valladolid college of the late Philip II's son and successor, Philip III, with his queen, Margaret of Austria. *A relation of the solemnetie wherewith the Catholike princes K. Philip the III and Quene Margaret were receyved in the Inglish Colledge of Valladolid the 22. of August. 1600* (1601) represents a partial translation by Francis Rivers of a Spanish original written by Antonio Ortiz and dedicated to the Infanta.[73]

Persons was partly prompted to compose *The King of Spaines receiving in Valliodolid* by an English government proclamation of October/November 1591, accusing Philip of waging an unjust war in France and of preparing to attack England.[74] The proclamation further alleged that the King of Spain, with the help of a new pope appointed personally by Philip, was harboring English Catholic exiles, "a multitude of dissolute young men," "for whom there are in

---

[72] *The King of Spaines receiving* (*ERL* 351), 15.

[73] Alison Shell, *Catholicism, Controversy and the English Literary Imagination, 1558–1660* (Cambridge: Cambridge University Press, 1999), 289 n. 26. Rivers, in dedicating his translation to George Carey, Second Baron Hunsdon ("the right honorable the Lord Chamberlayn") asserts the "good will of the King of Spaine and his people to our countrymen" and looks forward to a return to a time when the Spanish will again "be our best frends." Rivers perhaps hoped that through Hunsdon he could reach those members of the Privy Council who favored peace with Spain. A peace treaty was signed between England and Spain in 1604. See Gustav Ungerer, "Juan Pantoja de la Cruz and the Circulation of Gifts between the English and Spanish Courts in 1604/5," *Shakespeare Studies* 26 (1998), 145–86. According to Paul C. Allen, in 1600 members of the Spanish Council still entertained hopes of putting the Infanta on the English throne (*Philip III and the Pax Hispanica, 1598–1621: The Failure of Grand Strategy* (New Haven: Yale University Press, 2000), 100).

[74] See Peter Milward, *Religious Controversies of the Elizabethan Age: A Survey of Printed Sources* (London: Scolar Press, 1977), 112–14. Also see Victor Houliston, "The Lord Treasurer and the Jesuit: Robert Persons's Satirical *Responsio* to the 1591 Proclamation," *Sixteenth Century Journal* 32 (2001), 383–401; and P. J. Holmes, "Robert Persons and an Unknown Political Pamphlet of 1593," *Recusant History* 17 (1985), 341–7.

Rome and Spain and other places certain receptacles made to live in and there to be instructed in school points of sedition, and from thence to be secretly and by stealth conveyed into our dominions with ample authority from Rome to move, stir up, and persuade as many of our subjects as they dare deal withal to renounce their natural allegiance due to us [i.e. Elizabeth]."[75] The college at Valladolid, although not actually named in the proclamation, was one of the main "receptacles" targeted by the government.

Persons's response to the proclamation in *The King of Spaines receiving in Valliodolid*, like William Allen's earlier defense of the English scholars at Douai and Rheims in 1581, upholds the reputation of the Valladolid students against allegations that they were malcontents, traitors, "unnaturall people."[76] Persons counters these charges by describing how the students study for the priesthood by engaging in religious controversy, scriptural exegesis, divinity, and philosophy. More poignantly, he tells how students prepare for the hardships of their future missions to England and the possibility of martyrdom by embracing a college regime characterized by rigor and discipline and organized by a "table . . . of the orders of the house, conteining the distribution of all the tyme from hower to hower, throughout the whole daie, and weeke, and yeare."[77] If the government hoped to damage the colleges by issuing the proclamation, Persons thought they had failed. The proclamation, he believed, had actually served as an advertisement for the colleges, inciting more zealous young Catholics to join.[78]

Immediately after its publication in English, *The King of Spaines receiving* was translated into Spanish in an expanded edition by Thomas James as a *Relacion de un sacerdote Ingles*, suggesting the importance Persons and his backers attached to gaining the support of the local Castilian community. Some Spaniards, we should remember, opposed Persons's college from its inception, fearing the presence of English spies and heretics among the students, as well as the financial burden a fledgling college would impose on the city. To combat these suspicions, Persons had earlier printed a pamphlet in Spanish about England's martyrs, *Relacion de algunos martyrios, que de Nuevo han hecho los hereges en Inglaterra, y de otras cosas tocantes a nuestra santa y Catolica religion* (1590).[79] The martyrology sought the sympathy of its Spanish readers for English Catholics by recounting the recent executions of recusants at Oxford. Persons concluded the pamphlet with a separate section that justified the new foundation at Valladolid in the context of the English seminary movement generally: *Informacion que da el Padre*

---

[75] Paul L. Hughes and James F. Larkin (eds.), *Tudor Royal Proclamations: The Later Tudors (1588–1603)* (New Haven: Yale University Press, 1969), 3: 86–93. The proclamation also appears in Robert Southwell, *An Humble Supplication to her Majestie*, ed. R. C. Bald (Cambridge: Cambridge University Press, 1953), 59–65.

[76] Southwell, *An Humble Supplication*, 60.

[77] *The King of Spaines receiving*, 23. See Williams, *St Alban's College Valladolid*, Appendix A, for details about the college rules.

[78] *The King of Spaines receiving*, 13.   [79] AR 1: 122–3.

Personio... acerca de la Institucion del Seminario en Valladolid.[80] In *The King of Spains Receiving*, Persons reminds readers of these earlier Spanish language texts and claims that, along with Spanish versions of Nicholas Sander's *De Schismatis Anglicani* and "the late booke of *Andreas Philopater*," they had met with "greedie acceptaunce" by Spanish readers.[81] Yet if Persons thought he had made headway in persuading Spaniards about the value of English colleges on their territory, he also realized there was still much work left to do in order to win their full backing for the cause of the English exiles.

Persons directs his narrative in *The King of Spaines receiving* in a way that gestures to the broadest possible readership, including English Catholics in England as well as in exile across the Continent. The narrative is framed as a report written by an English priest at Valladolid "to a Gentleman and his wyf in Flaunders, latelie fled out of Ingland, for profession of the Catholique religion."[82] By this device, Persons connects the geographically isolated community of exiles at Valladolid to the diaspora of English Catholics scattered throughout Europe and the Atlantic archipelago. This larger body of believers is held together by material and spiritual means: by the correspondence that circulates between Spain, Flanders, England, and other sites of exile, and by the prayers and acts of intercession by fellow Catholics for each other.[83]

The fictional scenario in the opening frame also locates the text on a historical continuum as well as in a geographical nexus. The recusant couple addressed by the narrator have departed England after they are discovered harboring a priest in their home—a treasonable act which connects them to "the most renowmd example of glorious S. Alban our first Martyr of England." Executed by the Emperor Diocletian for sheltering a priest, St Alban and his cult were central to the identity of the Valladolid college which was named in his honor.[84] A relic of St Alban, "the protomartyr of England," encased in gold and crystal and placed on the high altar was, along with paintings of English martyrs and a statue of the Virgin and Child (the Madonna Vulnerata), one of the main devotional objects that attracted visitors to the college.[85] The kindness shown by St Alban and the recusant couple to fellow believers emerges as a central value in *The King of Spaines receiving*—a work that focuses on Philip's extraordinary generosity to the beleaguered Catholic youth of England. Typologically, Philip is imagined

---

[80] Leo Hicks, "Father Persons, S.J., and the Seminaries in Spain," *The Month* 157 (1931), 499–502, and 158 (1931), 27–8.

[81] *The King of Spaines receiving*, 58. AR 1: 123.

[82] *The King of Spaines receiving*, Title Page.   [83] Ibid. 5.   [84] Ibid. 4, 26.

[85] See Ortiz, *A relation of the solemnetie*, 16 and 38 on the relics of St Alban donated to the college by Philip II. Lewis Owen claimed that "a piece of old Tyburne" also functioned as a relic at Valladolid, in memory of the gallows outside London upon which so many Catholics suffered (*The Running Register*, 54). On the martyr paintings, see Michael E. Williams, "Images of Martyrdom in Paintings at the English College Valladolid," in Margaret A. Rees (ed.), *Leeds Papers on Symbol and Image in Iberian Arts* (Leeds: Trinity and All Saints College, University of Leeds, 1994), 51–71. On the Vulnerata, see Shell, *Catholicism, Controversy*, 200–7.

by Persons as the good King Abdias, sheltering the righteous prophets from the wrath of the wicked Jezebel—a popular biblical type for Elizabeth in Catholic polemic.[86]

In *The King of Spaines receiving*, Persons depicts Philip II as a non-threatening and humble figure, the antithesis of Philip's image as the tyrannical nemesis of Elizabeth that circulated in anti-Spanish rhetoric. Persons's Philip is a deeply pious man who prefers to visit churches and monasteries than attend "shewes, maskes, [and] running of Bulles" performed for his entertainment.[87] When the king arrives at the Valladolid college and offers to stand up for an embrace of each student in turn, his attendants are alarmed because of their master's recent attack of gout. In fact, the staff Philip carries is a reminder of his aging, feeble body.[88] However, if Philip's physical body is mortal, Persons reminds us that it is merely the earth-bound container of the Godly ruler's spiritual, immortal body— the non-corporeal sovereign essence that passes at Philip's death to his successor. Hence, in Ortiz's later account of the visit to the college of Philip III, one of the English students tells the new king that "this your presence so reneweth" the memory of the father's visit, "that it seemeth we see agayne that most glorious and pious king memorable to all ages, in this very place, giving eare againe to the stammering speeches of children...We see agayne in your Magestie that most wise and potent monarch of the world, though then languishing in yeares." In Philip III, both the characteristics of his father and the essence of Spanish sovereignty are preserved.[89]

As a riposte to the lurid propaganda of the Black Legend, both Persons and Ortiz present their Habsburg rulers as reassuringly magnanimous father figures. Persons's discussion of Philip II as father to his nation and to two model children—the Prince and the Infanta—implicitly highlights the shortcomings of Queen Elizabeth in the early 1590s with her failure to produce an heir. Likewise, Persons's portrayal of the future Philip III on the threshold of manhood seems calculated to remind English readers of what their country lacks and of the sterile female rule that has so long oppressed them. The Prince, who with his "wonderfull comlines of bodie" proves "much more manlyke then [Persons] could have supposed," enters the town on horseback—a gesture of male authority acclaimed by the people.[90] Blessed with all the graces of royalty, and "prepared

---

[86] *The King of Spaines receiving*, 74. For Catholic representations of Elizabeth I as Jezabel, see my " 'A Pestilent and Seditious Book': Nicholas Sander's *De Origine ac Progressu Schismatis Anglicani* and Catholic Histories of the Reformation," in Paulina Kewes (ed.), *The Uses of History in Early Modern England* (Berkeley: University of California Press, 2006), 147–67.

[87] *The King of Spaines receiving*, 18.   [88] Ibid. 51–2.

[89] Ortiz, *A relation of the solemnetie*, 43–4. For this idea, see Ernst Kantorowicz, *The King's Two Bodies: A Study in Mediaeval Political Theology* (Princeton: Princeton University Press, 1957).

[90] *The King of Spaines receiving*, 18. For the topos in seventeenth-century English art, see Roy Strong, *Van Dyck: Charles I on Horseback* (London: Allen Lane, 1972). Lewkenor describes Prince Philip as "pale and weak of complexion, and not of the greatest vivacitie of spirit" (*The Estate of English Fugitives*, Ri^r).

for a pillar to all Christianitie," the future monarch of the Habsburg empire becomes the sort of earthly savior of Catholics that Prince Henry Stuart would later, briefly, become in English Protestant mythology.

In *The King of Spaines receiving*, Philip II's parental benevolence also extends to the English students. When a 14-year-old boy whose father "dyed in prison for his religion" offers to kiss the king's hands, Philip "would not suffer him, but imbraced him tenderlie about the head and so dismissed him." Symbolically, Philip takes the place of the boy's absent father.[91] Later, other father-surrogates step forward from the ranks of the Spanish nobility. In return for the prayers of the scholars, noblemen offer to support the English boys in their studies, adopting these outcasts from home and country.[92] Philip's "peculiar love to all Catholiques of the Inglish nation" makes him in effect England's unofficial patron and protector against heresy.[93] In fact, Philip has been helping Englishmen in his territories before the Valladolid seminary was founded: when a group of English exiles is imprisoned by Spaniards who have conceived a "just hatred...against the Inglish name," Philip orders that the Englishmen be released and "most tenderlie cherished and favored."[94] Philip becomes a figure of the ideal androgynous sovereign who can both protect and nurture his subjects and friends. He is, in Persons's formulation, both the masculine royal eagle of the House of Habsburg defending innocent pigeons (English Catholics) against birds of prey (Protestants) as well as the maternal "Egle that protecteth hir litle ones, and as the hen that gathereth together her yong chickens."[95] At one point in the narrative, Philip is marked as a virtual divinity, the earthly equivalent of Christ, for the protection he offers English youth.[96]

As vividly as Persons depicts Philip II's masculine protection and feminine support of the English students, Ortiz carries even further the emphasis in his narrative on the conceit of the English students as orphan children, defending their innocence against charges that the students were political malcontents. The students, like the baby Moses, have been "violently drawn from [their] mothers breastes," cast out of their country, and "taken up" by a "new father and mother...pious and loving parents."[97] In Ortiz's text, the protective and nurturing functions that Persons assigns to Philip II alone, are divided between Philip III and his wife, Margaret, who is described as the "potent daughter of Pharo," succoring "with motherly affection" the abandoned Moses. Ortiz, by pressing the parent–child conceit on the royal couple effectively imposes an obligation on the Spanish rulers to continue their patronage of the college. Moreover, Ortiz's depiction of "a litle youth that in semblance seemed a very angell," again evokes Bede's story of the Angelic English youths in the Roman marketplace and the

---

[91] *The King of Spaines receiving*, 30–1.   [92] Ibid. 58–9.   [93] Ibid. 10.
[94] Ibid. 9–10.
[95] Ibid. 55–6, 44. James I famously tapped into discourses of androgyny, styling himself a "loving nourish-father." See Curtis Perry, *The Making of Jacobean Culture: James I and the Renegotiation of Elizabethan Literary Practice* (Cambridge: Cambridge University Press, 1997), ch. 4.
[96] *The King of Spaines receiving*, 47.   [97] Ortiz, *A relation of the solemnetie*, 44–5.

beginning of Pope Gregory's quest to convert their homeland. What Gregory and Augustine had begun in planting the Roman Catholic faith in England, Ortiz's text suggests, Philip and Margaret will finish by expediting England's final reconversion to the one true church.[98]

Beyond standard encomium of Philip, Persons's narrative of the earlier royal visit amplifies the Habsburgs' beneficial effect upon English Catholics by "stealing" a heritage long appropriated by Protestants for their cause: the memory of the first Christian Emperor Constantine the Great. Persons's close attention to the king and his two children, he writes, "made me to imagen that I saw present our noble Britishe Emperour Constantine the greate, with his renowmed two Catholique children, Constans, and Constantia."[99] Persons here stakes a claim for Catholics to the powerful figure of Constantine against Protestant writers like John Foxe, who famously opened the first edition of his *Actes and Monuments* (1563) with the word "Constantine" and an extended analogy between the Roman emperor and Elizabeth I. Like so many figures from early Church and British history, as well as the Bible, Constantine was a malleable figure in Reformation polemic; in 1603, Persons would again evoke him, but this time as a precursor to King James—the first ruler "that hath bene absolutely Lord of the whole ilande of Britany (with the parts annexed therunto) since Constantine."[100]

For an English readership, however, the analogy between Constantine and Philip was both comforting and problematic because if, on the one hand, it had the effect of disarming the Spanish ruler by giving him a veneer of Englishness, on the other hand it could also suggest Philip's imperial ambitions. According to Eusebius's "Life of Constantine" (a major source for Foxe and Persons), the emperor was English by virtue of his English mother, Helena, and British by virtue of his dominion over the whole of the British Isles. But as a Roman emperor, even a Christian one, Constantine's vast territorial sway would have resonated suspiciously for Protestants with Philip's similarly far-flung possessions that stretched from the Iberian Peninsula, to northern and central Europe, the Italian states, and the New World.[101]

---

[98] Ibid. 46. As Philip III and his queen are about to leave the college, the Duke of Lerma describes the English students as "a quire of angells" (64).

[99] *The King of Spaines receiving*, 20.

[100] *A treatise of three conversions of England from paganisme to Christian religion* (St Omers, 1603. ERL 304), *2[r–v]. For commentary, see Michael S. Pucci, "Reforming Roman Emperors: John Foxe's Characterization of Constantine in the *Acts and Monuments*," in David Loades (ed.), *John Foxe: An Historical Perspective* (Aldershot: Ashgate, 1999), 29–51; Patrick Collinson, "If Constantine, then also Theodosius: St Ambrose and the Integrity of the Elizabethan *Ecclesia Anglicana*," *Journal of Ecclesiastical History* 30 (1979), 205–29; Richard Koebner, "'The Imperial Crown of this Realm': Henry VIII, Constantine the Great, and Polydore Vergil," *Bulletin of the Institute of Historical Research* 26 (1953), 29–52; and Winifred Joy Mulligan, "The British Constantine: An English Historical Myth," *The Journal of Medieval and Renaissance Studies* 8 (1978), 257–79.

[101] Geoffrey Parker, "The Place of Tudor England in the Messianic Vision of Philip II of Spain," *Transactions of the Royal Historical Society*, 6th ser. 12 (2002), 167–221. My thanks to the author for sharing this essay with me in pre-publication form.

The Constantine analogy receives a further twist in Persons's *The King of Spaines receiving* when Philip's daughter, the Infanta, is likened to both Constantine's mother, the saintly Helena, and to his daughter, Constantia. Persons's double identification of the Infanta intensifies a sense of the assimilation of Spanish royalty to an English/British heritage in a way that counteracts Protestant arguments about the assimilation of the English and their values to Iberian culture. Persons's use of the Constantine analogy, then, helps not only to transform Philip from the "stranger and...demi-Moore" imagined by his enemies, the ruler "whose language we understand not, and whose humours and fashions we shall never be able to abide," into a nominal Englishman, but also Anglicizes the Infanta.[102] In fact, Persons's handling of the Infanta in *The King of Spaines receiving* prepares English readers for the case he was about to lodge on her behalf as a legitimate successor to Elizabeth in *A conference about the next succession to the crowne of Ingland* (1595).

Persons's efforts to narrow or bridge the gap between England and Spain by assimilating Philip and the Infanta to English culture harks back to the earlier attempts of English writers to domesticate the Habsburg prince at the time of his marriage to Mary Tudor.[103] Even in the 1590s, Persons continued to resurrect memories of this short-lived Anglo-Hispanic alliance as a way of reassuring skeptical readers that Philip's intentions toward England had always been good. Persons praises Philip's "princely behaveour and pious government, during the few yeares he lived amongst us and ruled over us," thus confuting the allegations of Protestants like Sir Francis Hastings that Philip had sought "an absolute power over poor England," that he had wished to impose a "bloody inquisition," root out the English nobility, and "make [the commons] slaves among the Moores."[104] Against Hastings's "absurd inventions," Persons describes Philip as the selfless benefactor of the English people and the "cheefest stay and defence" of their new queen, Elizabeth, whom he was instrumental in freeing during her half-sister's reign from imprisonment at Woodstock.[105]

In light of the past goodwill shown by Philip and other Spaniards to England as well as the dynastic alliances that had cemented relations between the realms, such as Philip's marriage to Mary and Katherine of Aragon's to Henry VIII, Persons implies that the presence of English subjects and colleges on the Iberian Peninsula are not dangerous aberrations but the reflection of a long and mutually beneficial relationship between two great nations whose identities are closely intertwined. Persons reinforces this vision of Anglo-Spanish harmony in his tract

[102] Copley, *Another letter of Mr. A.C. to his dis-Jesuited kinesman*, 17.

[103] Among the Spanish, it was not only monarchs who claimed consanguinity with English nobility. At the English college in Seville, the narrator of Persons's *Newes from Spayne and Holland* meets "Don Rodrigo de Castro, the Cardinal and Archbishop of that citie, who estemeth himself and his house (which is very honorable and of the most auncientest Grandes of Spayne) to be discended of your old Dukes of Lancaster" (4ʳ).

[104] *A temperate ward-word*, 107, 113, 114, 115.   [105] Ibid. 116–17.

Newes from Spayne and Holland, published the year after *The King of Spaines receiving*. Persons's narrator (born in the Low Countries but raised in England) sets out to defend "the estate, residence, and exercises of the English nation in Spaine."[106] En route to see the new English college in Seville, he stops in San Lucar where he visits the English church of St George that the town's community of English merchants have bequeathed to English seminary priests ("together with all the houses, groundes, and other emoluments belonging therunto").[107] For the narrator, the existence of this English church in San Lucar gestures to the larger patterns of commercial, religious, and political/dynastic exchange that have historically bound the two countries together. The ancient and continuing presence of the English in Spain reveals to the narrator (and to the reader) that notions of an essential incompatibility between the two peoples and of a threat of contamination to English visitors in Spain are simply Protestant fictions.

In *Newes from Spayne and Holland*, Persons looks forward to a time after the lifting of anti-Catholic laws in England when the country's historically amicable relations with Spain will be restored, along with England's rightful place in international circuits of commerce and culture. This will be a time, argues Persons,

when the Catholique man and woman in England may deale with their neighbour in love and confidence; when our noble and worshipful gentlemen abrode may returne home, and shew their loyal duties to their Soveraigne without offence or peril, or force offred to their conscience for matters of religion; when our English merchantes may traffique freely throughout the world without peril of piracie or confiscations, when our home gentlemen may travel with lyke libertie where it seemeth them best for increase of their experience to serve their country, when our English students may visit forrayne universityes without restraint, and strangers come to ours and speake, confer, dispute, and reason with modestie without danger of intrapping.[108]

In a Europe increasingly polarized by confessional divisions, Persons's fantasy of open borders, freedom of conscience, and the unimpeded circulation of people, goods, and ideas between England and the Continent, was to remain just that, a fantasy, but a potent Catholic fantasy nonetheless.

THE ENTERTAINMENT AT VALLADOLID

The King of Spaines receiving is a testament to the English Catholic students' ingenuity and resourcefulness in the art of collective self-presentation. Philip's hosts at the college face a daunting task if they are to emulate the many magnificent entertainments the king has already witnessed on his summer itinerary.

---

[106] *Newes from Spain and Holland* (*ERL* 365), A2^r.   [107] Ibid. 3^r.
[108] *A temperate ward-word*, 128–9.

With the college refectory still under construction, the English students cover half-built walls with timber and canvas, which they decorate with "grene and redd taffatie…abundance of verses of manie languages, Emblemes, Hieroglyphicks, and other learned inventions, as was most beutifull and delectable to behold."[109] They stage the heart of the entertainment in the "greate hall or theater" where the royal entourage listens to a series of orations by the students in various ancient and modern languages. Taking Psalm 71 as their text, selected students read a verse each, and through the art of "application," gloss it in relation to Habsburg power and "the state of our afflicted countrie," England.[110]

Persons explains that the psalm, which begins, "O Lord geve judgement unto the King, and justice unto the Kings son," "though it were written properlie and peculiarlie of Christ himself, yet by secondarie application, and by some similitude, it maie also verie apteie be accommodated to this most christian King, and his son, that are so principall ministers of Christ, and do imitate so manifestlie his kinglie virtues, which in this Psalme are expressed."[111] This provocative subject matter poses a potential problem to Persons who must have realized that the idea of Philip as a type of Christ would not have been well received by many English readers, some of whom would already have been familiar with Philip's own rhetoric of Messianic imperialism.[112]

For strategic reasons, then, the English students do not recite (or Persons does not record them reciting) all twenty verses of the psalm, so as not to overplay Philip's reputation as "rex imperii." The students omit verse 5, "And he shal continew with the sunne and before the moone in generation and generation," possibly on the grounds that it could be construed as ascribing an immortality to Philip that was Christ's alone. They also leave out verses 8 through 11, perhaps because they could heighten the anxieties of English readers about Philip's alleged dream of establishing a universal empire:

> And he shal rule from sea unto sea, and from the river even to the
>   ends of the round world.
> Before him shal the Æthiopians fal downe: and his enimies shal lick
>   the earth.
> The kinges of Tharsis, and the ilands shal offer presentes: the kings
>   of the Arabians, and of Saba shal bring giftes.
> And al kinges of the earth shal adore him: al nations shal serve him.

"The Ilands" in verse 10, according to the annotations in the Douai–Rheims Old Testament, include Great Britain, and the words prophesy the territory's conversion to Christianity. In the interpretive framework established at Valladolid by the presence of Philip, these lines could be understood as forecasting Great Britain's conquest and reconversion by Spain—a scenario that Persons wished

[109] *The King of Spaines receiving*, 24.   [110] Ibid. 26, 25.   [111] Ibid. 32, 25.
[112] Parker, "The Place of Tudor England in the Messianic Vision of Philip II," 167–221.

to play down in the interests of presenting the college as a purely religious venture.[113]

Persons, as the orchestrator of the entertainment and author of the commemorative tract, carefully selected the ten languages spoken by the students in order to highlight their erudition and diversity. The learned languages of Hebrew, Greek, and Latin are obvious choices—vehicles for demonstrating the students' scholarly training—while French, Italian, Spanish, and Flemish are the languages of territories within Philip's sphere of influence. "Three vulgar languages" are also represented: English, Welsh or British, and Scottish.[114] Persons includes Welsh because of the presence of "divers" Welsh students in the college, but also as a way of reassuring his royal audience that the frictions between English and Welsh Catholics in the college in Rome a decade earlier would not flare up again in Spain.[115] Other students speak in a lowland Scots dialect, but are careful not to use that of "the mountaine parts and Ilands of Orchades and Hebrides [where] the naturall language is Irish."[116] The omission of Gaelic reminds us of Persons's determination both to keep Irish students out of his college in Valladolid and to prevent the erection of a separate Irish college in the town.[117] Persons knew only too well what advantages the Irish already enjoyed over the English in Spain and he had no intention of adding to them. Persons, in fact, seems to have conceived of the Valladolid college in exclusive, Anglocentric terms, despite the linguistic inclusiveness of the entertainment. In *The King of Spaines receiving*, he still refers to all members of the college as "us persecuted and banished Inglish Catholiques," and calls Valladolid "a College of one onlie Nation."[118] Persons's act of national imagining treats the multicultural diversity of Britain as merely a sideshow to the central focus on Catholic Englishness.[119]

When the young Prince Philip returned for a second visit to the college as King Philip III in 1600, the students presented a reading of Psalm 20. According to Ortiz's narrative of the accompanying ceremony, the students again spoke in ten different languages, only this time substituting Cornish for Welsh.[120]

---

[113] *The Second Tome of the Holie Bible*, 131–3 (*ERL* 266). The students also cut verses 15 through 17, as well as verse 20. The psalm is number 72 in the Geneva Bible. For related instances of writers adapting the psalms to fit religio-political agendas, see Hannibal Hamlin, *Psalm Culture and Early Modern English Literature* (Cambridge: Cambridge University Press, 2004).

[114] *The King of Spaines receiving*, 36.

[115] Persons also refers to the recent publication at Valladolid of a Welsh grammar and catechism (Ibid. 38–9).

[116] Ibid. 40.

[117] See Beales, *Education under Penalty*, 46. Patricia O'Connell claims that "An Irish college was founded in Valladolid in 1589 but it did not survive long" ("The Early-Modern Irish College Network in Iberia, 1590–1800," in Thomas O'Connor (ed.), *The Irish in Europe, 1580–1815* (Dublin: Four Courts Press, 2001), 52 n. 12).

[118] *The King of Spaines receiving*, 47, 25.

[119] John Bossy, "Catholicity and Nationality in the Northern Counter-Reformation," in *Religion and National Identity*, ed. Stuart Mews (Oxford: Blackwell, 1982), 285–96.

[120] *A relation of the solemnetie*, 48.

Perhaps the change reflects nothing more than the backgrounds of the students available to take reading parts, but the fact that the Cornish dialect, observes Ortiz, had "a certaine grace and reddynes of speach not unlike to that of the Biscaies" also helps to suggest a larger consonance between England and Spain.[121] The harmony that Ortiz seems keen to demonstrate between the English youth and their Spanish hosts is emblematized by the "sweet and artificial song made after [the English] country manner of musicke and the ditty in Spanish to the purpose." In this performance of an English song in the Spanish tongue, Ortiz projects the wished-for reunification of two cultures forced apart by misplaced prejudice and distrust.[122]

In both Persons's and Ortiz's texts, nothing about these extraordinary students is either narrowly English or dangerously hispaniolized. Instead, the students' multilingual performances mirror the dispersal of the Catholic diaspora in "divers contries and nations," while also affirming the students' membership of religious, scholastic, and humanistic communities that transcend national borders.[123] Their participation in an international community is also evident from the emblems and hieroglyphics they devise for decorating the walls of the college. These impresa "speak" in a Catholic *Lingua Franca* by employing a visual language accessible to all educated Europeans.[124] One notable emblem described by Persons depicts the "armes of Valliodolid, which are certaine flames of fyar, and nighe to this, were painted two ships, one cominge and the other going to an Island in the sea, that represented Ingland, and both ships full of schollers, the one coming with torches out, to light them at the saide flames, and the other sorte retourning home, with their torches lighted and burning."[125] The emblem's imagery of sea passage captures the students' exilic identity based on movement between home and abroad, while also recalling the idea of the Ship of the Church wending its way back to England. The flames on the emblem signify more than the civic identity of Valladolid, recalling Christ's defiant motto, "Ignem veni mittere in terram" ("I came to cast fire on the earth: and what

---

[121] Ibid. 55–6. Psalm 20 is about the nature of Solomonic kingship and God's promises to the good ruler. As a new Solomon, Philip III is urged by the students to extend Catholic religion "beyond the fardest seas, to the east and west and to the north from whence we come" (50). The godly monarch must be active beyond his borders. Philip is credited with bringing peace to France, waging wars against heresy in Flanders, and caring for England's recusants. Philip's seminaries for English youth are seen as a "holesome hearbe calleth Brittanica, to chase away and put to flight those venomous serpentes, the infernal spirites that have infected and poisoned England with heresy" (59).

[122] *A relation of the solemnetie*, 60. Andrew Breeze, "Welsh and Cornish at Valladolid, 1591–1600," *The Bulletin of the Board of Celtic Studies* 37 (1990), 108–11.

[123] *The King of Spaines receiving*, 31–2.

[124] See Karl Josef Hltgen, "Henry Hawkins: A Jesuit Writer and Emblematist in Stuart England," in John W. O'Malley, SJ, Gauvin Alexander Bailey, Steven J. Harris, and T. Frank Kennedy, SJ (eds.), *The Jesuits: Cultures, Sciences, and the Arts 1540–1773* (Toronto: University of Toronto Press, 1999), 600–26.

[125] *The King of Spaines receiving*, 54.

wil I, but that it be kindled?").[126] Moreover, in the context of the entertainment's performance of multiple languages, the flames evoke the biblical story of Pentecost:

And when the daies of Pentecost were accomplished, [the Apostles] were al together in one place: and sodenly there was made a sound from heaven, as of a vehement winde coming: and it filled the whole house where they were sitting. And there appeared to them parted tonges as it were of fire, and it sate upon every one of them: and they were al replenished with the Holy Ghost, and they began to speake with diverse tonges, according as the Holy Ghost gave them to speake.[127]

Just as the apostles are granted the gift of speaking in tongues, so the students at Valladolid—a breed of new apostles—enact their own form of glossolalia, speaking in languages "learned," "barbarous," and "vulgar."[128] Ortiz's later account makes the Pentecostal context explicit by likening the English college at Valladolid to "the holy Colledge of the Apostles" that received "divers tonges and languages."[129]

Though Persons celebrates the English students' ability to balance their Englishness with a cultivated European sensibility, Persons's detractors, like the secular priest Christopher Bagshaw, refused to believe that "these Spanish schollers" had preserved an autonomous English identity in Spain. Bagshaw alleged that for political reasons Persons had left out of "the printed copy" of *The King of Spaines receiving*, "that part of the youths oration" in which the student offered Philip "not only himselfe, but in the name of the rest, all his fellowes: nay their whole Countrey, their parents, and friends, with all their Allyes, confederates, and acquaintance."[130] Bagshaw could not imagine the possibility of a reciprocal, equitable mingling of Englishmen and Spaniards: instead, he imagines Englishness capitulating to a voracious Spanishness that converts everything it touches. Persons, on the contrary, debunks this fantasy of hispaniolization by showing how the exiled students uphold an Englishness enriched outside England by contact with the cultural currents of European Christendom.[131] Previously, Persons had revealed in a private letter that the first English students at Valladolid had become worryingly immersed in the study of Hispanic language and culture.[132] In *The King of Spaines receiving*, however,

---

[126] Douai–Rheims Bible, Luke 12: 49. See also Carol M. Richardson, "Durante Alberti, the *Martyrs' Picture* and the Venerable English College, Rome," *Papers of the British School at Rome* 73 (2005), 252–3; Jason A. Nice, "Being 'British,' in Rome: The Welsh at the English College, 1578–1584," *The Catholic Historical Review* 92.1 (2006), 1–24.

[127] Douai–Rheims Bible, Acts 2: 1–4.   [128] *The King of Spaines receiving*, 41.

[129] *A relation of the solemnetie*, 48.

[130] *A sparing discoverie of our English Jesuits* (1601), 54.

[131] Beales discusses the "uncompromisingly English" nature of the college at St Omers and the insistence of students there upon "stolidly angliciz[ing] the pronunciation of the name St 'Omers' " (*Education under Penalty*, 126).

[132] *Calendar H.M.C. Salisbury MS*, vol.4, 69. Quoted in Loomie, *Spanish Elizabethans*, 189.

he deliberately avoids giving the impression that the students had developed a singleminded fascination with their host culture by stressing, for instance, how Spanish is only one of the ten languages they use.[133] Similarly, Ortiz downplays the students' familiarity with Spanish: although they understand it, he tells us, they are not competent enough to compose verses in it.[134] For both Persons and Ortiz there is nothing unnatural, hispaniolized, or "out of place" about English Catholics in Spain—on the contrary, their Protestant enemies are the "unnatural" ones for "vex[ing] . . . theyr owne naturall countriemen."[135]

A SATIRICAL IMAGE AT SEVILLE

Whereas in *The King of Spaines receiving*, Persons emphasizes the loyalty of the Valladolid students to the English crown, he shows elsewhere how the other colleges on the Iberian Peninsula could foster political resistance to the Tudor state, very much as the Protestant authorities feared. This is the case in *Newes from Spayne and Holland* that describes the celebration at the English college in Seville of the feast of St Thomas of Canterbury. As part of this celebration, students display various papers, poems, and "lerned devises" around the college, the most striking of which—and the one that may have formed the centerpiece of a larger iconographical program—juxtaposes contrasting images of Henry II and Henry VIII. The device's complex visual scheme is divided horizontally into four "rancks." In the first rank, beneath the title, "the triumph of St Thomas of Canterbury over two king Henryes of Ingland," are four images. On the extreme right side of the paper, Henry II is shown "armed and angry and striking at St Thomas" who appears to the left, fleeing from the king. On the extreme left side of the paper, Henry VIII is shown "very fatt and furious," and to his right the body of Thomas is depicted "with the ensignes of glory." Inscriptions above and between each of the images explicate the scenes. In the "second ranck" of the picture are three images: the two Henrys appear again on the right and left sides of the paper, but they are divided by a single central image of "the tombe and sepulcre" of Thomas. This time Henry II is painted "leane and repentant, barefooted kneeling on his knees, and whipping himselfe severly," while Henry VIII is shown "more fatt and monstrous them [*sic*] before sweating and chaffing and in great fury digging downe the sepulcre with a pickaxe."[136] In the "third ranke" of the picture on the right hand side, beneath the image of Henry II, angels are shown "expecting him to glory and salvation," while in

---

[133] *The King of Spaines receiving*, 25.   [134] *A relation of the solemnetie*, 21.

[135] *The King of Spaines receiving*, 41. The statutes of the English College, Rome, required that all students learned Italian—an indication that they were not necessarily expected to return to England as missionary priests, but instead to seek church offices in Rome and Italian-speaking lands. See Anthony Kenny, "From Hospice to College," in *The English Hospice in Rome*. The Venerabile Sexcentenary issue. May 1962. Vol. 21 (Exeter: Catholic Records Press), 233, 245 n. 68.

[136] *Newes from Spayne and Holland*, 11ᵛ–12ᵛ.

the corresponding position on the left side, devils are shown "with instruments of torments" preparing to receive Henry VIII into Hell. Elizabeth I is depicted between the two Henrys, "beholding sadly the one and the other example"; beneath her are the words "choose which you wil of thes two." Finally, at the bottom of the picture, two English students of the college are shown on either side in a pose of "holding up the said paper." They offer Latin verses to Elizabeth "for explication of their meaning in this representation."[137]

What makes this extraordinarily sophisticated and "witty" propaganda piece so effective is its aesthetic quality. The passers-by who flock "to looke upon it," find it "pleasant to behold, being large and fayrely paynted to the eye." No wonder the narrator thinks it will soon "be engraved and printed."[138] The picture is a repudiation of Elizabethan modes of legitimation, a radical rewriting of the officially sanctioned view of the Tudor past. It encodes two alternative models of kingship: one identified with Henry II's resubmission to the medieval Church and his accompanying acts of bodily penance, the other with Henry VIII's foolish reenactment of Henry II's crimes. The satirical indignity of the unflattering image of Henry VIII's corpulent body and disordered mind is consistent with other negative representations of the king by Catholic polemicists like Nicholas Sander. This treatment of Henry was especially galling to Elizabeth given her investment in preserving the memory of her father as the resolute embodiment of the Tudor dynasty and nation. Catholic images of a physically grotesque Henry VIII undermined the officially sanctioned image of a vigorous and commanding king derived from Holbein that loyal subjects continued to display in their homes throughout Elizabeth's reign.[139]

The picture asks Elizabeth to choose between the contrasting courses of action taken by her predecessors, between whom she is shown sitting pensively. If she chooses her father's precedent, she will not be able to persecute St Thomas of Canterbury, but she will be able to persecute his symbolic successors: the English Catholic students. As *Newes from Spayne and Holland* makes clear, the students explicitly identify themselves with Thomas. Like the saint, they suffer temporary banishment from England, and like him they are prepared to return home to face persecution and a possible martyr's death.[140]

ENGLISH NUNS IN LISBON: EXILED FROM THEIR EXILE

Persons's involvement with and representations of the English exiles on the Iberian Peninsula extended beyond the all-male seminaries at Valladolid and Seville to the community of Bridgettine nuns that settled in Lisbon in 1594.

---

[137] Ibid. 12[v].   [138] Ibid. 11[v].

[139] Xanthe Brooke and David Crombie, *Henry VIII Revealed: Holbein's Portrait and its Legacy* (London: Holberton, 2003), 59–60.

[140] *Newes from Spayne and Holland*, 9[r].

Shortly after the nuns' arrival in Portugal, Persons wrote the preface to an account of the sisters' long and troubled exile from England. Known as "The Wanderings of Syon," the narrative was printed in Spanish as *Relacion que embiaron las religiosas del monesterio de Sion... al Padre Roberto Personio* (1594) and was later partly incorporated into Diego de Yepes, *Historia particular de la persecucion de Inglaterra* (Madrid 1599).[141] Persons recounts the history of the Bridgettines, beginning with their foundation at Syon Abbey by Henry V in 1415. The dissolution of the monasteries in 1539 forced the nuns to flee to Flanders, but they returned to England when Catholicism was restored under Mary and Philip. However, the sisters enjoyed only a brief respite from exile because, with the return of "heresy" under Elizabeth, they left England a second time for the Continent. In 1563 the Bridgettine nuns acquired their own house in Flanders, but were forced to move again because of an "unwholesome" climate and lack of funds.[142] Their next destination was close to Antwerp in the Duchy of Brabant where conditions were at first more favorable to the religious life. But in time the aggression of "heretics" forced them to take refuge inside the city. Unable to find suitable lodging there, the sisters moved once more, this time to Mechlin (Malines), where they remained seven years until again forced to flee by "heretics."[143] The nuns—in the words of a sympathetic observer— were, like other exiles in the region, "thrust from their homes and so from their monasteries, and, as it were, again exiled from their exile, that they consider it a great benefit that they are expelled and not killed, and that they can in safety escape together elsewhere."[144] The sisters finally left Flanders, traveling by sea to Rouen in France where they stayed for fourteen years until the defeat of the Catholic League precipitated their departure for Lisbon in 1594, their eighth move in fifty-five years.[145]

Throughout their wanderings, the nuns clung tenaciously to their unique institutional and national identity. During their second period of exile in Spanish Flanders, they found a home "in a distinct quarter" of a Flemish Bridgettine monastery, "making as it were two monasteries, one of the Flemish, the other of the English nuns, each with their own different Abbess."[146] This segregation of the English and Flemish sisters signals the Bridgettines' determination to ward

---

[141] For an English translation of Persons's preface, see Adam Hamilton, *The Angel of Syon: the Life and Martyrdom of Blessed Richard Reynolds, Bridgettine Monk of Syon, Martyred at Tyburn, May 4, 1535. To which is added a sketch of the History of the Bridgettines of Syon, written by Father Robert Persons, S.J., about the year 1595*, edited from a MS copy at Syon abbey, Chudleigh (Edinburgh: Sands, 1905); AR 1: 741. Also see John Rory Fletcher, *The Story of the English Bridgettines of Syon Abbey* (South Brent, Devon, 1933); Nancy Bradley Warren, "Dissolution, Diaspora, and Defining Englishness: Syon in Exile and Elizabethan Politics," in *Women of God and Arms: Female Spirituality and Political Conflict 1380–1600* (Philadelphia: University of Pennsylvania Press, 2005), 139–67.

[142] Hamilton (ed.), *The Angel of Syon*, 106.   [143] Ibid. 108–9.

[144] Quoted in Peter Guilday, *The English Catholic Refugees on the Continent, 1558–1795* (London: Longmans, Green, and Co., 1914), 58 n. 6.

[145] Hamilton (ed.), *The Angel of Syon*, 110.   [146] Ibid. 104–5.

off potentially corrupting foreign influences. As Claire Walker explains, "many women [exiles] saw themselves primarily as members of the English Catholic community, and only secondly as members of the universal Catholic Church." Typically, English nuns objected to admitting local foreign women to their ranks and to sharing premises with foreign sisters even of the same order. When native women were admitted, they tended to be appointed as lay or converse sisters, inferior in rank to the socially elevated English choir nuns. These lay or converse sisters were responsible for the menial work of the nunnery and for communicating with the surrounding community in the local language that the English sisters were unlikely to know.[147]

By insulating and segregating themselves in these ways, the Bridgettines, like other English women religious in Habsburg territories, could claim to be protecting themselves against the dangers of hispaniolization. Nunneries functioned in effect as little self-enclosed Englands that shut out the foreign cultures around them. Furthermore, the nuns' lives behind the convent walls represented a condition of self-imposed internal sequestration added to the external exile from England itself. When relatives and curious visitors from England came to see the nuns in their overseas "receptacles," the sisters could only communicate through a grill, curtain, or other screen—after gaining the approval of their superiors.[148] And on these occasions, if the nun was willing to keep her head bowed and her eyes averted, she was promised "a grete crowne in heven."[149]

If the nuns thought they were shunning the dangers of hispaniolization by detaching themselves from their foreign surroundings, they could not so easily distance themselves from their Spanish patrons. Indeed, Persons's narrative of the Bridgettine nuns stresses the help they have received from Philip II as a sign of their divine blessing. Philip not only helped the sisters gain safe passage out of England at Elizabeth's accession, but he continues to support them financially (even if payments were somewhat irregular).[150] Philip's contribution to the nuns' survival in exile is also foregrounded in another history of the Bridgettines

---

[147] Claire Walker, *Gender and Politics in Early Modern Europe: English Convents in France and the Low Countries* (New York: Palgrave Macmillan, 2003), 13–15, 38–42; quotation at 40. Peter Guilday discovered "the apostolic Brief of Pius IV. (1559–1565), dated May 8, 1564, to the Archbishop of Cambrai, asking him to secure a separate house for [the sisters] in his diocese, where they could carry out their Rule with all the privileges, indulgences and prerogatives granted to the English branch of the Order since 1415" (*The English Catholic Refugees*, 57 n. 2). The nuns' introspective Englishness would have been reinforced by the resentment of the local community. John Rory Fletcher records an occasion when the nuns' house in Rouen was besieged by angry demonstrators, shouting "the Bridgettines were strangers and English...our old enemies, why should they be among us?" (*The Story of the English Bridgettines*, 78).

[148] On the fascination of English travelers with the nunneries of their countrywomen, see C. D. Van Strien, "Recusant Houses in the Southern Netherlands as seen by British Tourists, c.1650–1720," *Recusant History* 20 (1991), 495–511.

[149] Quoted in Ann M. Hutchison, "Eyes cast Down, But Self Revealed: Letters of a Recusant Nun," in Bonnie Wheeler (ed.), *Feminea Medievalia: Representations of the Feminine in the Middle Ages* (Academia, 1993), 331.

[150] Warren, "Dissolution, Diaspora," 150–1.

produced in the early seventeenth century. The unique manuscript of this text includes nine "rectangular miniatures painted in gold and colors" that tell the story of the Bridgettines, beginning with an image of St Bridget of Sweden embarking on her pilgrimage to Rome from "the furthest ends and capes of the world," to the sisters' recent arrival in Lisbon.[151] Three of the images depict Philip in person greeting the nuns into his territories. He first welcomes them back to England after their initial exile under Edward VI; then he welcomes them to Flanders at the beginning of Elizabeth's reign; and finally he greets them as they disembark at Lisbon.[152] Each image depicts Philip as an imposing royal figure standing on the sea-shore, guarding the borders of his lands, yet holding out his hands in a gesture of welcome to the wandering nuns. The miniatures paint the nuns as diminutive by contrast, huddled together in groups of two and three, and looking beseechingly at the king their protector.

As related by Persons, the nuns' arrival in Lisbon was a providential moment: just as the Bridgettines had been founded by the Lancastrian King Henry V, so in Lisbon they were effectively refounded by the Lancastrian descended royal house of Portugal. Persons here recycles the subversive genealogy he had used so effectively in *A conference about the next succession to the crowne of Ingland* in which he traced the royal houses of Spain and Portugal back through a Lancastrian genealogy to their progenitor John of Gaunt. This bit of Catholic "Lancastrianism" is, as Nancy Bradley Warren argues, a deft appropriation by Persons of one of Elizabeth's own potent mythologizing strategies of linking herself to Henry V and the Lancastrian inheritance.[153] Persons's reference to the nuns finally finding a "home" in Portugal also reminds readers that in 1581 Philip had added "King of Portugal" to his other titles, after the Portuguese royal line died out.[154]

In Lisbon the nuns would at last find the safe-haven they had sought in their years of wanderings. The city was an attractive destination for Catholic exiles from all parts of the Atlantic archipelago in the late sixteenth and early seventeenth century. Lisbon was easily accessible by ship from the north Atlantic and already had long-established trading ties with Britain and Ireland. Lisbon was also a relatively safe place for Catholic refugees and, unlike France and the Low Countries, "not liable to be disturbed by European religious wars." By the time the Bridgettines arrived, several religious institutions catering to other exiles already existed in the city, including a residence for English clergy as well as an Irish College of St Patrick founded in 1592.[155] However, even in

---

[151] Christopher De Hamel, *Syon Abbey: The Library of the Bridgettine Nuns and their Peregrinations after the Reformation* (London: Roxburghe Club, 1991), 26.

[152] Another image shows Philip watching over the nuns as they leave England upon the accession of Elizabeth, after he has secured their safe conduct out of the country.

[153] "Dissolution, Diaspora," 151–4.   [154] Walker, *Gender and Politics*, 13.

[155] Michael E. Williams, "The Origins of the English College, Lisbon," *Recusant History* 20 (1991), 478–9, quotation at 487; Guilday, *The English Catholic Refugees*, 30.

ENTRADA EN FLANDRES.

El mismo Rey Phelippe las Recibio en flandes y despues en el
ano de 1563 les dio vn monasterio en Zelandia llamado Beta-
nia. Ps. 30. statuisti in loco spacioso pedes meos.

Fig. 7. The arrival in Flanders of the Bridgettine nuns, from a manuscript history of the
wanderings of the nuns of Syon, compiled in Lisbon in the early seventeenth century
(vellum) by Portuguese School. His Grace the Duke of Norfolk, Arundel Castle.

Lisbon, the nuns encountered problems at first because they wished to retain their order's distinct English heritage, something the Archbishop of Lisbon claimed "was contrary to the Roman Pontifical and the decrees of the Council of Trent." Matters were only resolved after the intervention of Persons and Pope Clement VIII.[156]

The Bridgettine nuns, as Persons points out, were the last surviving congregation of women religious from pre-Reformation England—"the only relics of all the Orders and Religious which in Catholick times were in England, which, as all know, were very many."[157] Along with their brothers in religion—the monks of Sheen—the nuns of Syon had

continued and preserved so many years so miraculously, in the midst of so many travels, persecutions, and perils in their banishment, even to our days, giving great hope that our Lord in His good pleasure will bring them once again home to their country, to be the seed and seminaries of many others ... Which hope is greatly confirmed by another succour which our Lord in these times of so great trouble hath given to this nation by the seminaries of English priests in France, Flanders, Rome, and Spain, whose design is to preach the Catholick Faith in their country, and to reduce it to the obedience of the Holy Apostolick See ... So that these two monasteries of religious persons giving themselves to prayer and contemplation, are Moses, Aaron, and Hur, lifting up their hands to God for redress of their country, and for victory over the enemies of the Church of God. And in like manner the five seminaries perform the office of Joshua and the other valiant captains of the People of God against the Amalakites, that is, against the hereticks.[158]

Persons's association of the female convent at Lisbon with the male seminaries elsewhere on the Iberian Peninsula and Europe reflects his conviction that the two ventures were part of a joint enterprise, sharing the goal of replanting the Catholic faith in England. While the sisters in Lisbon could not train as priests or join the mission to England, they could offer their own form of political resistance to the Protestant nation-state. As Claire Walker argues, the English communities of exiled women religious understood their acts of prayer, meditation, and devotion as forcefully connected to the spiritual revival of England and the overthrow of "heresy."[159] The fact that militant Catholics like Nicholas Sander advised and financially supported the nuns during their time in Flanders underscores the important role they were accorded by leading expatriates in the task of winning England back to the Old Faith.[160]

[156] Guilday, *The English Catholic Refugees*, 59 n. 4, 60.
[157] Hamilton (ed.), *The Angel of Syon*, 112.   [158] Ibid. 112–13.
[159] *Gender and Politics.* Walker, however, does not discuss the convents on the Iberian Peninsula (6, 115–19). Nancy Bradley Warren also argues that the political activism of the Sion nuns meant that "women of God" became "women of arms." Some of the nuns, including Elizabeth Sander (sister of Nicholas Sander), returned "illegally to England to work for the Catholic cause" by collecting alms and distributing Catholic books, as well as by planning military action and plotting to depose Elizabeth in favor of Mary Stuart ("Dissolution Diaspora," 141–9).
[160] Hamilton (ed.), *The Angel of Syon*, 106. Nicholas Sander's sister, Elizabeth, was a member of the Bridgettine congregation at this time.

The convents in Habsburg lands were no less an object of Protestant fascination and anxiety than were the all-male seminaries. And the Brigettine nuns in Lisbon, as the last remaining pre-Reformation order of women religious from England, attracted special attention. To Protestants, the Bridgettines' longevity was an embarrassing reminder of the vestigial presence of English Catholics on the European political scene; to Catholics, the community's continuation through so many displacements was a sign of their faith's righteousness. The Lisbon convent may have been materially inconsequential, but it remained symbolically pivotal to the narratives of both Catholics and Protestants.[161]

---

[161] Walker, *Gender and Politics*, 118–19.

Epilogue

The most detailed Protestant exposé of the Bridgettine convent in Lisbon was Thomas Robinson's *The anatomy of the English nunnery at Lisbon in Portugall: Dissected and laid open by one that was sometime a yonger brother of the convent* (1622). This first-person account describes Robinson's own misadventures in the convent where he is "inticed" by its confessor, "father Seth, alias, Joseph Foster." There, Robinson claims that his identity is gradually taken from him. First the Bridgettines deprive him "of meanes to depart . . . by taking away my apparell and putting me into a disguized foolish habite." Then Father Seth and the Abbess persuade him "to become a holy Brother and Masse-priest in the house."[1] Whereas the ease with which Robinson succumbs to these Catholic entreaties no doubt disturbed some Protestant readers, Robinson's freedom within the house allowed those same readers the vicarious pleasure of gaining access to its inner secrets. Robinson works first copying "out certaine Treatises of Obedience, which [Foster] had composed for the Nunnes," but later he becomes the convent's scribe and copyist, "writing over divers bookes for them, and amongst the rest, the Register of their House." Robinson has gained access to privileged, inside information about the nuns' "estate, beginning and successe untill this present"— information that can embarrass and ruin the convent in the eyes of the outside world.[2]

Robinson's infiltration of the convent perfectly serves *The anatomy*'s project of exposing what it sees as fraudulent Catholic claims about the sanctity of the Lisbon convent and, by extension, all religious houses. The women Robinson discovers here are nothing like the original well-born sisters of Syon described in the Order's own accounts of itself. Instead, they are a "meaner" breed of "Recusants daughters . . . silly tender-hearted chambermaids . . . [and] a rabble of such like stuffe."[3] In spite of the women's humble status, Robinson still urges their relatives and friends to rescue them from the convent's superstitions and male tyranny; at the end of the text he lists the sisters' names as a way of shaming their families into taking action.[4]

---

[1] *The anatomy of the English nunnery*, 1–2. [2] Ibid. [3] Ibid. 7.
[4] Ibid. 31–2. Allegedly, many of the women have been conveyed over from England after sexually servicing priests in recusant households (7, 12, 28).

The text's project of revealing a hidden world of Catholic corruption is reinforced by the woodcut that was added to the title page of the work's second edition of 1623. At the center of the image, Robinson opens a heavy curtain and points accusingly at a nun and friar who embrace on a bed in the background. A banderole issuing from Robinson's mouth reads simply, "Behold." The text's voyeuristic impulse, opening to public scrutiny a secretive and ostensibly all-female Catholic institution that had not existed on English soil since the late 1530s, resonates with earlier Reformation polemics like John Bale's *The actes of Englysh Votaryes* (Antwerp, 1546). Bale's tract focused its charges against the alleged sexual improprieties of the Catholic religious.[5] More recently, William Fennor's *Pluto his Travels or the Devil's Pilgrimage to the College of Jesuits lately discovered by an English Gentleman* (1612), followed the steps of "many of our countrymen...which for some offense are constrained to leave the sweet and wholsome aire of their native country, and live in the abhominations of the Babilonious Mistresse." Fennor's destination was the English Jesuit College at Louvain that proved especially enticing to young gentlemen. Louvain also featured "an English cloister of Gentlewomen, and the Lady Abbesse much respected for her hidden vertues, in which Cloyster their dwelleth a young man called Raph." Fennor tells the story of how the English Jesuit "Ralph" impregnates the maid: "Thus you see, though they are not content a woman should enter their Cloyster, yet they themselves will vouchsafe to enter their closets."[6]

Like Fennor and Bale before him, Robinson figures the religious closet, cell, or confessional as the site of "unchaste practices."[7] In Father Seth's chamber, the nuns entertain their confessor with "ribaldrous Songs and jigs, as that of Bonny Nell, and such other obscene and scurrilous Ballads"; here the father reads "Venus and Adonis, the jests of George Peele, or some such scurrilous booke," and has sex with "his dearling Kate Knightley" or "Sister Mary Brooke, or some other of his last-come Wags."[8] In a passage mocking the nun's use of relics, Robinson reveals the convent's darkest secret of all: hidden in the building's walls are the body parts of the murdered bastards of the nuns and friars.[9]

Published in 1622, Robinson's *Anatomy* appeared at a critical moment in the negotiations for a dynastic alliance between the heir to the throne of Great Britain, Prince Charles, and the Infanta Maria of Spain. The work was a timely reminder to English readers keenly aware of the negotiations of the presence of English Catholics in Spanish territories and of the dangers that awaited any unsuspecting Englishman unfortunate enough to get embroiled in Iberno-Catholic affairs. Then, in February of 1623, the Spanish match took an

---

[5] Also see John Gee, "A Discourse of English Nunnes," in *New shreds of the old snare* (1624) (113–20), where he lists the names of recently "transported" girls (113–20); also relevant is Thomas Scott, *The second part of Vox populi, or Goudomar appearing in the likenes of Matchiavell* (1624), 56.

[6] *Pluto his Travels*, 17–18.   [7] *The anatomy of the English nunnery*, 17.

[8] Ibid. 13, 17, 19.   [9] Ibid. 12.

THE ANATOMIE OF THE ENGLISH NVNNERY AT Lisbon in PORTVGALL:

Diſſected and laid open by one that was ſometime a yonger Brother of the *Couent*.

Who (if the grace of God had not preuented him) might haue growne as old in a wicked life as the oldeſt amongſt them.

Publiſhed by Authority.

The frier Confeſſor.

A Nun att Confeſſion.

Printed for Philemon Stephens & Chriſtopher Meredith. 1630.

Fig. 8. Thomas Robinson, *The anatomie of the English nunnery at Lisbon in Portugall: Dissected and laid open by one that was sometime a yonger brother of the convent* (London, 1637). STC 21126. Title page.

unexpected turn when Charles, frustrated by the "interminable" negotiations, embarked on a sensational journey to Madrid in order personally to secure the Infanta's hand in marriage.[10] Traveling incognito, Charles and his small party took a perilous overland journey that was not finally completed until the prince's safe homecoming in October. In the prince's absence, alarming rumors and gossip about his impending hispaniolization and apostasy spread uncontrollably. Charles's Spanish hosts, claimed one report, were "starving the prince into submission and isolating him from his Protestant chaplains," in order to bring about his conversion to Catholicism.[11] The court newsmonger John Chamberlain based similar misgivings upon his view of the prince's youthful impressionability: "all the world wishes him here again," wrote Chamberlain, "for the Spanish delayes are like to weare out his patience as well as ours, unlesse his affection be more strong then can be lookt for upon so little incouragement. Besides there is a *periculum in mora* many wayes, specially in regard of his religion which is no small daunger considering his age, the cunning of those he hath to deale withall, and other circumstances."[12]

Robinson's *Anatomy* was reissued in a second edition in 1623, no doubt to take advantage of heightened public interest in the fate of the absent Charles and to exploit the even closer resemblance that now emerged between the Iberian adventures of Robinson and the heir to the throne of Great Britain. To the relief of many Protestant readers, Robinson finally eludes the threat of hispaniolization and the associated danger of apostasy. After two and half years spent in the convent, he plots his escape, concerned for the health of his soul and inspired by "a naturall affection to my kindred and countrey." But extricating himself is no easy task: he continues to be pressured into becoming "a profest brother of the Covent," and fears he will be poisoned if caught leaving.[13] Readers of *The anatomy* would have to wait longer for news of the similar homecoming of Charles, which was eventually greeted with ecstasy by London's anti-Catholic crowds. The Puritan Stephen Jerome described Charles's return to

the English Court, his own center in health and honour, prosperitie, and safetie both in bodie and soule, not so much as the least infected dust cleaving to his feete, much lesse any corrupted Popish ayre infect his royall bloud, such was the antydote and preservative of grace, of which his highnesse hath given more then Mathematicall demonstration, even since his comming home.[14]

---

[10] Glyn Redworth, *The Prince and the Infanta: The Cultural Politics of the Spanish Match* (New Haven: Yale University Press, 2003), 39. Also see Thomas Cogswell, *The Blessed Revolution: English Politics and the coming of War, 1621–1624* (Cambridge: Cambridge University Press, 1989); and id., "England and the Spanish Match," in Richard Cust and Ann Hughes (eds.), *Conflict in Early Stuart England: Studies in Religion and Politics, 1603–1642* (London: Longman, 1989), 107–33.

[11] Cogswell, *The Blessed Revolution*, 47.

[12] *The Letters of John Chamberlain*, ed. Norman Egbert McClure (Westport, Conn.: Greenwood Press, 1979), 2:504. Charles's experiences in Spain are discussed in Gordon Albion, *Charles I and the Court of Rome: A Study in Seventeenth Century Diplomacy* (London, 1935), 25–48.

[13] *The anatomy of the English nunnery*, 26, 22.

[14] *Ireland's Jubilee, or joyes Io-paean, for Prince Charles his welcome home* (Dublin, 1624), 212.

With divine assistance, according to Jerome, Charles had been inoculated against the contaminating influences of Spanish earth and air. He had ventured to a land riddled with religious error yet returned "whole." And to the delight of militant Protestants, he had come back home without a Spanish bride but resolved to declare war on Spain and its allies.

Robinson's *Anatomy* was part of an outpouring of writing and speech by Protestants opposed to what they perceived as James I's pro-Spanish foreign policy and his willingness to sacrifice the country's heir to an ill-conceived Habsburg alliance. Other texts that took a more directly polemical approach in denouncing the Hispano-Catholic threat to English national identity included the pamphlets of John Gee and Thomas Scott as well as Puritan sermons, anonymous verse libels, and Thomas Middleton's notorious production of *A Game at Chess*.[15]

The Spanish match of the early1620s takes us back to an issue with which this book began, with another vexed Marian moment—the troubled compact between Mary Tudor and Philip II of Spain. Although the earlier match was successfully concluded, briefly uniting the Houses of Tudor and Habsburg, and the later one was eventually abandoned, both moments crystallized competing Protestant and Catholic imaginings of English/British national identity. While a pro-Spanish Protestant lobby led by James existed at this time, most Protestants shared a vision of Englishness/Britishness as an easily contaminated commodity that could survive only by resisting cross-cultural intercourse with its "traditional" religio-political enemies. Even within the anti-Spanish Protestant community, however, differences emerged between those content to see the English/British withdraw into their island home and those more belligerent, internationalist Protestants who favored confronting the Habsburg menace on its own territories. After 1618, these militant Protestants focused their energies on the plight of James's Calvinist son-in-law, Frederick the Elector Palatine, and his struggle with imperial Habsburg forces for control of Bohemia.

Unlike most Protestants, Catholics at home and abroad welcomed the prospect of a dynastic alliance with Spain in the hopes that it would bring about the relaxation or abolition of anti-Catholic laws across the British Isles and Ireland.[16] Already during the drawn-out negotiations with the Spanish, Charles's father, James I, had taken a conciliatory stance toward his Catholic subjects: he

[15] Roberta Anderson, " 'Well Disposed to the Affairs of Spain?' James VI and I and the Propagandists: 1618–1624," *Recusant History* 25 (2000), 613–35. A selection of verse libels relating to the Spanish match can be found at "Early Stuart Libels" http://www.earlystuartlibels.net/htdocs/index.html. On *A Game at Chess*, see Richard Dutton, "Receiving Offence: *A Game at Chess* Again," in Andrew Hadfield (ed.), *Literature and Censorship in Renaissance England* (New York: Palgrave, 2001), 50–71.

[16] The Catholic response to the Spanish match has been largely ignored in the scholarship. Thomas Cogswell claims that in 1623 "some Catholics openly gloated" that they would soon have freedom of religion, but in support of this view he cites only Protestant sources ("England and the Spanish Match," 120). The government's relaxation of its anti-Catholic initiatives during the years of the Spanish match encouraged overseas Catholic printers to reissue many devotional, catechetical, and controversial works from the Elizabethan period. See A. F. Allison, "John Heigham of St Omer

clamped down (unsuccessfully) on inflammatory anti-Catholic and anti-Spanish sermons and pamphlets, he relaxed financial penalties against recusants, and he released imprisoned priests. James offered these measures as gestures of goodwill toward the Spanish who insisted that the marriage treaty include provisions to end the repression of Catholics in all the Stuart kingdoms, not just England.[17] Catholics dared to hope that the arrival of the Infanta in Britain would be the first step toward the eventual restoration of their faith's official status. Rumors that Charles might convert to his wife's religion were as welcome to Catholics as they were painful to Protestants. Catholics could also hope that Charles and Maria's children would be raised Catholic, at least in their formative years, and that a future Catholic monarch might one day rule over a Great Britain obedient once more to Rome.

In the more hospitable religious climate of the early 1620s, Catholics at home and in exile positioned themselves to take advantage of a major realignment in Britain's religio-political landscape. The Bridgettine nuns in Lisbon, for example, presented a manuscript history of their order to the Infanta on "the special occasion" of her impending marriage to Prince Charles.[18] Written in Spanish and signed on behalf of the nuns by their Abbess, Barbara Wiseman, the manuscript begins with a petition to the Infanta, whom Wiseman prematurely addresses as "Her Royal Highness the Princess of Wales." In what turned out to be a ludicrously optimistic analysis of the political situation, Wiseman argues that of all the Catholics in exile the Bridgettines were the most deserving of immediate repatriation because "more than all other English religious Sisters we are able to say with the devout Mordecai, *who knoweth*, because our case is unique, since not only were we the first exiles for our Holy Catholic Faith, but also the only ones, of all the orders and convents of English nuns, who have continued and persevered in this very hard exile from its first inception until now." Just as the exiled Mordecai had urged his adopted daughter Queen Esther to "help and defend the people of God" against extermination, so the nuns ask the Infanta, as a type of Esther, to help "put an end to our exile, and lead us back to happy and greatly desired rest in our former home, Syon." Wiseman appeals to the Infanta

---

(*c*.1568–1632)," *Recusant History* 4 (1958), 226–42, esp. 234; and id., "The Later Life and Writings of Joseph Cresswell, S.J. 1556–1623," *Recusant History* 15 (1979) 79–144, esp. 119–24.

[17]   On the implications of the Spanish match for the Catholics of Ireland and Scotland, see Glynn Redworth, "Perfidious Hispania? Ireland and the Spanish match, 1603–1623," in Hiram Morgan (ed.), *The Battle of Kinsale* (Bray, Ireland: Wordwell, 2004), 255–64; and id., "Beyond Faith and Fatherland: 'The Appeal of the Catholics of Ireland,' c.1623," *Archivum Hibernicum* 52 (1998), 3–23.

[18]   "The Mirror of the Peregrinations of the English Nuns of the Order of Saint Bridget," in Christopher De Hamel, *Syon Abbey: The Library of the Bridgettine Nuns and their Peregrinations after the Reformation* (London: Roxburghe Club, 1991), 23. An earlier version of the nuns' history was evidently presented to the Infanta's father, Philip III, when he visited the convent, possibly in 1600 (23). The petition states that the nuns had been in exile for sixty-one years. Since they first left England in 1539, this would mean the petition was composed in 1600 (33). Philip died in 1621 in the midst of the marriage negotiations.

by assimilating the Bridgettines not only to Mordecai but also to Abraham and the Israelites, as well as to their founder, St Bridget, whose nomadic sufferings the nuns allegedly share. Through all these trials, declares Wiseman, the nuns have preserved a heart-felt Englishness, expressed in an "aching loss of [their] native land, families and mother tongue."[19]

Whereas the Bridgettines' manuscript petition pled their community's special case directly to the Infanta, printed Catholic works about the Spanish match tried to persuade a wider English-reading public about the benefits of Anglo-Spanish union. As Catholic writers looked forward to a new dynastic compact, they also looked back to earlier ones, and not just the reign of Mary and Philip. For William Pateson, the impending marriage of Charles and Maria brought to mind the betrothal of the Spanish princess Katherine of Aragon during the reign of Henry VII, first to Prince Arthur and then to Prince Henry. Although Henry VIII's twenty-two year marriage to Katherine had ended in a shameful divorce with the added insult of the king's second marriage to Anne Boleyn, Pateson imagined Charles and Maria's marriage as wiping away these stains to national honor and returning Anglo-Spanish relations to their earlier positive footing.[20] Catholic writers argued, in fact, that hostilities between England and Spain were of recent origin: "That England and Spayn have anciently remayned in great amitie together Histories and Chronicles wil witnes, and the divers alliances and mariages often made between those two countries can also give testimonie thereof... the great breach and hostillitie between England and Spayn began but in these our dayes." Contrary to Hispanophobic stereotypes, English Catholics reassured a nervous public that the Spaniards did not have "unreconciliable and revengefull natures," but were ready to forgive past indignities and seek peace.[21]

As usually happened at times of proposed Anglo-Spanish rapprochement like Philip II's marriage to Mary Tudor or Persons's promotion of the Infanta Isabella's claim to the English throne, Catholics prominently displayed the Lancastrian descent of the Kings of Spain to confirm that the two countries' rulers at least were no strangers but blood relatives. Pateson argued, for example, that because the kings of Spain were "as floorishing brainches of the tree and stock of Lancaster," Charles's marriage to the Infanta meant that he was effectively "warm[ing] his bedd with his own blood."[22]

Catholic writers stressed not only that Anglo-Spanish alliances had until recently been the norm, but so too had Protestant-Catholic ones. "Is it so

[19] De Hamel, *Syon Abbey*, 24–5.

[20] William Pateson (alias Matthew Pattenson), *The image of bothe churches, Hierusalem and Babel* (Tornay, 1623. *ERL* 362), 8–9. According to Protestant John Gee, Pateson was a Jesuit priest living in London (AR 2: 116).

[21] Richard Verstegan, *A toung-combat, lately happening, between two English soldiers; in the tilt-boat of Gravesend* (np, 1623. *ERL* 7), 23, 27. See also A. F. Allison, "A Group of Political Tracts, 1621–1623, by Richard Verstegan," *Recusant History* 18 (1996), 128–42.

[22] Pateson, *The image of bothe churches*, 7–8.

strainge," asked Pateson, "to heare that a protestant should match with a Catholick?" In the last reign, the Protestant Elizabeth had come very close to marrying the French Catholic Duke of Alençon ("Monsieur"), while during Edward VI's reign, the king's Protestant advisers had no misgivings about marrying him to the Scottish Catholic princess Mary. At this time of potential reconciliation, Catholic writers saw the advantages of stressing what Catholics and Protestants had in common rather than what separated them. Both were Christians, after all, sharing one creed and one pater noster. To Pateson, the differences between Catholics and Protestants seemed insignificant compared to the radical differences of opinion within the Protestant camp, among Lutherans and Calvinists for example.[23]

For Catholics, the marriage of Charles and Maria not only promised to transform the domestic political scene within James's dominions, easing the penalties on Catholics and decriminalizing their faith, but it also opened up the nation to the world beyond its own borders. Richard Verstegan, no doubt glancing at Protestant imaginings of the nation as a "hortus conclusus," pronounced in a memorable formulation that "Englishmen cannot live pen'd in within the compasse of their countrey, as those of China, between the sea and a huge wall, but must travayle and traffique abroad in so many flourishing Countreyes and places of Christendome as are Catholike."[24] Verstegan, like other supporters of Charles's Spanish marriage, turns to an economic conception of English nationalism that defines the country on the basis of its trade and commerce. Verstegan and other Catholics were confident that a Spanish match could only boost England's economy, strengthening existing trade routes and opening up new markets. Catholics argued that the economic advantages to England of renewed friendship with Spain would more than offset the economic losses suffered when England severed ties with the Dutch—Protestant England's most important trading ally. The Dutch, according to Verstegan, were no friends to the English, as Protestants asserted, but "caterpillers and destroyers of our comon welth."[25]

As well as bringing economic benefits to England, the opening up of the country to the outside world as a result of the Spanish match promised an improvement in the national character. Catholics alleged that the common people of England had grown barbarous, especially in the way they treated foreign visitors. English xenophobia had recently been directed against the Spanish Ambassador, Gondomar, when his coach was attacked by angry apprentices on the streets of London. The mistreatment of foreign visitors in England is a main topic of conversation among the representatives of various nations who meet in a French tavern in Verstegan's pamphlet, *Londons looking-glasse. Or the copy of a*

---

[23] Ibid. 5.

[24] Richard Verstegan, *The copy of a letter sent from an English gentleman, lately become a Catholike beyond the seas* (St Omers, 1622. *ERL* 7), 48.

[25] Verstegan, *A toung-combat*, 31.

letter, written by an English travayler, to the apprentices of London (1621). The one Englishman present attributes his countrymen's abuse of foreigners to the fact that the English for the most part "live pen'd in within the compasse of their countrey," never venturing "into the mayne continent [and] beholding the civill carriage of other Nations."[26] Although Verstegan's interlocuters do not mention the Spanish match directly, it is present as a subtext, the implication being that England's alliance with Spain would allow more English people to travel "out of the Realme." Once English travelers experience civil treatment overseas, they will be more likely to treat visitors to England with a similar generosity. In this way, England will be brought back in line with the norms of civility and "the generall law of al Nations" in Europe.[27]

   The arguments in favor of Anglo-Spanish union set out by Catholic writers like Pateson and Verstegan are also interwoven and embellished in a rambling poetic defense of Catholic doctrine, *Jesus praefigured: or a poeme of the holy name of Jesus in five bookes* (Antwerp, 1623. *ERL* 54). Written by John Abbot, a one-time Jesuit turned secular priest, the poem is the only printed work I have found by an English Catholic that includes a dedication to the Infanta.[28] The dedication, written in Spanish, again hails her prematurely as "Princesa de Gales" (Princess of Wales). It is followed by a dedication in English to Prince Charles. Abbot only printed the first two books of the projected five, no doubt because of the intervening breakdown of the marriage negotiations. Ostensibly a meditation in praise of the power and mystery of Jesus's name, Abbot's poem also contains a seam of topical allusions to Anglo-Habsburg relations and the Spanish match.

   While praising the greatness of the House of Austria, Abbot exclaims:

> But shall the world be warm'd by Austrias son,
> And to our Britaine shall no good be done?
> Must wee be over-past, as if wee stood
> Under the Arctike Pole, where comes no good?
> Yee gentle heav'ns forbid, now is the time,
> When Austria shall give our Northerne Clime
> A Marie, who like the fourth Edwards heire,
> In whom combin'd the diff'rent Roses weare,
> Shall make wars Trumpet ever more to cease;
> And blesse our England with eternall peace.[29]

Abbot appeals here to the idea of the north as a zone of spiritual darkness. Britain, situated on the edge of this zone, can only be redeemed by the intervention of a saving grace from the more securely Catholic regions to the south. The Infanta Maria embodies this grace, bringing through her union with Charles international peace to Britain just as an earlier union between the warring Houses of York and Lancaster had brought domestic peace.

---

[26] *Londons looking-glasse*, 6.   [27] Ibid. 5.
[28] D. M. Rogers, "John Abbot, (1588?–1650)," *Biographical Studies* 1 (1951), 22–33; AR 2: 3.
[29] Abbot, *Jesus praefigured*, 110, 37, 27.

In Abbot's bold prophetic vision, the coupling of Charles and Maria (when "England and Spaine eternally shall wed") promises more than an end to international hostilities. Their union represents the rebirth of the Catholic Church in Britain: "Our Church beginnes to live, | It is a Babe, in England newlie borne," nursed and protected by the royal couple. As a new beginning for the Catholic Church in Britain, the marriage compensates for past crimes against the Roman faith: Henry's VIII's "lawlesse" marriage to Anne Boleyn, to be sure, as well as Elizabeth's execution of Mary Queen of Scots—a crime so heinous that the narrator wonders why "waters doe not over-whelme our land, | And Neptune swim, where Englands Isle doth stand." Yet "Englands Isle," instead of suffering destruction by a second flood, can now look forward to a glorious future in which James, the "just Noah," steers the ship of state toward a Habsburg alliance.[30]

With a daring that few other Catholics could muster at the time of the marriage negotiations, Abbot's poem envisages this Anglo-Spanish entente bringing about far more than just the relaxation of anti-Catholic laws. Abbot looks beyond the present to predict that Charles and Maria will not only rekindle the Catholic faith in Britain, but that inspired by his wife, Prince Charles will go on to become a Confessor of the Catholic Church, taking his place alongside the Apostles as a pillar of Christendom. Charles will achieve this status, the poem suggests, by leading a crusade against schismatics and infidels: "Let us behold thee with thy conq'uring bands, | Revoke to Jesus, faith revolting landes." Abbot's vision of Charles the Catholic warrior links "Great Charles the second Hope of Northern clime," to two other "patrons" of the same name: "Charles surnam'd great," or Charlemaigne, the first Holy Roman Emperor, and "fift Charles" or Charles V, the last Holy Roman Emperor to preside over a unified empire before its division between two branches of the Habsburg dynasty at his death.[31]

In the most daring move of all, the poem does more than liken Charles Stuart's future accomplishments to the past achievements of the emperor Charles V. Abbot in fact suggests that Charles should actually become Charles V's successor by taking upon himself the mantle of Holy Roman Emperor:

> With the fift Charles Achilles of our daies,
> Beyond Alcides Pillars, Tropheies raise,
> Plus ultra be thy motto, thy armes tend,
> And where the world, there let thy Empire end.
> Bee evermore victorious, ever great,
> Ever obedient to Saint Peters seate.[32]

---

[30] Ibid. 17.
[31] Ibid, 19; William Maltby, *The Reign of Charles V* (New York: Palgrave, 2002), 26.
[32] *Jesus praefigured*, 19–20. Maltby observes that "When he became king of Spain in 1516, [Charles V] adopted his famous personal device: the motto *Plus Oultre* ('Yet Further') above a representation of the Pillars of Hercules" (*The Reign of Charles V*, 29). Abbot also imagines Charles Stuart adopting the motto *non ultra* ("none further") as a sign that his achievements will never be equaled (*Jesus praefigured*, 41).

Abbot confirms his wish one day to see Charles as the emperor, when he imagines how the pope will bestow on the House of Stuart a symbolic eagle to join to its insignia of the royal lion. The eagle in question here is the double-headed eagle adopted by the Holy Roman Emperor at his installation by the pope. Abbot's vision of Charles Stuart as future Holy Roman Emperor is perhaps not as far-fetched as it might first seem. After all, through his marriage to the Infanta, Charles would become a Habsburg ruler, the family that for several generations had supplied the emperor. In fact, before Charles V became emperor in 1519, an earlier English king, Henry VIII, had coveted the title for himself, briefly entering a three-way competition with Charles and the French king, Francis I.[33] Because the position of emperor was in theory elective rather than hereditary, there was nothing in principle to bar Charles Stuart from one day receiving an honor that would require him above all else to defend Catholic Christendom from its enemies both within and without. In 1623, moreover, the idea that the heir to the throne of Britain would one day become the Catholic Holy Roman Emperor gained extra frisson from the fact that the current emperor, Ferdinand II, was at war with Charles's own brother-in-law, Frederick V, Elector Palatine.

Abbot's poetic vision, of course, is an outrageous fantasy: Charles remained a committed Protestant during his time in Spain; once the marriage negotiations collapsed and Charles was safely back in England, he declared war on Spain while pushing for an alternative alliance with the Habsburg's main dynastic rivals, the French Bourbons. Abbot's random inconsistency in referring to Charles's future kingdom by the various titles of England, Britain, and Albion, suggests the uncertain identity of the nation in the poem. Indeed in the future envisaged by Abbot, Great Britain (to use the Stuart's preferred title) is effectively absorbed within a Habsburg super-state and ruled by a sovereign whose international priorities as emperor would leave little time for protecting his homeland's specifically Catholic heritage. As such, Abbot's fantasy of the nation was one that very few readers, Protestant or Catholic, would have approved.

---

[33] J. J. Scarisbrick, *Henry VIII* (Berkeley: University of California Press, 1968), 97–105.

Bibliography

PRIMARY SOURCES

Abbot, George. *The reasons which Doctour Hill hath brought, for the upholding of papistry* (1604).

Abbot, John. *Jesus praefigured: or a poeme of the holy name of Jesus in five bookes* (Antwerp, 1623. *ERL* 54).

An advertisement and defence for trueth against her backbiters (1581).

Alabaster, William. *Unpublished Works of William Alabaster (1568–1640)*, ed. Dana F. Sutton (Salzburg University, 1997).

Allen, William. *An apologie and true declaration of the institution and endevours of the two English colleges, the one in Rome, the other now resident in Rhemes* (Rheims, 1581. *ERL* 67).

—— *A true, sincere, and modest defence, of English Catholiques that suffer for their faith both at home and abrod* (np, 1584. *ERL* 68).

—— *An Admonition to the people and nobility of England and Ireland concerning the present warres* (np, 1588. *ERL* 74).

—— *The Letters and Memorials of William Cardinal Allen (1532–1594)*, ed. Thomas Francis Knox (London, 1882).

—— *Letters of William Allen and Richard Barret, 1572–1598*, ed. P. Renold. Catholic Record Society 58 (London, 1967).

Anderton, Roger. *The converted Jew* (np, 1630. *ERL* 206).

Archangel, Father. *The life of the reverend Fa. Angel of Joyeuse, Capucin preacher . . . Together with the lives of the reverend fathers, Father Bennet Englishman, and Father Archangell Scotchman* (Douai, 1623. *ERL* 70).

Ascham, Roger. *The Schoolmaster*, ed. Lawrence V. Ryan (Folger Shakespeare Library: University of Virginia Press, 1967).

Bagshaw, Christopher. *A sparing discoverie of Our English Jesuits and of Fa. Persons proceedings under pretence of promoting the Catholicke faith in England* (1601. *ERL* 39).

Bale, John. *The actes of Englysh Votaryes* (Antwerp, 1546).

—— *The image of both churches after the most wonderfull and heavenly Revelation of sainct John the Evangelist* (1570).

Barthlett, John. *The pedegrewe of heretiques* (1566).

Bede, The Venerable. *The history of the church of Englande* (Antwerp, 1565. *ERL* 162).

—— *Bede's Ecclesiastical History of the English People* ed. Bertram Colgrave and R. A. B. Mynors (Oxford: Clarendon Press, 1969).

Bell, Thomas. *The anatomie of popish tyrannie* (1603).

Bisse, James. *Two Sermons Preached, the one at Paules Crosse the eight of Januarie 1580, The Other, at Christes Churche in London the same day in the afternoone* (1581).

Bluet, Thomas. *Important considerations which ought to move all true and sound-Catholikes . . . to acknowledge that the proceedings of her Majesty . . . have been both mild and mercifull* (np, 1601. *ERL* 31).

Bodin, Jean. *Method for the Easy Comprehension of History by John Bodin*, trans. Beatrice Reynolds (New York: Columbia University Press, 1945).

—— *Six Books of a Commonweal: A Facsimilie Reprint of the English Translation of 1606 Corrected and Supplemented in the Light of a New Comparison with the French and Latin Texts*, ed. Kenneth Douglas McRae (Cambridge, Mass.: Harvard University Press, 1962).

Boys, John. *The autumne part from the twelfth Sundy after Trinitie, to the last in the whole yeere dedicated unto the much honoured and most worthy Doctor John Overal* (1613).

A briefe discoverie of Dr Allens seditious drifts (1588).

A briefe relation of the late martyrdrome of the five Persians converted to the Catholique faith by the reformed Carmelites (Douai, 1623. *ERL* 67).

Broughton, Richard. *A just and moderate answer to a most injurious, and slaunderous pamphlet* (np, 1606. *ERL* 93).

Calendar of State Papers and Manuscripts Relating to English Affairs Existing in the Archives and Collections of Venice, vol. 2: *1558–1580*, ed. Rawdon Brown and G. Cavendish Bentinck (London, 1890; Kraus Reprint, 1970).

Calendar of the State Papers, Domestic Addenda 1566–79, ed. Mary Anne Everett Green (London: Longman, 1871).

Calendar of the State Papers, Relating to Ireland, of the Reign of James I, vol. 2: *1606–1608*, ed. C. W. Russell and John P. Prendergast (Nendeln/Liechtenstein: Kraus Reprint, 1974).

Calfhill, James. *An Answer to the Treatise of the Cross* (1565).

Camden, William. *Britain* (1637).

Campion, Edmund. *Edmund Campion,* A Historie of Ireland (*1571*), ed. Rudolf B. Gottfried (New York: Scholars' Facsimiles and Reprints, 1940).

Canisius, Peter. *Certayne necessarie principles of religion*, trans. T.I. (Secret press, 1578–9. *ERL* 2).

Cecil, William. The Execution of Justice in England *by William Cecil, and* A True, Sincere, and Modest Defence of English Catholics *by William Allen*, ed. Robert M. Kingdon (Ithaca, NY: Cornell University Press, 1965).

Certayn and tru good nues, from the syege of the isle of Malta, wyith the goodly vyctorie, wyche the Christenmen… have ther latlye obtayned, agaynst the Turks (1563. *ERL* 170).

Chamberlain, John. *The Letters of John Chamberlain*, ed. Norman Egbert McClure, 2 vols. (Westport, CT: Greenwood Press, 1979).

Charke, William. *An answere to a seditious pamphlet lately caste abroade by a Jesuite, with a discoverie of that blasphemous sect* (1580).

Charnock, Robert. *An answere made by one of our brethren, a secular priest* (np, 1602. *ERL* 112).

Chauncy, Dom Maurice, *The Passion and Martyrdom of the Holy English Carthusian Fathers: A Short Narration*, ed. G. W. S. Curtis (London: The Church Historical Society, 1935).

Christopherson, John. *An exhortation to all menne to take hede and beware of rebellion* (1554).

Clarke, William. *A Replie unto a certaine libell* (np, 1603. *ERL* 115).

Cochlaeus, Johannes, *Sieben Kopffe Mertini Luthers* (Leipzig: V. Schumann, 1529).

Constable, Henry. *A discoverye of a counterfecte conference* (Paris, 1600. *ERL* 6).

The Conviction of Novelty (1632. *ERL* 138).

A copie of a letter lately sent by a gentleman, a student in the lawes of the realme, to a frende of his concernyng D. Story (1571).

Copinger, John. *A mnemosynum or memoriall to the afflicted Catholickes in Irelande* (np, 1606. *ERL* 129).

—— *The theatre of Catholique and Protestant religion* (St Omers, 1620. *ERL* 191).

Copley, Anthony. *An answere to a letter of a Jesuited gentleman* (1601. *ERL* 31).

—— *Another letter of M.r A C. to his dis-jesuited kinseman* (1602. *ERL* 100).

Copley, Sir Thomas. *Letters of Sir Thomas Copley*, ed. Richard Copley Christie (London, 1897).

Craig, Sir Thomas. *De Unione Regnorum Britanniae Tractatus*, ed. and trans. C. Sanford Terry (Edinburgh: Scottish History Society, 1909).

Craigie, James, ed. *The Poems of James VI of Scotland* vol. 1 of 2 (1955).

Crashaw, William. "A sermon preached in London before the right honourable the Lord Lawarre, Lord Governour and Captaine Generall of Virginia" (1610).

Daunce, Edward. *A briefe discourse of the Spanish state* (1590).

Declaration of the lyfe and death of John Story, late a Romish canonicall doctor by professyon (1571).

Dorman, Thomas. *A disproufe of M. Nowelles reproof* (1565. *ERL* 234).

Drant, Thomas. *Impii cuiusdam epigrammatis quod edidit R. Shacklockus in mortem Cuthberti Scoti apomaxis, also certayne of the speciall articles of the epigramme, refuted in Englyshe* (1565).

An Edict or Ordonance of the French King, conteining a Prohibition and Interdiction of al preaching and assembling, and exercise of any other Religion, then of the Catholique, the Apostolique, and the Romaine Religion [and] *an other Edict of the same king, removing al Protestants from bearing any Office under the king, in the Realme of France* (Louvain, 1568. *ERL* 97).

Elder, John. *The copie of a letter sent into Scotlande* (1554).

An Elizabethan Recusant House, Comprising the Life of the Lady Magdalen, Viscountess Montague (1538–1608). Translated into English from the Original Latin by Cuthbert Fursdon, in the Year 1627, ed. A. C. Southern (London: Sands, 1954).

Evans, Lewis (trans.). Gulielmus Lindanus, Bishop of Ruremunde, *Certaine tables... wherein is detected and made manifeste the doting dangerous doctrine, and haynous heresyes, of the rashe rabblement of heretikes* (Antwerp, 1565. *ERL* 52).

An extract of the determinacion, and censure of the doctours of the universities of Salamanca and Valledolid touching the warres of Ireland, and declaracion of the poape his breve concerning the same warres (np, 1603. *ERL* 200).

Fen, John (trans.). Osório da Fonseca, *A learned and very eloquent treatie* (Louvain, 1568. *ERL* 318).

Fennor, William. *Pasquils jestes mixed with Mother Bunches merriments. Whereunto is added a bakers doozen of guiles. Very prettie and pleasant, to driue away the tediousnesse of a winters evening* (1609).

—— *Pluto his Travels or the Devil's Pilgrimage to the College of Jesuits lately discovered by an English Gentleman* (1612).

Fitzherbert, Thomas. *A defense of the catholyke cause* (np, 1602. *ERL* 146).

Fitzsimon, Henry. *A catholike confutation of M. John Riders clayme of antiquitie* (Roan, 1608. *ERL* 182).

The flowers of the lives of the most renowned saincts of the three kingdoms England Scotland, and Ireland Written and Collected out of the best authours and manuscripts of our nation, and distributed according to their feasts in the calendar (Douai, 1632. *ERL* 239).

Foley, Henry. *Records of the English Province of the Society of Jesus* (7 vols. in 8, London, 1877–83).

Forbes-Leith, William, SJ (ed.). *Narratives of Scottish Catholics Under Mary Stuart and James VI* (Edinburgh: William Paterson, 1885).

Foxe, John. *Actes and Monuments* (1563, 1570, 1583).

Frarinus, Peter. *An oration against the unlawfull insurrections of the Protestantes of our time* trans. John Fowler (Antwerp, 1566. *ERL* 226).

Fulke, William. *A treatise against the Defense of the censure given upon the bookes of W. Charke and Meredith Hanmer, by an unknowne popish traytor* (1586).

Gee, Edward. *The Jesuit's memorial for the intended reformation of England* (1690).

Gee, John. *The foot out of the Snare: with a detection of sundry late practices and impostures of the priests and Jesuits in England* (1624).

—— *New shreds of the old snare* (1624).

Geoffrey of Monmouth, *The History of the Kings of Britain*, trans Lewis Thorpe (Harmondsworth: Penguin, 1987).

Gerard, John. *John Gerard: The Autobiography of an Elizabethan*, trans. Philip Caraman (Oxford: Family Publications, 2006).

Gosson, Stephen. *Playes Confuted in Five Actions* (1582).

Harding, Thomas. *An answere to Maister Juelles Chalenge* (Louvain, 1564. *ERL* 229).

—— *A confutation of a booke intituled An apologie of the Church of England* (Antwerp, 1565. *ERL* 310).

Harington, Sir John. "A Short View of the State of Ireland," in *Anecdota Bodleiana: Gleanings from Bodleian MSS*, ed. W. Dunn Macray (Oxford: James Parker, 1879).

—— *A Tract on the Succession to the Crown (A.D. 1602) by Sir John Harington*, ed. Clements R. Markham (London: J. B. Nichols, 1880).

—— *The Letters and Epigrams of Sir John Harington*, ed. Norman Egbert McClure (Philadelphia: University of Pennsylvania Press, 1930).

—— *Orlando Furioso. Translated into English Heroical Verse by Sir John Harington*, ed. Robert McNulty (Oxford, Clarendon Press, 1972).

Hartwell, Abraham. *A sight of the Portugall pearle* (1565).

Heywood, Thomas. *Troia Britanica: or, Great Britaines Troy* (1609).

Hide, Thomas. *Consolatorie Epistle to the afflicted Catholikes* (Louvain, 1580. *ERL* 105).

Hogarde, Miles. *The displaying of the Protestantes* (1556).

The holie bible faithfully translated into English (Douai, 1609. *ERL* 265, 266).

Holinshed, Raphael. *Chronicles of England, Scotlande, and Irelande* (1577).

Holland, Thomas. *Paneguris D. Elizabethae, Dei gratiâ Angliae, Franciae, & Hiberniae Reginae* (Oxford, 1601).

Howson, John. *A sermon preached at St Maries in Oxford, the 17. day of November, 1602. in defence of the festivities of the Church of England, and namely that of her Majesties coronation* (1603).

Hughes, Paul L., and James F. Larkin (eds.). *Tudor Royal Proclamations: The Later Tudors (1588–1603.)*, vols. 2–3 (New Haven: Yale University Press, 1969).

Hull, John. *The unmasking of the politike atheist* (1602).

Injunctions giuen by the most reverende father in Christ, Edmonde by the providence of God, Archbishop of Yorke primate of England, and Metropolitane, in his Metropoliticall visitation of the prouince of Yorke, aswell to the clergie, as to the laytie of the same province. Anno do. 1571.

James, Thomas. *The Jesuits downefall threatned against them by the secular priests for their wicked lives, accursed manners, hereticall doctrine, and more then Matchiavillian policie. Together with the life of Father Parsons an English Jesuite* (Oxford, 1612).

James VI and I. "The Lepanto of James the Sixt, King of Scotland," in *His Majesties Poeticall Exercises at Vacant Hours* (Edinburgh, 1591).

Jerome, Stephen. *Ireland's Jubilee*: or *joyes Io-paean, for Prince Charles his welcome home* (Dublin, 1624).

Jewel, John. *An Apologie, or aunswer in defence of the Church of England* (1562).

—— *A replie unto M. Hardinges Answeare* (1565).

—— *A defence of the Apologie of the Churche of Englande* (1567).

Jocelinus, *The life of the glorious bishop S. Patricke apostle and primate of Ireland* (Louvain, 1625. *ERL* 210).

Keating, Geoffrey. *Foras Feasa ar Eirinn (The History of Ireland)*, trans. and ed. John O'Mahony (Kansas City: Irish Genealogical Foundation, 1983).

King, Henry. *A sermon preached at Pauls Crosse, the 25. of November. 1621 Upon occasion of that false and scandalous report (lately printed) touching the supposed apostasie of the right Reverend Father in God, John King, late Lord Bishop of London* (1621).

Knolles, Richard. *The generall historie of the Turkes* (1603).

Knox, Thomas Francis (ed.). *The First and Second Diaries of the English College, Douay* (London: David Nutt, 1878).

Las Casas, Bartolomé de. *The Spanish colonie, or Briefe chronicle of the acts and gestes of the Spaniardes in the West Indies, called the newe world*, trans M.M.S (1583).

Law, Thomas Graves, ed. *The Archpriest Controversy: Documents Relating to the Dissensions of the Roman Catholic Clergy, 1597–1602., ed. from the Petyt Mss. of the Inner Temple* (Westminister: Camden society, 1896–8).

Lemnius, Levinus, *The touchstone of complexions*, trans. Thomas Newton (1576).

Leslie, John. *A treatise of treasons against Q. Elizabeth, and the croune of England* (Louvain, 1572. *ERL* 254).

—— *A treatise towching the right, title, and interest of the most excellent princesse Mare, Queene of Scotland, and of the most noble King James, her graces sonne, to the succession of the croune of England* (np, 1584).

Lewkenor, Lewis. *A discourse of the usage of the English fugitives by the Spaniards* (1595).

—— *The estate of the English fugitives under the king of Spaine and his ministers* (1595).

Lewkenor, Samuel. *A discourse not altogether unprofitable, nor unpleasant for such as are desirous to know the situation and customes of forraine cities without travelling to see them Containing a discourse of all those citties wherein doe flourish at this day priviledged universities* (1600).

Lombard, Peter. *The Irish War of Defence 1598–1600: Extracts from the* De Hibernia Insula Commentarius *of Peter Lombard, Archbishop of Armagh*, ed. and trans. Matthew J. Byrne (Cork: Cork University Press, 1930).

Lunn, David. *The English Benedictines, 1540–1688: From Reformation to Revolution* (New York: Barnes and Noble, 1980).

Marshall, George. *A compendious treatise in metre declaring the firste originall of sacrifice, and the building of aultares and churches, and the firste receaving of the Christen faith here in Englande* (1554).

Martiall, John. *A replie to M. Calfhills blasphemous answer made against the Treatise of the crosse* (Louvain, 1566. *ERL* 203).

Martin, Gregory. *Roma Sancta (1581)*, ed. George Bruner Parks (Rome: Edizioni di Storia e Letteratura, 1969).

Moore, Andrew. *A compendious history of the Turks: containing an exact account of the originall of that people* (1659).

More, Thomas. *A dialogue of cumfort against tribulation*, trans. John Fowler (Antwerp, 1573. *ERL* 25).

Mornay, Philippe de, seigneur du Plessis-Marly. *A woorke concerning the trewnesse of the Christian religion, written in French: against atheists, Epicures, Paynims, Jewes, Mahumetists, and other infidels. By Philip of Mornay Lord of Plessie Marlie. Begunne to be translated into English by Sir Philip Sidney Knight, and at his request finished by Arthur Golding* (1587).

Munday, Anthony. *Palmerin of England, part 1* (1596).

—— *The English Roman Life*, ed. Philip J. Ayres (Oxford: Clarendon Press, 1980).

—— *Pageants and Entertainments of Anthony Munday*, ed. David M. Bergeron (London: Garland, 1985).

Mush, John. *A dialogue betwixt a secular priest, and a lay gentleman* (Rheims, 1601. *ERL* 39).

Newes from Spaine: The king of Spaines edict, for the expulsion & banishment of more then nine hundred thousand Moores out of his kingdome, which conspired and plotted to bring the kingdome of Spaine under the power and subjection of the Turkes and Saracens (1611).

Nichols, John Gough (ed.). *The Chronicle of Queen Jane, and of Two Years of Queen Mary* (London: Camden Society, 1850).

Norton, Thomas. *A Warning agaynst the dangerous practices of papistes* (1569).

Nowell, Alexander. *A reproufe written by Alexander Nowell* (1565).

Ormerod, Oliver. *The Picture of a Papist* (1606).

Ortiz, Antonio. *A relation of the solemnetie wherewith the Catholike princes K. Philip the III and Quene Margaret were receyved in the Inglish Colledge of Valladolid the 22. of August. 1600*, trans. Francis Rivers (1601).

O'sullivan Beare, Philip. *Historiae Catholicae Iberniae Compendium* (*Compendium of the Catholic History of Ireland*) (Lisbon, 1621).

Owen, Lewis. *The running register: recording a true relation of the state of the English colledges, seminaries and cloysters in all forraine parts* (1626).

A particular declaration or testimony, of the undutifull and traiterous affection borne against her Majestie by Edmond Campion, Jesuite, and other condemned priestes (1582).

Pateson, William (alias Matthew Pattenson). *The image of bothe churches, Hierusalem and Babel* (Tornay, 1623. *ERL* 362).

Peron, Cardinal. *Luthers Alcoran* (np, 1642).

Persons, Robert. *A brief discours contayning certayne reasons why Catholques refuse to goe to church* (Douai, 1580. *ERL* 84).

—— *An epistle of the persecution of Catholickes in Englande* (Douai, 1582. *ERL* 125).

—— *Relacion de algunos martyrios, que de Nuevo han hecho los hereges en Inglaterra, y de otras cosas tocantes a nuestra santa y Catolica religion* (1590).

—— *A relation of the King of Spaines receiving in Valliodolid* (Antwerp, 1592. *ERL* 351).

—— *Newes from Spayne and Holland* (Antwerp, 1593. *ERL* 365).

—— et al. *A conference about the next succession to the crowne of Ingland* (Antwerp, 1595. *ERL* 104).

—— *A temperate ward-word, to the turbulent and seditious Wach-word of Sir Francis Hastinges knight* (Antwerp, 1599. *ERL* 31).

—— *A briefe apologie, or defence of the Catholicke ecclesiastical hierarchie* (Antwerp, 1601. *ERL* 273).

—— *A manifestation of the great folly and bad spirit of certayne in England calling themselves secular priestes* (Antwerp, 1602. *ERL* 169).

—— *A relation of the triall made before the King of France, upon the yeare 1600. betwene the Bishop of Eureux, and the L. Plessis Mornay* (St Omers, 1604. *ERL* 305).

—— *A treatise of three conversions of England from paganisme to Christian religion*, 3 vols (St Omers, 1603–1604. *ERL* 304–6).

—— *A treatise tending to mitigation towardes Catholicke – subjectes in England* (St Omers, 1608. *ERL* 340).

—— "Of the Life and Martyrdom of Father Edmond Campian," *Letters and Notices* 11 (1877), 219–42, 308–39; 12 (1878), 1–68.

—— "The Memoirs of Father Robert Persons," ed. J. H. Pollen, SJ, in *Miscellanea II*, Catholic Record Society 2 (London, 1906).

—— "Father Persons' Memoirs (concluded)... Punti per la Missione d'Inghilterra," ed and trans J. H. Pollen, SJ, as "Notes Concerning the English mission," in *Miscellanea IV*, Catholic Record Society 4 (London, 1907).

—— *Letters and Memorials of Father Robert Persons, SJ: Volume I (to 1588)*, ed. L. Hicks, SJ, Catholic Record Society 39 (London, 1942).

Pole, Reginald. *Pole's "Defence of the Unity of the Church*," trans. Joseph G. Dwyer (Westminster, Md., 1965).

The policy of the Turkish empire (London, 1597).

Pricket, Robert. *The Jesuits miracles, or new popish wonders. Containing the straw, the crowne, and the wondrous child, with the confutation of them and their follies* (1607).

Proctor, John. *The historie of wyates rebellion* (1554).

Prouninck, Gerard. *A short admonition or warning, upon the detestable treason wherewith Sir William Stanley and Rowland Yorke have betraied and delivered for monie unto the Spaniards, the town of Deventer, and the sconce of Zutphen* (1587).

Rainolds, William. *Calvino-Turcismus id est, Calvinisticae perfidiae, cum Mahumetana collatio, et dilucida utriusque sectae confutation* (Antwerp, 1597).

Rastell, John. *A treatise intitled, Beware of M. Jewel* (Antwerp, 1566. *ERL* 255).

Rich, Barnaby. *A new Irish prognostication, or popish callender* (1624).

Robinson, Thomas. *The anatomy of the English nunnery at Lisbon in Portugall: Dissected and laid open by one that was sometime a yonger brother of the convent* (1622).

Rochford, Robert (trans.). Jocelinus, Prior of Furness, *The life of the glorious bishop S. Patricke apostle and primate of Ireland* (St Omers, 1625. *ERL* 210).

Rollins, Hyder E. (ed.). *Old English Ballads 1553–1625* (Cambridge, 1920).

Sander, Nicholas. *A treatise of the images of Christ, and of his saints* (Louvain, 1567. *ERL* 282).

Sander, Nicholas. *De visibili monarchia Ecclesiae* (Louvain, 1571).

—— "Dr Nicholas Sander's Report to Cardinal Moroni on the Change of Religion in 1558–9 (1561)," in *Miscellanea I*, ed. John H. Pollen, SJ, Catholic Record Society 1 (London, 1905).

—— "Some Letters and Papers of Nicolas Sander 1562–80" in *Miscellanea XIII*, Catholic Record Society 26 (London, 1926).

—— *The Rise and Growth of the Anglican Schism by the Rev. Nicolas Sander*, ed. and trans. David Lewis (London: Burns and Oates, 1877; Rockford, Ill.: Tan Books, 1988).

Scott, Thomas. *The second part of Vox populi, or Gondomar appearing in the likenes of Matchiavell* (1624).

Shacklock. Richard, trans. Hosius, Cardinal Stanislaus, *A most excellent treatise of the begynnyng of heresyes in oure tyme* (Antwerp, 1565. *ERL* 24).

——, trans. Osório da Fonseca, Jerónimo, Bishop of Sylva, *An epistle of the reverend father in God Hieronimus Osorius* (Antwerp, 1565. *ERL* 329).

Southwell, Robert. *An Humble Supplication to her Majestie*, ed. R. C. Bald (Cambridge: Cambridge University Press, 1953).

Spenser, Edmund. *Edmund Spenser: A View of the State of Ireland*, ed. Andrew Hadfield and Willy Maley (Oxford: Blackwell, 1997).

Stapleton, Thomas, trans. *The apologie of Fridericus Staphylus* (Antwerp, 1565. *ERL* 268).

—— *A returne of untruthes upon M. Jewelles Replie* (Antwerp, 1566. *ERL* 308).

——, trans. Hosius, Stanislaus, *Of the expresse worde of God* (Louvain, 1567. *ERL* 73).

—— *A counterblast to M. Hornes vayne blaste against M. Fekenham* (Louvain, 1567. *ERL* 311).

—— *De vita S. Patricii, Hiberniae apostoli* (Antwerp, 1587).

—— *Thomas Stapleton: The Life and Illustrious Martyrdom of Sir Thomas More*, trans. Philip E. Hallett (London: Burns Oates and Washbourne, 1928).

Stocker, Thomas, trans. *A tragicall historie of the troubles and civile warres of the lowe Countries... together [with] the Barbarous crueltie and tyrannie of the Spaniard* (1583).

The Supplication of certaine Masse-Priests falsely called Catholikes (1604).

Sutcliffe, Matthew. *De Turcopapismo* (1599).

—— *The subversion of Robert Parsons his confused and worthlesse worke, entituled, A treatise of three conversions of England from paganisme to Christian religion* (1606).

—— *The blessings on Mount Gerizzim, and the curses on Mount Ebal. Or, The happie estate of Protestants compared with the miserable estate of papists under the Popes tyrannie* (1625).

A treatise with a kalendar (1608. *ERL* 109).

The true reporte of the prosperous successe which God gave unto our English souldiours against the forraine bands of our Romaine enemies, lately arived... in Ireland (1581).

Verstegan, Richard. *Descriptiones quaedam illius inhumanae et multiplicis persecutionis, quam in Anglia propter fidem sustinent Catholice Christiani* (*Several Illustrations of that Inhuman and Manifold Persecution which the Catholic Christians are Suffering in England for the Sake of their Faith.* Rome, 1584).

—— *An advertisement written to a secretarie of my L. Treasurers of Ingland, by an Inglishe intelligencer as he passed throughe Germanie towardes Italie* (Antwerp, 1592. *ERL* 166).

—— *A declaration of the true causes of the great troubles, presupposed to be intended against the realme of England* (Antwerp, 1592. *ERL* 360).

—— *A restitution of decayed intelligence: in antiquities. Concerning the most noble and renowmed English nation* (Antwerp, 1605. *ERL* 323).

—— *Londons looking-glasse. Or the copy of a letter, written by an English travayler, to the apprentices of London* (St Omers, 1621. *ERL* 7).

—— *The copy of a letter sent from an English gentleman, lately become a Catholike beyond the seas* (St Omers, 1622. *ERL* 7).

—— *A toung-combat, lately happening, between two English soldiers; in the tilt-boat of Gravesend* (Mechlin, 1623. *ERL* 7).

—— *The Letters and Despatches of Richard Verstegan, c.1550–1640*, ed. Anthony G. Petti, Catholic Record Society 52 (London, 1959).

Wadsworth, James. *The English Spanish pilgrime. Or, a new discoverie of Spanishe popery and Jesuiticall stratagems* (1629).

A warnyng for Englande conteynyng the horrible practises of the Kyng of Spayne, in the kyngdome of Naples (Emden, 1555).

Watson, William. *A decacordon of ten quodlibeticall questions* (1602. *ERL* 197).

Wilson, John. *The English martyrologe conteyning a summary of the lives of the glorious and renowned saintes of the three Kingdomes, England, Scotland, and Ireland* (St Omers, 1608. *ERL* 232).

Wright, Thomas. *The Passions of the Minde in Generall. A Reprint Based on the 1604 Edition*, ed. Thomas O. Sloan (Urbana: University of Illinois Press, 1971).

The Zurich Letters, comprising the correspondence of several English bishops and others, with some of the Helvetian reformers, during the early part of the reign of Queen Elizabeth. Translated from authenticated copies of the autographs preserved in the archives of Zurich, Parker Society, ed. Revd. Hastings Robinson. 2 vols. (Cambridge: Cambridge University Press, 1842).

SECONDARY SOURCES

Adams, Simon. "A Patriot for Whom? Stanley, York and Elizabeth's Catholics," *History Today* 37 (1987), 46–50.

Albion, Gordon. *Charles I and the Court of Rome: A Study in Seventeenth Century Diplomacy* (London, 1935).

—— "An English Professor in Louvain: Thomas Stapleton (1535–1598)," *Miscellanea historica in honorem Alberta de Meyer* (Louvain and Brussels: University of Louvain, 1946), 895–913.

Allen, Paul C. *Philip III and the Pax Hispanica, 1598–1621: The Failure of Grand Strategy* (New Haven: Yale University Press, 2000).

Allison, A. F. "John Heigham of St Omer (*c.*1568–1632)," *Recusant History* 4 (1958), 226–42.

—— "The Later Life and Writings of Joseph Cresswell, SJ, 1556–1623," *Recusant History* 15 (1979), 79–144.

—— "A Group of Political Tracts, 1621–1623, by Richard Verstegan," *Recusant History* 18 (1996), 128–42.

Anderson, Roberta. " 'Well Disposed to the Affairs of Spain?' James VI and I and the Propagandists: 1618–1624," *Recusant History* 25 (2000), 613–35.

Anstruther, Godfrey. "Owen Lewis," in *The English Hospice in Rome*. The Venerabile Sexcentenary issue. May 1962. Vol. 21 (Exeter: Catholic Records Press), 274–94.

Antwerp, Dissident Typographical Centre: The Role of Antwerp Printers in the Religious Conflicts in England (16th century). (Antwerp: Plantin-Moretus Museum, 1994).

Arblaster, Paul. *Antwerp and the World: Richard Verstegan and the International Culture of Catholic Reformation* (Leuven, Belgium: Leuven University Press, 2004).

Bagchi, David V. N. *Luther's Earliest Opponents: Catholic Controversialists, 1518–1525* (Minneapolis: Fortress Press, 1991).

Baker, David J. *Between Nations: Shakespeare, Spenser, Marvell and the Question of Britain* (Stanford: Stanford University Press, 1997).

Bartlett, K. "The English Exile Community in Italy and the Political Opposition to Mary I," *Albion* 3 (1981), 223–41.

Bartlett, Robert. "Medieval and Modern Concepts of Race and Ethnicity," *Journal of Medieval and Early Modern Studies* 31 (2001), 39–56.

Baskerville, Edward J. *A Chronological Bibliography of Propaganda and Polemic Published in England between 1553 and 1558 from the Death of Edward VI to the Death of Mary I* (Philadelphia: The American Philosophical Society, 1979).

Baumer, Franklin L. "England, the Turk, and the Common Corps of Christendom," *The American Historical Review* 50.1 (1944), 26–48.

Beales, A. F. C. *Education under Penalty: English Catholic Education from the Reformation to the Fall of James II 1547–1689* (London: The Athlone Press, 1963).

Bell, Sandra, "Writing the Monarch: King James VI and *Lepanto*," in Helen Ostovich, Mary V. Silcox, and Graham Roebuck (eds.), *Other Voices, Other Views: Expanding the Canon in English Renaissance Studies* (Newark: University of Delaware Press, 1999), 193–208.

Bireley, Robert. *The Refashioning of Catholicism, 1450–1700: A Reassessment of the Counter Reformation* (Washington, DC: Catholic University of America, 1999).

Boeckl, Christine M. "Plague Imagery as Metaphor for Heresy in Rubens' *The Miracles of Saint Francis Xavier*," *Sixteenth Century Journal* 27 (1996), 979–95.

Bossy, John. *The English Catholic Community, 1570–1850* (Oxford: Oxford University Press, 1975).

—— "Catholicity and Nationality in the Northern Counter-Reformation," in Stuart Mews (ed.), *Religion and National Identity* (Oxford: Blackwell, 1982), 285–96.

Bowen, Geraint. *Welsh Recusant Writings* (Cardiff: University of Wales Press, 1999).

Bradshaw, Brendan. "The English Reformation and Identity Formation in Ireland and Wales," in Brendan Bradshaw and Peter Roberts (eds.), *British Consciousness and Identity: The Making of Britain 1533–1707* (Cambridge: Cambridge University Press, 1998), 43–111.

—— Andrew Hadfield, and Willy Maley (eds.). *Representing Ireland: Literature and the Origins of Conflict, 1534–1660* (Cambridge: Cambridge University Press, 1993).

Breeze, Andrew. "Welsh and Cornish at Valladolid, 1591–1600," *The Bulletin of the Board of Celtic Studies* 37 (1990), 108–11.

Brennan, Michael G. "English Contact with Europe," in Andrew Hadfield and Paul Hammond (eds.), *Shakespeare and Renaissance Europe* (London: Thomson, 2005), 53–97.

Bridgett, T. E. *Our Lady's Dowry: How England Gained that Title* (London: Burns and Oates, nd).

Brooke, Xanthe, and David Crombie. *Henry VIII Revealed: Holbein's Portrait and its Legacy* (London: Holberton, 2003).

Burton, Jonathan. "Anglo-Ottoman Relations and the Image of the Turk in *Tamburlaine*," *Journal of Medieval and Early Modern Studies* 30 (2000), 125–56.

Busse, Daniela. "Anti-Catholic Polemical Writing on the 'Rising in the North' (1569) and the Catholic Reaction," *Recusant History* 27 (2005), 11–30.

Calderwood, David (ed.). *The History of the Kirk of Scotland* (Edinburgh, 1845).

Canny, Nicholas. "Taking Sides in Early Modern Ireland: The Case of Hugh O'Neill, Earl of Tyrone," in Carey and Lotz-Heumann (eds.), *Taking Sides*, 94–115.

Caraman, Philip. *The Other Face: Catholic Life under Elizabeth I* (London: Longmans, 1960).

—— *Henry Garnet, 1555–1606 and the Gunpowder Plot* (London: Longmans, 1964).

Carey, John. "Did the Irish Come from Spain? The Legend of the Milesians," *History Ireland* 9.3 (2001), 8–11.

Carey, Vincent P. *Surviving the Tudors: The Wizard Earl of Kildare and English Rule in Ireland, 1537–1586* (Dublin: Four Courts Press, 2002).

—— "A 'Dubious Loyalty': Richard Stanihurst, the 'Wizard' Earl of Kildare, and English-Irish Identity," in Carey and Lotz-Heumann (eds.), *Taking Sides*, 61–77.

—— and Ute Lotz-Heumann (eds.). *Taking Sides: Colonial and Confessional Mentalites in Early Modern Ireland. Essays in Honour of Karl S. Bottigheimer* (Dublin: Four Courts Press, 2003).

—— (ed.) *Voices for Tolerance in an Age of Persecution* (Washington, D.C.: Folger Shakespeare Library, 2004).

Carrafiello, Michael L. "*Rebus Sic Stantibus* and English Catholicism, 1606–1610," *Recusant History* 22 (1994), 29–40.

—— *Robert Persons and English Catholicism, 1580–1610* (London: Associated University Presses, 1998).

Carroll, Clare. "Irish and Spanish Cultural and Political Relations in the Work of O'sullivan Beare," in Morgan (ed.), *Political Ideology in Ireland*, 229–53.

—— *Circe's Cup: Cultural Transformations in Early Modern Writing about Ireland* (Notre Dame, Ind.: University of Notre Dame Press, 2001).

Casway, Jerrold. "Henry O'Neill and the Formation of the Irish Regiment in the Netherlands, 1605," *Irish Historical Studies* 18 (1973), 481–8.

The Catholic Encyclopedia, vol. 4 (New York: Robert Appleton Company, 1908) (http://www.newadvent.org/cathen/04215a.htm).

Chadwick, Hubert. "The Scots College, Douai, 1580–1613," *The English Historical Review* 56.224 (1941), 571–85.

Chew, Samuel. *The Crescent and the Rose: Islam and England during the Renaissance* (Oxford: Oxford University Press, 1937).

Christianson, Paul. *Reformers and Babylon: English Apocalyptic Visions from the Reformation to the Eve of the Civil War* (Toronto: University of Toronto Press, 1978).

Clancy, Thomas H., SJ. *Papist Pamphleteers: The Allen-Persons Party and the Political Thought of the Counter-Reformation in England, 1572–1615* (Chicago: Loyola University Press, 1964).

Claydon, Tony, and Ian McBride. "The Trials of a Chosen People: Recent Interpretations of Protestantism and National Identity in Britain and Ireland," in Tony Claydon and Ian McBride (eds.), *Protestantism and National Identity: Britain and Ireland, c.1650–c.1850* (Cambridge: Cambridge University Press, 1998), 3–32.

Cleary, J. M. "Dr. Morys Clynnog's Invasion Projects of 1575–1576," *Recusant History* 8 (1966), 300–22.

Cogswell, Thomas. *The Blessed Revolution: English Politics and the coming of War, 1621–1624* (Cambridge: Cambridge University Press, 1989).

—— "England and the Spanish Match," in Richard Cust and Ann Hughes (eds.), *Conflict in Early Stuart England: Studies in Religion and Politics, 1603–1642* (London: Longman, 1989), 107–33.

Collinson, Patrick. "If Constantine, then also Theodosius: St Ambrose and the Integrity of the Elizabethan *Ecclesia Anglicana*," *Journal of Ecclesiastical History* 30 (1979), 205–29.

Coppens, Christian. *Reading in Exile: The Libraries of John Ramridge (d. 1568), Thomas Harding (d. 1572) and Henry Joliffe (d. 1573), Recusants in Louvain* (Cambridge: LP Publications, 1993).

Corthell, Ronald. "Robert Persons and the Writer's Mission," in Arthur F. Marotti (ed.), *Catholicism and Anti-Catholicism in Early Modern English Texts* (New York: St Martin's Press, 1999), 48–56.

Corthell, Ronald, Frances E. Dolan, Christopher Highley, and Arthur F. Marotti (eds.). *Catholic Culture in Early Modern England* (Notre Dame, Ind.: University of Notre Dame Press, 2007).

Cowdrey, H. E. J. "Bede and the 'English People'," *Journal of Religious History* 11 (1981), 501–23.

Cuddy, Neil. "Anglo-Scottish Union and the Court of James I, 1603–1625," *Transactions of the Royal Historical Society*, 5th ser. 39 (1989), 107–24.

Cunningham, Bernadette. *The World of Geoffrey Keating: History, Myth and Religion in Seventeenth-Century Ireland* (Dublin: Four Courts Press, 2000).

—— and Raymond Gillespie, " 'The Most Adaptable of Saints': The Cult of Patrick in the Seventeenth Century," *Archivium Hibernicum; or, Irish Historical Records* 49 (1995), 82–104.

Curran, John E. *Roman Invasions: The British History, Protestant Anti-Romanism, and the Historical Imagination in England, 1530–1660* (Newark: University of Delaware Press, 2002).

Davidson, Peter. *The Idea of North* (London: Reaktion Books, 2005).

—— "Recusant Catholic Spaces in Early Modern England," in Corthell, Dolan, Highley, and Marotti (eds.), *Catholic Culture in Early Modern England*, 19–51.

Dawson, Jane. "Anglo-Scottish Protestant Culture and Integration in Sixteenth-Century Britain," in Ellis and Barber (eds.), *Conquest and Union*, 87–114.

De Hamel, Christopher. *Syon Abbey: The Library of the Bridgettine Nuns and their Peregrinations after the Reformation* (London: Roxburghe Club, 1991).

De Nave, F. "Antwerp, Dissident Typographical Centre in the 16th Century: General Synthesis," in *Antwerp, Dissident Typographical Centre*, 11–20.

De Vocht, Henry. *History of the Foundation and the Rise of the Collegium Trilingue Lovaniense, 1517–1550* (Louvain: Bibliotheque de l'Universite, Bureaux du Recueil, 1951–5), 4 vols.

Dillon, Anne. "The Construction of Martyrdom in the English Catholic Community to 1603" (Cambridge Ph.D. thesis, 1998).

—— *The Construction of Martyrdom in the English Catholic Community, 1535–1603* (Aldershot: Ashgate, 2002).

—— "Praying by Number: The Confraternity of the Rosary and the English Catholic Community, *c.*1580–1700," *History* 88 (2003), 451–71.

Dimmock, Matthew. *New Turkes: Dramatizing Islam and the Ottomans in Early Modern England* (Aldershot: Ashgate, 2005).

Dolan, Frances E. *Whores of Babylon: Catholicism, Gender, and Seventeenth-Century Print Culture* (Ithaca: Cornell University Press, 1999).

Donaldson, Peter. "Machiavelli, Antichrist, and the Reformation: Prophetic Typology in Reginald Pole's *De Unitate* and *Apologia ad Carolum Quintum*," in Richard L. DeMolen (ed.), *Leaders of the Reformation* (Selinsgrove, Pa.: Susquehanna University Press, 1984), 211–46.

The Downside Conference. "Recusant Archives and Remains from the Three Kingdoms, 1560–1789. Catholics in Exile at Home and Abroad." Downside Abbey June 23–24, 2004. http://www.catholic-heritage.net/recusant/

Duffy, Eamon. *The Stripping of the Altars: Traditional Religion in England, 1400–1580* (New Haven: Yale University Press, 1992).

—— "William, Cardinal Allen, 1532–1594," *Recusant History* 22 (1995), 265–90.

—— *Saints and Sinners: A History of the Popes* (New Haven: Yale University Press, 1997).

Dutton, Richard. "Receiving Offence: *A Game at Chess* Again," in Andrew Hadfield (ed.), *Literature and Censorship in Renaissance England* (New York: Palgrave, 2001), 50–71.

Edwards, David. "A Haven of Popery: English Catholic Migration to Ireland in the Age of Plantations," in Alan Ford and John McCafferty (eds.), *The Origins of Sectarianism in Early Modern Ireland* (Cambridge: Cambridge University Press, 2005), 95–126.

Edwards, Francis, SJ (ed. and trans.). *The Elizabethan Jesuits: Historia Missionis Anglicanae Societatis Jesu (1660) of Henry More* (London: Phillimore, 1981).

—— *Robert Persons: The Biography of an Elizabethan Jesuit 1546–1610* (St Louis, Missouri: Institute of Jesuit Sources, 1995).

Edwards, John. "Carranza in England," in Edwards and Truman (eds.), *Reforming Catholicism*, 11–20.

——, and Ronald Truman (eds.). *Reforming Catholicism in the England of Mary Tudor: The Achievement of Friar Bartolomé Carranza* (Aldershot: Ashgate, 2005).

Edwards, T. M. Charles, "The Social Background of Irish *Peregrinatio*," *Celtica* 11 (1976), 43–59.

—— "Bede, the Irish, and the Britons," *Celtica* 15 (1983), 42–52.

Elliot, Neil. " 'The Heresy of the Saracens' to 'The War against the Turk': A study of later medieval understandings of Islam from Peter the Venerable to Martin Luther." Centre for the Study of Islam and Christian-Muslim Relations, Department of Theology, University of Birmingham. Occasional papers, No. 9, September 2001. www.theology.bham.ac.uk/research/CSICPapers/Elliott1.htm

Ellis, Steven G. and Sarah Barber (eds.). *Conquest and Union: Fashioning a British State, 1485–1725* (London: Longman, 1995).

Elton, G. R. *The Tudor Constitution: Documents and Commentary*. Second edition (Cambridge: Cambridge University Press, 1982).

Enos, Carol. "Catholic Exiles in Flanders and *As You Like It*," in Richard Dutton, Alison Findlay, and Richard Wilson (eds.), *Theatre and Religion: Lancastrian Shakespeare* (Manchester: Manchester University Press, 2003), 130–42.

Fissel, Mark Charles. *English Warfare, 1511–1642* (New York: Routledge, 2001).

Flanagan, Marie Theresa. "The Contribution of Irish Missionaries and Scholars to Medieval Christianity," in Brendan Bradshaw and Daire Keogh (eds.), *Christianity in Ireland: Revisiting the Story* (Dublin: Columba Press, 2002), 35–43.

Fletcher, John Rory. *The Story of the English Bridgettines of Syon Abbey* (South Brent, Devon, 1933).

Floyd-Wilson, Mary. "Temperature, Temperance, and Racial Difference in Ben Jonson's *The Masque of Blackness*," *English Literary Renaissance* 28 (1998), 183–209.

Flynn, Dennis. "The English Mission of Jasper Heywood, SJ," *Archivum Historicum Societatis Jesu* 54 (1985), 45–76.

Ford, Alan. "Martyrdom, History and Memory in Early Modern Ireland," in Ian McBride (ed.), *History and Memory in Modern Ireland* (Cambridge: Cambridge University Press, 2001), 43–66.

Forse, James. "How 'Black' was the 'Black Legend' in Elizabethan England?" *Shakespeare and Renaissance Association of West Virginia Selected Papers* 25 (2002), 13–33.

Foster, Brett. "Gregory Martin's 'Holy Latinate Jerusalem': Roman English, Romanist Values, and the *Rheims New Testament* (1582)," *Prose Studies* 28.2 (2006), 130–49.

Frantzen, Allen J. *Desire for Origins: New Language, Old English, and Teaching the Tradition* (New Brunswick: Rutgers University Press, 1990).

—— "Bede and Bawdy Bale: Gregory the Great, Angels, and the 'Angli'," in Allen J. Frantzen and John D. Niles (eds.), *Anglo-Saxonism and the Construction of Social Identity* (Gainesville, Fla.: University Press of Florida, 1997), 17–39.

Fraser, Antonia. *Faith and Treason: The Story of the Gunpowder Plot* (New York: Doubleday, 1996).

Fuchs, Barbara. "Conquering Islands: Contextualizing *The Tempest*," *Shakespeare Quarterly* 48 (1997), 45–62.

Fumerton, Patricia. "Subdiscourse: Jonson Speaking Low," *English Literary Renaissance* 25 (1995), 76–97.

Galloway, Bruce R. *The Union of England and Scotland, 1603–1608* (Edinburgh: John Donald, 1986).

—— and Brian P. Levack (eds.). *The Jacobean Union: Six Tracts of 1603* (Edinburgh: Scottish History Society, 1985).

Gardiner, David. " 'These Are Not the Thinges Men Live by Now a Days': Sir John Harington's Visit to the O'Neill, 1599," *Cahiers Elisabéthains: Late Medieval and Renaissance Studies* 55 (1999), 1–15.

Garret, C. H. *The Marian Exiles* (Cambridge: Cambridge University Press, 1938).

Garstein, Oskar. *Rome and the Counter-Reformation in Scandinavia* Vol. 2 1583–1622 (Oslo: Universitetsforlaget, 1980).

Gillespie, Raymond. *Devoted People: Belief and Religion in Early Modern Ireland* (Manchester: Manchester University Press, 1997).

Gillingham, John. "The English Invasion of Ireland," in Bradshaw, Hadfield, and Maley (eds.), *Representing Ireland*, 24–42.

Gillow, Joseph (ed.). *The Haydock Papers: A Glimpse into English Catholic Life under the Shade of Persecution and in the Dawn of Freedom* (London: Burns and Oates, 1888).

Greenfeld, Liah. *Nationalism: Five Roads to Modernity* (Cambridge: Harvard University Press, 1992).

Gregory, Brad S. *Salvation at Stake: Christian Martyrdom in Early Modern Europe* (Cambridge: Harvard University Press, 1999).

Gregory, Jeremy. "The Making of a Protestant Nation: 'Success' and 'Failure' in England's Long Reformation," in Nicholas Tyacke (ed.), *England's Long Reformation 1500–1800* (London: University College London, 1998), 307–34.

Griffin, Eric. "Un-Sainting James: Or, *Othello* and the 'Spanish Spirits' of Shakespeare's Globe," in Stephen Orgel and Sean Keilen (eds.), *Shakespeare and History* (New York: Garland, 1999), 278–320.

—— "From Ethos to Ethnos: 'Hispanizing' the Spaniard in the Old World and the New." *CR: the new centennial review* 2:1 (2002), 69–116.

—— "The Specter of Spain in John Smith's Colonial Writing," in Robert Appelbaum and John Wood Sweet (eds.), *Envisioning an English Empire: Jamestown and the Making of the North Atlantic World* (Philadelphia: University of Pennsylvania Press, 2005), 111–34.

Guilday, Peter. *The English Catholic Refugees on the Continent, 1558–1795* (London: Longmans, Green, and Co., 1914).

—— "The English Catholic Refugees at Louvain, 1559–1575," in *Mélanges d'histoire offerts à Charles Moeller* 2 (1914), 175–89.

Hadfield, Andrew. "Translating the Reformation: John Bale's Irish *Vocacyon*," in Bradshaw, Hadfield, and Maley (eds.), *Representing Ireland*, 43–59.

—— (ed.). *Amazons, Savages, and Machiavels: Travel and Colonial Writing in English, 1550–1630. An Anthology* (Oxford: Oxford University Press, 2002).

Haigh, Christopher. "The Continuity of Catholicism in the English Reformation," *Past and Present* 93 (1981), 37–69.

—— *English Reformations: Religion, Politics, and Society under the Tudors* (Oxford: Oxford University Press, 1993).

Haile, Martin. *An Elizabethan Cardinal, William Allen* (London: I. Pitman, 1914).

Hall, Kim F. *Things of Darkness: Economies of Race and Gender in Early Modern England* (Ithaca: Cornell University Press, 1995).

Halloran, Brian M. *The Scots College in Paris, 1603–1792* (Edinburgh: John Donald, 1997).

Hamilton, A. C., et al. (eds.). *The Spenser Encyclopedia* (Toronto: University of Toronto Press, 1990).

Hamilton, Adam. *The Angel of Syon: the Life and Martyrdom of Blessed Richard Reynolds, Bridgettine Monk of Syon, Martyred at Tyburn, May 4, 1535. To which is added a sketch of the History of the Bridgettines of Syon, written by Father Robert Persons, SJ, about the year 1595*, edited from a MS. copy at Syon abbey, Chudleigh (Edinburgh: Sands, 1905).

Hamilton, Donna. "Richard Verstegan's *A Restitution of Decayed Intelligence* (1605): A Catholic Antiquarian Replies to John Foxe, Thomas Cooper, and Jean Bodin," *Prose Studies* 22 (1999), 1–38.

—— "Catholic Use of Anglo-Saxon Precedents, 1565–1625," *Recusant History* 26 (2003), 537–55.

—— "The Persecution of Catholics in Renaissance England," in Carey (ed.), *Voices for Tolerance*, 109–20.

—— *Anthony Munday and the Catholics, 1560–1633* (Aldershot: Ashgate, 2005).

Hamlin, Hannibal. *Psalm Culture and Early Modern English Literature* (Cambridge: Cambridge University Press, 2004).

Hammerstein, Helga. "Aspects of the Continental Education of Irish Students in the Reign of Queen Elizabeth I," in *Historical Studies: Papers Read Before the Irish Conference of Historians* 8 (Dublin: Gill and MacMillan, 1971), 137–53.

Harris, P. R. "The Reports of William Udall, Informer, 1605–1612," *Recusant History* 8 (1966), 192–284.

Hastings, Adrian. *The Construction of Nationhood: Ethnicity, Religion, and Nationalism* (Cambridge: Cambridge University Press, 1997).

Heal, Felicity. "Mediating the Word: Language and Dialects in the British and Irish Reformations," *Journal of Ecclesiastical History* 56.2 (2005), 261–86.

Helgerson, Richard. *Forms of Nationhood: The Elizabethan Writing of England* (Chicago: University of Chicago Press, 1992).

Hendricks, Margo. "Race: A Renaissance Category?" in Michael Hattaway (ed.), *A Companion to English Renaissance Literature and Culture* (Oxford: Blackwell, 2000), 690–8.

Henry, Grainne. "The Emerging Identity of an Irish Military Group in the Spanish Netherlands, 1586–1610," in R. V. Comerford, Mary Cullen, Jacqueline R. Hill, and Colm Lennon (eds.), *Religion, Conflict, and Coexistence in Ireland* (Dublin: Gill and Macmillan, 1990), 53–77.

—— *The Irish Military Community in Spanish Flanders, 1586–1621* (Dublin: Irish Academic Press, 1992).

Hernán, Enrique García. "Philip II's Forgotten Armada," in Morgan (ed.), *The Battle of Kinsale*, 45–58.

Hicks, Leo. "Father Persons, SJ, and the Seminaries in Spain," *The Month* 157 (1931), 193–204, 410–17, 497–506; ibid.158 (1931), 26–35, 143–52, 234–44.

—— "The Catholic Exiles and the Elizabethan Religious Settlement," *The Catholic Historical Review* 22 (1936), 129–48.

—— "Father Robert Persons SJ and *The Book of Succession*," *Recusant History* 4 (1957–8), 104–37.

Higham, N. J. *An English Empire: Bede and the Early Anglo-Saxon Kings* (Manchester: Manchester University Press, 1995).

Highley, Christopher. "John Copinger and the Counter-Reformation: The Writings of a Forgotten Exile from Ireland," *Prose Studies* 24 (2002), 1–14.

—— "Richard Verstegan's Book of Martyrs," in Highley and. King (eds.), *John Foxe and his World*, 183–97.

—— " 'A Pestilent and Seditious Book': Nicholas Sander's *De Origine ac Progressu Schismatis Anglicani* and Catholic Histories of the Reformation," in Paulina Kewes (ed.), *The Uses of History in Early Modern England* (Berkeley: University of California Press, 2006), 147–67.

—— and John N. King (eds.), *John Foxe and his World* (Aldershot: Ashgate, 2002).

Hltgen, Karl Josef. "Henry Hawkins: A Jesuit Writer and Emblematist in Stuart England," in John W. O'Malley, SJ, Gauvin Alexander Bailey, Steven J. Harris, and T. Frank Kennedy, SJ (eds.), *The Jesuits: Cultures, Sciences, and the Arts 1540–1773* (Toronto: University of Toronto Press, 1990), 600–26.

Holleran, James V. *A Jesuit Challenge: Edmund Campion's Debates at the Tower of London in 1581* (New York: Fordham University Press, 1999).

Holmes, Peter. "The Authorship and Early Reception of *A Conference about the Next Succession to the Crown of England*," *Historical Journal* 23 (1980), 415–29.

Holmes, P. J. *Resistance and Compromise: The Political Thought of the Elizabethan Catholics* (Cambridge: Cambridge University Press, 1982).

—— "Robert Persons and an Unknown Political Pamphlet of 1593," *Recusant History* 17 (1985), 341–7.

Honigmann, E. A. J. *Shakespeare: The "Lost Years."* 2nd edn. (Manchester: Manchester University Press, 1998).

Houliston, Victor. "The Polemical Gravitas of Robert Persons," *Recusant History* 22 (1995), 291–305.

—— "The Hare and the Drum: Robert Persons's Writings on the English Succession, 1593–6," *Renaissance Studies* 14 (2000), 234–50.

—— "The Lord Treasurer and the Jesuit: Robert Persons's Satirical *Responsio* to the 1591 Proclamation," *Sixteenth Century Journal* 32 (2001), 383–401.

Hulse, Clark. "Dead Man's Treasure: The Cult of Thomas More," in David Lee Miller, Sharon O'Dair, and Harold Weber (eds.), *The Production of English Renaissance Culture* (Ithaca: Cornell University Press, 1994), 190–225.

Hurstfield, Joel. "The Succession Struggle in Late Elizabethan England," in S. T. Bindoff, Joel Hurstfield, and C. H. Williams (eds.), *Elizabethan Government and Society* (London: Athlone Press, 1961), 369–96.

Hutchinson, Ann M. "Eyes cast Down, But Self Revealed: Letters of a Recusant Nun," in Bonnie Wheeler (ed.), *Feminea Medievalia: Representations of the Feminine in the Middle Ages* (Academia, 1993), 329–37.

Jackson, Peter. "Herwagen's Lost Manuscript of the *Collectanea*," in Martha Bayless and Michael Lapidge (eds.), *Collectanea Pseudo-Bedae* (Dublin, 1998), 101–20.

James, Edward. "Bede and the Tonsure Question," *Peritia* 3 (1984), 85–98.

Jenkins, Gary W. *John Jewel and the English National Church: The Dilemmas of an Erastian Reformer* (Aldershot: Ashgate, 2006).

Jenkins, Gladys. "The Archpriest Controversy and the Printers, 1601–1603," *The Library* (1948), 180–7.

Jennings, Brendan. "Irish Students in the University of Louvain," *Measgra I gcuimhne Mhichil Ui Chleirigh* (Dublin, 1944), 74–83.

Johnston, Andrew G., and Jean-François Gilmont, "Printing and the Reformation in Antwerp," in Jean-François Gilmont (ed.), *The Reformation and the Book* (Eng. edn. and trans. by Karin Maag. Aldershot: Ashgate, 1998), 188–213.

Kantorowicz, Ernst. *The King's Two Bodies: A Study in Mediaeval Political Theology* (Princeton: Princeton University Press, 1957).

Kendrick, T. D. *British Antiquity* (London: Methuen, 1950).

Kenny, Anthony. "Anthony Munday in Rome," *Recusant History* 6 (1962), 158–62.

—— "From Hospice to College," in *The English Hospice in Rome*. The Venerabile Sexcentenary issue. May 1962. Vol. 21 (Exeter: Catholic Records Press), 218–73.

Kesselring, K. J. " 'A Cold Pye for the Papitses': Constructing and Containing the Northern Rising of 1569," *Journal of British Studies* 43 (2004), 417–43.

Kidd, Colin. *British Identities before Nationalism: Ethnicities and Nationhood in the Atlantic World, 1600–1800* (Cambridge: Cambridge University Press, 1999).

Kilroy, Gerard. *Edmund Campion: Memory and Transcription* (Aldershot: Ashgate, 2005).

King, John N. *English Reformation Literature: The Tudor Origins of the Protestant Tradition* (Princeton: Princeton University Press, 1982).

—— (ed.). *Voices of the English Reformation: A Sourcebook* (Philadelphia: University of Pennsylvania Press, 2004).

—— *John Foxe's* Book of Martyrs *and Early Modern Print Culture* (Cambridge: Cambridge University Press, 2006).

Kingsley-Smith, Jane, *Shakespeare's Drama of Exile* (New York: Palgrave Macmillan, 2003).

Koebner, Richard. " 'The Imperial Crown of this Realm': Henry VIII, Constantine the Great, and Polydore Vergil," *Bulletin of the Institute of Historical Research* 26 (1953), 29–52.

Kritzeck, James. *Peter the Venerable and Islam* (Princeton: Princeton University Press, 1964).

Kumar, Krishan. *The Making of English National Identity* (Cambridge: Cambridge University Press, 2003).

Kupperman, Karen Ordahl. "Fear of Hot Climates in the Anglo-American Colonial Experience," *William and Mary Quarterly* (1984), 213–40.

—— "Climate and the Mastery of the Wilderness in Seventeenth-Century New England," *Seventeenth-Century New England* (Boston, 1988), 3–37.

Lake, Peter. "Religious Identities in Shakespeare's England," in *A Companion to Shakespeare*, ed. David Scott Kastan (Oxford: Blackwell, 1999), 57–84.

—— , and Michael Questier. "Puritans, Papists, and the 'Public Sphere,' in Early Modern England: The Edmund Campion Affair in Context," *The Journal of Modern History* 27 (2000), 587–627.

Lakowski, Romuald I. "Thomas More, Protestants, and Turks: Persecution and Martyrdom in *A Dialogue of Comfort*," *Ben Jonson Journal* 7 (2000), 199–223.

Lander, Jesse M. *Inventing Polemic: Religion, Print, and Literary Culture in Early Modern England* (Cambridge: Cambridge University Press, 2006).

La Rocca, John J., SJ. "Time, Death, and the Next Generation: The Early Elizabethan Recusancy Policy, 1558–1574," *Albion* 14 (1982), 103–117.

—— " 'Who Can't Pray with Me, Can't Love Me': Toleration and the Early Jacobean Recusancy Policy," *Journal of British Studies* 23 (1984), 22–36.

Lavezzo, Kathy (ed.). *Imagining a Medieval English Nation* (Minneapolis: University of Minnesota Press, 2004).

Leatherbarrow, J. Stanley. *The Lancashire Elizabethan Recusants* (Manchester: Chetham Society, 1947).

Lennon, Colm. *Richard Stanihurst the Dubliner 1547–1618* (Dublin: Irish Academic Press, 1981).

—— "Edmund Campion's *Histories of Ireland* and Reform in Tudor Ireland," in McCoog (ed.), *The Reckoned Expense*, 67–84.

—— "Political Thought of Irish Counter-Reformation Churchmen: The Testimony of the 'Analecta' of Bishop David Rothe," in Morgan (ed.), *Political Ideology in Ireland*, 181–202.

—— "Taking Sides: The Emergence of Irish Catholic Ideology," in Carey and Lotz-Heumann (eds.), *Taking Sides*, 78–93.

Leuven University 1425–1985 (Leuven University Press, 1990).

Levack, Brian P. *The Formation of the British State: England, Scotland and the Union, 1603–1707* (Oxford: Clarendon Press, 1987).

Levine, Joseph M. *Humanism and History: Origins of Modern English Historiography* (Ithaca: Cornell University Press, 1987).

Loach, Jennifer. "Reformation Controversies," in James McConica (ed.), *The History of the University of Oxford*, vol. 3: *The Collegiate University* (Oxford: Oxford University Press, 1986), 363–96.

Loades, David. *The Reign of Mary Tudor: Politics, Government, and Religion in England, 1553–1558* (London: Benn, 1979).

—— "The Origins of English Protestant Nationalism," in Stuart Mews (ed.), *Religion and National Identity* (Oxford: Blackwell, 1982), 297–307.

—— "Philip II and the Government of England," in Claire Cross, David Loades, and J. J. Scarisbrick (eds.), *Law and Government under the Tudors* (Cambridge: Cambridge University Press, 1988), 177–94.

—— *Politics, Censorship, and the English Reformation* (London: Pinter, 1991).

—— "The English Church during the Reign of Mary," in Edwards and Truman (eds.), *Reforming Catholicism*, 33–48.

—— *The Chronicles of the Tudor Queens* (Stroud, Gloucestershire: Sutton, 2002).

Loomba, Ania. " 'Delicious Traffick': Alterity and Exchange on Early Modern Stages," *Shakespeare Survey* 52 (1999), 201–14.

—— *Shakespeare, Race, and Colonialism* (Oxford: Oxford University Press, 2002).

Loomie, Albert J., SJ. *The Spanish Elizabethans: The English Exiles at the Court of Philip II* (New York: Fordham University Press, 1963).

—— "Richard Stanyhurst in Spain: Two Unknown Letters of August 1593," *Huntington Library Quarterly* 28 (1965), 145–56.

—— *Guy Fawkes in Spain: The "Spanish Treason" in Spanish Documents* (Bulletin of the Institute of Historical Research, Special Supplement No. 9. Nov. 1971).

—— *Spain and the Early Stuarts, 1585–1655* (Aldershot: Ashgate, 1996).

Lotz-Heumann, Ute. "Tolerance and Intolerance in the Protestant and Catholic Reformations in Germany," in Carey (ed.), *Voices for Tolerance*, 31–44.

Low, Anthony. "Recent Studies in the English Renaissance," *Studies in English Literature 1500–1900* 37 (1997), 191–236.

Löwe, J. Andreas. "Richard Smyth and the Foundation of the University of Douai," *Nederlandsch Archief voor Kerkgeschiede* 79 (1999), 142–69.

Lunn, David. *The English Benedictines, 1540–1688: From Reformation to Revolution* (New York: Barnes and Noble, 1980).

McCarthy-Morrogh, Michael. *The Munster Plantation: English Migration to Southern Ireland 1583–1641* (Oxford: Clarendon Press, 1986).

McClain, Lisa. *Lest we be Damned: Practical Innovation and Lived Experience among Catholics in Protestant England* (NewYork: Routledge, 2004).

MacColl, Alan. "Richard White and the Legendary History of Britain," *Humanistica Lovaniensia* 51 (2002), 245–57.

MacColl, Alan. "The Construction of England as a Protestant 'British' Nation in the Sixteenth Century," *Renaissance Studies* 18 (2004), 582–608.
—— "The Meaning of 'Britain,' in Medieval and Early Modern England," *Journal of British Studies* 45 (2006), 248–69.
McConica, James Kelsey. *English Humanists and Reformation Politics Under Henry VIII and Edward VI* (Oxford: Clarendon Press, 1965).
—— "The Recusant Reputation of Thomas More," in R. S. Sylvester and G. P. Marc'hadour (eds.), *Essential Articles for the Study of Thomas More* (Hamden, Conn.: Archon Books, 1977), 137–49.
—— (ed.). *The History of the University of Oxford*, vol. 3: *The Collegiate University* (Oxford: Oxford University Press, 1986).
McCoog, Thomas M., SJ, "Establishment of the English Province of the Society of Jesus," *Recusant History* 17 (1984), 121–39.
—— *The Society of Jesus in Ireland, Scotland, and England, 1541–1588: "Our Way of Proceeding?"* (New York: Brill, 1996).
—— (ed.). *The Reckoned Expense: Edmund Campion and the Early English Jesuits* (Woodbridge: Boydell Press, 1996).
—— "The Society of Jesus in Wales, The Welsh in the Society of Jesus," *The Journal of Welsh Religious History* 5 (1997), 1–27.
—— "Harmony Disrupted: Robert Parsons, SJ, William Crichton, SJ, and the Question of Queen Elizabeth's Successor, 1581–1603," *Archivum Historicum Societatis Jesu* 73 (2004), 149–220.
Mac Craith, Mícheál. "The Gaelic Reaction to the Reformation," in Ellis and Barber (eds.), *Conquest and Union*, 139–61.
MacCulloch, Diarmaid. *The Boy King: Edward VI and the Protestant Reformation* (New York: Palgrave, 1999).
—— *The Reformation: A History* (New York: Penguin, 2004).
McDougall, Hugh. *Racial Myth in English History: Trojans, Teutons, and Anglo-Saxons* (London: University Press of New England, 1982).
McEachern, Claire. *The Poetics of English Nationhood, 1590–1612* (Cambridge: Cambridge University Press, 1996).
Maginn, Christopher. "The Baltinglass Rebellion, 1580: English Dissent or a Gaelic Uprising?" *Historical Journal* 47 (2004), 205–32.
McGinnis, Paul, and Arthur H. Williamson, "Britain, Race, and the Iberian World Empire," in Allan I. Macinnes and Jane Ohlmeyer (eds.), *The Stuart Kingdoms in the Seventeenth Century: Awkward Neighbours* (Dublin: Four Courts Press, 2002), 70–93.
McGrath, Patrick, and Joy Rowe, "The Marian Priests Under Elizabeth I," *Recusant History* 12 (1984), 103–20.
McGurk, John. *The Elizabethan Conquest of Ireland: The 1590s Crisis* (Manchester: Manchester University Press, 1997).
Maley, Willy. " 'Another Britain'? Bacon's *Certain Considerations Touching the Plantation in Ireland* (1609)," *Prose Studies* 18 (1995), 1–18.
Maltby, William S. *The Black Legend in England: The Development of Anti-Spanish Sentiment, 1558–1660* (Durham, NC: Duke University Press, 1971).
—— *The Reign of Charles V* (New York: Palgrave, 2002).

Manning, Roger B. *Religion and Society in Elizabethan Sussex* (Leicester: Leicester University Press, 1969).

Marshall, Peter. *Religious Identities in Henry VIII's England* (Aldershot: Ashgate, 2006).

—— "The Other Black Legend: The Henrician Reformation and the Spanish People," *English Historical Review* 116 (2001), 31–49.

—— "Is the Pope Catholic? Henry VIII and the Semantics of Schism," in Shagan (ed.), *Catholics and the "Protestant Nation"*, 22–48.

Mason, Roger A. "Scotching the Brut: Politics, History and National Myth in Sixteenth Century Britain," in Roger A. Mason (ed.), *Scotland and England 1286–1815* (Edinburgh: John Donald, 1987), 60–84.

—— "The Scottish Reformation and the Origins of Anglo-British Imperialism," in Mason (ed.), *Scots and Britons*, 161–86.

—— (ed.). *Scots and Britons: Scottish Political Thought and the Union of 1603* (Cambridge: Cambridge University Press, 1994).

Matar, Nabil. *Turks, Moors and Englishmen in the Age of Discovery* (New York: Columbia University Press, 1999).

Mayer, Thomas F. *Reginald Pole: Prince and Prophet* (Cambridge: Cambridge University Press, 2000).

—— *The Correspondence of Reginald Pole Vol. 2 A Calendar, 1547–1554: A Power in Rome* (Aldershot: Ashgate, 2003).

Milward, Peter. *Religious Controversies of the Elizabethan Age: A Survey of Printed Sources* (London: The Scolar Press, 1977).

Monta, Susannah Brietz. *Martyrdom and Literature in Early Modern England* (Cambridge: Cambridge University Press, 2005).

Morey, Adrian. *The Catholic Subjects of Elizabeth I* (Totowa, NJ: Rowman and Littlefield, 1978).

Morgan, Hiram. *Tyrone's Rebellion: The Outbreak of the Nine Years War in Tudor Ireland* (Woodbridge, Suffolk: Royal Historical Society, 1993).

—— "Faith and Fatherland or Queen and Country? An Unpublished Exchange between O'Neill and the State at the Height of the Nine Years War," *Du'iche Ne'ill: Journal of the O'Neill Country Historical Society* 9 (1994), 9–65.

—— "Faith and Fatherland in Sixteenth-Century Ireland," *History-Ireland* 2 (1995), 13–20.

—— " 'Un Pueblo Unido . . .': The Politics of Philip O'Sullivan Beare," in Enrique García Hernán et al. (eds.), *Irlanda y la Monarquía Hispánica: Kinsale 1601–2001. Guerra, Política, Exilio y Religión* (Madrid: Universidad de Alcalá, 2002), 265–82.

—— (ed.). *The Battle of Kinsale* (Bray, Ireland: Wordwell, 2004).

—— (ed.). *Political Ideology in Ireland 1541–1641* (Dublin: Four Courts Press, 1999).

Morrissey, Thomas. "The Irish Student Diaspora in the Sixteenth Century and the Early Years of the Irish College at Salamanca," *Recusant History* 14 (1978), 242–60.

Muller, J. A. *Stephen Gardiner and the Tudor Reaction* (New York: Macmillan, 1926).

Mullett, Michael A. *The Catholic Reformation* (London: Routledge, 1999).

Mulligan, Winifred Joy. "The British Constantine: An English Historical Myth," *The Journal of Medieval and Renaissance Studies* 8 (1978), 257–79.

Murphy, Andrew. *"But the Irish Sea Betwixt Us": Ireland, Colonialism, and Renaissance Literature* (Lexington, KY: University Press of Kentucky, 1999).

Neale, J. E. *Elizabeth I and her Parliaments 1559–1581* (New York: St Martin's Press, 1958).

Neill, Michael. " 'Mullatos,' 'Blacks,' and 'Indian Moors': *Othello* and Early Modern Constructions of Human Difference," *Shakespeare Quarterly* 49 (1998), 361–73.

Netzloff, Mark. "The English Colleges and the English Nation: Allen, Persons, Verstegan, and Diasporic Nationalism," in Corthell, Dolan, Highley, and Marotti (eds.), *Catholic Culture in Early Modern England*, 236–60.

Ni Chathain, Proinseas, "Bede's Ecclesiastical History in Irish," *Peritia* 3 (1984), 115–30.

Nice, Jason A. "Being 'British,' in Rome: The Welsh at the English College, 1578–1584," *The Catholic Historical Review* 92 (2006), 1–24.

—— "Cross-Confessional Features of English Identity: The Ditchley Portrait of Queen Elizabeth I and the High Altarpiece of the English College in Rome," in Philip M. Soergel (ed.), *Studies in Medieval and Renaissance History: Nation, Ethnicity, and Identity in Medieval and Renaissance Europe*. 3rd ser. vol. 3 (New York: AMS Press, 2006), 185–209.

Noreen, Kirstin. "*Ecclesiae Militantis Triumphi*: Jesuit Iconography and the Counter-Reformation," *Sixteenth Century Journal* 29 (1998), 689–714.

North, Marcy L. "N. D. versus O. E.: Anonymity's Moral Ambiguity in Elizabethan Catholic Controversy," *Criticism: A Quarterly for Literature and the Arts*, 40 (1998), 355–75.

Norwood, Frederick A. *Strangers and Exiles: A History of Religious Refugees*. 2 vols. (New York: Abingdon Press, 1969).

ó Buachalla, Breandán. " 'James our True King': The Ideology of Irish Royalism in the Seventeenth Century," in D. George Boyce, Robert Eccleshall, and Vincent Geoghegan (eds.), *Political Thought in Ireland Since the Seventeenth Century* (London: Routledge, 1993), 7–35.

O'Connell, Marvin R. *Thomas Stapleton and the Counter-Reformation* (New Haven: Yale University Press, 1964).

O'Connell, Patricia. "The Early-Modern Irish College Network in Iberia, 1590–1800," in O'Connor (ed.), *The Irish in Europe*, 49–64.

O'Connor, Thomas. "Irish Migration to Spain, and the Formation of an Irish College Network, 1589–1800," in Luc François and Ann Katherine Isaacs (eds.), *The Sea in European History* (Pisa, Italy: Università di Pisa, 2001), 109–23.

—— "Hugh O'Neill: Free Spirit, Religious Chameleon or Ardent Catholic?" in Morgan (ed.), *The Battle of Kinsale*, 59–72.

—— "A Justification for Foreign Intervention in Early Modern Ireland: Peter Lombard's *Commentarius* (1600)," in Thomas O'Connor and Mary Ann Lyons (eds.), *Irish Migrants in Europe after Kinsale, 1602–1820* (Dublin: Four Courts Press, 2003), 14–31.

—— (ed.). *The Irish in Europe, 1580–1815* (Dublin: Four Courts Press, 2001).

Ord, Melanie. "Representing Rome and the Self in Anthony Munday's *The English Roman Life*," in *Travels and Translations in the Sixteenth Century*, ed. Mike Pincombe. Studies in European Cultural Transition 20 (Aldershot: Ashgate, 2004), 45–61.

O'scea, Ciaran. "The Devotional World of the Irish Catholic Exile in Early Modern Galicia, 1598–1666," in O'Connor (ed.), *The Irish in Europe*, 27–48.

Palmer, William. *The Problem of Ireland in Tudor Foreign Policy 1485–1603* (Woodbridge, Suffolk: Boydell, 1994).

Parker, Geoffrey. "The Place of Tudor England in the Messianic Vision of Philip II of Spain," *Transactions of the Royal Historical Society*, 6th ser. 12 (2002), 167–221.

Parry, Graham. *The Trophies of Time: English Antiquarians of the Seventeenth Century* (Oxford: Oxford University Press, 1995).

Patterson, W. B. *King James VI and I and the Reunion of Christendom* (Cambridge: Cambridge University Press, 1997).

Perry, Curtis. *The Making of Jacobean Culture: James I and the Renegotiation of Elizabethan Literary Practice* (Cambridge: Cambridge University Press, 1997).

Peters, Robert. "Some Catholic Opinions of King James VI and I," *Recusant History* 10 (1970), 292–303.

Pettersen, Alvyn. " 'To Flee or Not to Flee': An Assessment of Athanasius's *De Fuga Sua*," in W. J. Sheils (ed.), *Persecution and Toleration* (London: Blackwell, 1984), 29–42.

Petti, Anthony G. 'Richard Verstegan and Catholic Martyrologies of the Later Elizabethan Period,' *Recusant History* 5 (1959), 64–90.

—— "A Bibliography of the Writings of Richard Verstegan (*c*.1550–1641)," *Recusant History* 7 (1963), 82–105.

Pilarz, Scott. " 'Campion dead bites with his friends' teeth': Representations of an Early Modern Catholic Martyr," in Highley and King (eds.), *John Foxe and His World*, 216–34.

Plowden, Alison. *The House of Tudor* (Stein and Day: New York, 1976).

Pocock, J. G. A. "The Atlantic Archipelago and the War of the Three Kingdoms," in Brendan Bradshaw and John Morrill (eds.), *The British Problem, c.1534–1707: State Formation in the Atlantic Archipelago* (New York: St Martin's Press, 1996), 172–91.

Pollen, J. H. "The Irish Expedition of 1579," *The Month* 101 (1903), 69–85.

Pucci, Michael S. "Reforming Roman Emperors: John Foxe's Characterization of Constantine in the *Acts and Monuments*," in David Loades (ed.), *John Foxe: An Historical Perspective* (Aldershot: Ashgate, 1999), 29–51.

Quadflieg, Helga. "Approved Civilities and the Fruits of Peregrination: Elizabethan and Jacobean Travelers and the Making of Englishness," in Hartmut Berghoff, Barbara Korte, Ralf Schneider, and Christopher Harvie (eds.), *The Making of Modern Tourism*: *The Cultural History of the British Experience, 1600–2000* (New York: Palgrave, 2002), 21–46.

Questier, Michael C. "What Happened to English Catholicism after the English Reformation?" *The Historical Journal* (2000), 28–47.

—— "Catholicism, Kinship and the Public Memory of Sir Thomas More," *Journal of Ecclesiastical History* 53 (2002), 476–509.

—— *Catholicism and Community in Early Modern England: Politics, Aristocratic Patronage and Religion, c.1550–1640* (Cambridge: Cambridge University Press, 2006).

Racaut, Luc. *Hatred in Print: Catholic Propaganda and Protestant Identity during the French Wars of Religion* (Aldershot: Ashgate, 2002).

Racine, Matthew. "*A Pearle for a Prynce*: Jerónimo Osório and Early Elizabethan Catholics," *Catholic Historical Review* 87 (2001), 401–28.

Redworth, Glyn. "Beyond Faith and Fatherland: 'The Appeal of the Catholics of Ireland,' *c*.1623," *Archivium Hibernicum* 52 (1998), 3–23.

—— *The Prince and the Infanta: The Cultural Politics of the Spanish Match* (New Haven: Yale University Press, 2003).

Redworth, Glyn. "Perfidious Hispania? Ireland and the Spanish Match, 1603–1623," in Morgan (ed.), *The Battle of Kinsale*, 255–64.

Rhodes, J. T. "English Books of Martyrs and Saints of the Late Sixteenth and Early Seventeenth Centuries," *Recusant History* 22 (1994), 7–25.

Rhu, Lawrene F. "Romancing the Word: Pre-Texts and Contexts for the Errour Episode," *Spenser Studies* 11 (1994 for 1990), 101–9.

Richardson, Carol M. "Durante Alberti, the *Martyrs' Picture* and the Venerable English College, Rome," *Papers of the British School at Rome* 73 (2005), 223–63.

Robinson, Benedict Scott. "John Foxe and the Anglo-Saxons," in Highley and King (eds.), *John Foxe and His World*, 54–72.

Rodriguez-Salgado, M. J. "Christians, Civilized and Spanish: Multiple Identities in Sixteenth Century Spain," *Transactions of the Royal Historical Society* 8 (1998), 233–51.

Rogers, D. M. "John Abbot, (1588?–1650)," *Biographical Studies* 1 (1951), 22–33.

Rollins, Hyder E. (ed.), *Old English Ballads 1553–1625* (Cambridge: Cambridge University Press, 1920).

Ronan Myles V. *The Reformation in Ireland Under Elizabeth 1558–1580 (From Original Sources)* (London: Longmans, 1930).

Rostenberg, Leona. *The Minority Press and the English Crown: A Study in Repression 1558–1625* (Nieuwkoop: B. De Graaf, 1971).

Rowlands, Marie B. "Hidden Peoples: Catholic Commoners, 1558–1625," in id. (ed.), *English Catholics of Parish and Town 1558–1778* (London: Catholic Record Society, 1999), 10–35.

Ryan, Salvador. "Steadfast Saints or Malleable Models: Seventeenth-Century Irish Hagiography Revisited," *Catholic Historical Review* 91 (2005), 251–77.

Safran, William. "Diasporas in Modern Societies: Myths of Homeland and Return," *Diaspora* 1.1 (1991), 83–99.

Samson, Alexander. " 'Changing Places': The Marriage and Royal Entry of Philip, Prince of Austria and Mary Tudor, July-August 1554," *Sixteenth Century Journal* 36 (2005), 761–84.

Scarisbrick, J. J. *Henry VIII* (Berkeley: University of California Press, 1968).

—— "Robert Persons's Plans for the 'true' Reformation of England," in Neil McKendrick (ed.), *Historical Perspectives: Studies in English Thought and Society* (London: Europa Publications, 1974), 19–42.

Scherb, Victor I. "Assimilating Giants: the Appropriation of Gog and Magog in Medieval and Early Modern England," *Journal of Medieval and Early Modern Studies* 32: 1 (2002), 59–84.

Schmuck, Stephan. "The 'Turk' as Antichrist in John Foxe's *Acts and Monuments*," *Reformation* 10 (2005), 21–44.

Scribner, R. W. *For the Sake of Simple Folk: Popular Propaganda for the German Reformation* (New York: Oxford University Press, 1994).

Scott-Warren, Jason. review of *Edmund Campion: Memory and Transcription*, by Gerard Kilroy, *Early Modern Literary Studies* 12.2 (2006). http://www.extra.shu.ac.uk/emls/12–2/revkilro.htm

Scully, Robert E. " 'In the Confident Hope of a Miracle': The Spanish Armada and Religious Mentalities in the Late Sixteenth Century," *Catholic Historical Review* 89 (2003), 643–70.

Sena, Margaret. "William Blundell and the Networks of Catholic Dissent in Post-Reformation England," in Alexandra Shepard and Phil Withington (eds.), *Communities in Early Modern England: Networks, Place, Rhetoric* (Manchester: Manchester University Press, 2002), 54–75.

Shagan, Ethan H., ed. *Catholics and the "Protestant Nation": Religious Politics and Identity in Early Modern England* (Manchester: Manchester University Press, 2005).

—— "Introduction: English Catholic History in Context," in Shagan (ed.), *Catholics and the "Protestant Nation"*, 1–21.

Shapiro, James. *Shakespeare and the Jews* (New York: Columbia University Press, 2005).

Sharpe, Kevin. *Sir Robert Cotton 1586–1631: History and Politics in Early Modern England* (Oxford: Oxford University Press, 1979).

Shell, Alison. " 'We are Made a Spectacle': Campion's Dramas," in McCoog (ed.), *The Reckoned Expense*, 103–18.

—— *Catholicism, Controversy, and the English Literary Imagination, 1558–1660* (Cambridge: Cambridge University Press, 1999).

Silke, John. J. "Hugh O'Neill, the Catholic Question, and the Papacy," *Irish Ecclesiastical Record*, 5th ser. 104 (1965), 65–79.

—— *Kinsale: The Spanish Intervention in Ireland at the End of the Elizabethan Wars* (New York: Fordham University Press, 1970).

—— "The Irish Abroad, 1534–1691," in T. W. Moody, F. X. Martin, and F. J. Byrne (eds.), *A New History of Ireland* (Oxford: Clarendon Press, 1976), vol. 3: *Early Modern Ireland, 1534–1691*, 587–633.

Simons, Jos. *Robert Persons, SJ Cartamen Ecclesiae Anglicanae: A Study of an Unpublished Manuscript* (Assen, Netherlands: Van Gorcum, 1965).

Simpson, Richard. *Edmund Campion, A Biography* (London, 1896).

Smith, Anthony D. " 'Set in the Silver Sea': English National Identity and European Integration," *Nations and Nationalism* 12: 3 (2006), 441–2.

Southern, A. C. *Elizabethan Recusant Prose, 1559–1582: A Historical and Critical Account of the Books of the Catholic Refugees Printed and Published Abroad and at Secret Presses in England together with an annotated Bibliography of the same* (London: Sands, 1950).

—— " 'The Best Wits out of England': University Men in Exile under Elizabeth," *The Month* 7 (1952), 12–21.

Southern, R. W. *Western Views of Islam in the Middle Ages* (Harvard University Press, 1962).

Spelman, Sir Henry. "Of the Union," in Galloway and Levack (eds.), *The Jacobean Union: Six Tracts of 1604*.

Stanford Encyclopedia of Philosophy http://plato.stanford.edu/entries/bodin/

Starkey, David. *Elizabeth: The Struggle for the Throne* (London: Harper, 2001).

Stoye, John. *English Travellers Abroad, 1604–1667* (New Haven: Yale University Press, 1989).

Stradling, R. A. *Europe and the Decline of Spain: A Study of the Spanish System, 1580–1720* (London, 1981).

Strong, Roy. *Van Dyck: Charles I on Horseback* (London: Allen Lane,1972).

Tait, Clodagh. "Adored for Saints: Catholic Martyrdom in Ireland *c.*1560–1655," *Journal of Early Modern History* 5 (2001), 128–59.

Tanner, Marie. *The Last Descendant of Aeneas: The Hapsburgs and the Mythic Image of the Emperor* (New Haven: Yale University Press, 1993).

Taylor, Bruce. "The Enemy Within and Without: An Anatomy of Fear on the Spanish Mediterranean Littoral," in William G. Naphy and Penny Roberts (eds.), *Fear in Early Modern Society* (Manchester: Manchester University Press, 1997), 78–99.

Ungerer, Gustav. "Juan Pantoja de la Cruz and the Circulation of Gifts between the English and Spanish Courts in 1604/5," *Shakespeare Studies* 26 (1998), 145–86.

Van Strien, C. D. "Recusant Houses in the Southern Netherlands as seen by British Tourists, *c.*1650–1720," *Recusant History* 20 (1991), 495–511.

Veech, Thomas McNevin. *Dr Nicholas Sanders and the English Reformation, 1530–1581* (Louvain: Bureaux du Recueil, Bibliothèque de l'Université, 1935).

Vitkus, Daniel. *Turning Turk: English Theater and the Multicultural Mediterranean, 1570–1630* (New York: Palgrave Macmillan, 2003).

Voss, Paul J. "The Making of a Saint: John Fowler and Thomas More in 1573," *Journal of English and Germanic Philology* 99 (2000), 492–512.

Walker, Claire. *Gender and Politics in Early Modern Europe: English Convents in France and the Low Countries* (New York: Palgrave Macmillan, 2003).

Walker, Julia M. *The Elizabeth Icon, 1603–2003* (London: MacMillan, 2004).

Walsh, Micheline Kerney. "The Military Order of Saint Patrick, 1593," *Seanchas Ard Mhacha* 9 (1979), 274–85.

—— *Hugh O'Neill: an Exile of Ireland, Prince of Ulster* (Dublin: Four Courts Press, 1996).

Alexandra Walsham, *Church Papists: Catholicism, Conformity, and Confessional Polemic in Early Modern England* (Woodbridge, Suffolk: Boydell, 1993).

—— "'Domme Preachers'? Post-Reformation English Catholicism and the Culture of Print," *Past and Present* 168 (2000), 72–123.

—— "Unclasping the Book? Post-Reformation English Catholicism and the Vernacular Bible," *Journal of British Studies* 42 (2003), 141–66.

—— "Translating Trent: English Catholicism and the Counter Reformation," *Historical Research* 78.201 (2005), 288–310.

—— "Holywell: Contesting Sacred Space in Post-Reformation Wales," in Will Coster and Andrew Spicer (eds.), *Sacred Space in Early Modern Europe* (Cambridge: Cambridge University Press, 2005), 211–36.

—— *Charitable Hatred: Tolerance and Intolerance in England, 1500–1700* (Manchester: Manchester University Press, 2006).

Warneke, Sarah. "A Taste for Newfangledness: The Destructive Potential of Novelty in Early Modern England," *Sixteenth Century Journal* 26 (1995), 881–96.

Warren, Nancy Bradley. "Dissolution, Diaspora, and Defining Englishness: Syon in Exile and Elizabethan Politics," in *Women of God and Arms: Female Spirituality and Political Conflict 1380–1600* (Philadelphia: University of Pennsylvania Press, 2005), 139–67.

Wiener, Carol Z. "'The Beleagured Isle': A Study of Elizabethan and Early Jacobean Anti-Catholicism," *Past and Present* 51 (1971), 27–62.

Williams, Michael E. *The Venerable English College Rome: A History 1579–1979* (London: Associated Catholic Publishers, 1979).

—— *St Alban's College Valladolid: Four Centuries of English Catholic Presence in Spain* (New York: St Martin's Press, 1988).

—— "The Origins of the English College, Lisbon," *Recusant History* 20 (1991), 478–92.

—— "Images of Martyrdom in Paintings at the English College Valladolid," in Margaret A. Rees (ed.), *Leeds Papers on Symbol and Image in Iberian Arts* (Leeds: Trinity and All Saints College, University of Leeds, 1994), 51–71.

—— "The Library of Saint Alban's English College Valladolid: Censorship and Acquisitions," *Recusant History* 26 (2002), 132–42.

—— "Campion and the English Continental Seminaries," in McCoog (ed.), *The Reckoned Expense*, 285–300.

Williams, Penry. "Elizabethan Oxford: State, Church, and University," in James McConica (ed.), *The History of the University of Oxford*, vol. 3: *The Collegiate University* (Oxford University Press, 1986), 397–440.

Williams, Richard. " 'Libels and Payntinges': Elizabethan Catholics and the International Campaign of Visual Propaganda," in Highley and King (eds.), *John Foxe and his World*, 198–215.

Williamson, Arthur H. "Scotland, Antichrist and the Invention of Great Britain," in John Dwyer, Roger A. Mason, and Alexander Murdoch (eds.), *New Perspectives on the Politics and Culture of Early Modern Scotland* (Edinburgh: John Donald, 1982), 34–58.

—— "From the Invention of Great Britain to the Creation of British History: A New Historiography," *Journal of British Studies* 29 (1990), 267–76.

—— 'Scots, Indians, and Empire: The Scottish Politics of Civilization 1519–1609," *Past and Present* 150 (1996), 46–83.

—— "Patterns of British Identity: 'Britain' and its Rivals in the Sixteenth and Seventeenth Centuries," in Glenn Burgess (ed.), *The New British History: Founding a Modern State, 1603–1715* (London: I. B. Tauris, 1999), 138–72.

Wizeman, William. "The Virgin Mary in the Reign of Mary Tudor," *Studies in Church History* 39 (2004), 239–48.

Wooding, Lucy E. C. *Rethinking Catholicism in Reformation England* (Oxford: Clarendon Press, 2000).

—— "The Marian Restoration and the Language of Catholic Reform," in Edwards and Truman (eds.), *Reforming Catholicism*, 49–64.

Wormald, Jenny. "Gunpowder, Treason and Scots," *Journal of British Studies* 24 (1985), 141–68.

—— "James VI and I, *Basilikon Doron* and *The Trew Law of Free Monarchies*: The Scottish Context and the English Translation," in Linda Levy Peck (ed.), *The Mental World of the Jacobean Court* (Cambridge: Cambridge University Press, 1991), 36–54.

—— "The Union of 1603," in Mason (ed.), *Scots and Britons*, 17–40.

Wormald, Patrick. "Bede, the *Bretwaldas* and the Origins of the *Gens Anglorum*," in id. (ed.), *Ideal and Reality in Frankish and Anglo-Saxon Society* (Oxford: Oxford University Press, 1983), 99–129.

Wright, Jonathan. "Surviving the English Reformation: Commonsense, Conscience, and Circumstance," *Journal of Medieval and Early Modern Studies* 29 (1999), 381–402.

—— "The World's Worst Worm: Conscience and Conformity during the English Reformation," *Sixteenth Century Journal* 30 (1999), 113–33.

—— "Marian Exiles and the Legitimacy of Flight from Persecution," *Journal of Ecclesiastical History* 52 (2001), 220–43.

Index